BRIAN LANE was an expert in the field of true crime. He came to writing via fine art, theatre and experimental music and also spent a number of years with the United Nations in Geneva and Vienna. He founded The Murder Club in 1987 and compiled the formidable six-volume series of *Murder Club Guides to Great Britain*. He sadly died in 1999.

By the same author:

The Encyclopedia of Women Killers
The Encyclopedia of Serial Killers (with Wilfred Gregg)
The Encyclopedia of Mass Murder (with Wilfred Gregg)
The Encyclopedia of Cruel and Unusual Punishment
The Murder Club Guides (6 vols)
The Murder Guide to Great Britain
The Murder Guide to London
The Butchers
Murder Update
The Murder Yearbook

The Encyclopedia of Forensic Science

Brian Lane

Magpie Books, London

Constable & Robinson Ltd
3 The Lanchesters
162 Fulham Palace Road
London W6 9ER

This edition published by Magpie Books,
an imprint of Constable & Robinson Ltd 2004

First published in the UK by Headline Book Publishing in 1994

A copy of the British Library Cataloguing in
Publication Data is available from the British Library

ISBN 1-84119-852-8

Printed and bound in the EU

Contents

vi **Contents**

viii **Contents**

Introduction

For a crime historian rather than a crime scientist to write a book such as this makes a great deal more sense than may at first appear. So far, books on the subject of forensic science have tended to fall into two main types – textbooks for the scientifically educated and trained, to be used by aspiring police cadets and those engaged in the various forensic disciplines; and those popular compilations of anecdote and story sprinkled with a heavy scientific seasoning lifted from the textbooks. What was required was a serious attempt to demystify for an informed readership of crime enthusiasts some of the minor miracles that are occurring in scientific detection today, and an attempt to place them in a familiar historical context – the DNA 'fingerprint' versus the 'ink and roll' fingerprint, for example – and emphasize the way techniques work through means of real-life case studies. Consequently, in order to present a lucid lay explanation, I have relied on a hundred and one sources and the patience of very many people in order to grasp the fundamentals of processes and instrumentation, both scientific and intuitive. In short, if I could understand it, there was a good chance my readers could.

Forensic Science

The basis on which the investigation of crime stands is the assembling of a sequence of facts which will allow the judicial process to be carried through to a satisfactory conclusion. It should prove that a crime was committed, and it should present evidence that a named person or persons were responsible for committing that crime.

It was as early as 1910 that Edmond **Locard*** at the University of

*Words in bold type refer to main entries in the alphabetical body of the *Encyclopedia*.

Lyon recognized the value of **Trace Evidence** and advanced his 'contact trace theory', which states simply that a criminal will always carry away with him some trace from the scene of his crime, and leave some trace of his presence behind. This is the very foundation of forensic science. It is these *objective* traces which the criminal deposits as clues, along with *subjective* traces such as witness statements, that conspire to prove that the 'named person or persons' was responsible for a crime. This tangible evidence will these days be subjected to analysis and comparison in one or other of the several specialized sections of the modern forensic science laboratory.

Forensic tools which remain in the control of specialized teams of police officers are **Fingerprint** identification, **Photo-FIT** (and its predecessor, **Identikit**), and the work of the **Police Artists**. In addition, the business of keeping centrally stored criminal records, and the use of computer-based detection aids such as **H.O.L.M.E.S**. are also police matters.

In 1984, the British Home Office carried out a research study into 'The Effectiveness of the Forensic Science Service',* a valuable result of which was an examination of the work-load passing through the Forensic Science Service during the study year:

WORK-LOAD PASSING THROUGH FORENSIC SCIENCE SERVICE, 1984

Category	Cases	%	Total recorded
Homicide	422	1	457
Woundings	1147	2	93,148
Sexual assault	1508	2	17,150
Burglary	3030	5	727,612
Robbery	343	1	11,245
Theft	1673	3	1,429,209
Arson	1370	2	15,051
Criminal damage	1332	2	223,949
		18	
Coinage	17	<1	
Explosives	150	<1	
Safes	10	<1	
Unclassified	816	1	
Sudden death (alcohol/toxicological)	1346	2	
Firearms	1210	2	
Documents	2236	4	
Tachographs	244	<1	

*The figures cover only England and Wales.

Category	Cases	%	Total recorded
Traffic accidents	2459	4	
		14	
Drink/driving	29,101	48	
Drugs	12,441	20	
		68	
TOTAL	60,855	100	

The statistics are important in the context of the way we view crime and its investigation. It is easy when reading books such as this to receive a distorted view of the prevalence of serious crime. The reality, as the figures show, is that almost fifty per cent of forensic laboratory cases are concerned with drink/driving, and another twenty per cent with mainly straightforward drug offences. The most serious crimes, those of homicide, wounding and sexual offences, account for only five per cent of the cases handled by the laboratories in an average year. It should be added, of course, that the amount of laboratory time expended on such cases is greatly in excess of that spent on semi-automatic blood/alcohol tests, and it will be noted that not all recorded crimes in the more serious categories were referred to the Forensic Science Service. Although these figures relate to the rate of crime in England and Wales, the underlying principles as they relate to, say, the European experience are still valid. The sheer size of the United States and the broad variation in crime patterns across the country makes it difficult to assemble useful comparative statistics. For example, the number of cases involving firearms was notably small in the Home Office survey compared with known figures for *homicidal* shootings in the United States for any given year (11,832 in 1989, for example), reflecting the freer accessibility of firearms.

Scene of Crime

Because the police and forensic scientists both have a single, common aim – to solve crime – it is vital that they work with a spirit of total cooperation and mutual respect. This is all the more important because it is at the most crucial stage in an investigation, the examination of the **Scene of Crime**, that scientist and policeman are likely to meet, literally, on common ground. It is at the crime scene and from victims and suspects that the contact traces which are so vital are found. If the evidence is badly handled, wrongly labelled or allowed to become contaminated by the specially trained Scenes-of-Crime Officers (SOCOs), by the detectives or by uniformed officers, it will be useless to the laboratory. One anecdote in circulation concerns the uniformed constable who was firmly under the impression that avoiding contamination meant protecting himself from contagious diseases by wearing rubber gloves. Worse, if clues are overlooked, the policemen will get no second chance.

There are some occasions on which scientists will be called to the scene of a crime by the police to undertake on-site investigation – almost always it is in the case of arson, where the origin of the fire needs to be established early. In the United States it is common for a mobile laboratory to be dispatched to the scene of a suspicious fire. On rarer occasions a scientist may be summoned to the scene because of some specialist knowledge, such as the interpretation of **Bloodstains**.

In cases of wounding and sexual assault, a **Police Surgeon** will be responsible for collecting the medical samples for dispatch to the laboratory, and in the case of homicide it will be the **Pathologist** who is in charge of the medical examination and report.

The Forensic Laboratory

Although for easy reference this *Encyclopedia of Forensic Science* is arranged in an alphabetical format, in preparing the material for the entries, the author had in mind a hypothetical 'visit' around an idealized forensic laboratory. Of course, there is no such place. In Britain, for example, there are eight Forensic Science Service laboratories scattered around the country, some of which are stronger on certain scientific disciplines and some on others – firearms, for example, are the specialty of the Nottingham laboratory, and Birmingham is known for document examination. Often cases will be sent to entirely other laboratories for analysis – some poisons go to the government microbiological research establishment at Porton Down, and some explosives cases end up at the Royal Armament Research and Development Establishment.

However, for the purpose of this overview there is a laboratory to which all evidence deriving from the police investigation and the pathologist's post-mortem will be sent. The following list covers the most usual pieces of detritus handled by forensic scientists:

Arson/Fire related
Biological/Sexual – semen, vaginal swabs, etc.

Biological/Other – saliva, faeces, etc.
Blood
Clothing, cloth
Documents
Drugs and associated paraphernalia
Dust traces
Explosives and explosive residues
Fibres
Firearms and associated material – bullets, cartridges, etc.
Forgery equipment
Glass
Glove-prints
Hair
Impressions – shoe-prints, tyre-prints
Paint
Poisons
Shoes/footwear
Soil
Tool-marks and tools
Vehicles
Weapons (other than firearms)

In whatever the section of the laboratory, the scientist will normally be at pains to answer two fundamental questions. First, what is it? – is that white powder cocaine, or only sucrose; is that stain blood or dried banana? Secondly, he will want to establish whether a clue left at the scene of the crime can be associated with a 'control' sample taken from a suspect – a hair perhaps, or a clothing fibre; does the bloodstain on his trousers share the same group as the victim?

Biology
Because it deals largely with the evidence connected with violent crimes such as homicide and rape, the biology section in many people's eyes is the forensic laboratory. It is true that all blood comes here, but it is only one aspect even of this section's work.

Although there are inevitable cross-overs, there are a number of identifiable sub-groups in biology. **Hair** and **Fibres** are one group of trace evidence examined, and a wide range of magnification techniques from the basic compound **Microscope** to the **Scanning Electron Microscope**, with its capacity to enlarge up to 150,000×. It often surprises people that the humble microscope is all that is needed in a great number of cases of analysis and comparison – for example, did that hair found in the boot of a suspect's car come from the victim's head or from the suspect's dog as he claims? Although most of what we still need to know about hair had already been encapsulated in Professor **Glaister**'s *Hairs of Mammalia from the Medic-Legal Aspect* in 1931, one recent discovery – **DNA Profiling** – can prove *specific* identity from a single hair.

Much of the **Instrumentation** used in the forensic laboratory is suitable for use in many sections; the **Comparison Microscope** used to match hairs will also be used to study bullets and cartridges recovered from a shooting incident. Similarly, the flexible technique of **Chromatography** is as valuable to the chemist analysing drugs as it is to the biologist determining the component dyes of a fibre.

Body fluids make up one very large division of the biology laboratory, and **Serology**, the study of those fluids, is a discipline that has developed most remarkably from the first discovery of the simple ABO blood grouping by Karl Landsteiner in 1900, to the modern miracle of genetic 'fingerprinting' discovered by Dr Alec Jeffreys in 1984. Although the refinement of the DNA analytical process has made a great deal of the former work on body fluids undertaken by the biology laboratory redundant, routine examination of possible **Semen** stains, saliva samples, and others are still carried out on samples passed on by the police surgeon or by the pathologist.

Other functions of the biologists are identification of botanical and sometimes zoological material. It is not entirely unknown for a forensic pathologist to send samples from the **Insect Infestation** of a dead body to the biology laboratory for identification and an estimate of the time since death based on the life-cycle of the maggots – a procedure first used by Dr Alexander Mearns during his work on the notorious Ruxton case (see page 149). Or the pathologist may require an accurate analysis of the stomach contents of one of his cases, to determine the composition of the last meal, or perhaps to see how far digestion had progressed as an aid in determining time of death.

Chemistry

The chemistry department is usually the largest single unit in a forensic laboratory (followed by the biologists). The kind of materials handled are **Paint** and **Glass** – often resulting from vehicle crashes or hit-and-run accidents. The chemist is also responsible for the examination and matching of **Impressions**, such as tyre- and **Shoe-Prints**, and **Tool Marks** left at the scene of a crime, normally during the process of illegal entry.

In cases of suspected **Arson**, it may be important that an experienced fire chemist visits the scene of the incident, not only to establish whether or not a crime has been committed, but also to oversee the collection of evidence from which he will later identify such clues as the nature of the accelerant – petrol, paraffin, etc.

Illegal **Drugs** are a growing international problem, and this is reflected in the case-load of the world's forensic chemistry laboratories. In the United States, official figures claim that in excess of seventy-five per cent of laboratory analysis work is drugs-related; in Britain, where the problem is for the time being thankfully less severe, a comparatively huge twenty per cent of laboratory cases is connected to drug misuse. The situation is complicated by the ever increasing number of new drugs that are finding their way from the pharmacist's shelf to the street, and the huge increase in what are called 'desiguer' drugs, a cocktail of existing substances in new combinations to satisfy a cultural or fashion need. In this respect, the forensic chemist will have not only substances to analyse, but the equipment from illegal drug factories and the paraphernalia of drug use; on top of which are the blood and urine samples from alleged users passed on by the police surgeon.

Drink/driving has become such a problem that chemistry laboratories have a special **Alcohol** unit, specifically for the analysis of blood and urine samples taken as the result of positive roadside breathalyser tests. In Britain such work comprises a staggering forty-eight per cent of all cases handled by the Forensic Science Service.

When a pathologist has completed his post-mortem examination of a suspected poisoning case, it is usual for the whole of the stomach contents – probably accompanied by the stomach itself – the small intestine, and most of the internal organs to be dispatched to the forensic science laboratory for qualitative and quantitative analysis of possible toxins. This least enviable of jobs is picked up by the chemist/toxicologist.

Firearms

The examination of **Firearms** as they relate to crime is the field of expertise of what are popularly called **Ballistics** experts, though the word more specifically refers to the study of projectiles. Overall the firearms expert is required to make judgements on the origin of evidence recovered either from the scene of a shooting or from a victim's body. This is usually done by the comparison of 'rifling' marks etched into the surface of a bullet as it passes down the barrel of a gun. Each bullet fired from the same gun will carry identical marks; it has, in forensic terms, put a 'fingerprint' on the projectile. This information will allow the specialist to determine whether or not a suspect gun has fired a fatal bullet. Similar evidence will be left on metal cartridge cases, and they too can be married with a specific weapon.

Working in close collaboration with the forensic pathologist, ballistics experts will also advise on matters connected with **Gunshot Wounds** – estimating the range from which shotguns were fired by the shape of the injury, and calculating the trajectory of bullets.

Documents

With headlines reserved for cases of violent death, and media attention attracted only by developments in new miracle techniques of identifying criminals, the section of the laboratory which deals with **Disputed Documents** has been cast in a Cinderella role. However, with the fraudulent use of cheques and cheque and credit cards running to millions of dollars worldwide every year, the scientific analysis of documents is increasingly engaging the time of forensic scientists, and new techniques devised for protection from fraud.

More recently a technique has been developed in the search for a better way of visualizing impressions of writing that have been transferred to the page underneath, which has had startling repercussions throughout the world of criminal law and law enforcement. In a number of notorious cases in England it was positively proved by the use of ESDA (Electrostatic Detection Apparatus) that supposed confessions and police statements had been tampered with in order to secure convictions. Several innocent people have already been released from custody, and a number of police officers, some of senior rank, have been disciplined or suspended from duty.

Forensic Medicine

Perhaps the best known of all the scientific detectives, and the ones whose names become legends, are the forensic **Pathologists**, the physicians whose job it is to carry out post-mortem examinations, often in the most appalling circumstances, in an attempt to solve the three fundamental riddles of homicide – **Cause of Death**, **Time of Death**, and the identity of the victim. Frequently the remains are skeletal or so badly decomposed as to defy visual means of identification; in these cases the post-mortem pathologist may call on other skills such as **Facial Reconstruction**, **Odontology** (Forensic Dentistry), and **Anthropology**.

It is impossible to put an exact date to the birth of forensic medicine; it evolved gradually as its component parts, medicine and law, evolved. We do know from the earliest manuscripts that the Ancient Egyptian civilization already had an extensive history of medicine and a highly developed system of law. The practice of examining the bodies of those who had died violently or mysteriously is ancient, and a brief synopsis of the early development of legal medicine will be found under the entry on **Post-Mortem Procedures**. It will be seen that while Europe already had a rudimentary tradition of forensic medicine centred on the universities in the seventeenth and eighteenth centuries, it was not until the nineteenth and early twentieth centuries that Britain and the United States developed anything like a coherent policy on what it called 'medical jurisprudence'.

At the turn of the twentieth century forensic pathology – called by its detractors 'the beastly science' – was attracting some of its first great luminaries. There were Professor John **Glaister** and his son, also John, who successively held the chair in Forensic Medicine at Glasgow University, the celebrated Sir Bernard **Spilsbury** and his equally highly respected contemporary Sir Sydney **Smith**. The pathologist in those days was still very much a 'jack-of-all-forensic-trades', it was only later that ballistics, toxicology, serology, metallurgy, and so on became separate disciplines. By that time a new generation of pathologists were earning their laurels; in England there was the trio known affectionately as the Three Musketeers – Keith **Simpson**, Francis **Camps**, and Donald **Teare**. In America the giants were Milton Helpern, Alan Moritz and Michael Baden.

As the understanding of physical medicine was advancing apace, so too was the investigation of the human mind, and in tandem with its rapid clinical advancement, *forensic* **Psychiatry** added yet another powerful weapon to the arsenal of criminal investigators. The forensic psychiatrist, however, does not simply pronounce on the **Insanity** or otherwise of apprehended suspects and their **Competence to Stand Trial**; increasingly they are becoming active in areas like constructing **Psychological Profiles** to assist in the identification of unknown criminals. This new development has enjoyed significant success in tracking down serial murderers.

A Question of Identity

It has been this ceaseless search for a suitable means of identifying criminals which has led to some of the most ingenious and, it must be said, most preposterous propositions. Some early researchers like Cesare Lombroso believed that there was such a person as **'Criminal Man'**, whose physiological features would reveal his predisposition to crime. Equally exotic claims were made for **Physiognomy**, and adherents to **Phrenology** were convinced that tendencies to criminality could be read in the bumps of the head. In 1882 Alphonse **Bertillon**, a junior clerk in the records office of the Paris Sûreté, was given the opportunity to put into practice his theory of **Anthropometry**. With the assumption that no two human beings shared the same physical measurements, Bertillon began keeping physiological records of the criminals that passed through the office. It was a system of criminal record which enjoyed some international success until the introduction of what at the time was the single greatest advance in scientific criminal investigation – the classification of **Fingerprints**. Fingerprints are still the world's most commonly used means of identifying felons, though there is every possibility that in the future some form of electronic record based on **DNA Profiling** will supersede it.

Basing his work on Bertillon's second brain-child, **Portrait Parlé**, Detective Thomas **Byrnes** of New York began to utilize the rapidly advancing science of photography to take 'mug-shots' of convicted criminals for what he called his Rogue's Gallery. In the 1940s another American, Hugh C. McDonald, invented **Identikit**, succeeded in 1970 by Jacques Penry's **Photo-FIT**; there have followed a number of variations on video-fit systems, and some early experiments with laser **Facial Reconstruction**.

The Future

For the future it is to be hoped that the forensic sciences will be used to a far greater extent across the spectrum of crime, since the advances made in DNA profiling are of huge significance not only in positively convicting the *guilty*, but also positively clearing the *innocent*.

So many alarming cases of miscarriage of justice have been highlighted recently by accusations that confessions have been obtained by coercion – sometimes long after an innocent person has begun their sentence – that far less emphasis can be placed on the reliability of confessions and that other notoriously unreliable evidence, witness

Identification, that in the future convictions *must* be made to rely on indisputable forensic proof.

Milestones in Forensic Science

Various dates and events in history have been advanced by their champions to celebrate the birth of legal science, but one thing is beyond dispute; that the requirement of scientific proof is most clearly seen in the development of medical knowledge, and that legal medicine (medical jurisprudence as it was called until the nineteenth century) was the foundation of all the other forensic sciences. Indeed, it was once the legal doctor's responsibility to be competent in many of the disciplines which technology has made the preserve of the specialist – toxicology, biochemistry, ballistics, etc., a situation that changed only comparatively recently.

The rapid advances made in technology over the past half-century have put ever more sophisticated facilities at the disposal of the forensic scientists. Some of these developments, like DNA (or genetic) 'fingerprinting' carry with them the opportunity to render redundant already existing techniques – in this example, conventional fingerprinting and serology. Other equipment, like the scanning electron microscope, has effected an inter-disciplinary revolution that has widened efficiency over the whole field of trace evidence examination.

The following chart serves as a chronological introduction to some of the landmarks in the history of forensic science that will be encountered in greater detail in the entries which follow.

1591   *Microscopy:* Zacharias and Hans Jansen design the first practical microscope.

1728   *Photography:* Johan Heinrich Schulze, a German physician, demonstrates the possibility of imposing photographic images of objects on a solution of chalk and silver nitrate. It was not until 1822 that Louis Daguerre perfected a reliable photographic process.

1804   *Physics:* J.W. Ritter discovers ultraviolet rays, the forensic significance of which was that erased writing and blemishes could be detected by their means.

1814   *Toxicology:* Mathieu Orfila, called the father of toxicology, publishes his monumental work on the classification of poisons, *Traité de Poisons*.

1835   *Ballistics:* Henry Goddard begins to make comparisons between bullet striations and the rifling in gun barrels.

1836   *Toxicology:* One of the founders of scientific toxicology, Alfred Swaine Taylor, publishes *Elements of Medical jurisprudence*. James Marsh develops a test for detecting small traces of arsenic in human tissue.

1858   *Fingerprints:* Introduced by Sir William Herschel.

1850   *Spectrography:* Bunsen and Kirchoff identify evaporable inorganic materials, discovering that gas fumes under fluctuating temperature give off light and energy in relation to the molecular structure of the gas.

1875   *X-rays:* Professor Wilhelm Konrad Röntgen of Wurtzburg discovers that solid objects placed so as to intercept cathode rays produce a secondary radiation which delineates the shapes of the solid matter.

1882   *Anthropomeny:* Alphonse Bertillon in Paris develops a criminal classification system based on body measurement.

1893   *'Criminalistics':* Austrian legal expert Hans Gross publishes his seminal work on the scientific investigation of crime, *Hanbuch für Untersuchungsrichter als System der Kriminalistik.*

1901   *Serology:* Karl Landsteiner establishes the first system of blood grouping, the so-called ABO system.
      Serology: Paul Uhlenhuth uses protein-composition factors to distinguish human from other animal blood.

1912   *Ballistics:* Balthazard improves comparison of bullets found at the scene of a crime and bullets from a suspect gun by using photographic enlargements.
      Microphotography: Lukas S. May compares tool prints with marks left on surfaces at the scene of crime.

1921   *Polygraph:* Larson designs a portable lie detector.

1923   *Casting of Traces:* A method by Hans Mullner for casting at the scene of crime.

1925   *Microscopy:* The comparison microscope by Philip O. Gravelle revolutionizes the comparison of traces by permitting two objects to be observed simultaneously.

1932   *Serology:* Swedish scientist Widmark observes the measurable content of ethyl alcohol in the blood as an indicator of intoxication.

1940   *Identikit:* Hugh C. McDonald begins work on the prototype.

1941   *Voice Spectrography:* Developed by Bell Telephone Laboratories and refined by L.G. Kersta.

1965   *Microscopy:* Using beams of electrons instead of beams of light, the Scanning Electron Microscope is capable of magnifications of the order of 150,000×.

1971 *Photo-FIT:* First launch of Jacques Penry's successor to Identikit.

1984 *DNA Profiling:* Dr Alec Jeffreys of the Lister Institute of Leicester University develops the first DNA 'fingerprint'.

A

ACID

Chemically, acids are defined as substances which in solution with (usually) water produce hydrogen ions. They are sharp to the taste (indeed, many are *lethal* if taken orally), turn litmus red, and are to a greater or lesser extent corrosive. The strength of an acid is measured by its hydrogen/ion concentration on a pH scale between 0 (extremely acid), through 7 (neutral) to 14 (extremely alkaline).

Among the organic acids (those containing carbon) are: acetic, benzoic, citric, formic, lactic, oxalic and salicyclic.

Inorganic (or mineral) acids include: boracic, carbonic, *hydrochloric, nitric,* phosphoric and *sulphuric*.

Although the acids rarely appear as *methods* by which murder is procured, the powerful corrosive properties of the inorganic acids have periodically been appreciated as a means of disposing of a tell-tale corpse.

The most commonly used are:

Hydrochloric (called Spirits of salts): A highly corrosive aqueous solution of the colourless gas hydrogen chloride (HCl). It has many industrial uses, as in the production of chlorides and chlorine, and in recovering zinc from galvanized scrap iron. In common with the other corrosives, poisoning with hydrochloric acid is invariably the result of accidental or suicidal ingestion.

It was the solution favoured by German-Swiss Erwin Spengler when he addressed the problem of disposing of the mortal remains of wealthy seventy-four-year-old Katharina Kornagel at her home on Lake Constance. Frau Kornagel was last seen on 6 December 1987, and in response to the anxieties expressed by friends and neighbours, an official search of her apartment was carried out by a forensic team from the State Criminal Investigation Office. The searchers found evidence of a life-and-death struggle resulting in a multitude of human bloodstains on walls and floors leading to the bathroom, where more blood was found along with clear traces of hydrochloric acid. The conclusion reached by investigating officers was that after her brutal murder, Frau Kornagel's chauffeur, Erwin Spengler, had dismembered his victim and rendered her remains liquid with acid before flushing them down the bath.

Nitric (Aqua fortis, or Red spirit of nitre): Usually colourless, though the presence of oxides of nitrogen can impart a reddish-brown tint. The usual strength of the acid (HNO_3) is 70 per cent by weight, although the powerful brownish 'fuming' nitric acid contains 94 per cent. Nitric acid is obtained either by the action of sulphuric acid on potassium nitrate, or by the oxidation of ammonia. Commercially used in the manufacture of plastics, dyes and fertilizer nitrates, as well as explosives (nitro-glycerine). Nitric is the only acid that will dissolve gold (hence the 'acid test'), and it is this property of dissolving metals that has caused nitric acid to be viewed unfavourably for use in acid-baths.

Nevertheless, a decidedly deadly use for it was found by the notorious Dr Geza de Kaplany. De Kaplany was a thirty-six-year-old Hungarian anaesthetist living and practising in California and married to a model of whose physical beauty he was insanely jealous. In August 1962, neighbours were so upset by the constant moaning and wailing sounds coming from the direction of the de Kaplany residence that the police were called in, and the source of the disturbance traced to Mrs Hanja de Kaplany.

In order, it seems, that no other man should ever enjoy his wife's beauty, de Kaplany had turned their bedroom into a virtual torture chamber. Tying Hanja to the bed, de Kaplany had made cut marks down and across her body and then systematically poured acid into the wounds. A note found in the room instructed the agonized woman: 'If you want to live – do not shout; do what I tell you or else you will die.' Thirty-six hours after her admittance to hospital for emergency treatment Hanja de Kaplany did die. At the scene of her ordeal, police found three one-pint bottles containing hydrochloric, sulphuric and nitric acid – the latter was almost empty, the bed had become a mass of soggy, disintegrating sheets and the carpet was burned through by the action of the acid. Although de Kaplany was eventually sentenced to life imprisonment for murder, he was paroled in 1976, in one of the most controversial decisions in Californian legal history.

Sulphuric (Oil of vitriol): In its pure state a colourless, dense oily liquid containing between 95 per cent and 98 per cent of the acid H_2SO_4. Extensively used in the chemical industry and in petrol refining, the deceptive oily consistency has not infrequently been mistaken for other oils, glycerine and syrup – with fatal consequences.

Sulphuric acid is a powerful dehydrating agent which extracts water from body tissue leaving a soft, fatty residue which can easily be flushed away. The intense heat generated by this chemical process will eventually destroy the bones as well. This interdependence of flesh and bone was a factor investigated by Dr Turfit, the deputy director of Scotland Yard's Forensic Laboratory, during his work on the Haigh case. Turfit found that a human foot, amputated from the body, completely dissolved in sulphuric acid in about four hours, while a sheep's femur, stripped of its fleshy covering, took four days.

Although it was John George Haigh who achieved lasting infamy as 'The Acid-Bath Killer', there had been a precedent across the channel in France in 1933. George Sarret, a lawyer, had concocted an elaborate insurance fraud with the willing collaboration of the Schmidt sisters, Katherine and Philomene. Katherine, who was Sarret's mistress, contrived to marry a man who was terminally ill with cancer, and arranged for a colleague named Chambon to pose as her husband for the purpose of taking out a life insurance policy for 100,000 francs (insurers being understandably reluctant to issue policies on those at death's door). In time death occurred naturally and Sarrett, Chambon and the Schmidts divided the spoils. Being of an instinctively greedy and naturally criminous disposition, Chambon sought to increase his portion with a little blackmail against his partners. Which was a pity for Chambon, because they shot him. They also dispatched Chambon's mistress who had been privy to the scene. The two bodies were then laid in a bath in Sarret's cellar and covered with twenty-five gallons of sulphuric acid. The second time the terrible trio attempted the insurance scam was their last; indeed, for Maître Sarret it was the last piece of dishonesty that he ever engaged in – sentenced to death for murder, he was later guillotined.

ACONITE

A drug derived from the common garden plant 'monkshood' *(Aconitum anglicum),* though in some parts of the country it is called 'wolfsbane', 'leopard's bane', 'women's bane', and 'Devil's helmet'; in Ireland it is known as 'blue rocket'.

The active constituent of aconite is an alkaloid called aconitine, contained in greater or lesser strength in the plant's foliage or root. In medicine it was formerly administered in the form of tincture of aconite or as a liniment – usually for the relief of sciatica and rheumatism, where its heat-producing and mildly anaesthetic properties gave comfort. Aconitine fell into disfavour when it was found that even rubbing preparations on the skin produced symptoms of poisoning as by ingestion.

Until well into the twentieth century it was the most virulent poison known, one-fiftieth of a grain having proved fatal, while it is certain that one-tenth of a grain will always result in death. It is a white powder without any definite crystalline structure, hardly soluble in water, but dissolved by alcohol or weak acids. Dilutions of one-thousandth of a grain can be distinguished by the tingling sensation set up by the drug.

The symptoms of aconitine poisoning are these: in a few minutes to an hour from the time of ingestion, the victim experiences a numbness and tingling sensation in the mouth and throat, which become parched. If a large quantity has been administered, this tingling becomes a severe burning extending down the throat and into the abdomen. The tingling rapidly extends to the hands and feet, and soon the whole surface of the body is affected. The skin of the extremities is cool and clammy to the touch, but at the same time the victim complains that he feels as though his limbs have been flayed. There is a loss of power in the legs, and sight and hearing are considerably dulled, though usually the victim remains in full possession of his mental faculties until death ensues. Occasionally, muscular twitching is followed by convulsions. The pulse becomes weak and variable, the pupils of the eyes dilated, and the least exertion may bring on a fatal syncope. Death usually results from failure of the respiratory organs. Aconitine paralyses all the organs in turn, and the fatal period can be from eight minutes to three or four hours.

The most notable case of aconitine poisoning in England is the case of Dr Henry Lamson, while in Scotland Dr Edward William Pritchard's use of aconite helped earn him a place in that country's Black Calendar as well as on the scaffold.

The aconite poisons have been known throughout the world from the earliest of times, and the use of aconitine recorded by the ancient Greeks, who called it the Queen of Poisons and believed that it was created from the saliva of the mythical guardian dog of the underworld, Cerberus. So popular was it as a means of familicide in Rome that Juvenal in his *Satires* wrote:

Murdering your stepson is the traditional thing to do, so wards with rich expectations should learn to look after themselves. Don't trust any of the dishes at dinner, those pies are black with the poison your dear mother has put in . . . You think I'm exaggerating? Listen to Pontia confessing all: 'Yes, I admit it, I gave aconite to my children. Everyone knew they were poisoned, and I did it.' 'What, you serpent, both at one meal?' 'Yes, and if there had been seven of them, I'd have done the lot.'

Perhaps Drs Lamson and Pritchard were scholars of the classics.

Case Study

DR HENRY GEORGE LAMSON

Lamson was born in 1849, and from an early age exhibited an adventurous spirit. At the age of eighteen he chose to study medicine in Paris. On the outbreak of the Franco-Prussian War he volunteered for the French Ambulance Corps and served with distinction. After qualifying in 1874, he worked for two years in a Paris hospital before volunteering again for active service in the Balkans. For this effort he was decorated both by the Serbian and the Romanian governments. In 1878, he elected to return to England and in the same year married a wealthy ward of Chancery, Kate John, and in the process inherited £1,500.

Unfortunately, while in the Balkans Lamson had developed an addiction to morphine. He invested his wife's money in a series of medical practices, each of which failed, eating up more and more of his capital. He had also begun to develop a dishonest streak in his character as his financial difficulties became more desperate. In Brighton he falsely added the name of a popular doctor to his brass plate, and in London he hired locals to call at his surgery to make it seem more successful when he was trying to sell the practice. By 1881 he was in a dire position, with no capital and no practice, and had resorted to issuing false cheques to tide himself over. He was badly in need of some new source of finance, and he found one readily to hand.

Mrs Lamson's mother, the widow of a Manchester merchant, had left her fortune in trust to her three sons and two daughters until they reached the age of twenty-one. One son, Herbert, had already died, and in 1879 the second son, Henry, would also die of a mysterious stomach complaint. This left the two daughters – Kate, Lamson's wife, and a married sister, Margaret Chapman and the youngest son, Percy. Percy John was only fifteen in 1878 and was crippled with a curvature of the spine and paralysis of the lower limbs. If he, too, were to die, Lamson would immediately inherit over £700 through his wife's interest.

Percy, who hero-worshipped Henry Lamson, was invited, with Margaret Chapman and her husband, to spend the summer holiday with the Lamsons on the Isle of Wight. Before they arrived Lamson bought quinine sulphate powder and one grain of aconitine, a highly toxic irritant vegetable poison, from a local Ventnor pharmacist. Lamson then announced to Percy and the Chapmans that he must leave that same evening on a trip to America in search of new employment. During the course of the afternoon he administered the quinine sulphate powder to Percy, saying that he didn't look well. That evening, when Lamson was well on his way out of the country, Percy was taken ill with severe vomiting and did not recover until the next morning.

Returning to England after a fortnight, Lamson continued to run up further debts to the point where another attempt on his nephew's life seemed the only solution. Lamson wrote to Percy John at Blenheim Special School, Wimbledon, where he was a pupil, to inform the boy that he wished to pay him a visit before travelling to Paris on business. The following day, 3 December 1881, he arrived at 7.00 p.m. and was shown up to see the headmaster, Mr William Bedbrook. Percy was carried into the room and Mr Bedbrook offered Lamson a glass of sherry. Lamson inexplicably asked to have sugar in it, and a bowl of caster sugar was brought to the room. From his black bag Lamson now produced three slices of Dundee cake, and selected one each for Bedbrook and Percy; he then turned the conversation to some empty gelatine capsules which he had discovered while he was in America. Filling one with the harmless caster sugar, he offered it to Percy saying 'Percy, you are a champion pill-taker, take this. Show Mr Bedbrook how easy it is to swallow.' He then quickly took his leave, stating that he had to catch a train for London Bridge to get to Paris that night. On the way out, he remarked to Bedbrook on how ill Percy was looking and how he might not last long.

Later that evening Percy was taken by a violent spasm of vomiting, and after lapsing into a coma died at twenty past eleven, despite all the efforts of the school physician. Next morning the police were called, and, the local doctors being unable to ascertain a cause of death, Dr Thomas Stevenson, the premier toxicologist of the day, was brought in to perform an autopsy and test various substances found at the school.

Grey patches on the stomach suggested the presence of a vegetable alkaloid poison and a raisin in the stomach contained traces of aconitine, as did a powder sent to Percy from Ventnor. At the inquest Lamson was mentioned by name and this jogged the memory of an assistant at Allen & Hanbury's, a pharmacy in the City of London, who recalled selling aconitine to a Dr Lamson on 2 November.

From the safety of Paris, Lamson had obviously decided that his crime was unprovable and that he could brazen the matter out. After writing a letter protesting his innocence, he set out for London, arriving at Scotland Yard in the company of his wife to discuss any misconceptions the police might have. To his chagrin, he was immediately arrested and lodged in Wandsworth Prison.

The trial opened at the Old Bailey on 8 March 1882 and lasted six days. The defence counsel, Mr Montagu Williams, claimed that nobody knew the exact effects of aconitine poisoning or how it had been administered, and cited Lamson's good relationship with the victim and his family as shedding doubt on any evil intention, but the circumstantial evidence was so strong that it only took the jury thirty minutes to reach a verdict of guilty.

Lamson's demeanour deteriorated considerably in prison, probably partly due to the withdrawal from morphine, and, towards the end, he confessed to the cold-blooded crime he had committed. On 18 April 1882, he was led in considerable trepidation from his cell in Wandsworth Prison to face righteous retribution at the hand of Marwood, the hangman.

ADIPOCERE

The result of a process called 'saponification' which arises when a body has been immersed in water or interred in damp soil for a long period of time.

The phenomenon is caused by the hydrogenization of normally semi-liquid body fats into a hard 'suety' substance varying in colour from white to yellowish-white. The process takes a long time – it is established on the face and neck between 4–5 months and on the trunk between 5–6 months if the body is in damp ground; the change in water is more variable, adipocere developing more slowly the lower the temperature.

Apart from serving as a broad indicator of time of death, the formation of adipocere once established is irreversible and can to some extent protect the internal organs of the body – sometimes to a remarkable degree, as in the case of the Hopetoun Quarry victims.

Case Study

HOPETOUN QUARRY MURDERS

It was a June afternoon in 1913, when ploughman Thomas Duncan, showing a new colleague around the locality, turned out of the hot sunshine in to the cool shade of greenery that surrounded the water-filled Hopetoun Quarry, just a mile from Winchburgh. It was less 'summery' here, almost gloomy, where the brooding stillness of the water's surface and the almost total silence created a sinister atmosphere.

When first they saw the bundle floating on the water's surface, the two men thought perhaps somebody had removed a scarecrow from one of the fields above the quarry and thrown it in. As they began to pull the package slowly nearer to the bankside it became obvious that it was no scarecrow, but two small, waterlogged bodies tied together.

When the remains were laid on the slab in the Linlithgow mortuary, the local police doctor was doubtful whether any attempt could even be made at a post-mortem. The bodies had been immersed in water for so long and had decomposed so badly, as to render them almost unidentifiable as human beings. The Chair at Edinburgh University's Department of Forensic Medicine was at the time held by Professor Harvey Littlejohn, who was also Chief Police Surgeon; and when Littlejohn arrived at the tiny mortuary he had as his assistant Sydney Smith. It was to be Smith's first major case in a career that would make his name a legend in forensic medicine.

Following the painstaking procedures of their science, the two pathologists were, against all odds, able to present local police with profiles of the two victims:

Body No. 1
Male; Height: three feet seven and a half inches; Age (determined by the rate of development of the permanent molars and the growing ends of the 'long bones'): between six and seven years. There was a small injury to the head, though it was impossible to state whether this was caused before or after death.

Body No. 2
Male; Height: three feet two inches; Age: between three and four years.

Death was estimated to have occurred around the late summer/early autumn of 1911 – about a year and a half previously.

In the case of the Hopetoun Quarry victims, the conversion of the body fats to adipocere was all but complete, and this had the effect of preserving the internal organs of the bodies to a remarkable degree – to the extent that Smith was able clearly to identify the constituents of their last meal – traditional Scotch broth – and further state that the meal had been eaten about one hour before death. This indicated that the boys had been locals, an opinion strengthened by a visit to the quarry, and the realization that the only practical way of getting the two victims to such an isolated spot was on their own two legs – lured to their death. This in turn indicated the grim possibility that the killer had been a close friend or relative.

While examining the clothing in which the bodies had been dressed, Smith had found the faded imprint of a stamp on one of the shirts – it had formerly been the property of the Dysart poorhouse, Fife.

Only a brief search of police files was required to ascertain that two young boys had gone missing from the area at about the estimated time of the quarry victims' deaths – November 1911. Their descriptions fitted perfectly the pathologist's profiles.

William Higgins had been born in December 1904, his brother John in August 1907. Their father, Patrick, an habitual drunkard, had so neglected his family that his young wife died in 1910, and in the same year his children were granted relief by the Inspectorate of the Poor in Fife. In January 1911, they were admitted to the Dysart poorhouse, with the provision that Higgins pay for their modest upkeep. This he failed to do, and in June 1911 he was imprisoned for two months.

When Patrick Higgins was released from gaol he removed his sons from Dysart and took lodgings for them in the house of Elizabeth Hynes in Broxburn – for which he also felt disinclined to hand over any of his drinking money. With some compassion and much anger, Mrs Hynes reported Higgins to the Inspector of the Poor, and he was again reminded of his responsibilities and the consequences of failing to meet them. At the beginning of November, William and John disappeared.

Higgins made several attempts to come up with a plausible explanation – to a fellow-worker he said the boys were on their way to a new home in Canada. He told James Daly a preposterous story about two ladies whom they had met on a train and who were so stricken with pity that they each took one of the children home with them. To Alexander Fairnie, Higgins lamented that the lads had 'gone to glory', and he told Elizabeth Hynes that they had drowned.

Higgins' defence at his trial in Edinburgh was temporary insanity caused by epilepsy, and the main evidence was concerned with proving or disproving this condition. In the end, the jury decided that Higgins was sane and found him guilty of murder. On 2 October 1913, without ever having shown the least remorse, Higgins was hanged at the prison on Calton Hill.

A footnote to this remarkable story of medical detection: Sydney Smith was so unpressed by the perfect formation of adipocere on the bodies of the Higgins children that he took the dismembered corpses back with him to Edinburgh, wrapped in small parcels, and lodged them in the Museum of Forensic Medicine at the university. It was a piece of 'body-snatching' for which Smith's mentor was lampooned in university doggerel:

> Two bodies found in a lonely mere,
> Converted into adipocere.
> Harvey, when called in to see 'em,
> Said 'Just what I need for my museum.'

ALCOHOL

While it is not *per se* an offence to be drunk, inebriety is of forensic importance partly because a drunken person is more likely to have and cause accidents and to sustain injury, and partly because there is well-documented evidence to connect alcohol with crime, particularly crimes of violence.

The fact that a person is drunk when he attacks another is no defence in law. However, if it can be proved that he was so hopelessly drunk that he was incapable of knowing what he was doing, or of forming any specific intention, then, in a case of homicide, it could reduce a charge of murder to one of manslaughter.

There are a number of quaintly archaic offences related to drunkenness – for example, being drunk while on a passenger steamer, in charge of a child under seven, horses or cattle, and loaded firearms – but it is usually in connection with driving a motor vehicle while under the influence of drink that criminal charges are brought.

Drink/Driving

Under the provisions of the Road Traffic Act of 1988 it is an offence for a person to be in charge of a motor vehicle on a road or other public place while unfit to drive through drink or drugs. It is an additional offence if the driver has an amount of alcohol in his blood equivalent to 80mg or more per 100ml of blood (the equivalent measurement for urine is 107mg in 100ml).

Breathalysers

Although breathalysers are the concern of police officers and not forensic scientists, they represent the first step in a very important function of the biology laboratory. When a driver who has been stopped and tested is shown by the breathalyser to exceed the permissible blood/alcohol level, a sample of blood is taken at the police station which is subsequently sent for analysis. The results of the laboratory test will be the basis of the case against the defendant charged with a drink/driving offence.

Physiology of Alcohol

Alcohol is absorbed from the stomach at roughly the rate of one unit (the equivalent of one measure of spirits) per hour, and is then distributed around the body. The elimination of alcohol from the body takes longer – about 15mg/100ml per hour.

How an individual will be affected by alcohol depends to a great degree upon how accustomed he is to imbibing large quantities; to a lesser extent such factors as heat and cold, illness or disease, the use of medications, a full stomach, etc. will also modify the effect.

The following is a rough guide to behaviour:

0–50mg* per 100ml of blood: Unlikely to be any adverse symptoms unless the subject is unused to alcohol, suffering some complicating illness or physically exhausted.

50–100mg: This is what is considered the 'social drinking' level, and the familiar effect is that, as a result of the alcohol depressing some of the inhibitions, the subject begins to be more talkative (he may also become more friendly or aggressive). The face will become flushed, and

*A general guide to quantities in terms of beer is:

50mg alcohol/100ml blood = approximately 1½ pints of beer
150mg alcohol/100ml blood = approximately 4 pints of beer
250mg alcohol/100ml blood = approximately 7 pints of beer
400mg alcohol/100ml blood = approximately 11 pints of beer

the eyes slightly suffused, with a tendency to nystagmus and dilated pupils. There may be some degree of muscular incoordination.

125–250mg: The state of full intoxication; bodily actions become uncoordinated, speech slurred; loss of memory. The skin appears flushed, the mouth dry, the pupils of the eye dilated and the breathing heavy.

250–400mg: Stage of pre-coma – gross uncoordination and incoherence. Pupils of the eye react sluggishly. The inexperienced drinker will become very ill with vomiting (possibly blood-stained).

400–500mg: Subject liable to slip into a coma with severe cerebral depression. Heavy, noisy breathing, pallid complexion, abnormally low body temperature; pupils contracted.

Over 500mg: Alcohol causes medullary paralysis followed, in the case of an inexperienced drinker, by death.

Recognition of Intoxication

A doctor (most usually a police surgeon) may be called to make an examination and provide a report on a suspected drunk's level of inebriety to determine, for example, his ability to drive; whether his condition is due to alcohol or to some illness or injury; whether it is safe to detain him in a police cell or whether he should be admitted to hospital; and so on. To assist the doctor, the British Medical Association has produced a check-list of what to look out for – *The Recognition of Intoxication;* the following is a synopsis:

1. The presence of any serious injury or illness requiring urgent attention should be excluded first.
2. Medical history; for example, of long-term illness or disability – diabetes, epilepsy, etc.; use of prescription drugs; the nature of any recent food or drink.
3. General demeanour – state of dress, speech, coordination; although a subject may be able to exercise a degree of self-control for a time, behaviour may become increasingly eccentric.
4. Memory and general mental performance – questions of time and place – what was he doing prior to being arrested.
5. Writing – quality when copying a passage from newspaper.
6. Pulse (should be taken at commencement and completion of examination); temperature, condition of skin (flushed, clammy).
7. Blood pressure; important to eliminate conditions such as cardiovascular disease.

8. Respiration; it is possible that a subject may have refused, or been unable to provide, a breath sample due to respiratory disease.
9. State of tongue (dry, coated); smell of breath.
10. Eye movements. Look for nystagmus, reaction of pupils to light, visual acuity; check wearing of spectacles or contact lenses.
11. Hearing – impairment.
12. Central nervous system – gait; ability to walk steadily in a straight line and to turn immediately when asked without losing balance. Ability to stand with eyes open or closed without swaying. Ability to perform finger-to-finger and finger-to-nose tests. These tests are especially important if there is any suspicion of head injury.
13. Examinations of cardiovascular, respiratory and alimentary systems.

Samples
These observations will support the analysis of blood or urine samples which the police will already have obtained. Blood samples may be requested by the police or the subject may offer them, but can only be taken with the consent of the subject. The sample must be divided in two, one part going to the laboratory, the other given to the subject enabling him if he wishes to obtain independent analysis.

Case Study

THE BOY AND THE BOTTLE
In his autobiographical *Forty Years of Murder*, Professor Keith **Simpson** recounts the strange case of the young boy found dead in suspicious circumstances on the Channel Island of Guernsey. Simpson was in England at the time and was woken early one morning by a telephone call from Detective Sergeant Brown of the Guernsey force. Brown had been summoned to an incident on the island where a fourteen-year-old youth was lying dead on the living room floor of his parents' house, blood smears everywhere. The boy's parents had gone out the previous evening at around eight, and returned some time after midnight to find their son covered with blood, apparently murdered. The police surgeon had arrived at the scene at 1.30 a.m. and from the stiffness of the body assumed rigor had set in and estimated the **Time of Death** as around six the previous evening – *while the parents were still in the house,* Sergeant Brown added significantly.

Simpson, troubled by the doctor's estimate of time of death and the seeming onset of rigor mortis, asked whether the body temperature had been taken. It had not. 'Then I suggest you call the doctor out and get him to take it at once. And ask him to take it again in an hour's time so that, if it is still falling, we can work out how fast. Ring me later.'

Taking the body temperature showed that over the hour it had fallen from 93°F at 4.00 a.m. to 92°F at 5.00, making death at six the previous evening impossible; Simpson offered a new estimate as between eleven and twelve at night – effectively depriving detective Brown of his suspects. As for the rigor mortis, Simpson explained: 'It must have been a cadaveric spasm, the stiffening that comes on sometimes at the moment death takes place. It means that the boy must have been very frightened or very taut at the time he died.'

The 'extensive bleeding' turned out on post-mortem examination to have originated from just one bad cut on the foot, which the policeman attributed to the shattered glass tumbler that was near the body. And now he came to recall, Sergeant Brown had been aware of a strong smell of whisky in the room, and noticed a half-empty bottle of Scotch on the dresser.

'Did the boy smell of alcohol?' Simpson asked when he next spoke to the Guernsey man.

'Come to think of it, he did.'

With his customary quick-wittedness, Professor Simpson now gave the verdict on his first 'telephone autopsy'. The boy, he suggested, taking advantage of his parents' absence to sample the contents of the whisky bottle, got very drunk, dropped the glass he was drinking from and in stumbling about cut his foot badly and spread blood around the room. It had been a combination of alcohol and panic that drove the lad into a cadaveric spasm and he died from loss of blood. The pathologist was soon proved correct when an analysis of the deceased's blood revealed 173mg of alcohol per 100ml of blood – enough to make a fourteen-year-old very drunk indeed.

ANTHROPOLOGY

The wider discipline of Anthropology can be broadly described as the study of humankind from its earliest evolution on earth (about five million years ago) to the present. Physical Anthropology is the narrower study of human beings themselves – literally their 'physique', their structure. It is this branch with its extensive experience in the field of osteology that has given birth to the youngest of the forensic sciences,

Forensic Anthropology. One specialist has defined the discipline as: 'That branch of physical anthropology which for forensic purposes deals with the identification of more or less skeletonized remains known to be or suspected to be human. Beyond the elimination of non-human elements, the identification process undertakes to provide opinions regarding sex, age, race, stature, and such other characteristics of each individual involved as may lead to his or her recognition.'

In many instances the experienced forensic pathologist will have acquired sufficient knowledge of human anatomy to serve his needs in post-mortem identification of partial or skeletal remains, but such sophistications as forensic anthropology represent one of the ways in which legal medicine is benefiting from the general trend towards specialization. This is particularly apparent in the United States where forensic anthropology is a certificated profession in its own right under the American Board of Forensic Anthropology, established through the American Academy of Forensic Sciences in the mid-1970s.

However, because it is customary in Great Britain and Europe (as well as in a large part of the United States) for the work of identification of skeletal remains to fall to the lot of the post-mortem pathologists, the bulk of the notes and examples on their aspect of forensic medicine will be found in the entry on **Post-Mortem Procedures** (Identification of the Dead). Nevertheless, the following brief scheme outlines the procedure for osteological identification according to the American Board of Forensic Anthropology:

1. Is the bone human or animal?
2. Length of time since death
3. Age of skeleton at death
   (See also **Post-Mortem Procedures** 'A Question of Identity')
   Maturation
   Degenerative changes
4. Sex of skeleton
   (See also **Post-Mortem Procedures** 'A Question of Identity')
   Pelvis
   Skull
   Rest of skeleton
5. Race of skeleton
   Anthropometric measurements
   Prognathism (in Negroid skulls)
   Nasal sill (in Caucasoid skulls)

> *Flat face* (in Mongoloid skulls)
> *Edge of bite in incisor region* (in Mongoloid skulls)

6. Estimation of stature

In addition to this information on general identity, forensic anththropology can indicate the existence in life of illnesses and diseases which have affected the bony structures, as well as healed fractures, wounds and operations.

Case Study

EDWARD, MARTYR KING

It is written that Edward was born around the year 963, son of Edgar the Peaceful, sovereign of all England, and his wife Ethelfleda. The queen died shortly after the birth of Edward, and Edgar remarried, to Elfrida by whom he had another son, Ethelred.

At the death of the king in 975 Edward, as the eldest son, succeeded the throne to begin a reign that was to be as unpopular as it was short. Though we know little of the political life of Edward, his adherence to the strict guidance of Dunstan (then Archbishop of Canterbury, later St Dunstan), and his own irrepressible ill-temper, made him many powerful enemies. Opposition was particularly strong among a group of anti-monastic thanes based in the influential kingdom of Mercia. In their disloyalty to Edward, they had a close ally in Elfrida, who since Edgar's death had sought to install her own son Ethelred – though he was barely ten years of age – on the throne of England.

According to the historian monk William of Malmesbury, in March 979 Edward had been on a hunting trip in what is now Dorset. Weary of the chase and thinking to visit his young step-brother Ethelred, Edward approached Elfrida's castle at Corfe. Warned of his arrival, Elfrida rode out with a party of servants to greet the king, and seeing that he was alone embarked on an impromptu plan that resulted in his death. Feigning pleasure at his unexpected visit, Elfrida called for refreshment for the king, and while he supped, one of her servants 'pierced him through' with a dagger. Although Edward spurred his horse to make an escape, he slipped from the saddle, and with one foot caught in the stirrup was dragged along 'his blood leaving a trail' until he died.

William of Malmesbury relates that Elfrida ordered the king's body to be thrown into a bog that it might not be discovered, but a miraculous pillar of light marked the spot, and the corpse was taken for burial in the church at Wareham. In 980, it is said, Dunstan had the relics removed to Shaftesbury Abbey.

In 1001, Ethelred (called 'Unraed' or 'The Unready' on account of his youth) signed a charter by which his later step-brother was dignified as 'Saint and Martyr'; in 1008 he further ordered the observance of an annual feast of St Edward, Martyr King.

As for Elfrida, overwhelmed by remorse she expiated her sin by becoming a nun and founding the monasteries of Amesbury and Wherwell, at the latter of which she died.

The relics of St Edward were protected by the nuns at Shaftesbury until the Dissolution of Monasteries, when they were buried. The bones were unearthed in 1931 by Mr John Claridge from his family's estate, which included the ruins of the abbey.

Enter Forensic Science

Confirmation of the manner of Edward's death came with the advances made in forensic science subsequent to the 1930s when the martyr king's relics were exhumed. Identity was established by Thomas E.A. Stowell, CBE, MD, FRCS, DIH, a leading pathologist. The task Stowell faced was to answer the basic questions of forensic anthropology – what is the age (or maturation) of the bones, their gender, stature, nationality, and if possible whether the condition of the bones was compatible with the traditional account of Edward's murder.

To start with, the bones when Thomas Stowell first confronted them in 1962 were in what he described as 'a deplorable condition of fragility'. Thanks to the expertise of Don Brothwell* of the British Museum's Department of Anthropology, the remains were first impregnated with the synthetic resin Alvar.

Maturation of the bones: It is interesting in the present context to note that Dr Stowell based his calculations for the age at which the victim died on the studies of two Americans, Dr T.W. McKern and Dr T.D. Stewart, who carried out the vital research into skeletal age change in human males in 1957. For obvious reasons what is quaintly called the

---

*It is only fair to mention that Don Brothwell has publicly dissociated himself from Stowell's findings. In his work on the archaeology of the peat-mummy called 'Lindow Man' (see Mummification) Brothwell states: 'Alas my own examination of the bones [of Edward] did not help to consolidate these claims. In my opInion, the age at death indicated by the skeletal remains seemed wrong, and the damage to the bones far more likely to have been sustained after death' *(The Bog Man,* 1987).

'cadaver population' is mainly composed of people of late middle-age to old age. McKern and Stewart were able to salvage some positive good from the tragedy of the Korean war by collecting data on American casualties – mostly young men.

Thomas Stowell's assessment of his victim's maturation was: a young man, over seventeen years of age but under twenty-one, and due to the presence of a number of 'green-stick' fractures, probably towards the lower end, say eighteen. This age was supported by examination of the skull, vertebrae, pelvis and sacrum.

Stature: Height can be determined with a good degree of accuracy (plus/minus one inch) from calculations based on the measurements of the long bones (see page 415), and despite the fact that in the case of the supposed remains of Edward Martyr the bones were badly fractured with some sections missing, it was possible to arrive at a height of between 5ft 5in and 5ft 8in.

Race: An examination of the reassembled fragments of the skull suggested that it was long-headed (dolichocephalic), a characteristic of the Saxons – as distinct from the Britons or Celts, who were 'round-headed'.

Cause of death: It was Stowell's treatment of the cause of death that illustrates the remarkable powers of deduction of the modern forensic pathologist. Examining the left forearm he found the radius had been broken in four places and the ulna suffered an almost complete transverse fracture, injuries consistent with the arm being violently twisted behind the victim's back. The left thigh-bone also bore tell-tale green-stick fractures of a nature according with the story of Edward's murder – that he had been forced backwards over the saddle cantle and dragged along the ground with his left foot trapped in the stirrup. Fortuitously, Stowell had recently treated just such an injury in a young man of seventeen whose foot had been caught up in the driving belt of a lathe – the fractures matched exactly. That the victim had fallen heavily from the saddle on to his left side was clearly indicated by fractures to the right shoulder blade, elbow and haunch bones.

Thomas Stowell concluded his detailed report: 'I cannot escape the conviction, on historical, anatomical and surgical grounds, that beyond reasonable doubt we have here the bones of Saint Edward, King and Martyr.'

ANTHROPOMETRY

It was in early nineteenth-century Paris that the celebrated arch-criminal-turned-policeman, Eugene Vidocq, encouraged his officers of the Sûreté to pay regular visits to the gaols to familiarize themselves with the faces of prisoners, so that, if the felon was imprudent enough to come into custody again, he would be recognized.

During his subsequent long career, Vidocq initiated the first documentary records of the descriptions of criminals in words and drawings. After Vidocq's retirement in the 1830s the records continued to expand and the practice of record-keeping spread throughout Europe.

The major failing of all this documentary material was that it lacked a key by which information could be quickly and reliably retrieved; no means existed of sorting the images save an ever-increasing staff of clerks who painstakingly sifted through an ever-increasing library of files.

Bertillonage

It was at this stage that Alphonse **Bertillon**, a junior records clerk with the Sûreté, frustrated with the seemingly hopeless task of identifying information, began to experiment with various systems of classification based on facial characteristics.

The breakthrough came when Bertillon recalled similar work undertaken years before by the Belgian biometrician Lambert Quetelet, who had advanced the hypothesis that no two human beings possessed the same body measurements. Bertillon reasoned that if this were applied to criminal detection and accurate cross-referenced records were kept of convicted criminals, then it should be all but impossible for an already known felon to escape capture if adequately described.

In October 1879, Bertillon presented a report on his work to Louis Andrieux, Prefect of Police. Andrieux, able to make little sense of Bertillon's complicated mathematics, passed the paper on to Gustave Macé, head of the Sûreté, who rejected it. Macé was a brilliant detective of the old Vidocq school, though lacking in imagination, and it was not for another three years – until Andrieux had been replaced by Jean Camecasse – that Bertillon, through the intervention of his doctor father, was grudgingly given the chance to try out his theory.

Camecasse gave the young man three months – from December 1882 to February 1883 – to prove that the system he called 'anthropometry' (and which later in his honour was named 'Bertillonage') was a practical proposition. With only two clerks to assist him in this enormous task, and a growing file of over 1,500 cards and no prisoners who matched, there is every likelihood that Bertillon would have failed the test. But the project was blessed with good fortune.

It happened that on 20 February 1883 – two weeks before his time ran out – Bertillon recorded the measurements of a thief named Dupont. In checking the index of known criminals he turned up the name of a thief called Martin, a man with exactly the same characteristics. When Dupont confessed to being Martin the future of Bertillonage was assured. By the end of the following year the system had identified no fewer than 300 prisoners with previous convictions, and its inventor had become a celebrity.

In February 1888, Bertillon was awarded the title Director of the Judicial Identification Service, and moved to a new headquarters with a large staff. But his present glory was to be short-lived. After one final triumph in 1892 when Bertillon was awarded the Legion d'honneur for his identification of the anarchist bomber Ravachol, the system of 'Bertillonage' was rapidly overshadowed by the new science of 'dactylography', or 'fingerprinting', and by the end of the century anthropometry was a quaint piece of police history.

Great Britain

Despite its imaginative response to most areas of criminology and the emerging forensic sciences, Great Britain had been slow to adopt the anthropometric identification system.

By 1893, the need was being felt for a more effective system of identifying criminals than the annual *Register of Distinctive Marks*; in June that year, Francis Galton, as a member of the Committee of the influential Council of the British Association for the Advancement of Science, wrote a lengthy letter to *The Times* in which he proposed a central card index of Anthropometric Records based on the 'Paris system' with the addition of the felon's **Fingerprints** (Galton's seminal work, *Fingerprints,* had been published the previous year). Three months later the Home Secretary, Mr Herbert Asquith, appointed Charles Edward Troup to head a committee to advise on which method – anthropometry or fingerprints – would be most suitable. If nothing else, the inquiry served to highlight the often disastrously inefficient situation prevailing in many regional police forces, and after a visit to Paris to meet representatives of the Sûreté and M. Bertillon himself, the committee found themselves more impressed by Mr Galton's persuasive fingerprint system. Nevertheless, with commendable British compromize, the Troup Committee recommended that a system incorporating both measurement and fingerprinting be introduced. And so on 4 July 1894, the Anthropometric Registry was founded with the Assistant Commissioner of Police, CID, Mr Robert Anderson, as its first Registrar and Dr G. Garson as its scientific adviser.

Whether for good or ill, the Registry proved less successful than had been hoped, and in many instances it met pockets of resistance which stubbornly adhered to the pre-Troup methods of identification. By 1900, the fingerprinting lobby led by Edward Henry (whose *Classification and Use of Fingerprints* had just been published) resulted in the Belper Committee recommendation to change to fingerprints; in July 1901 the Anthropometric Office gave way to Scotland Yard's Fingerprint Branch.

ANTIMONY

Like arsenic, antimony is one of the historic poisons – its name derives from the Greek *anthemonium,* 'flower-like', from the shape of its crystals. Legend tells that the poisonous properties of antimony were really discovered accidentally; under the original name of stibium, it was greatly used by Egyptian beauties to darken their eyelids and eyebrows. One of the princesses of the house of Urs-maat-Ra was apparently given to experimenting, and selected one of her handmaids to try the effect of an oral dose of stibium. Needless to say, the girl did not survive the ordeal, and from that occasion, it is said, dates the use of antimony as a poison. The early Roman physicians fashioned little goblets from the silver-like metal, which were sold as emetic cups. The cups were filled with wine and left fermenting until such time as the bloated reveller could eat and drink no more – he then took a quaff from the cup, vomited violently, and was ready to continue feasting.

Antimony is found naturally in a metallic state, mixed with arsenic and silver, and for years the great difficulty in purifying the metal was getting rid of the arsenic.

The poisoner commonly obtains antimony in the form of a tartar emetic, or antimony tartrate, a white powder which leaves a strong taste of metal in the mouth. In doses of more than a grain at a time it is a strong emetic, and for that reason may not have a poisonous effect, being rejected before it has had time to exhibit its lethal properties. However, where a deadly dose has been retained, the patient exhibits all the symptoms of poisoning with a strong irritant. There is a sensation of burning in the throat, accompanied by difficulty in swallowing. This is followed by violent pain in the stomach, incessant vomiting and diarrhoea, faintness and extreme depression apparently provoked by the premonition of death. At the onset the pulse is accelerated, but blood-pressure begins to fall and the pulse becomes slow and irregular. Perspiration is profuse, and the skin cold and clammy to the touch; the extremities of the body and the face exhibit a general cyanosis (blueness). Cramps in the calves of the legs may be followed by spasmodic contractions, vertigo and repeated syncope, until the victim finally loses consciousness and death follows from heart failure. It is, in short, a most painful death, and the chance of survival in cases of acute antimony poisoning is slim.

So much for the poison when administered in large doses. From the virulence of the symptoms, and the distinctive metallic taste of antimony, the drug is very easily recognized, and for that reason not thought much of by poisoners, who prefer a medium which is slower in its operation, but none the less sure. However antimony, unlike most poisons, is far more deadly when administered in repeated small quantities than when one large dose is given, and by regulating the doses, a victim can be killed without attracting unfavourable attention – presenting symptoms of sickness, abdominal pam, loss of appetite and diarrhoea entirely compatible with common diseases of the stomach.

Case Study

DR EDWARD WILLIAM PRITCHARD

In many ways the story of Dr Pritchard is typical of what has come to be known as the Classic Victorian Poisoning Case. The slow murder of an unwanted spouse, the illicit amours, the final revelations behind the mask of respectability and crime's just reward on the gallows. Cliché it may be, but in Dr Pritchard's case absolutely true.

Pritchard graduated from King's College Hospital, London, and the Royal College of Surgeons in 1846. Four years later he married Mary Jane Taylor and via private practice in Yorkshire, bought a practice in Glasgow in 1859, and began actively to pursue his ambition to become 'a leading public figure'.

In May 1863, a fire at the Pritchards' house destroyed part of the attic storey, and in the subsequent investigation the body of the maid was found: 'The face, arms and trunk were badly charred, and only the legs encased in stockings had resisted the action of the flames. The police believe that the girl, while reading in bed by candlelight, fell asleep and that the bed-clothes caught fire.'

Further information raised a series of questions which put Dr Pritchard in a decidedly embarrassing position:

1. Was there any link between the girl's death and the fact that she was, though unmarried, pregnant?
2. Why, at the beginning of May and with no heating in the room, should she have been sleeping naked but for a pair of stockings?
3. Was it simply coincidence that the fire started when the girl was alone in the house with Pritchard?
4. Why was there no trace of the book which she was supposed to have been reading?
5. Why was the bedroom door locked – from the outside?
6. Why was the girl lying straight out in bed? Surely a conflagration in the bedding would at least have caused her to jump out of bed.

Could it have been, Pritchard's critics asked, that it was the good doctor who had made the girl pregnant, and then murdered her to avoid the scandal? Might he have given her a drug to render her more compliant to being burned alive in her bed; and then locked the door from outside lest the wretched girl recover and entertain ideas of saving herself?

At any event the insurance company had their own suspicions, and refused to pay up on the fire damage. It was a scandal that Pritchard could do without, and cutting his losses, he moved the family across town to Clarence Place. Here the medical practice began to shrink and the loss of clients was accompanied by inevitable financial difficulties. Such was the anxiety of Mrs Pritchard's parents over their daughter's security that the good folk gave Pritchard the sum of £500 in order to buy a house.

By this time the doctor was up to his old tricks with the servants again – this time fifteen-year-old Mary McLeod, whom he first made pregnant and then aborted. Mary Jane Pritchard seemed to take this latest indignity in her stride, but in October 1864 she was taken suddenly ill – a malady which her husband diagnosed as a chill. However, the symptoms of vomiting and diarrhoea became so acute that only a period of extended care in the capable hands of her parents in Edinburgh effected a recovery.

Mary Jane had not been back home with her husband more than a couple of weeks before the symptoms returned, this time complicated by severe stomach cramps. At the beginning of February 1865 she was in a critical state; critical enough for old Mrs Taylor to journey across to Glasgow to be at her daughter's bedside. The good lady's suspicions cannot have failed to be aroused when she, Mary Jane and the cook all fell violently ill after eating some tapioca pudding. Whether Mrs Taylor confronted Pritchard with trying to poison them all we will never know, but by 24 February the old lady herself was also confined to bed – in fact, she was in a coma. Dr Patterson, a local man much under the influence of Pritchard, responded to a call to Mrs Taylor's sick-bed, and wrote later:

> Her face was rather pale, but the expression was calm and placid. The eyelids partially closed; the lips rather pale and livid; the breathing slow and laborious; the skin cool and covered with a clammy perspiration; the pulse almost imperceptible, and she seemed to be perfectly unconscious. On my opening up the eyelids I found both pupils very much contracted. From the symptoms and judging from her general appearance, my conviction was that she was under the influence of opium or of some other powerful narcotic.

This latter observation would by no means have been unreasonable under normal circumstances – Mrs Taylor had suffered for some years with neuralgia, and was in the habit of imbibing Battley's Sedative Solution, one of those popular patent concoctions that relied for its efficacy on a high morphine content. It was discovered afterwards that it also contained two ingredients not specified by Mr Battley – aconite and antimony salts. Mrs Taylor was by now dead. Three weeks later, on 17 March, after progressively aggravated symptoms, her daughter also succumbed.

Egg flip had finally sealed Mary Jane Pritchard's fate. Prepared as a nourishing pick-me-up by her husband, it was taken not only by Mary Jane, but also by a servant who had been unwise enough to 'taste' it; it made her very ill indeed – but not as ill as her mistress, for whom it was fatal.

It was the apparently grief-stricken Pritchard himself, in his professional capacity, who signed the death certificate – it stated that his wife had been the tragic victim of gastric fever. No one could have given a more convincing performance of the bereaved spouse; Pritchard even went so far as to have Mary Jane's coffin opened just before burial so that, through a veil of crocodile tears, he might give her one last kiss.

An anonymous letter to the Procurator-Fiscal finally exposed Dr
Pritchard for the callous murderer that he was. It may have come from
Dr Patterson – feeling guilt at not having voiced his misgivings over
Mrs Taylor's condition more publicly, and thus probably saving the life
of her daughter. Be that as it may, the letter was enough to persuade the
police to ask for an exhumation order on the bodies of Mrs Taylor and
Mrs Pritchard. The internal organs of both were found to contain high
levels of antimony – the distribution of the poison in Mary Pritchard's
case indicating that she had been progressively dosed over several
months.

At his trial at the beginning of July 1865, before Lord Justice-Clerk
Inglis, Edward Pritchard was found guilty of two charges of murder,
and sentenced to hang at Glasgow on 28 July.

While awaiting sentence at North Prison, Duke Street, Pritchard
made three separate and different confessions:

1. That he had murdered his wife with the willing collaboration of the
   servant Mary McLeod, his mistress.
2. That he had killed his wife with chloroform, and that McLeod was
   merely a witness to the act; but that he was not responsible for Mrs
   Taylor's death. And
3. That he had killed both Mary Jane and her mother, and that Mary
   McLeod was innocent of any involvement.

On the day of execution, Edward Pritchard achieved the national
fame to which he had for so long aspired. Not only was the concourse
of some 100,000 spectators come to see him hang one of the largest
audiences in Scottish criminal history, but he had the doubtful privilege
of being the last man publicly hanged in the city of Glasgow.

The motive for Pritchard's murder of his wife remains a mystery. When
in good health she seems to have fullfiled all the requirements of a
dutiful wife, and was by all accounts a good mother to their five
children. Indeed, Mary Jane Pritchard's constant stoicism in the face of
her husband's infidelity and financial incompetence might be seen to
put her a step or two ahead of the average partner. More extraordinary
still was the fact that her life was not insured for a single penny.

It is equally difficult to understand why Pritchard should have used
both aconite and antimony. Antimony, as we have seen, was readily
identifiable both in the bodies and, as confirmation, revealed through

the symptoms of vomiting and other stomach disorders. Aconite alone, as found in Mrs Taylor's bottle of Battley's Sedative Solution, would have defied detection given the contemporary state of the science of toxicology.

ARSENIC

No poison has been so much used by criminals throughout the ages as arsenic. In the earliest days it was administered in the form of yellow sulphide, the bright colour of which had already convinced the ancient alchemists that it must be a source of gold.

However, the more common white oxide of arsenic was traditionally prepared by roasting the metallic ore slowly then putting the product into a vessel and applying even greater heat; the vapours produced condense as a heavy white powder, or a crystalline mass. The vapour, which smells strongly of garlic, is very poisonous, and the greatest care has to be taken to avoid inhaling it.

In fact arsenic occurs naturally in many living organisms, particularly fish and crustaceans, and in a number of ores, in coal and in common soil. It is naturally present in the human body, notably in the blood, heart, lungs and liver, and the hair and fingernails – an estimated total of about one ten-millionth of the body's weight.

The symptoms of arsenic poisoning vary a great deal, according to the form and dose which is administered. In a typical case of poisoning by white oxide the patient begins by experiencing an irritation and burning in the throat, faintness, nausea and a feeling of depression accompanied by sickness. These symptoms are followed by vomiting, first of food then of mucus, frequently specked with blood. Abdominal pain follows, described as like red-hot coals placed on the stomach, which is aggravated by touch. By now the tongue has become covered in a white 'fur' and there is a feeling of constriction in the throat. Diarrhoea develops after twelve to eighteen hours, which is more or less violent, and accompanied by pain and tenesmus. At the same time cramp sets in to the calves of the legs and the pulse is weak, rapid and irregular. Collapse rapidly comes on, and the patient dies, still conscious. One of the most marked external characteristics is cyanosis – blueness of the skin caused by lack of oxygen in the bloodstream. Post-mortem examination reveals the lining membrane of the stomach to be very much inflamed, and in many cases badly ulcerated. Arsenic is therefore a distinct irritant poison.

There are several curious points about arsenic. It can be found in every part of the body of a person poisoned by it, and even after the body has been buried for years it may be found in the bones and hair.

Arsenic can be administered in almost any form, but its post-mortem effects are the same. The poison can pass through the skin, and yet the stomach will be inflamed. It can be inhaled as a vapour, and the same symptom will be found. It is one of the strongest of the irritant poisons.

Of its use to poisoners, one must note that even in comparatively large doses arsenic is virtually tasteless, and the faintly metallic sweetness can easily be masked by administering it in food. Arsenic can also have a cumulative effect, so that the toxin can be built up in the body (particularly the kidneys and the liver) over a period of time until a quite small dose is lethal. The symptoms are so like cholera and dysentery that when those conditions were common in Europe murder could quite easily be attributed to 'natural causes'. Similarly, many cases must have been classed as food poisoning, many of whose symptoms arsenic poisoning shares.

The Arsenic Act

So prevalent was arsenic poisoning in England during the nineteenth century that in 1851 it was felt necessary to introduce a specific Arsenic Act. The Act forbade the sale of any arsenic compound unless the purchaser was known to the pharmacist. More important, all arsenic compounds were required to be mixed with a colorant – either soot or indigo – in the proportion of one ounce per pound of arsenic. This went a long way to reducing the large number of deaths caused by mistaking arsenic for sugar or other innocuous white powders; and made it considerably more difficult to hide the homicidal presence of arsenic in food and drink.

Case Study

BLUE FOOD

Shortly after her separation from Leonard Hearn, his wife Sarah returned to the bosom of her family and in 1921 could be found with her aunt and her sister Minnie enjoying the uneventful country life that revolved around the small Cornish village of Lewannick. Towards the end of the decade, Mrs Hearn's aunt died, followed early in 1930 by Minnie, who had succumbed to a long illness marked by severe gastric pains.

Throughout these troubled times Sarah Hearn had derived great comfort from the friendly attentions of her neighbours William and Alice ('Annie') Thomas. The Thomases had always been on good terms with the family, but now, in her isolation, they began to show Sarah extra little attentions; taking her on outings with them in their car, and when Annie was baking there were always a few extra treats for her neighbour.

On 18 October 1930, William and Annie Thomas invited Mrs Hearn to accompany them on a trip to the seaside town of Bude, a little to the north of Lewannick. Sarah's contribution was to make some tinned salmon sandwiches which they all enjoyed during a break in the journey for afternoon tea. On the return drive Mrs Thomas became violently ill with stomach cramps and vomiting, which once home became so severe that she was admitted to Plymouth Hospital where she died on 4 November. A post-mortem examination revealed the presence of white arsenic.

It is inevitable, especially in small insular communities, that tongues should begin to wag in the face of such mysterious events as Annie Thomas's death; and that fingers should begin to point. They were pointing at Sarah Hearn.

Indeed, so distressed did Mrs Hearn become that she fled the village, and some days later sent a letter to William Thomas postmarked 'Launceston'. In it she accepted that the sandwich connection did make her an obvious suspect, and indicated that she might be about to commit suicide. Meanwhile, the police had obtained an exhumation order, and the bodies of Sarah Hearn's aunt and sister were found to contain traces of arsenic.

Mrs Hearn did not take her own life – though she did leave her coat and hat on a cliff-top at Looe to give the impression that she had. Instead, she took up employment as housekeeper to an architect who recognized her photograph on the 'wanted' notices. And that is how Mrs Sarah Hearn came to be standing before Mr Justice Roche at the Bodmin Assizes in July 1931.

To present her case, Mrs Hearn was fortunate to have the services of Mr Norman Birkett KC, one of the most successful defence attorneys of his day.

The prosecution, led by Mr H. du Parcq KC (later Lord du Parcq) assisted by Mr Patrick Devlin (later Lord Devlin), opened its case by presenting evidence relating to the fatal sandwiches. Under cross-examination, William Thomas insisted that there had been nothing suspicious about the circumstances, no attempt to 'force' his wife to eat a particular sandwich, and that neither he nor Mrs Hearn had suffered the slightest discomfort as a result of eating their share. The chief chemist of the firm who manufactured the tinned salmon agreed that, though every care was taken to sterilize food before canning, it was always possible that toxins *could* remain and cause food poisoning. Furthermore, there *were* cases on medical record in which one person might succumb to such poisoning while others might not.

Mr Birkett, in contesting the medical testimony on the deaths of Mrs Hearn's aunt and sister, was able to establish that the soil in which both bodies were interred yielded a high concentration of natural arsenic – higher, in fact, than that found in either of the corpses. Attacking the evidence of Dr Eric Wordley, the pathologist responsible for the exhumation and post-mortems, Birkett suggested that it was possible for contaminated soil to have found its way into the jars in which the organs used for analysis were stored, concluding with the question: 'Am I right in saying that a piece of soil, so small you could hold it between your fingers, dropped on to the body would make every single calculation wrong?' 'Yes.'

In reply, Mr du Parcq quoted the findings of the redoubtable Dr Roche Lynch, senior Home Office analyst, who held that the pathological evidence indicated that Minnie had been ingesting small doses of arsenic for about seven months before her death.

The one piece of solid, undisputed evidence that underpinned the Crown case was that Mrs Hearn had once purchased a packet of arsenic-based weed-killer; however, as Norman Birkett was to emphasize in his cross-examination of Dr Roche Lynch, it was arsenic which had, according to the law, been mixed with a blue dye.

Mr Norman Birkett: You say that in your opinion the weed-killer was used in solid form? – *Dr Roche Lynch:* I suggest so.

Have you taken a sandwich and put 14.3 grains in it? – No.

You have shown that arsenic put in Benger's Food discolours the white food? – Yes.

Seven times as much as would greatly discolour it? – Yes.

If you put 14 grains of blue weed-killer on a sandwich and carried it for hours, I suggest it would be blue? – I have not tried it; but my opinion, for what it is worth, is that it would not be.

But you have not tried it! On the theory of the prosecution, surely it was a most terrible risk to run? – Personally I do not think so.

If you have sandwiches in two piles of three each, assume for the moment that the topmost sandwich in one of these piles contains arsenic, am I right in assuming that the sandwich with the blue weed-killer would stain downwards? – Yes.

The white bread, like the white Benger's Food, would make the stains instantly discernible? – I agree, and the white bread being more localized the blue would come through in spots and stains.

Norman Birkett called only one witness for the defence, Mrs Hearn herself. A modest, straightforward woman she defied the best efforts of the prosecution to shake her testimony – on the matter of motive, the only one that the Crown could offer, Mrs Hearn was emphatic that there was not, had never been, any hint of passion – 'guilty or otherwise' – between herself and William Thomas.

Following a summing-up by the judge as sympathetic to the defendant as his impartial role would allow, Sarah Ann Hearn was acquitted by the jury.

So how did Annie Thomas come to be poisoned? By whom? And why?

A Very Victorian Death

One thing that the Arsenic Act of 1851 did not do was define 'pharmacists', and so anybody who chose to do so could set up shop selling poisons. It was not until the sequence of Pharmacy and Pharmacy and Poisons Acts were introduced between 1868 and 1972 that poisons like arsemc were gradually brought under control.

It is therefore no great surprise to find arsenic poisoning remaining a popular method of homicide right through the reign of Queen Victoria and beyond into the 1920s and 1930s – a steady flow of shadowy figures emerging from the dark annals of murder, the rat-poison, weed-killer, and flypapers in their hands.

Christina Gilmour, who killed her husband in Scotland in 1843; and Madeleine Smith, who poisoned her lover in that same country six years after England had introduced the Arsenic Act. Dr Thomas Smethurst, sentenced to death for the murder of his bigamous wife in 1859, but reprieved when the poison tests were found to be faulty. Mary Ann Cotton, poisoned as many as fifteen members of her immediate family in the 1870s – all certified victims of 'gastric fever'. The tragic Florence Maybrick, convicted – some say wrongly – of spiking her husband's meat extract with arsenic in 1889. Frederick Heury Seddon, who killed his wealthy lodger in 1910 with the juice extracted from flypapers. In

1922 Herbert Rowse Armstrong was executed for murdering his wife with poison reserved for killing the weeds on his lawn; and in the same year Edward Ernest Black kept his appointment with the hangman for the murder of Mrs Black. Charlotte Bryant reversed the role in 1935 when she poisoned her husband with a dose of Eureka weed-killer.

Meanwhile, in the United States, Johann Hoch poisoned his way through the terms of office of five presidents, with a total of around a dozen victims between 1892 and 1905. In 1898 Cordelia Botkin murdered her lover's wife and sister-in-law with candy laced with arsenic; and in 1917 Amy Archer-Gilligan went several better when she was convicted of the murder of at least five of the patients at her home for elderly people.

All of which seems understandable in view of the vast range of cosmetic, domestic, medicinal and horticultural products on general sale, all of which contained enough arsenic to kill off the population of a small village, let alone an unwanted spouse. As late as 1939, the eminent forensic toxicologist Dr Gerald Roche Lynch listed the arsenical compounds then 'used for various purposes and most of them available to the public':

Sodium and potassium arsenite, sold as such and in arsenical sheep-dips, weed-killers, cattle-dips, hide preservers, worm powders and tablets for animals, fly powders for external application to sheep, preparations for foot-rot of sheep, and preservative solutions for wood; arsenous oxide in arsenical sheep-dips, powder for the destruction of ants, and fly powders for external application to sheep; sodium arsenate in arsenical sheep-dips and fly powders for external application to sheep; arsenic sulphides and thioarsenates in arsenical sheep-dips and fly powders for external application to sheep; arsenic acid in arsenical weed-killers; copper arsenite and arsenate in arsenical worm powders for animals; lead arsenate – either $PbHAsO_4$ or $Pb_3(AsO_4)_2$ – in horticultural spray or dust; calcium arsenate, magnesium arsenate, manganese arsenate, and zinc arsenite in horticultural spray or dust; London purple – calcium arsenate and arsenite – in horticultural spray or dust; and Paris green – copper aceto-arsenite – in horticultural spray. Arsenical soaps also are probably in fairly general use, and certain arsenical compounds are used as ingredients in anti-fouling paints for ships' bottoms. With the possible exception of soaps and anti-fouling composition, all the above-mentioned compounds can

produce fatal poisoning if taken by man.
Toxicology: I. Homicidal, Suicidal, and Accidental Poisoning,
London, 1939

Case Study

FREDERICK HENRY SEDDON

Seddon has the well-deserved reputation of being the meanest murderer in the annals of crime. Over the years, his name has become synonymous with cold, calculated greed, although his crime was no more vicious or horrifying than many others. Edward Marshall Hall, his defence counsel, described Seddon as the ablest man he had ever defended on a capital charge, and he was undoubtedly cunning. Yet he was also remarkably vain and totally insensitive, qualities which he unwisely displayed at his trial.

Seddon was forty years old, married, with five children and an aged father who lived with him. At the time of his notoriety he was a Superintendent of Collectors for a national insurance company, and the acquisition of money had become his great obsession – to the extent that he supplemented his income by running a second-hand clothes business from his home using his wife's name. He also speculated in the buying and selling of property, and 63 Tollington Park, Holloway, was substantial enough to tempt him to move in himself. There was room enough for his whole family and for an office on the ground floor (for which he charged his employers five shillings per week) while still leaving space to let the whole second floor at twelve shillings a week. His choice of tenant was Miss Eliza Barrow, a forty-nine-year-old spinster in comfortable circumstances, but who was sour, argumentative, sluttish, deaf, partial to alcohol, and Seddon's perfect match in meanness.

In July 1910, she brought with her two family friends, a Mr Hook and his wife, and their ten-year-old nephew, Ernest Grant, whom she had more or less adopted. Within a fortnight a row between Miss Barrow and Mrs Hook led to the Hooks being asked to look for alternative lodgings. Soon Seddon was advising Miss Barrow on financial matters, and after just two months in the house she had transferred £1,600 of India Stock into Seddon's name in return for a small annuity and a remission of rent. This was all the more singular in that it was a most casual arrangement for a man who was a professional in the business of annuities. In January 1911, the leases of two properties in Camden were likewise transferred to Seddon; Miss Barrow's annuity rose to £3 a week. Later that year, Miss Barrow became alarmed by Lloyd George's Budget and the Birkbeck financial crash; on Seddon's advice she withdrew £200 in coin from her Savings Bank and placed it into his safe hands. The old maid's remaining assets, a tidy sum in coin, notes and jewellery also found their way into Seddon's grasp, so he now had his hands on the entire £4,000 that constituted Eliza Barrow's worldly goods. It was around about this time that Mrs Seddon was observed changing thirty £5 notes in local shops, using the name 'Mrs Scott, of Evershot Street'.

In early August 1911, the Seddons went on a short holiday to Southend, taking Miss Barrow and young Ernie Grant with them. Following their return, Seddon sent his daughter Maggie to a chemist's shop in Crouch Hill to purchase a threepenny packet of flypapers, which was prominently labelled 'Poison' and contained a considerable quantity of arsenic. On 1 September, Miss Barrow was taken ill.

Seddon's own physician, Dr Sworn, was sent for and diagnosed epidemic diarrhoea. Miss Barrow was a heavy woman who suffered with asthma, and the risk of heart failure being evident, she was advised to keep to her bed. With sickness compounding her natural lack of basic hygiene, it took just a few days for her room to develop a most disgusting atmosphere, and it was buzzing with flies. The Seddons claimed that they placed saucers of water containing the poisonous flypapers on the mantelpiece and this was the reason for their purchase, though Dr Sworn on his visits failed to notice this detail. Miss Barrow's solution to the problem was to abandon her room and move in with young Ernie Grant, sharing his bed.

At midnight on 13 September Eliza Barrow was heard to cry out 'I'm dying!' Mrs Seddon went up to attend to her, but when Seddon returned from an evening at a music hall, his main concern was to moan to his sister-in-law about a man who had, heaven knows how, swindled him out of sixpence. While Mrs Seddon continued to minister to Miss Barrow, her husband settled down to a smoke. At 6.30 a.m., Miss Barrow died.

Seddon did not bother to call the doctor, though the next morning he obtained a death certificate from Dr Sworn, who did not bother to examine the body. Seddon then set about winding up Miss Barrow's affairs – not surprisingly in his own best interest. He arranged the funeral of Eliza Barrow at Islington Borough Cemetery, pocketing a commission of 12s 6d from the undertaker for his trouble. Only the Seddons and Ernie Grant attended.

Seddon did contact Miss Barrow's only known relatives some time later, when he produced her will, signed three days before her death, appointing him sole executor and guardian to Ernie Grant and Ernie's sister, who was away at school. This was accompanied by the documents detailing the transfer of stocks and property to himself. Finally, there was an account explaining that only £10 in cash and valuables had been found in Miss Barrow's room and that Seddon was actually out of pocket to the tune of £1 1s *10½d* after deducting the funeral expenses and the cost of Ernie's upkeep!

The Vonderahes, whose affection for Miss Barrow had always been firmly based on hopes of future advancement, were outraged, and immediately conveyed their suspicions about cousin Eliza's sudden death to the police. The exhumation and autopsy were carried out by Bernard Spilsbury, the young pathologist who had so recently made his reputation in the Crippen case. Although the symptoms of epidemic diarrhoea and arsenic poisoning are very similar, the unnatural preservation of the body so characteristic of arsenic suggested foul play. This was confirmed when Dr William Willcox, the senior Home Office analyst, found traces of arsenic in the tissues and organs. On 4 December, Frederick Seddon was arrested; in mid-January, the name of Margaret Ann Seddon, his wife, was added to the indictment.

The trial, which opened at the Old Bailey on 4 March 1912, lasted ten days, a record for a murder trial at that time. The counsel for the prosecution, as is traditional in poisoning cases, was the Attorney General, Sir Rufus Isaacs. Edward Marshall Hall represented Seddon and Mr Gervais Rentoul represented Mrs Seddon.

The first part of the trial was taken up with the medical evidence. The defence claimed that the ingestion of arsenic into Miss Barrow's body had been chronic, rather than acute; that is, the poison had been taken in small quantities over a protracted period, presumably by means of some relatively harmless medicinal preparation. Seddon was later to propose the additional theory that Miss Barrow might have drunk the flypaper water in her room by accident!

Willcox and Spilsbury, however, remained united in their initial assessment of acute arsenical poisoning. Willcox first weighed the remains of Eliza Barrow – the corpse itself and the organs which had already been removed for analysis – which added up to 60lbs, as compared with 140lbs in life (a reduction caused by moisture loss). Using Marsh's test for arsenic, Willcox calculated that the stomach contained 7.3 milligrams of the poison, 41 milligrams in the intestines, and 11.13 milligrams in the liver. Calculating from the accepted standard that muscle tissue accounts for about two-fifths of the body's weight, Miss Barrow's muscles contained 67.2 milligrams of arsenic; the hair contained 18 milligrams of poison for every 100 grams. In all, Dr Willcox accounted for 131.57 milligrams of arsenic in the remains – sufficiently damning proof of deliberate poisoning.

Nevertheless, it was said by many who attended the trial that Seddon's performance in the witness box, more than any of the evidence, condemned him to the gallows; the odiousness of his personality evident for all to see. His bearing was arrogant and vain. His hypocrisy and calculated poverty of spirit shone out at every opportunity. At one point, asked whether it was true that he had been seen by one of his agents counting Miss Barrow's money on the morning after her death, he vehemently denied the suggestion then, after a pause, added, 'I would have had all day to count the money.'

The outcome of the trial was uncertain to the end, but when the jury announced their verdict, it was evident that they had been greatly influenced by the conduct of the accused in the witness box. Frederick Seddon was found guilty; Mrs Seddon was acquitted. The final humiliation for Seddon, however, was the selling of his properties while he waited in the condemned cell. Seeing the meagre price fetched by the fruits of all his acquisitiveness, he exclaimed in desperation, 'That's finished it!' Frederick Seddon was hanged in Pentonville Prison on 18 April 1912.

Lewisite

In 1917, towards the end of the First World War, an American chemist, W. Lee Lewis, developed a compound of arsenic eponymously named 'Lewisite'. It was a powerful poison gas with effects similar to the notorious mustard gas – but more deadly. As little as thirty drops of the liquid compound on the skin could kill a man within half an hour. In fact, the conflict was over before Lewisite could be used as a weapon in the Great War, though it did resurface during the Manchurian campaign of 1937–43 when it was used in a small way by the Japanese against the Chinese.

The Marsh Test

Although the identification of arsenic by analytical means had been pioneered as early as the 1770s – notably by the Swedish chemist

Karl Wilhelm Sheele – it was not until much later that a test was developed which was held to be reliable enough for its results to be accepted as evidence in a court of law. In October 1836, James Marsh, an Englishman working at the Royal Arsenal in Woolwich, published a paper in the *Edinburgh New Philosophical Journal* detailing a method for converting arsenic traces into arsine gas, which itself was revealed as a metallic 'mirror' on a piece of glass or porcelain. So sensitive was the test that amounts of arsenic as small as one-fiftieth of a milligram could be identified. The principles of the Marsh Test are still used, though improvements and developments of Marsh's equipment made the later Reinsch and Gutzeit tests more reliable and easier to conduct.

The apparatus is a simple glass tube open at both ends and bent in the form of a syphon. A stop-cock ending in a fine jet passes through a hole made in a cork, which fits airtight into the opening of the lower bend of the tube.

When the apparatus is used, a bit of glass rod about an inch long is dropped into the shorter leg, followed by a piece of clean sheet zinc about an inch and a half long and half an inch wide, bent double so that it will run down the tube until it is stopped by the piece of glass rod. The stop-cock and jet are now fixed and the handle turned so as to leave the cock open. The fluid to be examined, mixed with a little dilute sulphuric acid, is poured into the long leg till it stands in the short one about a quarter of an inch below the bottom of the cork. Bubbles of gas will rise from the zinc, which are pure hydrogen, if no arsenic is present; but if the sample contains arsenic in any form in solution, the gas will be arsenuretted hydrogen. The cock is closed and the gas accumulates in the shorter leg, driving the fluid up the longer one, till the liquor has descended in the short leg below the piece of zinc, when further production of gas will cease. When the stop-cock is opened the gas will be propelled with some force through the jet and, on igniting it as it issues and then holding horizontally a piece of glass over it, in such a manner as to retard slightly the combustion, the arsenic (if any be present) will be found deposited in the metallic state on the glass.

ARSON
Arson – the deliberate burning of property for malicious or fraudulent purposes – shares with only the crime of murder itself a range of motives so broad that it traverses emotions from the cold calculating

greed of the insurance swindler to the psychopathic frenzy of the pyromaniac. The main motives for arson can be summarized:

1. To defraud an insurance company.
2. To destroy business records – possibly before an audit which would have revealed trading discrepancies, or attempts to evade tax.
3. To eliminate business competition.
4. Revenge – perhaps by a disgruntled employee, a dissatisfied customer, a spurned lover.
5. To camouflage or conceal another crime, such as burglary, embezzlement, murder.
6. Vandalism and thrill-seeking – usually by youths, often as an accompaniment to alcohol or drug abuse.
7. A psychotic need – the excitement, sometimes sexual gratification, of a pyromaniac.

Fires caused by arson are responsible worldwide for the loss of billions of dollars worth of goods and property every year, and many deaths and serious injuries. This does not include the large number of incidents which are suspected but cannot be proved.

Fraud

It has often been observed that the incidence of arson serves as an accurate barometer of a nation's economy. When times are difficult and businesses are in danger of bankruptcy the number of arson cases rises; when prosperity returns the figures fall. The most prominent example of this was the Great Depression of the 1930s in the United States, when arson reached almost epidemic proportions. In Britain, as recently as the summer of 1991, one major insurance company, Commercial Union, was obliged to raise its premiums because of the rash of suspicious claims made after fires had damaged or destroyed property. The company's assessors placed the probable extent of arson in recession-hit Britain as high as one in every four fires. In the investigation of a suspicious fire it is a wise detective who makes his first priority an inquiry into the financial status of the business that has been destroyed.

The Morphology of Fire
Types of Fire
It is customary for fire-fighters to classify fire according to the nature of the predominant combustible material:

Class A fires: The commonest materials in fires – wood, paper, fabric

Class B fires: Hydrocarbons – a wide variety including mainly petroleum products

Class C fires: Electrical systems and equipment

Class D fires: Combustible metals such as might be found in large industrial premises – zinc, potassium, magnesium

Class E fires: Radioactive materials

Colour of Flame

Although the interpretation of colour tends to be subjective, some authorities place faith in an interpretation of the effects of flame and smoke. There are several charts available, most of them originating in the United States.

Combustible	Flame colour	Smoke colour
Combustible	Flame colour	Smoke colour
Acetone	Blue	Black
Benzene	Yellow to white	Grey to white
Cloth	Yellow to red	Grey to brown
Cooking oil	Yellow	Brown
Gasoline (Petrol)	Yellow to white	Black
Kerosine (Paraffin)	Yellow	Black
Lacquer thinner	Yellow to red	Grey to brown
Lubricating oil	Yellow to white	Grey to brown
Naphtha	Straw to white	Brown to black
Nitrocellulose		Reddish-brown to yellow
Paper	Yellow to red	Grey to brown
Phosphorus		White
Rubber		Black
Wood	Yellow to red	Grey to brown

One of the most useful functions of these observations would be if the flame/smoke colours were inconsistent with materials supposed to have been stored in the burning building.

Accidental Causes

Most fires do not have an incendiary origin, and are entirely accidental (though they may be due to carelessness or irresponsibility). Some of the more common causes of accidental fires are:

Faulty electrical wiring and equipment
Faulty gas piping and equipment
Careless storage of flammable materials near open heat
Children playing with matches
Gas or electric cookers left on
Smoking in bed
Improperly extinguished cigarettes
Lightning strike
Spontaneous combustion

It is a fact that, by and large, accidental fires show a clear source of origin, as distinct from arson where the source may have been deliberately obscured or, more supicious still, there may be *several* sources.

Investigation of Fire
For obvious reasons it may be some time into the life-cycle of a fire before police or fire-service investigators are called to the scene. The most important objective is to put out the fire and secure the building against collapse; only when this has been done can the investigators, specially trained in suspicious fires, begin sifting the debris for clues. Like all other scenes of crime the site must be sealed off and nothing disturbed unnecessarily. At this stage any attempt to 'clean up' must be discouraged.

The first questions to be asked in any arson inquiry are: how and where did the fire start? As there is unlikely to be anything as helpful as an obvious place of origin, it will be necessary to base the investigation on the known factors of fire. For example, fire always travels upwards, so the search for a source should begin at the lowest level at which burning has occurred. If the conflagration was deliberately started with some combustible such as petrol or turpentine the heavy smell may still linger in the air around the place of origin. Although most of the flammable liquid will have burned off, some may have soaked into suffaces which can be treated in the laboratory. Frequently a bulkier than average concentration of burned debris and ash will indicate where a pile of combustible material was gathered to start the fire. If the fire was lit by means of a long-fuse a charred trail of twisted rag or paper 'streamer' may lead to the point at which the blaze started.

Search for Clues
One of the first indications that a fire may have been deliberately set is evidence of forcible entry to the building, and investigators must pay

particular attention to broken doors and windows, **Tool Marks** around forced locks, intercepted alarm systems, etc. Even such obvious clues as holes knocked through walls and ceilings from adjacent property have sometimes been overlooked.

Electrical systems, oil and gas pipes and equipment should all be checked by experts for signs of tampering and nothing but suspicion could attach to a sprinkler system that has been rendered inactive. The location of any valuable papers, cash or jewellery should be checked and any burned evidence carefully collected for examination by the laboratory **Documents** department. If such valuables as these, or any trace of them, are absent from where they should be then an accidental origin to the fire looks less likely, and the possibility arises that the blaze was set to conceal the true motive of robbery or embezzlement. Accident is also unlikely if flammable materials and accelerators are discovered in a part of the building where there is no legitimate reason to find them.

In arson, unlike most other crimes, motive is of vital importance in the search for suspects, and the experienced investigator will be alert to apparent inconsistencies at the scene of the fire. For example, if valuable possessions or commercial stock are supposed to have perished in the conflagration it would be suspicious indeed if there were no trace of their charred remains. One specialist cites the case of a tailor who claimed to have lost a fortune in garments when his factory burned down. When fire investigators learned that fireproof material had been used to make the buttons, they set about trying to find them in the ashes; not one was found. Which was hardly surprising as the enterprising manufacturer had already moved his stock on before torching the factory.

One of the greatest horrors that can be encountered at the scene of a fire is the remains of human victims caught in the blaze. This is tragic enough in cases of accident, but after an arson attack there is a very real possibility that the fire was set in order to conceal the crime of murder. Where a body is found, priority must be given to answering these questions:

1. Who was the victim; can he or she be identified?
2. Did the person have a lawful reason to be on the premises – if not, it may be that the arsonist was trapped by his own wickedness
3. The police must be called *immediately* if they are not already in attendance; they in turn must lose no time in summoning the police surgeon or a pathologist. Subsequent post-mortem examination will determine whether the victim died before or after the fire was started (see the entry on **Burning** for an explanation of the procedure).

Potentially valuable clues should be treated in exactly the same way as at any other scene of crime – photographed *in situ*, carefully packaged and labelled and transferred to the forensic laboratory.

The area *around* the site of the fire should also be painstakingly searched for clues such as footprints and tyre-prints, discarded tools and containers of flammables.

Testing for Flammables
Petrobst and Rhodakit

Before the development of sophisticated laboratory tests such as Chromatography, there were very few tools available to the arson investigator which would provide incontrovertible proof of a crime; suspicious flammables would either have been consumed in the fire or, because of their volatile nature, have evaporated into the air. However, as soon as it was recognized that hydrocarbons such as petrol and paraffin have a high affinity to fat, two detecting materials were developed named Petrobst and Rhodakit. These fine powders were sprayed on to surfaces at the scene of a fire and left for a day to soak in. The presence of hydrocarbons could then easily be seen by a change of colour in the powder. The problem was that the effect was the same for every fatty substance, and with the greater demand for accuracy these old methods were discarded.

Odour Tests

Other simple tests still practised depend on releasing enough of the hydrocarbon from whatever it has soaked into to the air to be detected by an experienced nose. One method is to heat the object in a container in water to a temperature of 70°C; when the container is opened the smell should be identifiable. Otherwise, pieces of the infected surface are distilled with water in a flask until the aroma wafts out.

Gas Chromatography

As the requirement of the test is to isolate positively one substance among many, the technique of **Chromatography** is ideally suited. The instrument will separate the components of a wide range of hydrocarbons and produce a chromatograph which will show graphically the characteristics of each one. Evidence is placed in a sealed jar and heated, causing the residues to be given off as a vapour which is separated in the chromatograph. It is possible by this method to achieve reliable results with infinitesimal traces of the substance.

Case Study

THE INNOCENCE OF BRUCE LEE

For Peter George Dinsdale life couldn't have been much crueller, nor his introduction to it less auspicious. He was born in 1960 with a deformed right arm and leg, and epilepsy. His prostitute mother, unable to cope with the pressures of trying to earn a living and looking after a new baby, increasingly left Peter in the care of her own mother to bring up. At the age of three, this became a permanent arrangement; permanent, that is, until the relationship between his grandmother and her common-law husband began to disintegrate. Then Peter was put into a home. Already showing signs of emotional instability, Peter would attend an educational institution for the handicapped until he was sixteen, where he was exposed to the homosexual practices that were to scar his young life further.

When Peter Dinsdale was released from school, he found himself regularly unemployed – and to a large extent unemployable; at this time he was living mainly in Salvation Army hostels, and was rapidly developing a drink problem. He would soon change his name to Bruce Lee, in tribute to the martial arts film star of that name.

In June 1980, a fire was deliberately started with paraffin at the home of Mrs Edith Hastie and her sons in Hull; the three children died in the blaze. By a process of elimination, suspects were narrowed down to local homosexuals who may have had contact with the late Charles Hastie. Not surprisingly they all denied having anything to do with murder by arson. Except Bruce Lee, who said: 'I didn't mean it.' Pressed further on the matter, Lee went on to confess to a series of other arson attacks around the west side of Hull between 1973 and 1979.

Although with one exception the fires had all been attributed by their respective inquests to natural causes, Lee was now claiming to have started them with paraffin. In the end he was charged with the manslaughter of twenty-six people, and with eleven cases of arson. His own worst enemy, Lee was reported as saying: 'I am devoted to fire. Fire is my master, and that is why I cause these fires.' In January 1981, he was ordered to be detained without limit of time in a special hospital.

But the case proved to be far more complex than the misdemeanours of a mentally unstable youth with a self-confessed love of fire. In fact, it was to transpire that the man who called himself Bruce Lee was almost certainly *not* guilty of many – if any – of the arson attacks to which he had so guilelessly confessed.

One of the worst fires in terms of loss of life destroyed the Wensley Lodge old people's home in 1977, causing the deaths of eleven elderly men. Following a year-long investigation by the *Sunday Times* newspaper, during which independent forensic experts contributed their findings to a new report on the case, an appeal was made by Bruce Lee's lawyers at the Court of Criminal Appeal. In December 1983, the Appeal Court cleared Lee of the charges arising from the fire. An earlier inquiry had concluded that the blaze started with a spark from a plumber's blow-lamp. Lee said he had broken into the home and poured paraffin on to the floor of the room above that in which the plumber had been working, and set fire to it. For this to have been true, it would have required the floorboards in the room to be so ill-fitting that the paraffin seeped through and allowed the fire to spread. In fact, forensic reconstructions and eye-witness reports of the fire were entirely inconsistent with Bruce Lee's story. Which indicates that, however emotionally disturbed Bruce Lee may be, it is very unlikely that he is a multiple killer.

ASPHYXIA
(see Cause of Death)

AUTOMATISM
Certain disorders may so disturb a person's state of consciousness that they behave 'automatically', and cannot, in law, be held responsible for their actions. Automatism may result from psychomotor epilepsy, sleeping, sleepwalking, concussion, brain tumour, hypoglycaemia or other dissociative states.

The law recognizes two states of automatism – insane and non-insane – and for a defence of 'guilty but insane' to be successful the automatic behaviour must be proved to originate in an organic or mental disease, such as hypoglycaemia, brain tumour, organic psychosis and epilepsy. Non-insane automatism does not result from any clearly defined disease, although the sufferer exhibits no control over his actions; these symptoms are commonly associated with states of sleeping or sleepwalking.

Insane Automatism

By far the commonest cause is epilepsy, which was one of the strongest considerations in drafting the amendments incorporated in the 1957 Homicide Act (see **Diminished Responsibility**).

Epilepsy

It is a well-known medical phenomenon that subsequent to an epileptic fit, the patient may enter a state known as 'epileptic automatism' where, as the name suggests, he behaves quite automatically, without rational premeditation, and with either no, or very imperfect, recollection of his actions. If it can be established that a crime was committed by the patient in this state, then a defence can be made that he was not responsible for the consequences of his actions.

In fact, it is only rarely that this defence is advanced in a case of murder; for it is not snfficient to prove (and the burden of proof here lies with the *defence*) that the prisoner is an epileptic, but also that the act of killing was performed in a state of automatism. However, there is a basic connection between murder and epilepsy beyond an expected numerical percentage. Drs Denis Hill and Desmond Pond, during research at the Maudsley Hospital in south-east London, observed that of 105 murderers in a sample, 18 exhibited symptoms of epilepsy. Given a normal population percentage of 0.5, this figure represents a staggering 32 times the expected incidence.

What may be more important is that, aside from the observable fits and subsequent automatism, the possibility of a complete personality change should be allowed for; we can see from encephalogram tracings that a fit involves a massive discharge of energy from the brain cells, which produces responses appropriate to whichever part of the brain from which it derives.

It may help to identify the three main clinical categories of what are collectively called epileptic fits:

Major epilepsy (called *Grand mal*): This is the most commonly encountered type of fit, and begins in the patient with an overpowering sensation that envelops the body, and can take the form of a burst of sound, or of light, or of heat. This is followed by loss of consciousness, and then the characteristic rhythmic 'convulsions'. This may be accompanied by foaming at the mouth and holding the breath. When consciousness returns, the patient feels tiredness usually accompanied by headache and confusion.

Minor epilepsy (called *Petit mal*): This is the minor loss of consciousness of which the patient himself may not even be fully aware. He may suddenly stop in the middle of speaking, or drop something that he is carrying; the eyelids and facial muscles may twitch slightly.

Psychomotor (or *Temporal Lobe*) *epilepsy:* This has been very adequately described in connection with a celebrated American murder case,* by Dr D.T. Davidson Jnr and Dr William Lennox:

> The behaviour of a person during an automatism, or automatic seizure, displays the greatest variety. He may appear to be fully aware of his surroundings and act as a normal person would, or he may be clumsy, speechless, or appear confused, act inappropriately or become surly or belligerent, or display excessive muscular activity such as violent running. In deciding as to whether a paroxysmal brain disorder is responsible for sudden and temporary abnormal actions, what the person did is not as important as whether he remembers what he did.
>
> The person's inability to remember what he did during this period may have three explanations: first his reputed amnesia may be simply feigned. The individual tries to dodge responsibility for his actions by saying he has no recollection of them. A plea for clemency is often based upon the false claim of amnesia. Such a lie may be exposed by indirect methods; a lie detector may be useful. The brainwave tracing should be normal.
>
> Secondly, the amnesia may be real, but hysterical based on some emotional disturbance such as the necessity of forgetting some horrible experience or escaping from an unpleasant dilemma. The person is not confused, but acts rationally and retains knowledge acquired in the past. He does not commit any major crimes in this state. Memory of events may often be recaptured under partial sedation with drugs or by hypnosis. The brainwave tracing taken during as well as before and after such episodes should be normal.
>
> The third type of amnesia is based on pathological rather than on psychological disturbance of brain function. Amnesia for events may attend such conditions as brain concussion, delirious states, complicating high fever, alcoholic intoxication or (in diabetics) an overdose of insulin. Such conditions are readily recognized.

*In May 1950, in Massachusetts, a man named Elwell stabbed and bludgeoned to death his aunt, wrapped her body in a sheet, loaded it into the boot of his car and drove out to a swamp to dispose of it. Arrested by the police, Elwell had but a fragmentary recollection of the events and was proved to have acted in a state of psychomotor epilepsy.

In addition, recurrent temporary periods of amnesia may occur in persons who are otherwise mentally and physically healthy, except for possible brainwave disturbance. These episodes may come without warning and without apparent cause. As already stated, actions may be extremely diverse.

These periods of amnesia and attendant actions come suddenly without premeditation or warning. They may last for half a minute, or many hours or even days. They are therefore termed seizure phenomena. The only laboratory examination that possesses significance is the finding of paroxysmal disturbance in the electrical rhythms of the brain. However, such abnormality may not be demonstrable always, because the electrical disturbance may not be continuously present or may be brought out only by means of sleep, by hard breathing or by injections of metrazol, a convulsive drug.

Case Study

LOCK AH TAM

Like all the world's great ports, Liverpool has a firmly established Chinese community; it developed in those years at the close of Victoria's reign, when the ships in England's docks were its lifeline to the world, and their crews came from all the races on earth.

One of those sailors was Lock Ah Tam. Born in Canton in 1872, he arrived in England on board ship in 1895, and quickly exchanged the wide ocean for the terra firma of Liverpool's dockland, and a job as a clerk in the Shipping Office.

Tam's command of the English language and his naturally industrious approach to his work endeared him as much to his employers as his generous, honest personality endeared him to the Merseyside Chinese community. As Tam's prestige grew, he was appointed European representative of the powerful Chinese stevedores organization, the Jack Ah Tai, and shortly afterwards became superintendent of Chinese labour to three major steamship companies. Above everything else, Tam was a family man; his integration into the country of his adoption was completed by his Welsh-born wife, the former Catherine Morgan, his two daughters Doris and Cecilia, and his son Lock Ling.

One of Tam's most characteristic virtues was his generosity to the Chinese community around him, and for them he founded the Chinese

Progress Club, where seamen far from home could be among their own people, to feel safe from suspicious and not always friendly Western eyes. It was this final act of kindness that was indirectly responsible for the tragedy that was to overtake Tam and his family.

On a February night in 1918 Tam had peacefully settled into the club for a couple of well-earned drinks and a game of snooker with friends. Without warning the door was broken down by a gang of drunken Russian sailors, and in the brawl that followed Tam was dealt a skull-cracking blow with a billiard cue. When the police arrived Tam was still bleeding profusely from his injury, and rather unsteady on his feet, but well up to the task of identifying his assailant.

For a while the attack seemed to have done no lasting damage. However, those close to the gentle Tam began to be aware of increasingly disturbing shifts in his once placid personality. For one thing he had begun to drink heavily and was on his way to becoming a chronic alcoholic. After these bouts of drinking (and later without them), Lock Ah Tam started to display uncontrollable paroxysms of manic rage, during which he would stamp his feet and foam at the mouth, bloodshot eyes almost popping from his swollen red face. And more than once he had attacked his own colleagues and friends over some imagined provocation.

Inevitably Tam's business suffered, and he never recovered from the crippling loss of more than £10,000 when a shipping venture failed in 1922. In 1924 Lock Ah Tam suffered the final humiliation of bankruptcy.

It was quite apparent now that Tam's brain had been severely unsettled by the blow that it had suffered during the fight at the Progress Club. He had become a sad, broken wreck, but none could have predicted the final outcome of his tragedy.

On 31 November 1925, Lock Ling Tam had only recently returned to Liverpool after nine years at school in China, and to celebrate this homecoming and to mark the boy's twentieth birthday the family gave a small party. Everything seemed uncannily normal; it was as though the calendar had dropped back seven years, with Tam acting the genial host of old as the festivities wound their merry way through to the early hours of the next morning.

The last of the guests had departed, and the household had retired exhausted but happy to their beds. Through encroaching sleep, young Lock Ling was aware of an enraged shouting. Startled into wakefulness he left his room and met his two sisters, who had also been brought from their beds by the sounds of fighting, now coming audibly from their parents' bedroom. Fearing for his mother's continued safety, Lock Ling suggested she spend what remained of the night next door with her friends the Chins. As Mrs Lock expressed reluctance, young Lock shunted his mother and sisters into the sitting-room, and went alone next door to secure the help of Mr Chin lest his father should again become violent.

Meanwhile, the three women trembled to hear Tam shouting to Margaret Sing, a young woman who occupied the double role as maid and part-time companion to Mrs Lock. Wisely, she had kept to her room during the nocturnal quarrelling; but now Tam was demanding his boots, demanding that Margaret get them for him! With more fear than devotion she took Tam's boots to his room, where she found him red-faced and foaming at the mouth, with a revolver in his hand. Margaret fled to the safety of the sitting-room and the comfort of her mistress, and between them the four women made a hasty job of barricading the door against the approaching sound of Tam's fury. Temporarily repulsed, the aggressor slunk back to his lair

By this time Lock Ling had returned with Mrs Chin, and the company retired to the downstairs kitchen while the son went out to find a policeman. Without warning there was a deafening explosion from the kitchen doorway, and Mrs Lock slumped to the floor; a second explosion felled Cecilia, and Doris had just enough time to see the spectre of madness standing before her, a gun in each hand, before she too was blasted to heaven.

When the telephone rang at Birkenhead Central police station the voice on the other end of the line requested simply: 'Send your folks, please. I have killed my wife and children.'

On 5 February 1926, Lock Ah Tam stood at the Chester Assizes charged with the murder of his wife and two daughters; on the bench sat Mr Justice (later Lord Justice) Mackinnon.

For Lock Ah Tam the Chinese community, who could never forget his past goodness, contributed to retain the formidable defender Sir Edward Marshall Hall. Hall's often moving defence pivoted on the injury suffered by Tam eight years previously, and with an expert witness, a specialist in psychiatric disorders, he sought to prove that Tam had been, at the time of the killing, a victim of 'epileptic automatism', in which condition he would appear conscious but have no knowledge of or control over what he was saying and doing. Sadly for Lock Ah Tam it was to take another thirty years and the introduction of

the Homicide Act before a defence on such grounds could be successfully advanced; and under the archaic McNaghten Rules (see **Insanity**)
he was clearly not, in the eyes of the law, 'insane' – the fact that he had
telephoned the police and confessed was adequate proof that not only
was he conscious of what he had done, but aware that it was wrong.

After a retirement of only twelve minutes, the jury found Lock Ah
Tam guilty of murder. It was said by observers that in a courtroom full
of Tam's sobbing friends, before a judge so moved he could scarcely
speak the words of the death sentence, only Tam remained apparently
calm – an inscrutable peace that stayed with him until the drop opened
beneath his feet, and the rope tightened around his neck.

Non-Insane Automatism

A defence plea to homicide based on the fact that the defendant was
asleep at the time of the offence is unlikely to receive a particularly
sympathetic hearing since the expert evidence presented to the court in
the case of Wills Eugene Boshears. It was the contention of Professor
Francis Camps that it was most unlikely that a person sleeping could
remain so while strangling another person to death.

The trance-like state of sleepwalking can affect any person at any
time – though it is more common in childhood, and at times when the
sufferer is under stress. Often a sleepwalker will appear disarmingly
normal, giving himself away only by responding to conversation with
apparent gibberish (he will in fact be responding to a dream conversation); the eyes will most often be open, and an electroencephalogram
reading will approximate the pattern of a waking subject.

Sleepwalking not associated with organic disease, although rare, is
not an unknown defence in law; it is, however, a difficult one to sustain.
Before any verdict can be given it is necessary for a jury to consider the
whole of the defendant's personality – it will be crucial, for example, to
know whether he has a previous history of violence. The unlikelihood
of such a defence succeeding was underlined early in 1991 when the
English Court of Appeal rejected an appeal against conviction brought
by Barry Burgess on the grounds that when he had killed a woman he
was suffering from non-insane automatism – he had been sleepwalking.

Case Study

GUILTY, BUT ASLEEP*

As a defence it stood unique. The prisoner in the dock was Wills Eugene Boshears, a twenty-nine-year-old Sergeant fitter with the American fighter-plane base at Wethersfield. The date was 4 January 1961; the place, the Essex Assizes at Chelmsford. The charge against Boshears was one of murder; his defence was that as he had killed in his sleep no 'crime' had been committed.

When trucker Sidney Ambrose pulled his lorry into the lay-by, murder could not have been further from his mind. What he needed was to relieve himself, and with that intention he walked the few yards into a field. There, lying under a blackberry bush, was the half-naked body of a young woman. Medical examination revealed that the girl had died of asphyxia due to manual strangulation, and the absence of mud on the soles of her feet indicated that she had met her death elsewhere and been dumped.

The victim turned out to be twenty-year-old Jean Sylvia Constable of Halstead, in Essex, and on New Year's Day she had left home saying she was going to a party in London. Jean Constable had been one of those young women for whom the free-spending American service personnel attached to the local US base proved an irresistible attraction, and much of her spare time was spent haunting the pubs in which they drank. The night of her death was no exception, and she had been seen, not for the first time, in the company of Staff-Sergeant Wills Eugene Boshears.

Boshears had started his drinking day early. He had risen at around 6.15 on that first morning of the new year in his flat in Great Dunmow. After drawing his pay at the base, Boshears breakfasted at the NCOs' club starting with a couple of vodka aperitifs, and concluding with a couple of vodka chasers. After spending the rest of the morning in convivial drinking, he left camp clutching a large bottle of 100 per cent proof vodka. On his way back to the flat, Boshears was diverted by a couple of beers at Great Bardfield, and after dropping in briefly at home for a large vodka and lemonade, the already merry Sergeant weaved his

*One repercussion of the Boshears case was that Lord Elgin enquired, during a Parliamentary discussion, whether the government had plans to make a change in the law to make possible a verdict of Guilty But Asleep, which would effectively prevent a similar defendant from walking free from punishment.

way into Braintree and the open doors of *The Bell*, *The Boar*, and back to *The Bell* again – which had by this time attracted the custom of Jean Constable and twenty-year-old David Salt, who were already well entrenched when Boshears joined them. After closing time the trio went back to Dunmow where the vodka bottle continued to dispense liquid happiness. Before long, driven no doubt by drink and passion, Salt and Jean Constable disappeared into the bedroom where they got to know each other a lot better. Wills Boshears, meanwhile, dragged a double mattress in front of the lounge fire, and when his companions returned from their love nest he suggested a night-cap before they all fell asleep on the mattress. At around 12.45 a.m. David Salt woke up, dressed, and departed, leaving Jean and Boshears much the worse for drink, sleeping.

Boshears takes up the narrative in his evidence given before the Essex Assizes:

I went to sleep almost immediately. The next thing I remember is that I felt something pulling at my mouth. I was not awake but this woke me up, and I found I was over Jean and I had my hands round her throat. Jean was dead, and I panicked. I started to cut her hair off. Then I took the body to the spare room and left it. I dressed her in the way in which she was later found. I took the sheets and blankets off the bed and put them in the bath tub to soak [Jean would have soiled them in her fear at being attacked] and went in and went to sleep.

The following day Boshears disposed of the body in the place where Sidney Ambrose found it.

This extraordinary defence could clearly not go unchallenged, and both Mr Stanley Rees QC, acting for the Crown, and Mr Justice Glyn-Jones, the presiding judge, made quite plain their mistrust of the proposition. And in this they were endorsed by the expert testimony of pathologist Professor Francis Camps. From the witness box, Camps declared that: 'Boshears would probably have felt the girl moving, even if he was half-asleep.'

Judge: He could not possibly have carried this through without waking up? – *Camps:* I should think that it is certainly within the bounds of improbability. My reason, from my findings, is this process would take a certain amount of time, and during that period the person would go through certain phases of movement, and from the description given of finding her suddenly dead like that I don't think it fits in with that type of death.

Summing up at the end of the trial, Mr Justice Glyn-Jones asked the jury: 'Have you ever heard of a man strangling a woman while he was sound asleep? We have no medical evidence that there exists any record in all the records of the medical profession that such a thing ever happened . . . You use your common sense and decide whether it happened.'

However, on the matter of the law as it applied to the case, he instructed them that if they believed that Boshears *had* been asleep and committed the act involuntarily, then he was entitled to be acquitted; if they had any doubts about whether he was asleep or not, then Boshears must be given the benefit of that doubt and be acquitted. But if they rejected the defence, only then could they convict. There were, he said, only two possible verdicts in the case – guilty of murder, or not guilty of anything at all.

Returning to the court after a deliberation lasting one hour and fifty minutes, the jury found Sergeant Boshears not guilty; he was released, and declared his complete satisfaction with British justice.

Only a week later another man, in London, stabbed his victim to death while, he claimed, he was asleep. This defence was obviously not destined to become fashionable, for the killer was convicted and sentenced to life imprisonment.

AUTOPSY
(see Pathologists, Post-Mortem Procedures)

B

BACTERIA POISONING

The biology department of a forensic laboratory will deal with matters of bacteriology as a matter of routine, though there are very few reliably attested cases of homicide by bacterial poisoning – by its very nature it is a death very open to confusion with 'natural causes'.

The first such murder was said to have been committed by the fraudulent French financier Henri Girard. In 1912 Girard took out an insurance policy on Monsieur Louis Pernotte for the sum of 300,000 francs; two years later Pernotte, his wife and two children became ill with what appeared to be typhoid. Coincidentally, Girard had not long before taken delivery of some cultures of that same bacteria from a Parisian laboratory supplier. In the end it was only Louis who perished, despite the frequent injections of 'camphorated camomile' administered by his old friend Girard. After he insured their lives for worthwhile sums of money, Henri Girard's next potential victims were fed on *Amanita phaloides*, a variety of poisonous **Fungi**. Both were very ill, as might be expected, but to Girard's great disappointment they proved hardy enough to recover their health. Which was more than poor Madame Monin could do when it fell to her turn to strengthen Henri Girard's bank balance. In April 1918 the unfortunate widow succumbed to an aperitif poisoned with bacteria – and Girard collected her insurance. By now the insurance companies had become suspicious that so many of the people on whom Girard had taken out policies were falling sick – even dying – so soon afterwards. He was arrested in August 1918, and while in custody made a number of statements which almost amounted to confessions, though Girard concluded that he was, underneath, a good man 'with a very warm heart'. The jury of his peers had no opportunity to make up their own minds about that because before his case came to trial Henri Girard took his own life – by swallowing germ cultures.

At around the time that Girard – 'The first scientific murderer' as he has been called – was experimenting with typhoid, Dr Arthur Warren Waite, a twenty-eight-year-old dentist from New York, was poisoning his mother-in-law by infecting her food with diphtheria and influenza germs. Two months later, in March 1916, Waite's father-in-law, Mr John Peck, followed his wife to the grave poisoned – according to Waite's subsequent admission – by 'similar methods'. He added rather proudly that a refinement had been a nasal spray infected with tuberculosis bacteria. In fact, the old man was tougher than Arthur Waite hoped, and he was obliged to administer the *coup de grâce* by the rather less inventive means of a hefty eighteen grams of arsenic. It was the arsenic that betrayed this greedy and callous killer when it was discovered at autopsy – had he persisted with the bacteria who knows but that it would have been yet another tragic death from 'natural causes'.

However, bacterial poisoning is not a method of murder confined to the 'gaslight' era of crime. Joan Robinson, daughter of oil millionaire Ash Robinson, married surgeon John Hill in the early 1960s, though by the end of the decade their relationship was in tatters. In March 1969, Joan Hill was rushed to hospital, where she died on the 19th. Although the hurried post-mortem suggested liver infection, Joan's father began openly accusing John Hill of *allowing* his daughter to die – that is, of committing murder by omission. In return Hill took out a five-million-dollar slander suit against Robinson. Just three months later John Hill married again, which served to refuel accusations of foul play, and a subsequent exhumation and autopsy on Joan's body revealed an apparent inconsistency when the brain which had been pickled after the first examination showed signs of meningitis, while the brain stem in the body did not; it was suggested that the preserved brain did not belong to Mrs Hill at all. So confusing did the situation become that it took three grand jury sittings to find sufficiently clear evidence on which to indict John Hill. Hill's trial was to open in 1971, when his second wife – now his ex-wife, and he had married for a third time – gave testimony that Hill had tried to kill her by driving his car into a wall while she was a passenger. She also claimed that he confessed to killing Joan with a bacterial culture made from 'every form of human excretion' even, she claimed, the pus drawn from a boil on one of his patients. She had fallen sick and he refrained from taking her to hospital until he was sure she was in irreversibie shock. It happened that all this information was made public rather prematurely, and the trial was declared void. Before he could be retried John Hill was assassinated by a hired gunman. In the continuing feud the Hill family accused Ash Robinson of hiring the killer, and despite his acquittal of the charge the case still generates considerable controversy.

BALLISTICS
History

In 1794 a Lancashire man was shot dead and the surgeon examining the body removed from his wound a wad of paper which had been used to pack the shot. This paper was later unfolded, and in its flattened state found to be an exact match with the torn corner of a ballad sheet still in the suspect's pocket; it was the first case of murder solved by 'ballistics' – or at least an ancestor of the science. Later, in 1854, a similar English case was proved by matching paper wads (on this occasion torn from *The Times),* and in 1891 a homicide was solved in France by matching wads made from the *Lorraine Almanach.*

It was in 1835 that 'bullet' evidence was discovered. In that year Henry Goddard, one of Fielding's Bow Street Runners, solved a case of burglary at Southampton during the course of which the butler claimed to have been shot at by the intruders as he lay in his bed. Goddard examined the supposed points of forced entry, but the **Tool Marks** made by the jemmy did not line up on the outside and inside, neither did the marks on the door of the closet containing the stolen plate. His suspicions aroused, detective Goddard demanded to see the builder's pistol and the mould in which he cast his bullets; he then dug the ball out of the servant's bed-head where he said he was shot at. Despite the bullet's slightly distorted condition, the eagle-eyed Runner found a singular mark on it, like a raised pin-head; a mark which was the result of a slight depression in the butler's mould and which was carried by all projectiles cast from it. Staggered by this proof that he had 'shot himself' the servant confessed to setting up the bogus burglary in order to rob his master. In France in 1869, a M. Roussin proved by the chemical analysis of a bullet removed from the victim's head that the precise melting point, weight and proportional composition of tin and lead made it identical with bullets found in the possession of the suspect, a clock-maker named Cadet.

However, it was during his investigation of the Echallier case in 1889 that the father of forensic science, Professor Alexandre **Lacassagne**, announced his conviction that the *marks* on a bullet recovered from the victim's body could be matched with the gun that fired it if only the gun could be found. Eventually, a suspect was detained and a search of his home revealed a gun whose seven rifling grooves matched the seven grooves on the projectile. Forensic ballistics had become a science; and over the next century it would became an *exact* science which, helped by a lot of experience and an increasing battery of new laboratory techniques, would prove that a fired bullet carries marks as unique as a fingerprint.

By this time, across the Atlantic in the United States, the gun factory set up by Samuel Colt in 1846 to supply the Texas Rangers with the first successful 'six-shooter' was revolutionizing crime. Cheap, lethal weapons – advertized by Colt as 'The Equalizer' – were finding their way into the nation's homes.

Perhaps it was appropriate, then, that over the next several decades the lead in forensic ballistics came from the United States. Charles Waite established his international reference collection of firearms and their specifications, by which he could ascertain from the appearance of a bullet the make, calibre and model of gun which fired it. It was Waite, in collaboration with Philip Gravelle, who founded the world's first Bureau of Forensic Ballistics, in New York in 1923. Two years later an army doctor with a specialist knowledge of guns joined the Bureau and went on to become America's leading expert on forensic ballistics; his name was Calvin Goddard.

It was Gravelle and Goddard who developed the single most important piece of apparatus in analytical ballistics – the **Comparison Microscope**. Using this new instrument, Goddard presented evidence to the inquiry sitting in judgement in the controversial Sacco and Vanzetti case.

The robbery and murder took place on 15 April 1920; just another payroll heist, two men shot dead and their killers the richer by $16,000. The consequences of the crime, however, were to reverberate around the world. Nicola Sacco, shoemaker, aged twenty-nine, and Bartolomeo Vanzetti, fish-seller, aged thirty-two, both Italian imnigrants, were picked up by the police as the result of descriptions given by witnesses to the robbery. Sacco and Vanzetti were both armed with pistols, but worse by far, they were known political activists – anarchists. The trial began in Dedham, Massachusetts, on 31 May 1921, and made news around the globe. Despite a complex and convincing defence, Sacco and Vanzetti were convicted of first-degree murder and sentenced to death. The trial judge, who had little time for 'these anarchist bastards' was continually criticized for his undisguised bias. Over the next seven years no fewer than seven motions for retrial were dismissed, and there were a number of official inquiries. It was to one of these that Goddard contributed the expert testimony that the fatal bullets *had* been fired by the gun carried by Nicola Sacco. Both prisoners exchanged their cell on Death Row for the Execution Chamber. Fifty years later, in 1977, the Governor of Massachusetts issued a special proclamation clearing the names of Sacco and Vanzetti, though the case continues to provoke strong emotions.

At about the time Goddard and Gravelle were developing the microscope, a physicist named John H. Fisher was inventing another instrument which would become vital to the study of ballistic evidence, the helixometer – a hollow probe fitted with a light and a magnifying glass for examining the insides of gun barrels.

In Britain it was Sir Sydney **Smith** who was championing the comparison microscope, which he had first used with conspicuous success in the case of the murder of the British Sirdar in Egypt, Sir Lee Stack, in 1924. Smith later introduced the instrument to his native Britain where it was enthusiastically received by expert gunsmith and leading ballistics expert Robert Churchill – nephew of Edward J. Churchill, the pioneer of English ballistics, who had died in 1910.

Identification and Comparison
Rifling Marks
The matching of bullets to guns is one of the simplest principles in forensic science. Since as early as the sixteenth century gunsmiths have been improving the speed and accuracy of **Firearms** by cutting spiral 'rifling' grooves around the insides of gun barrels. The effect is to make the bullet, propelled at great speed down the barrel, spin on its axis thus increasing its speed and force. Bullets are made *slightly* oversize for a particular gun, thus ensuring a tight fit (though the calibre will be matched to the weapon); it is this tight fit which causes the characteristic 'rifling' marks.

The deep furrows are engraved by the lands, and the striations between them are caused by the tool marks in the bottoms of the grooves.

Because the internal features remain constant, *any* suitable bullet that passes through will be marked in an *identical* way; so if a 'control' bullet is fired from a suspect gun it can, with the aid of a comparison microscope, be matched with a bullet recovered from the scene of a crime or from the body of a victim.

It was Calvin Goddard who wrote in 1924 that the individuality of a gun barrel would leave on every bullet fired 'the fingerprint of that particular barrel'.

Types of rifling vary considerably – in the number of grooves, in the relative widths of the lands and the grooves, and whether the 'twist' is right- or left-handed. Thus a knowledge of these specifications will help the ballistics examiner to identify the type of gun from which an individual bullet was fired.

For example, revolvers and self-loading pistols (see **Firearms**) are divided into five types:

Steyr type: Used in all the earlier self-loading pistols such as the Borchardt. Four grooves; grooves and lands of equal width; right-hand twist.

Browning type: The most common. Six grooves; narrow lands, broad grooves; right-hand twist.

Colt type: Used in all Colt revolvers and self-loading pistols, Bayard pistols, and Spanish copies of Colt pistols. Six grooves; narrow lands, broad grooves; left-hand twist.

Webley type: Used in all Webley revolvers. Seven grooves; narrow lands, broad grooves; right-hand twist.

Smith and Wesson type: Used in all Smith and Wesson revolvers, Harrington and Richardson revolvers, and Iver Johnson revolvers; (not used in any self-loaders). Five grooves; grooves and lands of equal width; right-hand twist.

Cartridge Marks

To understand the way in which cartridge cases become marked with a gun's 'fingerprint' it is necessary to appreciate the way in which the projectile is fired.

Breech blocks are machine-cut from steel and each example will carry with it the unique imperfections imposed by a variety of cutting and finishing operations – marks from the cutter-blades, those left by manual and mechanical grinding and filing, and so on. In addition, there are the accidental knocks and scratches collected both in the factory before use and during use that will endow a breech block with a unique face. Quite often the careless use of a cleaning rod will leave tell-tale indentations on the breech block. The firing pin is also cut and shaped and it too will leave identifiable marks on the base of the cartridge. When a cartridge is fired a huge pressure is generated (anything between two and twenty tons per square inch) which forces the cartridge case back against the face of the breech block. As the brass of the case is softer than the steel of the breech face it will be imprinted with any imperfection, no matter how fine; in other words, it will bear its 'finger-print'.

Case Study

THE MAJOR AND THE PASTRY COOK

As crimes go, the death of 'Doctor' Angelos Zemenides was as commonplace as could be. Zemenides, who had no professional entitlement to call himself Doctor, was a leading figure in the London Cypriot community, and on the night of 2 January 1933, he was safely at home in his Hampstead lodgings. About 11.20 a knock at the door was answered by a fellow lodger, a Mr Deby, who admitted a stranger asking to speak to Zemenides. Within minutes the two men were locked in a life and death struggle, the result of which was that the young visitor shot the doctor dead and fled out into the darkness. The police subsequently took into custody a young pastry cook named Theodosius Petrou, recently arrived from Cyprus and even more recently swindled out of his modest savings by Zemenides; he had been heard uttering threats of revenge.

A search of the cellar of the house where Petrou lodged was rewarded by finding a .32 self-loading Browning pistol with five cartridges still in the magazme. Of these remaining cartridges two were standard self-loading pistol cartridges, rimless with nickel-jacketed bullets; the other three were .32 revolver cartridges with the rims filed off and lead bullets.

Meanwhile, a search of the scene of the crime had resulted in the finding of two fired cartridge cases, one a rimless self-loading pistol cartridge, the other a .32 revolver cartridge with the rim filed down. The projectile removed from the victim's body was a nickel-jacketed pistol bullet, and a lead revolver bullet was later found embedded in the wainscoting at the scene of the shooting. On the balance of probability it seemed obvious that the bullets fired during the attack on Zemenides had come from the weapon hidden at Petrou's lodgings. Indeed, it was little more than a formality that Robert Churchilll, the expert retained by the prosecution, now handed over the ballistics evidence to the experts acting for the defence.

It was a very lucky day for young Petrou when the expert chosen was Major Sir Gerald Burrard, like Churchill one of the country's foremost ballistics specialists. Assisted by the handgun expert Dr R.K. Wilson, Burrard began with the cartridge cases. Using the suspect gun he fired no fewer than fifty shots into water using self-loading pistol ammunition with nickel-jacketed bullets; examination of the cartridge cases showed in every case an identical ejector mark in the rim, and running across the surface of the cap at a tangent to the striker indentation a pronounced ridge which had clearly been imparted by a deep tool cut on the pistol's breech face. Finally, the striker indentation in every case appeared off-centre at the 'one o'clock' position when all the cases were oriented with the ejector mark at 'nine o'clock'.

These consistent findings were compared with the cartridge cases recovered from the scene of the crime and were found by Burrard to be 'totally and utterly different from those of any of my test cases'. For a start there was no ejector mark at all, there was no ridge caused by the marked breech face, and finally the ex-centricity of the ejector mark was at 'six o'clock'.

Burrard and Wilson next repeated the experiments using the other type of cartridges found in the gun – the .32 revolver ammunition with filed-down rims. The results were identical. Thus on *every* test cartridge case – 110 of them – the 'fingerprint' was the same and totally different from the two cases found at the scene of the crime.

The experts then turned their attention to the bullets themselves. The test shots showed that the pistol's bore was of a very large diameter, and in every case the engraving caused by the rifling lands was relatively weak and barely reached above the cannelure of the bullet. In no case was there groove engraving all round the circumference – proving that the bullets were a loose fit in the gun's barrel. Comparison with the fatal bullet showed a pronounced difference – the bullet clearly having been fired from a pistol in which it had fitted the bore tightly all round and become heavily engraved all round by both the lands and by 'bottoming' the grooves; the land engraving was etched deeply up beyond the cannelure.

In short, despite the early coincidences that had seemed so suspicious, scientific examination proved beyond any possibility of doubt that the 'Petrou' gun had *not* fired the bullet that killed Angelos Zemenides.

Petrou himself had maintained his innocence from the outset, claiming: 'I am innocent and God will help me.' On this occasion God was wise in his choice of Major Burrard and Dr Wilson to act as experts. The jury, thoroughly convinced by the photographic enlargements of the bullets and cartridges shown to them acquitted Theodosius Petrou. The real killer, however, was never brought to justice.

BARBITURATES
(see Drugs, Poisons)

BAREFOOT PRINTS
Although 'footprints' are usually found classified under **Impressions** (or sometimes **Shoe-Prints**), it is worth recognizing that on some occasions the imprint of the bare foot itself will be found at the scene of a crime. Like the ridge patterns of **Fingerprints** and **Palmars**, those on the soles of the feet are unique to every individual; however, their infrequency as a contact trace means police forces keep no central register of barefoot prints. Any usefulness is therefore restricted to comparison with the print of a suspect.

Even when ridge patterns are indistinct, the application of 'micro-**Anthropometry**' provides a remarkably specific set of dimensions. The scheme illustrated opposite is from a contemporary Russian work on criminalistics and shows how points of measurement can contribute to evidence of identity.

In many countries it is the normal practice in maternity hospitals to use a baby's barefoot print as a means of identity, for though the papillary ridge patterns on the fingers have already been formed for life, they are too small to be of practical use.

Stockinged-Foot Prints
Although the value of such prints can be seen as a definite rarity in criminal investigation, the astute scenes-of-crime officer will always be aware of their possibilities as a means of helping identify the wearer. 'Points of comparison' are similar to those used to identify **Glove Prints** – namely imperfections in manufacture (uneven weave, knots in thread, etc.), seam stitching patterns, wear damage and repairs, and so on.

The Case of Peter Griffiths

Prints made by stockinged feet may be rare in the annals of homicide, but they made an important contribution to one of England's most distinguished fingerprint cases (see Case Study, page 248) – the detection of Peter Griffiths after his savage killing of June Anne Devaney in 1948. One of the notable features of the case was that Griffiths, after he had broken into the Blackburn hospital from which he abducted three-year-old June, took off his shoes to avoid being heard and proceeded in stockinged feet. Detective Chief Inspector Colin Campbell, head of Lancashire's Fingerprint Bureau, found a perfect set of the images imprinted into the waxed surface of the ward floor. Beginning at the entrance to Children's Ward CH3 the tracks went to the side of Cot No. 1, then to the instrument trolley from which the killer took a large storage bottle, back to Cot No. 2, then Cot No. 3 and Cot No. 4 where June Devaney was sleeping. Griffiths left the storage bottle by the bed, lifted the child from her cot and proceeded to the door leading out into the corridor. At this point he must have heard a noise outside the door because the footprints turned and walked back the length of the ward to the point of entry.

Colin Campbell had the prints photographed and then forensic experts were called in to scrape the wax from beneath them for further laboratory tests for miscroscopic fibres and other particle traces. It was the fingerprint left on the storage bottle that finally trapped Griffiths, and he was later hanged at Liverpool; but in building up the sequence of events leading to the murder, the trail of stockinged-foot prints played a significant part.

BERTILLON, ALPHONSE (1853–1914)

Born in 1853, son of the physician Dr Louis Adolphe Bertillon, President of the Paris Anthropological Society. Although he showed some aptitude for mathematics, the young Alphonse must, by his father's standards, have proved something of a disappointment. After Alphonse was expelled from school, and then dismissed from his first job with a Parisian bank, Louis secured his son a post as assistant clerk in the records office at the Prefecture of Police. It became Alphonse's job to take down the particulars of arrested felons and enter them on a record card. Perhaps it was the almost mathematical nature of the problem that fired the young man's enthusiasm to find a solution to the difficulties of keeping criminal records using the anthropometrical methods being studied by his father and his father's friend, the Belgian statistician Lambert Quetelet. It was Quetelet's theory that no two individuals shared the same physical characteristics, and in October 1879, Bertillon prepared a report on the system that would eventually bear his name, 'Bertillonage'. It appears that his suggestions were turned down by the Prefect of Police. It required a further three years, a change of prefect, and the intervention of Bertillon senior before Alphonse's system of **Anthropometry** was given a chance. There followed a year or two of relative success accompanied by encouragement from the newspapers which ensured that Bertillonage had a secure place in French criminal procedure.

From here Alphonse Bertillon turned his attention to the science of photography, making use of modern developments to improve the recording of mug-shots by taking both the frontal and profile portraits – a system still in use throughout the world. He also began to instruct detectives in making the **Portrait Parlé** – an excellent shorthand for classifying the shapes of facial features.

In 1888 Alphonse Bertillon was honoured with the title Director of the Judicial Identification Service. Four years later, in recognition of his identification and capture of the anarchist assassin known as Ravachol, Bertillon was awarded the Legion of Honour.

Although at the time of the scandal Bertillon was seen as a patriot among patriots, his was a large part of the blame for sending a perfectly innocent man to prison for a dozen years. In 1894 French military secrets were finding their way into enemy German hands with alarming regularity. A woman in the pay of the French, but employed to clean at the German embassy found in one of the embassy's waste-baskets a torn-up letter referring to the sale of secrets. There was clearly a spy among the officers of the French General Staff. In what was to become an international outrage, Captain Alfred Dreyfus, a Jew among a fiercely anti-Semitic General Staff, was taken into custody as a scape-goat. He was obliged to write out the words of the discovered letter and it was Alphonse Bertillon himself – the Director of Identification – who despite expert opposition gave evidence that both texts were in the same hand. In fact they were not, but Dreyfus was found guilty of treason anyway, and spent the next twelve years a prisoner on the notorious Devil's Island in French Guinea; until 1906 when the real traitor, a man named Esterhazy, was identified.

Bertillon was in many respects a victim of his own stubborn short-sightedness. Already in England the police authorities were experimenting with the newly published system of identification called

'Dactylography', or **Fingerprints**, as an alternative to the more cumbersome anthropometric records. Bertillon's active opposition to fingerprinting ('My measurements are surer than any fingerprint pattern'), and his refusal to incorporate it into French criminal procedure proved to be his downfall.

In 1911, what was arguably the world's best-known painting, Leonardo da Vinci's *Mona Lisa,* was stolen from the Louvre. Bertillon had been summoned to the gallery to oversee the investigation in person, and despite finding a clear set of fingerprints on the glass of the picture's frame he was unable to identify them. The problem was that despite having reluctantly agreed to add fingerprints to his anthropometric records he had dismissively relegated them to the category of 'special marks' – in other words, he had no means of classification by which to retrieve information on the prints. It was two years before a mentally unbalanced Italian named Vincenzo Perugia, who wanted to return the painting to its native Italy, was taken into custody and the painting recovered. Ironically, it transpired that Perugia had been arrested several times in Paris, and Bertillon had once taken his measurements and his fingerprints.

For Alphonse Bertillon the solution to the case had come far too late, and he had been lambasted for his incompetence in the newspapers which had once idolized him. Bertillon's health had already begun to fail, and the emotional pressure of his fall from grace was taking its toll. Gradually his eyesight began to fail, and on 13 February 1914, Alphonse Bertillon died of pernicious anaemia.

BERTILLONAGE
(see Anthropometry)

BITE-MARK ANALYSIS
Introduction
The investigation of bite marks is a comparatively recent development of forensic **Odontology**, although specific cases have provided convincing proof of its possibillties.

This ascendancy is due entirely to increased knowledge and awareness on the part of medical examiners in recognizing bite marks for what they are and not as simply bruising whose characteristics bite marks can share.

BITE MARKS: SIGNIFICANT LOCATIONS

NON-SEXUAL ASSAULT	SEXUAL ASSAULT			
	Heterosexual		*Homosexual*	
Extremities (ears, nose, fingers, etc.)	Female victim:	Male victim:	Female victim:	Male victim:
Chest	Neck	Arm	(No data)	Posterior shoulders
Thorax	Anterior shoulder	Chest		Upper back
	Breast	Abdomen		Armpit
	Arm			Breast
	Pubic area			Arm
	Buttocks			Penis
	Thigh			Scrotum

Types of Bite Mark

Bite marks can be divided, for forensic purposes, between two categories:

1. Human-on-human bites on the skin of one or more participants in an assault. It is necessary to describe the bite this circuitously as it may not be the victim of an attack who has been bitten but the perpetrator *by* the victim in self-defence. The primary value of the bite marks is to identify (or exclude) a suspected assailant.
2. Bite marks on food (cheese, chocolate, fruit, etc.), which may establish the presence of a person at a particular location, scene of crime, etc.

By far the greatest number of cases involve human-on-human bite marks, and of these by far the greatest number are associated with sexual assault (either heterosexual or homosexual) and the non-accidental injury of children.

Sexually Oriented Bite Marks

Quite distinct from bite marks not involving sexual activity. Bites tend to be inflicted slowly and deliberately, with the application of suction. Although there can be no absolute set of rules in such cases, evidence suggests that the table on the previous page may be useful in identifying bite marks on the body.

Child Abuse Cases
Characteristic of this type of violent assault is the presence of bite marks, either alone or in combination with other injuries. Like sexually motivated sadism, this category seems to be a manifestation of some deep primal rage.

Bite-mark Analysis
Collecting and Processing the Evidence
The first job of the forensic dentist called to assess bite marks on a human body is to answer the following questions:

1. Is this a bite mark and if so, is it of human origin?
2. Is the injury contemporary with the crime under investigation, and consistent with it?
3. Are there any characteristics that individualize the mark sufficiently to base a comparison on?

Assuming an affirmative answer to these questions can be given, the following procedures will be undertaken:

Saliva Swabs
A vital first step is to collect specimens of saliva that may still be present around the bite (saliva will show under ultra-violet light, but after five hours there is little chance of a positive reaction). These are taken with pure cotton swabs moistened with distilled water and stored in closed, sterile test tubes. Approximately 80 per cent of the population are 'secretors', people whose other body fluids (including saliva) contain blood antigens. It may therefore be possible to either exclude from the inquiry a suspect of a different blood group, or provide supporting evidence that a suspect with identical blood grouping *could* have been responsible for the bite.

Photographing the Evidence
Recognizing the fugitive nature of bite marks, a primary consideration must be the preservation of as much visual evidence as possible. This means, in the first instance, photographing the marks in such ways as will, when they have become obscured, retain an accurate record. Photographs should always include a linear scale to establish size and distance.

Sketching

A sketch and/or tracing of the area can be immediately annotated with such information as distances between marks, angles, etc.

Taking Impressions

It may, in some circumstances, be possible and useful to take cast impressions of the bite marks if they are of sufficient prominence.

Characteristics of Bite Marks

Human vs. Animal

The most obvious determinant, if a whole impression is available, is the overall pattern of the bite mark. Human dentition will make an ovoid, or elliptical, pattern, while other aninials will leave a V-shaped or oblong-shaped mark. Furthermore, only in human bite marks will there be evidence of a 'sucking' action.

Patterns of Teeth

Although biting, in this context, is rarely a precise action, being governed more by spontaneous passion, there is a broad pattern that can be useful in identifying the shapes of individual toothmarks:

Incisors: Rectangular, sometimes perforating the skin.
Canines: Triangular, with apex towards the labial and base the lingual of the elipse.
Premolars: Single or double triangles, or diamond.
Molars: By reason of their position at the back of the mouth, they rarely make contact or leave marks.

The teeth of animals tend to puncture the skin deeply, tearing the tissue, while the human bite is 'blunt' and superficial, the teeth abrading rather than tearing.

Comparison of Bite Marks

It has already been emphasized that bite-mark evidence is only of value in comparison with the marks made by the teeth of a suspect. It must also be recognized at the outset that, at the present state of the art at any rate, it is only through extremes of 'abnormality' that any *positive* identification may be made. More commonly, bite-mark comparison will tend to *exclude* certain suspects from an inquiry.

Having obtained impressions from a suspect's teeth (if not by consent, then by court order), they must be matched with the tracings and photographs taken of the marks on the victim's skin.

The first obvious step is exclusion; if the two are clearly incompatible then another suspect must be sought. Only if there are no discrepancies should the examination progress to the finer details.

As far as evidence presented to a court as expert testimony is concerned, the forensic odontologist will be expected to have arrived at one of three possible conclusions:

1. That there is a high degree of probability that the bite marks left on the victim's skin and the 'exemplar' (impression of the suspect's dentition) have a common origin.
2. That the bite mark and exemplar are *consistent* with having a common origin.
3. That the two marks are not consistent, and do not have a common origin.

Unlike fingerprint evidence, there are no recognized minimum 'points of resemblance', the science of bite-mark analysis being still at an early stage of development. Although new techniques common to all the sciences are enlarging the potential for accuracy, it is possible that the advancement of DNA profiling from saliva (see page 173) will render at least some of the observational practices obsolete.

Bite Marks in Food
By comparison with human-on-human bite marks, human-on-food is simple to deal with and accurate as long as an impression is cast in sufficient time to preserve against corruption by shrinkage and decay. It follows that the process of comparison will also be that much simpler and more accurate.

Case Study

TOOTH AND CLAW
THE GORRINGE CASE
Two fundamental cases launched the science of bite-mark analysis. Both were murders, both occurred in Britain (one each in England and Scotland), and both were investigated by Professor Keith Simpson, the pathologist who had already been responsible for great advances in

forensic dentistry throughout the world.

In the early hours of New Year's Day 1948, the body of a young woman was found in the car park adjoining a dance hall in which she had recently been celebrating the birth of a new year. The woman was identified as a Mrs Gorringe; she had been bludgeoned and strangled, her chest had been exposed and on the right breast there was a wound identified as a bite mark. Professor Simpson, summoned to examine the body, offered an opinion that such a distinctive mark – made by two upper front teeth and four lower teeth – should be comparable with the dentition of a suspect if and when one could be found. Fortunately the police did not have long to wait or far to look. Mrs Gorringe had been observed arguing heatedly with her husband at the New Year's Eve dance, and they had left together still quarrelling.

It was Simpson himself who took the wax impression of Gorringe's teeth, and casts made from it proved, to the satisfaction of a jury, a convincing match for the marks on the dead woman's breast. Gorringe was sentenced to death (though later reprieved) and Professor Simpson added another laurel to his already large collection.

THE MURDER AT BIGGAR

A second, altogether more complex case was tackled by Keith Simpson in collaboration with Dr Warren Harvey.

It began on 7 August 1967, with the discovery of the battered and strangled corpse of fifteen-year-old Linda Peacock in a cemetery in Biggar, a small town between Edinburgh and Glasgow. The girl had not been raped, though the clothing on the upper part of her body had been disarranged, and the police photographer whose job it was to record the scene of the crime and the victim's position was particularly impressed by an oval bruise-type mark on one of her breasts; consistent, he believed, with a bite mark. The fact was quickly confirmed by the pathologist, and Scotland's foremost forensic dentistry expert, Dr Warren Harvey, was assigned to the team investigating Linda Peacock's murder.

Police officers had already eliminated the 3,000 people so far interviewed in the area, and there remained a single group of twenty-nine youths, all inmates of a local detention centre. Harvey suggested as a first step taking dental impressions of each of the men in an attempt to match a set of teeth to the distinctive bite mark on the victim's body. One mark in particular looked as though it might have come from an uncommonly sharp or jagged tooth.

Dr Harvey was now able, on general observation, to reduce to five the number of impressions that could not yet be eliminated from suspicion. At this stage he consulted with Professor Simpson and the two experts concentrated their attention on the 'jagged' tooth.

Of the five suspects, only one had a match. Investigations now centred on seventeen-year-old Gordon Hay, who had now been proved missing from the borstal dormitory at the time of Linda Peacock's murder; he had been seen returning just before 10.30, dishevelled, breathless, and with mud on his clothes. Equally incriminating was the fact that Hay had met Linda at a local fair on the previous day, and had observed to a friend that he would like to have sex with her.

Hay – willingly, almost eagerly, it must be said – submitted to a further set of impressions being made of his teeth. From these the water-tight evidence that would convict Gordon Hay of murder was assembled. Closer examination revealed to Warren Harvey the sharp-edged, clear-cut pits, like small craters on the tips of the upper and lower right canines, due to a rare disorder called hypo-calcination. The upper pit was larger than the lower, which agreed with the bite mark on the victim's breast.

Patient examination of no fewer than 342 sixteen- and seventeen-year-old boys revealed only two with pits, one with a pit and hypo-calcination, and none with two pits. Harvey went on to extrapolate these findings graphically, arriving at the result that even if seventeen people could be found with two pitted canines, it is quite possible that none of them could have left marks identical to those found on the girl's body.

In February 1968, throughout a whole day, Dr Warren Harvey spoke from the witness box at Edinburgh's High Court of Justiciary. It was the first time that a Scottish jury had needed to consider bite-mark evidence, and clearly they were impressed. Gordon Hay was found guilty of murder and, on account of his youth, sentenced 'to be detained during Her Majesty's pleasure'.

Recent Developments
Scanning Electron Microscopy

Introduced in the late 1960s, the **Scanning Electron Microscope** has revolutionized many areas of forensics and is now a vital piece of equip-ment in the odontology laboratory. Main fields of use are:

1. Comparison of bite-mark evidence with the dentition of a suspect. The photomicrograph's image of minute surface variations, hugely magnified in three dimensions, reveals imperfections not observable by the naked eye or standard microscopy.
2. Comparison of broken surfaces of teeth or dentures, and the study of the patterns of dental wear.

(For a description of the Scanning Electron Microscope see page 442.)

Electronic Image Enhancement
The electronic enhancement of images has a wide variety of applications to the forensic sciences. In bite-mark analysis, enhancement of a bite pattern will render previously indistinct marks 'readable' by an experienced forensic dentist.

The instrument was developed by the Californian electronics company Stanford Technology Corp., and has the impressive name of Occlused Video Density Analyser and Edge Enhancer. Basically, a sophisticated closed circuit video system measures the density levels, or 'grey scale', of a photograph (or object) which is the area of the spectrum which the human eye cannot easily comprehend. Of course, combined with the ever increasing sophistication of modern-day computer image analysis programs, such techniques will soon make bite-mark identification as accurate as fingerprinting.

BLOOD
(see Bloodstains, DNA Profiling, Semen, Serology)

BLOODSTAINS
New Bloodstains
At the scene of most violent homicides there is an overwhelming presence of blood – not only on the body of the victim and any murder weapon that may have been left, but if the crime has been committed in a building, on walls, floor, furnishings and furniture surfaces, even the ceiling. In such cases it is important that a forensic scientist experienced in interpreting bloodstains is summoned to the scene as a great deal can be deduced from the quantity, distribution and shape of the stains.

Although the distinctive shapes of bloodstains had already been noted by Alexandre **Lacassagne**, it was Professor John **Glaister** in his *Medical Jurisprudence and Toxicology* who described the six patterns into which he grouped the marks:

Drops
Found on horizontal surfaces, caused by blood dripping from directly above. The shape of the drop will change according to the height from which it has fallen, the crenellations or 'starring' being more pronounced the greater the fall.

Splashes
Most commonly occurring where droplets of blood have travelled through the air – perhaps as a bludgeoning instrument is swung – and hit a surface such as a wall at an angle. This tends to leave a stain shaped like an elongated exclamation mark, the 'blob' indicating the direction of travel. These stains may provide useful information as to the scenes of assault where a victim has been struck in more than one location, and the *aciual* location of the assault when a body has been moved after death.

Spurts
Because blood is pumped by the heart around the body under great pressure it is obvious that if a major vein or artery is severed there will be a forceful outflow of blood which, in addition to staining the attacker, will also travel some distance around the victim – up walls, sometimes even to the ceiling.

It follows that if the victim is already dead (that is to say the heart has stopped pumping), then injuries inflicted will not result in such widespread 'spurting'. This fact could be an important indicator in distinguishing the scene of a killing from that of a subsequent dismemberment.

Pools
A pool of blood marks the spot where a heavily bleeding victim will have lain dead or, if more than one pool is apparent with a single victim, where he has dragged himself or been dragged from one place to another, remaining sufficiently long in each location to form a pool. The route between pools will be indicated by blood smears or drops.

Smears

Smears can be left either by a wounded victim or his assailant stained with fresh blood, gripping or brushing against the sides of furniture, doors, walls, etc., depositing blood. It could also be caused by the smearing of existing fresh stains.

Trails
If a bloody corpse is moved from the scene of the killing to another location by dragging it will leave a smeared trail along the route; a body carried from one place to another may leave a trail of 'drops', as would an injured person moving from one place to another.

Case Study

GRAHAM BACKHOUSE
In February 1985, forty-three-year-old Graham Backhouse appeared at Bristol Crown Court, charged with the attempted murder of his wife Margaret in order to collect the sum of £100,000 on her life insurance, and the murder of neighbour Mr Colyn Bedale-Taylor in order to divert police suspicion from himself.

Mr James Black QC, prosecuting, told the court that Backhouse had invented a scenario whereby he and his family were the victims of a supposed village vendetta; he had gone as far as to impale a sheep's head on a stake close to the house, bearing a note reading 'You Next'. The police had constant complaints from Mr Backhouse of threatening letters and telephone calls.

On 9 April 1984, Margaret Backhouse climbed into the driver's seat of the family's Volvo estate car and turned on the ignition; the resulting explosion left her with severe injuries to her legs and buttocks. Although they were 'extensive and extremely serious', the wounds were mercifully not fatal. Believed at the time to be the intended victim, Graham Backhouse was given twenty-four-hour police protection.

On 18 April, at Backhouse's request, the police watch was removed and a 'panic button' linked to the local police station fitted at the farmhouse. On 30 April the alarm went off.

When PC Richard Yeadon arrived at the farm he found sixty-three-year-old Colyn Bedale-Taylor dead from shotgun wounds to the chest; in his hand was a Stanley handyman's knife. Graham Backhouse was lying in the entrance to the lounge sobbing and stained with blood from wounds to the face and chest.

In a statement read to the court by Mr Lionel Read QC, acting for Backhouse, he claimed that Bedale-Taylor had called at the farmhouse on the evening of the 30th and told him that he had come to repair furniture: 'I told him there was no furniture to repair, and he said that God had sent him.' Bedale-Taylor then accused Backhouse of being responsible for the death of his son Digby – who had in fact died as the result of a car crash some eighteen months previously. The visitor later went on to confess to planting the car bomb, and then lunged at Backhouse with the Stanley knife and a violent struggle ensued in the kitchen during which Backhouse received his injuries.

Backhouse then claimed he fled from the kitchen, down the hall to the place where he kept a shotgun: 'I ran into the hallway and grabbed a gun; Bedale-Taylor was still after me. I shouted I had got a gun but he still kept coming and I shot him. He fell back and I shot him again and that was it.'

However, this version of the events leading to Bedale-Taylor's death was at variance with the findings of the forensic investigation, and Geoffrey Robinson from the Home Office Forensic Laboratory at Chepstow, Gwent, took the jury through his own re-creation of the murder according to the evidence of bloodstaining. Most damaging to Backhouse's claim that there was a struggle in the kitchen was the relative shortage of blood. Such a 'frenzied' attack would, according to Robinson, have left bloodstains of the 'splash' type on walls and furniture. In fact, quite contrary evidence presented itself in the number of *drops* of blood on the plastic floorcovering, indicating that Backhouse had been standing *dripping* blood. It was true that chairs in the kitchen had been knocked over, but some had landed *on top* of blood drops suggesting that the moving of the chairs was an afterthought. One of the chairs had blood smears along the top (identified as Backhouse's which differed in group from the victim's), an effect that could have been created if he had grabbed hold of the chairback with a bloody hand and pushed it over. If this were the case, how could a man already with bloody hands have picked up and fired a shotgun *afterwards* without leaving a single trace of blood? Furthermore, despite Backhouse's insistence that he had fled bleeding from the kitchen to the end of the hall, there was no trail of blood in the hallway itself – an impossibility given his injuries. All this led Geoffrey Robinson to advance the proposition that Graham Backhouse's wounds were self-inflicted, and that he placed the knife in his victim's hand after death. Backhouse, he suggested, must have dripped blood around the kitchen after the shooting to simulate an attack on himself. But when Backhouse had placed the knife in the dead man's hand, he could not have noticed that the palms were completely covered with blood through clutching at his gunshot wounds. If his story was true, and Bedale-Smith had been holding the knife all the time, then at least part of the palm should have been clear of blood. These doubts were confirmed by examining pathologist Dr William Kennard, who expressed misgivings at finding the knife clasped so firmly in the victim's hand; for this to have occurred rigor *mortis* would need to have set in instantaneously at the moment of death – an extremely rare phenomenon. Besides, a preliminary examination of the body on the night of the murder revealed no onset of *rigor*.

Dr Kennard's view of Backhouse's wounds concurred with the self-inflicted theory of the forensic experts; he confirmed that if the cut which was made diagonally downwards from Backhouse's left shoulder to the right side of his waist had been inflicted by another person then Backhouse would have had to stand still and neither offer resistance nor try to protect himself.

Evidence was then offered indicating that even after his arrest Backhouse continued in his efforts to incriminate Bedale-Taylor. The jury was told that Backhouse persuaded a fellow-prisoner to smuggle out an unsigned letter addressed to the Bristol *Evening Post* implicating the deceased in the car bombing. Forensic-document examiners proved that the handwriting matched the threatening letters supposed to have been *received* by Graham Backhouse, and that both matched the handwriting of Backhouse himself.

On 19 February 1985, after a retirement of five-and-a-half hours, the jury returned a majority verdict of guilty on both charges, for which Backhouse received two terms of life imprisonment.

Old Bloodstains

In the majority of homicide cases no attempt has been made to dispose of the victim's remains permanently or to clean the scene of crime. Bodies are for the most part left where they fall, surrounded by the mess and disorder created by their untimely death. In those cases where a killer, anxious to 'get away with murder', takes the trouble to try to thwart justice by covering his tracks, he is confronted by the bewildering problem of the bloody corpse.

Apart from the psychological problem created by a profusely bleeding body, murder victims present their killers with appalling logistical difficulties. Blood accounts for around nine per cent of human bodyweight – in effect about ten pints. When spilt it is, with modern detection techniques, impossible to eradicate. Bleach, that old kitchen standby so beloved of fictional killers, simply stains the blood a pale greeny-brown. In fact, cold water is by far the best solvent for stubborn bloodstains – hot water having the opposite effect of fixing the stain. Even in cases where all trace has apparently been removed – say on ceramic or plastic – there are chemicals which, if sprayed as a mist on the surface, will reveal the former presence of blood. The reagent leuco-malachite green will indicate traces diluted so as to be invisible to the eye, and sprays of orthotolidine and phenolphthalein produce the same result – the former revealing 'invisible' stains as bright green, the latter pink.

More frequently the suspicions of the scenes-of-crime experts are aroused by those minute tell-tale dark spots which have escaped the murderer's attention. However, because blood itself undergoes colour changes in certain circumstances, and many other substances can *look* like blood, there is the need for a simple, rapid, on-the-spot test to ensure that only blood stains are marked for later examination. The most common is the so-called Kastle-Meyer test where a piece of filter paper is rubbed on the stain so that some of the substance transfers to the paper; this is then treated with a drop in turn of the reagents alcohol, phenolphthalein and hydrogen peroxide. If the paper shows pink, blood is present, and the test is sensitive enough to give positive results with even minute samples.

BLUDGEONING

This is the method of killing most commonly associated with unpremeditated attacks – murderous assaults carried out during moments of blind passion when the first heavy implement that comes to hand becomes the instrument of death, the notorious 'blunt instrument'. Bludgeoning is frequently encountered in acts of homicide, and almost every conceivable blunt instrument has at one time or another been used to kill.

Battering is rarely fatal unless it involves the head, for the greatest damage is inflicted where a vital organ is so directly under the bone. However, it is not a simple matter to kill with a single blow, and often a rain of blows will make ruin of the head, creating as it does so a very bloody scene of crime, which is likely to have heavily stained the assailant with blood.

The laceration wounds caused by bludgeoning are characteristically ragged, with strands of skin, tissue and blood vessels deeply impacted into the bone, which may be smashed or may show depressed fractures; indeed, it is often possible to judge the nature and shape of the implement which caused the fracture from the wound it leaves.

Death after bludgeoning of the head almost always results from brain injury. When the skull is badly fractured, splinters of bone become embedded in the brain, and if the hole created is large enough an area of brain tissue may be pulped by the weapon itself. However, even in cases where the skull remains intact the haemorrhaging of blood vessels beneath the bone will result in internal bleeding between the skull and the dura, or membrane, covering the brain.

The nature of the weapon and the circumstances under which it is normally used, predispose the crimes to be brutal, lacklustre affairs, frequently the result of a bungled burglary or a mugging that went wrong. However, two of the most enduring mysteries of true-crime are the as-yet unsolved murders of Sir Harry Oakes and of Marilyn Sheppard. Oakes, an American-born millionaire was found burned and bludgeoned to death in his home in the Bahamas in 1943. The case is still shrouded in conspiracy theories and accusations of official cover-ups; even the nature of the blunt instrument used has never been established. Ten years later in Cleveland, Ohio, Mrs Marilyn Sheppard went to bed alone one night while her surgeon husband slept off the results of a supper party, on the downstairs couch. Sam Sheppard claimed that he had awoken to hear his wife screaming, and as he ran to her room was knocked unconscious by an intruder. When he came round, Dr Sheppard found his wife lying on her blood-soaked bed, her head savagely smashed by a blunt weapon. Sheppard was tried for his wife's murder in 1954, found guilty and sentenced to life. At a second trial, in 1966, the former conviction was over-turned and Sam Sheppard was released. Although he regained his licence to practice medicine, he never recovered his practice, and after two more marriages and a spell as a professional wrestler, Dr Samuel Sheppard died in 1970.

BOG PEOPLE
(see Mummification)

BRUISES

Bruises – or 'contusions' to give them their correct medical term – are the most commonly encountered injuries, in life as in crime. Although bruises vary in their severity and their cause, the condition always results from a haemorrhaging of the small blood vessels beneath the skin without actually breaking the skin.

Bruising can be caused by many kinds of injury, and is often simply an accompaniment to them. There is no hard and fast rule governing the speed or extent to which an individual will bruise – some people, particularly the elderly, bruise very easily; and different parts of the body will bruise more or less easily. The rapidity with which a bruise shows depends on the size of the blood vessels which have been broken and the subsequent speed with which blood escapes from them into the tissue.

Although it is an unreliable indicator of exact times, the colour of a bruise will show its age, from the first red or purple (depending upon size and depth), through a brownish colour as chemical changes in the underlying blood occur during the healing process, later becoming green, then yellow, until the bruise fades. In a healthy person the cycle will take a few weeks, though the older the individual the more slowly the bruise will clear. This gradual but marked colour change over time is of particular significance in cases of baby battering, where bruises in different stages of healing will indicate repeated physical abuse.

One vexing problem that as yet has no simple solution is the determination of whether a bruise occurred before or after death, because a heavy impact will cause blood vessels to rupture even after death (particularly areas engorged with post-mortem **Hypostasis**) and ooze blood into the tissues; the visual effect of this is similar to ante-mortem bruising. The most reliable test for distinguishing between damage caused after death and before is that in bruising caused during life a microscopic examination of the blood will reveal an abnormally high number of white cells (leucocytes) which the body's self-protection system had dispatched to the site of the injury to begin the healing process.

Bruises, both external and internal, are of particular importance to the pathologist in cases of **Strangulation**, where bruises on the neck can help to reconstruct the way in which the attack was carried out and the relative positions of the attacker and the victim.

BULLETS
(see Ballistics, Firearms, Gunshot Wounds)

BURNING

Burning is a comparatively common form of accidental death, though rare as a means of suicide and even rarer as a means of homicide. Burns can be caused by a number of agents and it is necessary to distinguish between them – this entry deals exclusively with burn deaths resulting from fire, while notes on burning by corrosive **Acid** and by some **Poisons** will be found in the appropriate entries.

The effects of fire on the body are graded according to six degrees of tissue damage as follows (from Glaister, *Medical Jurisprudence):*

First degree: Inflammation of the skin, transitory swelling and subsequent falling off in scales of the surface layers of the epidermis.

Second degree: Blistering.

Third degree: Partial destruction of the true skin.

Fourth degree: Total destruction of the true skin.

Fifth degree: Destruction of the subcutaneous tissue and involvement of muscular tissue.

Sixth degree: Extension in depth with involvement of large blood vessels, nerve trunks, serous cavities and bone.

Although victims removed from burning buildings, cars, etc. may exhibit many of the lesions defined as burns, it is often the case that death was due to some other cause connected with the fire – notably the inhalation of poisonous gases such as **Carbon Monoxide** and carbon dioxide.

In a few cases the cause of death may be quite unconnected with the blaze, indeed the fire may have been started in order to mask a homicide. With this in mind, it is obvious that for the pathologist there is an urgent need to answer the following fundamental questions:

1. Are the injuries caused by burning?
2. Were the injuries caused before or after death?
3. Were the injuries responsible for death?
4. If other injuries than those caused by burning are present, were they responsible for death?
5. Are the burn injuries accidental, suicidal or homicidal?

The vital question of whether a victim was alive or dead when the fire started can be answered by some very simple tests. Samples of blood are taken and tested for the presence of carbon monoxide; a positive reaction will prove that the victim was breathing *after* the fire was started. The presence of particles of carbon (soot) in the air passages and lungs is a similar indicator.

Whether burn injuries were suffered before or after death can be demonstrated by the presence or absence of 'vital reactions'. When a body sustains injury during life the natural protection system responds by sending thousands of white blood cells (leucocytes) to surround the wound and begin the job of healing. This activity results in the familiar inflammation, or hyperaemia, that surrounds the injury site. This is a clear indication that the body was alive when the injury was inflicted. In the case of burns received in life, hyperaemia will be found and the skin will have blistered. Fluid from the blisters will be tested by placing an amount in a test-tube and heating it; the protein will solidify if the burns were suffered during life. Burns received by the body after death show no signs of vital reaction – they are hard and yellowish in colour, and if blisters are present they will contain little or no fluid, and that which is found will not give a positive protein reaction.

Exposed to intense heat, areas of the body are subject to splitting of the soft tissues, particularly in places where bone is closely underlying, such as the skull.

These 'heat ruptures' on first inspection resemble lacerations such as might have been caused during a homicidal attack, so it is important to subject them to the closest examination. If the lesions are caused by heat they will show no sign of recent haemorrhage because blood has been coagulated in the vessels; below the surface of the rupture, nerves and vessels will be intact, and there will be no sign of bruising around the site.

One of the characteristic features of bodies exposed to intense heat is heat-stiffening – the so-called 'pugilistic attitude' with the arms extended from the shoulders and the forearms partially flexed, like the posture adopted by a boxer; generally the legs are also flexed accentuating the likeness. The effect is caused by coagulation of the muscles on the flexor surface of the limbs.

By far the greatest majority of deaths by burning is accidental. The death is so slow and comparatively painful that few suicides favour it – though mention must be made of incidents where people have soaked themselves in petrol and set fire to themselves as a political or religious protest.

Homicide by burning is rare, though the use of fire to try to *dispose* of the remains of homicide is well documented, as are instances of fires being set around already dead victims in an attempt to give the impression of accidental death – one of the motives for **Arson**.

BYRNES, THOMAS (died 1919)

Called by some 'America's most famous policeman', Byrnes was responsible for establishing the country's first scientifically based criminal identification system in the 1880s. As the chief of New York's detective force in the late nineteenth century he assembled a huge cross-referenced archive of tintype photographs of crooks of every description. The categories included: Bank Robbers, Bank Sneak Thieves, Forgers, Hotel and Boarding-house Thieves, Store and Safe Burglars, Shoplifters and Pickpockets, Confidence and Banco Men, Receivers of Stolen Goods, Sawdust Men, and Horse Sale Fraudsters.

Byrnes' time spent among the denizens of the twilight world of crime had taught him to mistrust any notion that there is such a thing as **'Criminal Man'**. Although he was prepared to admit that 'river thieves and low burglars are as hard-looking brutes as can be found', he would always reply to questions as to whether **Physiognomy** was any guide to the criminal class: 'A very poor one. Look for yourself. Look through the pictures in the Rogues' Gallery and see how many rascals you find there who resemble the best people in the country. Why, you can find some of them, I dare say, sufficiently like personal acquaintances to admit of mistaking one for the other. By the by, that is no uncommon occurrence, and the more you consider it the more readily you will come to appreciate how easy it is for a detective to pick up the wrong man.'

Accompanied by expansive and often unintentionally humorous descriptions of their character and crimes, the Byrnes collection of mug-shots was selectively published in New York in September 1886 in order, the detective claimed, that 'bankers, brokers, commercial and business men, and the public' should have access to information that might help them combat crime: 'With the view of thwarting thieves, I have taken this means of circulating their pictures . . . Hoping that this volume will serve as a medium in the prevention and detection of crime.'

So close were Inspector Byrnes' links with the underworld against which he did constant battle, that it is said he could order the return of a victim's stolen property within the day and it would be done. He claimed: 'The detective's trade consists not in pursuing but in forming friendships with criminals.' And there is no doubt that even so ardent a thief-taker as New York's Thomas Byrnes entertained some professional respect for his adversaries: 'The common thief will steal anything from a needle to a ship's anchor,' he once declared, 'The burglar masters a safe's combination with almost mathematical accuracy, and manipulates its complex machinery with the same dexterity and precision that a music teacher touches the keys of a piano. He is trained to detect one false note in a swelling chorus produced by the click of reverberating ratchets within the lock.'

It was this very 'kinship' which was to be the cause of Inspector Byrnes' ignominious fall from grace. In 1896 he was obliged to resign following his confession to an official inquiry that his police force had been turning a blind eye to the activities of some of New York's gambling dens and brothels in exchange for a cut of the takings. Byrnes died in 1919, but not before reminding an ungrateful city that he had notched up more years of convictions against criminals than the combined detective forces of 'Scotland Yard, Paris and New Jersey – nearly 10,000 years'.

C

CADAVERIC SPASM
(see Alcohol, Drowning, Time of Death)

CAMPS, FRANCIS EDWARD (1905–72)

Young Francis Camps first saw the light of day in Teddington, Middlesex, on 27 June 1905. His father was a general practitioner and surgeon whose fashionable practice was also a lucrative one. With this shining example it is little surprise that after a distingnished schooling at Marlborough, Francis chose medicine as his future means of support, qualifying at Guy's Hospital Medical School and joining a thriving clinic in Chelmsford.

In 1935, Camps took the decision to specialize in pathology, a field in which, inspired by the work he was doing with the Essex police force, he soon narrowed down to forensic pathology.

Fame came to Francis Camps through his work developing the department of forensic medicine at the London Hospital Medical School, which became in its day the finest in the world. It was a sad characteristic of this brilliant and enthusiastic teacher and practitioner that he was frequently the most unlikeable of men – a bully to those who worked under him and arrogant and overbearing to his peers. It has been said that to Francis Camps, his fellow men took a very poor second place to his own prestige and power. To achieve this Camps worked tirelessly and single-mindedly in the cause of forensic medicine, dismissing those less enthusiastic as 'scabs and bandits'.

But whatever anybody might have said or thought, Camps produced results; and he produced them fast – he himself estimated that by the time he retired in 1970 he had performed around 88,000 post-mortems while also carrying out a heavy lecture schedule at the Middlesex, Royal Free, and University College Hospitals.

This formidable 'body-count' can best be understood from the way in which Camps hit the mortuary like a whirlwind, brushing aside any common courtesies and basic safety measures that might lose him precious minutes. He would frequently rush in, perform the post-mortem in his everyday clothes, and dash on to his next engagement. In his biography of Camps,* Robert Jackson recalls an occasion on which 'Camps ripped a rubber glove while opening a rib cage and caused a scratch which bled. Most pathologists aware of the danger of septicaemia would have had the scratch treated immediately . . . not Camps. He refused the offer of a new glove and continued the post-mortem, commenting "I used to do autopsies with my bare hands.'

Of the many murder cases in which he was involved, Camps' most celebrated work was on the identification of the remains of six women found at the notorious 10 Rillington Place, and for whose murder John Reginald Christie was hanged in 1953. Camps' brilliance also illuminated a variety of other cases where, by reason of mutilation or decomposition, positive identification of the victim could only be made with considerable difficulty – Stanley Setty's 'Essex Marsh Torso', Hella Christofi, and Wills Eugene Boshears who claimed to have murdered in his sleep.

But one, almost sentimental, departure from his ceaseless search for accolades was Camps' persistent undertaking – with little financial reward – to give expert testimony on behalf of the defence, often unwisely, frequently without success.

The brief months between his retirement and his death on 8 July 1972, were for Professor Camps troubled times as he became increasingly dependent upon drugs to kill the unbearable pain that had developed in his abdomen. Camps believed, quite wrongly, that he had cancer. Characteristically, he refused to consult a physician – a profession of which he had a genuine, if irrational, fear. In fact, he was suffering from a stomach ulcer which, if treated, would have responded to surgery, and saved his life.

But if Francis Camps had exhibited an absurd stubbornness in respect of his health, his inexplicable obsession with fellow pathologist Keith Simpson verged on the ludicrous. For much of his working life Camps

*Francis Camps, Robert Jackson, Hart-Davies McGibbon, London, 1973.

had regarded Simpson as an arch enemy, and never passed up the opportunity to vilify him in public. Approaching death, Camps developed a terror that Simpson would be asked to perform the post-mortem – a fear that he took with him to the grave, though no autopsy was necessary to certify his death from natural causes.

So ended the career of a great forensic visionary; for all his human failings and eccentricities, a man whose dedication to spreading excellence in forensic medicine throughout the world, and whose impression on the British medico-legal profession has assured him of a place among the great names in forensic pathology.

CANTHARIDES (Spanish Fly) (see Poisons)

CARBON DATING
(see Radiocarbon Dating)

CARBON MONOXIDE POISONING

Carbon monoxide is an odourless, colourless non-irritant gas which is formed when carbon is oxidized in a limited supply of air. The gas once had a bewildering number of sources, mostly from industrial processes, and was a major agent of accidental poisoning.

Formerly the coal-gas used for lighting, heating and cooking in most of Britain's dwellings contained as much as fourteen per cent carbon monoxide, and 'putting one's head in the gas oven' was so common a cause of suicide that it became a euphemism. In addition, large numbers of people perished accidentally as a result of slow leaks from pipes and faulty appliances; indeed, up to the year 1965 carbon monoxide was the most common source of accidental and suicidal poisoning in Britain. The following chart plots the rise over forty-five years.

'Natural gas' pumped to the whole of Britain from the North Sea since 1967 is odourless and non-toxic, but because it is still highly combustible, and explosive if allowed to escape into a room and accidentally ignited, an artificial smell reminiscent of coal-gas had to be added.

Current sources of carbon monoxide include faulty gas water-heaters and paraffin stoves used in unventilated rooms, accounting for a small but significant number of accidental deaths each year. In outbreaks of

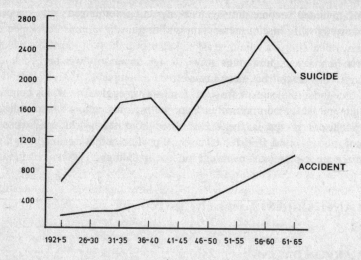

fire, it is carbon monoxide fumes that kill more frequently than heat and flame.

However, by far the readiest source of carbon monoxide is the exhaust from motor vehicles, and the hose leading from the exhaust pipe is a familiar scenario of modern suicide as well as sometimes claiming the lives of those working on cars with the engine running in unventilated garages.

Carbon monoxide kills by combining with haemoglobin in the blood, forming carboxyhaemoglobin, which effectively prevents the blood from transporting life-sustaining oxygen to the body tissues and nerve cells. The affinity of carbon monoxide for haemoglobin is an alarming 300 times greater than that of oxygen.

The symptoms of carbon monoxide poisoning depend on the level of saturation of the blood: twenty per cent will cause headache, dizziness and shortness of breath if the body is exerted; thirty per cent will produce the same symptoms in a body at rest, plus nausea and throbbing of the heart. Fifty to sixty per cent affects coordination and balance, and with exertion, collapse; involuntary voiding of the bowel and bladder may occur. Between sixty and eighty per cent absorption will prove lethal. One of the great dangers is that carbon monoxide poisoning is cumulative, so that even though only a small amount of the gas is present in the atmosphere it is progressively built up until the onset of carboxyhaemoglobin formation. Thus a person unaware of the presence of carbon monoxide (perhaps from the blocked flue of a water-heater) will gradually become drowsy, and suspecting nothing fall into sleep, followed by unconsciousness, coma and death.

Post-Mortem Appearances

In cases where gas had been inhaled over a comparatively long period of time there is no sign of physical distress or struggle. The skin is rather pink, and the blood uniformly cherry-red in veins, arteries and tissues (and also apparent in the colouring of **Hypostasis**); blood is also uncommonly fluid and free from clotting. The organs are also bright cherry-red and oedematous; lungs are congested and oedematous, and upper air passages contain a frothy fluid.

Where large concentrations of the gas have been inhaled and death has come rapidly, there may have been convulsions and vacuation of the faeces. The heart is dilated and viscera congested. Blood is highly carboxylated and the bright cherry-red colour is prevalent as described above. After death, carbon monoxide may still be detected in the blood for as long as six months.

Case Study

THE RITUAL BURIAL CASE

Carbon monoxide poisoning as a means of homicide is extremely rare, and in those cases where it has been used (for example, in the murder of James Pullen by his son-in-law Reginal Hinks in 1933) it has been dressed up to give the appearance of suicide. One tragic English case combined coal-gas and barbiturate poisoning.

On Monday, 19 October 1953, a Coroner's jury at Twickenham sat in silence as Detective Superintendent Leslie Watts described finding the body of thirteen-year-old John Michael Conroy – the subject of the current inquest – in what had become popularly known as The Ritual Burial Murder.

Watts had gone to the house in Denton Road on 26 September, where he saw the body 'buried' in the base of a divan; the bed had been ripped open along the centre, forming two flaps. The boy had been wrapped in a dark brown blanket and placed in among the upholstery of the bed and the flaps closed over it, but folded back in the area of the head rather like the lapels of a jacket. Two mattresses, four blankets, an eiderdown, and sheets – presumably from the divan – were piled in a heap on the floor.

Subsequent to the examination by pathologist Dr Donald **Teare**, the boy's mother, forty-four-year-old Teresa Miriam Conroy, had been accused of his murder. In mitigation, it was later observed that Mrs Conroy was not very sound in her mind at the best of times, and in all probability they were dealing with a case of **Diminished Responsibility**; the principal Medical Officer of Holloway Prison, Dr Thomas Christie, stated, 'She is of low intelligence, only slightly above the level at which certification as a mental defective would be considered.'

The circumstances that emerged from the evidence of the father, Michael Oliver Conway, were that on Friday 25 September his wife announced that she intended to visit a cousin of hers in Muswell Hill, and that she was taking their son with her. When he asked to see the boy that evening she told her husband not to worry him as he was sleeping, and that he would see the child in the morning. The following morning, however, there was no sign of Mrs Conroy or of John, and William Conroy assumed that they had left early for Muswell Hill. The family's irregular sleeping arrangements make this a reasonable explanation – Teresa Conroy and her son occupied beds in one room, and Mr Conroy slept in another.

'When I did my shopping,' continued Conroy, 'and returned on Saturday afternoon, I thought the boy was enjoying himself on Muswell Hill, but I found him dead in his own bedroom.' He immediately called a doctor to the house, and the doctor pronounced that the body had been dead for about forty-eight hours. It was at this point that police and pathologist took over the responsibility for attaching some reason to the bizarre discovery in the bed.

Dr Teare was provisionally of the opinion that the symptoms of death were consistent with asphyxia during an epileptic fit, from which John Conroy was known to suffer; the subsequent post-mortem, however, had a more sinister tale to tell. Asphyxia it certainly was, but an examination of blood samples revealed from fifty-five to sixty per cent carbon monoxide saturation – a fatal concentration. John Michael Conroy had been gassed to death. Furthermore, a quantity of a barbiturate drug used to treat epilepsy was found in the body in far too great a concentration for normal use; this almost certainly resulted in unconsciousness before death.

On 27 September, Teresa Conroy made a statement in which she claimed: 'Last Tuesday he had a fit. About midnight he had a bad turn for about an hour. Then he went off to sleep. I was awake practically all night looking after him. The next day he had another bad turn while he was still in bed. He just choked, and his hands and legs shook. This lasted five minutes, and then he appeared to go to sleep. I know I should have gone for a doctor, but I was so tired and worn out I did not know what I was doing. I did nothing to him or about him until Tuesday morning, by which time I realized he was dead. I stripped my bed [the divan] and ripped the covering with a pair of scissors. I don't know why I did this. I lifted him from his bed. I put the divan mattress on top of him, and made the bed in the usual way.'

On 15 October Leslie Watts had arrived at Denton Road to arrest Mrs Conroy on a charge of murder. She replied simply: 'Shall I have to stay at the police station long?'

Teresa Conroy appeared before the bench at the Old Bailey on Tuesday 8 December 1953. In its essentials, the prosecution case was outlined by Mr Christmas Humphries as follows:

It may be that in her mind was a mixture of three reasons as a motive for killing her son. The boy, who was epileptic, was getting worse. She was bound to him as a person whom she had nursed night and day. It would be a relief to her to be rid of the burden of the boy. There may have been some element of mercy killing, and that would seem to be true of some of the phrases in her statement to the police. There is a less kind allegation, but it is a fact that the boy had in a Post Office savings bank account more than £600 which had come to him in a will. Only he could touch that money. On his dying without making a will his next of kin would get it. If the police did not discover he had been murdered, the mother would be rid of a burden and she and her husband would be £600 better off. Possibly she gave the boy a dose of the drug, which was used for treating epilepsy, in a drink. Finding that he did not die, she carried him into the kitchen and put his head into the gas oven. When she turned on the gas he would die in three to four minutes. Then she probably took him back to the bedroom and ritually buried him in the divan by cutting open the top cover, pressing the body between the springs, and putting the mattress back on top of the divan.

In defence of Mrs Conroy, Mr Elliott Gorst QC said: 'She was a loving mother who cared for her child by day and by night. She must have got to breaking point. There was never a tear to the very end . . . this woman had no apprehension of what she was doing.' Mr Gorst said that the defence would not contest the facts of the murder, but asked for a verdict of 'Guilty but Insane'.

And it was an **Insanity** verdict that the jury returned, after a twelve-minute retirement. The prisoner was ordered to be detained during Her Malesty's pleasure, and it is unlikely that we will get any more help in making our selection from Christmas Humphries' three options; or of ever understanding the significance, if there was any, of the ceremonial 'burial'.

CAUSE OF DEATH
Proximate Causes
All deaths can be attributed to one of three proximate causes which relate to the failure of one of the organs essential to life: coma (brain), syncope (heart) or asphyxia (lungs).

Coma
Arrest of the brain's functions is principally caused by:

1. Compression of the brain resulting from a depressed fracture (homicidally, most commonly the result of **Bludgeoning**).
2. The effects of poisoning, either suicidally, homicidally or accidentally introduced into the body.
3. The effects of narcotic and hypnotic drugs usually self-introduced to the body accidentally in the form of overdose or impurities in the substance.
4. Medical conditions such as cerebral haemorrhage, brain tumour and diseases, the by-products of which may poison the brain and produce coma.

Syncope
1. 'Natural' heart failure is associated with many degenerative diseases of the organ, often accelerated by shock or powerful emotion.
2. Homicidal syncopes can be induced by certain poisons, or by extensive injury caused to the heart.

Asphyxia
Anoxia, meaning simply 'lack of oxygen', is the principal cause of death and widely encountered in acts of homicide. The condition results

from several causes, of which the first, anoxic anoxia, is usually known as asphyxia, or manual asphyxia.

Anoxic Anoxia (Asphyxia)
1. Associated with breathing an atmosphere with insufficient oxygen.
2. Obstruction of the oxygen supply by occlusion of the air passages.
3. Pressure on the chest or abdomen preventing breathing.
4. Paralysis of the respiratory function due to electric shock, the action of some poisons (morphine, barbiturates), etc.

Anaemic Anoxia
1. An insufficient supply of oxygen to the tissues as the result of heavy loss of blood and obstruction of the arteries; possible homicidal causes are extensive cut and stab wounds (i.e. bleeding to death).
2. Obstruction of the supply of oxygen to the blood, as in the case of **Carbon Monoxide Poisoning**.

Histotoxic Anoxia
Toxic materials paralyse the body tissues preventing them from utilizing the oxygen released by the blood; for example, **Cyanide**.

Stagnant Anoxia
Where blood circulation is stopped as the result of shock: heart failure or **Embolism**.

Specific Causes
It may be quite obvious to the pathologist from the state of the body at a homicide scene what the most likely cause of death was – the victim may, for example, still have a ligature tied tightly around his neck, or the skull may have been smashed with the bloody brick lying close by. The wise medic, however, always waits until he has performed a thorough **Post-Mortem** examination before committing himself to the precise cause of death; to do otherwise could seriously mislead investigating officers in the early stages of their inquiry. The most commonly encountered specific causes of death are:

Bludgeoning
In which for convenience are included not only the typical 'blunt instruments', but also other weapons which inflict impact injuries

(usually to the head) resulting in death – a motor-car, for example, and 'personal weapons' such as feet and fists.

Burning
Although death can result instantly from burning in the case of events such as flash fires, the most common cause of death associated with fire is asphyxia from smoke inhalation.

Drowning
One of the categories of asphyxia, caused by obstructing the respiratory channels with liquid.

Embolism
Clogging of the blood vessels by bubbles of air (or more rarely by fat) which causes an obstruction to the heart or to the brain where it blocks the blood supply.

Explosives
Proximity to explosive blasts results in a variety of injuries connected with the effects of the explosive itself – disintegration of the body, flash burns, effects of air pressure; and others associated with the *result* of the blast – flying glass and debris, collapsing buildings, etc.

Gunshot Wounds
The result of shooting with all types of firearms.

Knife Wounds
Damage to the body tissue of an extent where physical functions are destroyed; to which for convenience is added Throat-cutting.

Poison
Where extensive tissue damage combined with shock and paralysis destroy the vital functions of the body.

Strangulation
Embracing the most common forms of asphyxia:

   Manual stragulation: Caused by direct pressure on the victim's trachea by the killer's hands (or forearm).
   Ligature strangulation: Caused by constriction of the neck by *direct*

application of pressure by means of a rope, scarf, etc. pulled tightly by the killer.

Hanging: Caused by constriction of the neck by an *indirect* application of pressure on the ligature by the weight of the body; more commonly encountered as suicide than homicide.

Suffocation and Smothering
External stoppage of the nose and mouth preventing air being taken into the lungs, resulting in asphyxia.

CHEILOSCOPY
Like fingerprints, it has been observed that lip prints are unique and do not change during a person's life (though the lip prints of twins are very similar).

Less commonly encountered at the scene of a crime than fingerprints, impressions from the 'labial surfaces' can nevertheless be found on drinking glasses and cups, facial tissues, letters, etc. The problem is that the scientific credibility of such evidence has yet to establish itself in courts of law.

Despite this, Japanese research proceeds apace, and has shown that lip prints can be classified into eight patterns, of which the most common are:

Vertical
Branched
Intersected
Reticulary

CHLOROFORM
Discovered by the German chemist Baron Justus von Liebig in 1831, chloroform is the result of adding chlorinated lime to alcohol, and then distilling the mixture. To look at, it is a heavy colourless liquid, with a sweet spirituous taste and a pleasant smell. In 1847 its properties as an anaesthetic were recognized by Professor James Simpson of Glasgow University, though it was not until some years later that prejudice was overcome sufficiently for chloroform to become accepted by the medical profession for this purpose.

To correct several popular misapprehensions regarding this useful drug, it must be stated that it is almost impossible to chloroform a sleeping victim without awakening them in the process. Furthermore, the time taken for its effects to become apparent is longer than implied by writers of detective fiction; two or three minutes is rarely sufficient, and there have been many cases where the patient was fully conscious of the drug taking fifteen minutes to produce results. As the drug begins to take effect the patient in many instances exhibits strong convulsions, and has to be held down by assistants. One has often read of a criminal laying a handkerchief saturated with chloroform over a sleeping house-holder's face to ensure his unconsciousness of the burglary about to take place; in reality the effect would be to either wake the sleeper or severely blister his face – this latter being a characteristic consequence of chloroform applied to the skin. Prolonged inhalation will result in death through heart paralysis, and ingestion causes death through heart and liver failure.

In only one murder trial has chloroform featured as an alleged poison, and that was the so-called Pimlico Mystery of 1886 where, strange to say, the drug was taken internally, and not by inhalation. The trial lasted for three days, at the end of which Adelaide Bartlett was acquitted of the killing of her husband. How it was possible to administer secretly such an extremely irritant poison without severe pain and damage to the digestive system is one of crime's enduring mysteries.

CHOKING
(see Suffocation)

CHROMATOGRAPHY
Liquid Chromatography
Most substances presented to the forensic chemist for analysis are in an impure state – that is, they are a mixture of several different substances, which require the identification of each component and a measurement of the quantity contained. Take the example of the drug heroin, which may also contain sugar, quiuine, and any number of other impurities.

The technique mainly used for the separation and measurement is chromatography. In the liquid technique, the substance is first dissolved in an appropriate solvent (the so-called 'mobile phase') which is passed through a finely divided adsorbent (the 'stationary phase'). On its way down the tube the elements in the liquid sample attach themselves to the solid particles of the adsorbent. The compounds become attached in different strengths and because each has a unique chemical structure they pass down at different rates. The process has been succinctly described as being like a race between the chemical compounds; at the start of the race all the components are together, but as the race progresses some with a preference for the mobile phase will pull ahead of those that prefer to remain in the stationary phase. At the end of the race all the competitors will cross the line at different times. At the end of the tube they are all collected separately, and a detection device measures the substances as electrical signals as they pass through. It is the electrical signals that record their presence on a chart.

Gas Chromatography

This is a technique for the separation of mixtures of liquids or of gases by passing them through a substance which, effectively, slows down the rate of passage of the different elements of which it is composed. The system is mostly used to resolve highly complex mixtures into their component substances relatively quickly.

In principle the technique is not dissimilar from liquid chromatography; the sample here is gaseous (if originally liquid it will be heated until it vapourizes) and at the mobile ('moving-gas') phase is moved by a carrier gas (such as nitrogen or hydrogen which, being chemically inert, does not affect the analysis) through the stationary phase. In this instrument (see above) the stationary phase column is a fine tube of either stainless steel or glass, usually in a lightly wound coil, which may be up to six metres long and about three millimetres in diameter. In order to maintain the gaseous state of a liquid sample the column is kept heated. As in the liquid chromotography 'race', the elements of the sample will separate themselves out on the journey along the column, at the end of which they will pass through a detection device in which each purified component generates its own identifiable electrical impulses which in turn are recorded as a chromatogram of response (vertical peaks) versus time (horizontal axis). Typically a chromatogram will show a sequence of uneven peaks, each of which can be identified with a known reference chromatogram or with a control sample.

Pyrolysis Gas Chromatography

Gas chromatography is also suitable for the analysis of solid samples providing they can be rendered gaseous. This is achieved when specimens, such as paint or fibre, are heated, or pyrolized, at temperatures as high as 1,000°C, at which point they decompose into different gaseous products. These are then carried through the column in the usual way. The final complex pyrogram is 'unique' enough to permit comparison with other pyrograms to prove a match.

Thin-Layer Chromatography
In this chromatographic technique a glass slide is coated on one side with a thin layer of a stationary phase (usually silica gel) and spots of the sample are applied along the lower part of the slide. The next stage is to lower the slide into a container in which a suitable liquid (the mobile phase) reaches just below the spots of sample. By capillary action the liquid climbs up the slide and as it passes the spots carries the components of the sample with it, separating them as it rises. At this point the separations will probably be colourless and must be 'visualized' under ultraviolet light. Alternatively the slide can be sprayed with a suitable reagent which will cause the 'trail' to become coloured.

The resulting chromatographic plate can be compared with other samples or a 'control' for similarities.

CHROMOSOME ABNORMALITY
Chromosomes are found in the nucleii of all human cells. Each nucleus contains coded information in the form of DNA (deoxyribonucleic acid) arranged into groups called genes. These are in turn arranged on entwined strands of DNA which are chromosomes. Each body cell contains forty-six chromosomes arranged in twenty-three pairs, of which one each comes from the father and mother.

According to their shape, chromosomes are designated X or Y – in females the chromosomes normally consist of twenty-three pairs of XX, in males twenty-three pairs of XY. It is the father's chromosome which determines a child's gender, and if an X-containing sperm fertilizes the X egg the child will be a girl (XX); if a Y-containing sperm fertilizes the egg the child will be a boy (XY).

However, in the 1960s it was discovered that some males carry an extra Y chromosome, making them XYY. Psychiatric research identified a higher than average percentage of XYY males confined in prisons and special hospitals, leading to the suggestion that it is the extra chromosome that is responsible for their anti-social behaviour. The only apparent physical peculiarity associated with XYY is unusual tallness, and though there is a frequently marked behavioural disturbance showing as violence and aggression, there appears to be no obvious neurological impairment.

Despite these preliminary findings, insufficient work has yet been carried out on *unselected* groups of the population to give definite evidence that XYY subjects are more violent and rebellious than their fellows. Research continues worldwide into the significance of the extra chromosome.

Dermatoglyphics and Chromosome Abnormality
Although far too few reports have yet been published on the subject of fingerprint abnormalities ('dermatoglyphics') associated with chromosome abnormality, one researcher cites the case of a pre-pubertal boy with XYY chromosome constitution who exhibited marked differences in palmar ridge patterns from his parents and brother:

1. Considerably lower finger ridge count.
2. Few patterns on the palms.
3. Ridges of the palms fall into normal patterns except for one area between the base of the left forefinger and the ball of the left thumb.

The implications of deviant behaviour being detected from dermal ridge patterns are overwhelming (indeed, potential proof of '**Criminal Man**'). However, as yet it remains only in the realm of the possible.

COMPARISON MICROSCOPE
(see Microscopy)

COMPARISON PROJECTOR
(see Disputed Documents)

COMPETENCE TO STAND TRIAL
Unfit to Plead
While most defence pleas based upon a state of temporary or permanent mental unbalance (**Insanity, Diminished Responsibility**) are available to a defendant before he stands trial, there is a further category of 'insanity' that excuses an accused even from the due process of law. In

this instance he is not advancing a defence, but stating that he is too mentally ill to stand trial.

As most people charged with homicide are remanded in custody, assessments of the offender's mental state are usually carried out at the hospital section of the prison in which they are detained. If psychiatric disorder is suspected, opinions will be sought from independent specialists outside the prison medical service.

The decision as to whether or not a prisoner is fit to plead is made by a special jury. Before the start of a trial either the prosecution or the defence may enter a plea of unfitness, and the special jury is empanelled to judge the psychiatric evidence – often conflicting – of the doctors who have assessed the defendant. If the jury finds the accused unfit, then the court advises the Home Secretary who will make an order for hospital confinement under the Criminal Procedures (Insanity) Act, 1964. If he subsequently recovers, an accused may be put on trial.

One of the strongest criticisms of the 'competence to stand trial' procedure in Britain is that a defendant – quite possibly innocent of any crime – is in effect confined to an institution 'without limit of time' and it is only at the discretion of the Home Secretary that he or she will be able to stand trial and, if convicted, be sentenced to a *definite* term of confinement.

US Practice

In the United States the modern principle of 'Competence to stand trial' was established by the precedent *Dusky* v. *United States* (1960), and with minor variations in wording is accepted by all States to define competence to stand trial.

In the *Dusky* case, it was held by the Supreme Court that:

> It is not enough for the district judge to find that 'the defendant is oriented to time and place and has some recollections of events' but that the test must be whether he has sufficient present ability to consult with his lawyer with a reasonable degree of rational understanding – and whether he has a rational as well as factual understanding of the proceedings against him.

The problem initially was that too few of the psychiatrists who carried out the assessments (usually employees of the state mental hospitals where evaluations were carried out) were competent to assess matters of law as it related to competence. To a great extent this has been remedied over the last two decades with more extensive training programmes for psychologists.

The issue of competence may be raised at any stage of the criminal process, and if the court agrees that a genuine doubt exists it will order a formal evaluation of the prisoner. Once this evaluation has been completed and a report submitted, the findings may either be accepted both by the defence and the prosecution attorneys, in which case no hearing on the matter is necessary; or, if it is felt necessary, a court hearing may be called to decide the issue. The evaluation of competence rests *entirely* with the court who are not obliged to accept the assessor's recommendations.

When the matter of acceptance or rejection has been resolved, the case against a defendant found competent will be proceeded with, and the trial of a prisoner found incompetent to stand will be postponed until either competence returns or charges are dismissed and he is made the subject of a treatment order.

Assessing Competence

Most methods of assessment now place less weight on mental health judgements than on a purely functional evaluation of the defendant's ability – in other words, his capacity for understanding and participating in the legal process.

One State (Florida) has formalized this into eleven requirements:

1. Understanding of the charge
2. Appreciation of the extent and nature of the possible punishment
3. Understanding of the broad nature of legal process
4. Ability to explain the facts surrounding the charge to his attorney
5. Ability to relate to an attorney
6. Ability to cooperate in planning a defence
7. Capacity to challenge prosecution witnesses
8. Ability to behave in an appropriate manner in court
9. Ability to testify relevantly
10. Possess sufficient motivation to help himself
11. Ability to cope with detention while awaiting trial

Florida Rule of Criminal Procedure 3.2 1(a)(1)

COMPUTERS
(see Police Computers, H.O.L.M.E.S.)

CONIUM (CONIIE)
(see Poisons)

CONTACT TRACE THEORY
(see Trace Evidence)

CORONER
There is some dispute over the exact date of origin of the English office of coroner, and although the first mention of the modern equivalent dates from an ordinance of 1194 requiring every shire to elect an officer to 'keep the pleas of the Crown', it is reliably thought that as a Crown office it was first instituted following the Norman conquest.

The *De Officia Coronatoris,* a statute of 1276, enumerated the coroner's duties and obligations: the coroner, or to give him his full title, *custos placitorum coronae,* or keeper of the king's pleas, was so called because his special duty was to keep pleas, suits or causes which more particularly affected the king's Crown and dignity, and were determined either by the king in person or by his immediate officers. As one of the king's officers, his function was not so much to hear and determine causes as to keep a record of all that went on in the county in any way connected with the administration of criminal justice, and, above all, to guard what may be called chance revenues falling to the king. The collection of such revenues depended to a great extent on the diligence of the coroner in seeking for such things as the forfeited chattels of felons, deodands, wrecks, royal fish and treasure-trove. In his early days the chief functions of the coroner, whilst guarding the king's revenues, were the holding of inquests on view of the body in cases of death from violence or accident and of those dying in prison.

So the medieval coroner's judicial authorities covered mainly the inquiry into matters of unexplained deaths, the forfeiture of land and goods, disposal of wrecks and deodands (the instruments that cause death forfeited to the king for charitable use), the escape of murderers, the declaration of outlawries and the inquest upon treasure-trove.

Because a convicted felon forfeited his possessions to the Crown, it was not uncommon for professional crooks to attempt to defeat the system by burying their valuables. The coroner was expected to hold an inquest into any gold or silver that had been hidden, seeking to secure it for the king. Subsequent changes in politics, society and the Church rendered many of the duties obsolete, though quaintly the coroner is still occasionally called upon to determine cases of treasure-trove.

The statute *De Officia Coronatoris* and its many subsequent repeals and amendments was replaced by the consolidating Coroner's Act of 1887, where the duties of the office were restated and defined. In 1926 the Act was amended to allow the coroner discretion whether or not to empanel a jury for each inquest, except in certain mandatory cases:

1. Where the deceased dies as the result of murder, manslaughter or infanticide.
2. Where the death occurred in prison.
3. Where the death was caused by an accident, poisoning or disease which requires notice to be given to a Government Department in pursuance of an Act.
4. Where the death was the result of an accident arising from the use of a vehicle on a street or public highway.
5. Where the death occurred in circumstances the continuance of which is prejudicial to the health and safety of the public.

Following the 1926 Coroners (Amendment) Act, a person is only eligible for appointment who is a solicitor, barrister, or a medical practitioner of five years' or more experience. In practice most posts are held by solicitors, and apart from in cities and large towns, the appointments are part-time. Full-time city coroners are usually qualified in medicine *and* the law.

The procedure by which deaths in unorthodox circumstances come to the attention of the coroner is as follows: every death, whether at home or in a hospital, must be certified by a doctor as to cause, and this certificate must be lodged with the local office of the Registrar of Births, Marriages and Deaths. If there is any suspicion about the nature of the death, then the registrar is legally obliged to inform the coroner who will call an inquest. However, it is common practise for a doctor, if he is unhappy about the cause of death, to advise the coroner himself. The circumstances in which a death should be reported were laid down in guidelines issued by the Medical Protection Society:

1. Deaths which are sudden or unexpected and where the doctor cannot certify the real as opposed to the terminal cause of death or where the doctor has not attended in the last illness or within fourteen days of death.
2. Abortions, other than natural abortion.
3. Result of accidents and injuries of any date if in any way contributory to the cause of death.
4. Death under anaesthetics and deaths following operations for injuries, or where the operation, however necessary or skilfully performed, may have precipitated or expedited death.
5. Result of crime or suspected crime.
6. Result of drugs, either therapeutic or addiction.
7. Ill-treatment such as starvation and neglect.
8. Industrial disease arising from the deceased's employment; all diseases covered by the Health and Safety at Work Act of 1974.
9. Infant deaths if in any way unusual.
10. Deaths of pensioners receiving disability allowance where the death is connected with the pensionable disability.
11. Persons in prison, borstal institutions, detention centres, etc.
12. Poisoning from *any* source.
13. Death from septicaemia, if arising from an injury.
14. Still births where there was the possibility of the child being born alive, or where there is suspicion.

It is then the duty of the coroner's inquest to ascertain:

1. The identity of the deceased.
2. How, where and when death occurred.
3. Particulars at the time required by the Registration Acts to be registered concerning the particular death.

Until 1978 a further, some said iniquitous, duty was:

4. [To ascertain] the persons, if any, to be charged with murder, manslaughter, infanticide, or with being accessories before the fact in cases where the jury might find that the deceased came by his death by murder, manslaughter or infanticide.

In 1976, the Broderick Committee reported its recommendations on Death Certification and Coroners. It had been convened to examine, among other more medical issues, the role of the coroner in making observations as to the guilt of a particular party and his power to commit that person for trial. The Committee recommended that he should have no such power, and the still-fugitive Richard Bingham, Lord Lucan was the last person to be named as a killer by the coroner at the inquest on Sandra Rivett in June 1975.

According to one author (Mr F.G. Hails, coroner for the city of Stoke-on-Trent): 'The office of coroner in England has been adapted to keep pace with the legal machinery and needs of the times, and it is probably now the most effective machine of medico-legal investigation to be found in the world.'

United States

In the United States the office of coroner was transplanted by the first English colonists, though perhaps because they were a rough and ready breed of men, and anyway unqualified, the first colonial coroners did little to enhance the office's reputation; the only requirement of a candidate was that he was not an ex-convict. It was a system that survived the War of Independence, after which coroners became established as *elected* county officers. Such was the unsatisfactory state of affairs in some districts that in 1877 the commonwealth of Massachusetts abolished the coroner and established the medical examiner system. In this way the governor was responsible for appointing physicians who were answerable solely to him and to him they owed their continued employment. In fact, in the early days the system proved almost as inefficient and open to corruption as the coroners – the slight benefit was that at least the physicians knew a little about medicine.

New York had its coroners since colonial times, mainly incompetent political self-seekers with an inclination to corruption. The coroner was paid according to his level of trade – that is, per corpse; $11.50 to certify death. Not surprising perhaps that a single body might go around several times. Worse still, it was not unknown for obvious murder victims to be certified natural deaths – for an appropriate fee. It was in 1914 that mayor John Purroy Mitchell, after a thorough investigation into the coroner system, replaced the office with that of medical examiner. Learning from the Massachusetts experience, for the first time the incumbent had not only to be a physician, but a pathologist capable of performing post-mortems – and he had to pass stringent examinations in both before appointment.

Today the nation is divided between those states which retain the coroner system (and some do not even expect their coroners to be forensic pathologists) and those which have adopted the medical examiner system. The coroner is still a purely political office dependent entirely upon the fortunes or otherwise of the political party to which an individual candidate for the post is affiliated. This is clearly not only an unstable situation but one which is open to abuse; for example, some of those who run for the office of coroner are undertakers seeking to enhance their share of local business.

For these, and other reasons, the medical examiner option is gradually replacing the coroner. Currently fully qualified and experienced forensic pathologists are employed full-time by the state in charge of custom-equipped buildings and teams of qualified scientific staff. In many respects the system is more reliable, and certainly more realistically funded and staffed than its English counterpart.

CORPUS DELICTI

A much misunderstood term meaning simply 'the body of the offence'.

'If I tell you the truth you would not believe it, it is too fantastic for belief. Mrs Durand-Deacon no longer exists. She has disappeared completely, and no trace of her can ever be found again. I have destroyed her with acid. You will find the sludge that remains at Leopold Road. Every trace has gone. How can you prove murder if there is no body?'

The speaker is John George Haigh, the notorious 'Acid Bath Murderer', and he is talking to Inspector Albert Webb at the Chelsea police station. Haigh, not unusually, is boasting; boasting of his 'perfect' murder. In fact, he was wrong about there being no trace of Olive Durand-Deacon; pathologist Keith Simpson found quite a number of identifiable traces in the 'sludge'. Haigh was also wrong about not being able to prove murder without a body.

It was while he was a guest of His Majesty King George the Sixth on Dartmoor that Haigh first began to lay the ground-plans of his future career: 'Go after women,' he would pompously advise his fellow-guests, 'Rich old women who like a bit of flattery. There's your market if you're after big money.'

Arrogant little cleverjack that he was, John Haigh repeated so often his conviction that a murder could not be proved without a body that he was awarded the nickname 'Old Corpus Delicti'. Had he known better,

Haigh could have avoided his collision course with disaster, and in the process saved his own life. For John George was labouring under the by no means uncommon misunderstanding that *corpus* meant, literally, a 'corpse'. In reality, this legal concept describes the 'body' not of the victim, but simply of the crime itself – the essence of the crime that has to be established by the Crown in order to bring a successful prosecution. It is necessary only to prove that a person has been killed, and that death was the consequence of unlawful violence.

Less than eighteen months before Haigh's arrest, ship's steward James Camb had laboured under the same misapprehension. In October 1947, he raped and murdered actress Gay Gibson aboard the *Durban Castle* out of South Africa. Although Camb disposed of his luckless victim out of one of the liner's portholes and the body was never found, fresh scratches on the suspect's arms and back indicated a fierce struggle, and blood-flecked saliva on the bed-linen was consistent with strangulation. Furthermore, in situations of abject fear and panic such as Gay Gibson must have felt at the hands of her manic attacker, it is common for the bladder to empty – which accounted for the extensive urine staining on the bed. In March 1948 James Camb was sentenced to death.

There have been a number of subsequent instances of successful prosecutions being brought where no body was ever discovered: Michael Onufrejczyc, the Polish soldier-turned-farmer who killed his business partner and fed him to the pigs on their lonely Cefn Hendre Farm in Wales. And the kidnapping and murder of Mrs Muriel McKay in 1968, for which the brothers Arthur and Nizamodeen Hosein were eventually imprisoned. Mrs McKay is also believed to have provided a gruesome meal for the pigs.

As recently as 1987, Kingsley Rotardier, a forty-six-year-old model and composer was committed for trial at the Old Bailey charged with the murder of David Hamilton, his homosexual lover. It was claimed that Hamilton's body, which was never found, had been cut into small pieces and incinerated.

CRIME KITS

Physicians, of course, have always carried the essential tools of their trade with them, and the 'little black bag' has become synonymous with the doctor's calling. It is not surprising then that the **Police Surgeon** and the forensic **Pathologist** on call to the scene of a crime arrive well equipped for the specialist task ahead. What *is* surprising is that the 'Murder Bag', so closely connected in the popular imagination with the investigation of violent crime, should only have been 'invented' in 1924. It was one of Sir Bernard **Spilsbury**'s many lasting contributions to the scientific detection of crime.

Origin of the Murder Bag

What is known as the 'Murder Bag' is now part of the equipment of a chief-inspector, who takes it with him whenever he is called upon to investigate a case of murder in the provinces. The origin of the 'Murder Bag' is interesting. The first murder case I had after my appointment as chief-inspector was the crime for which Patrick Mahon was hanged – the murder of Miss Emily Kaye at Eastbourne. When Sir Bernard Spilsbury visited the bungalow on the Crumbles, he expressed astonishment that I had been handling portions of putrid flesh with my bare hands, and he pointed out that I had run a grave risk of septic poisoning. He said that no medical man outside a lunatic asylum would dream of doing such a thing, and that I ought to have at least worn rubber gloves. I told him we were not provided with rubber gloves. Sir Bernard, who is nothing if not practical, had a very serious talk with me and Dr Scott-Gillett, who had been of great assistance to me.

We police officers not only had no rubber gloves, but we lacked many other things which were essential to the efficient performance of our duties. If we wanted to preserve human hair on clothing, or soil or dust on boots, we had to pick it up with our fingers and put it in a piece of paper. We had no tapes to measure distances, no compass to determine direction, no apparatus to take fingerprints, no first-aid outfit, no instrument to find the depth of water, no magnifying glass. In fact, we had no appliances available for immediate use on the scene of a crime. And so it came about that the 'Murder Bag' was evolved. With the assistance of Sir Bernard and Dr Scott-Gillett, I made out a list of necessary articles for inclusion in the bag, and each chief-inspector now takes one with him on every occasion he is called on to investigate a crime in the country.

Ex-Superintendent Percy Savage, *Savage of Scotland Yard* (1934)

The general 'Murder Bag' was gradually refined over the years to take account of advances in technique as well as the requirements of the times. The 1949 edition of Hans **Gross**'s *Criminal Investigation* (edited by Ronald Martin Howe) cautions healthful cleanliness after the fashion of Spilsbury; among the equipment 'available for the detectives of a well-known English force', he lists: '*A piece of soap*. Soap is useful to take small impressions, as of keys, teeth (in the case of bites), etc. It is also a great comfort to have a wash after a search, handling dirty clothes and perhaps dirty bodies.'

Present-day scene-of-crimes officers will have a routine established which most effectively makes use of their time and experience, and will carry the familiar equipment and materials which that experience has taught may be required. Many of these items – even in the specialist kits – are simple everyday things such as bottles and bags, tweezers and test-tubes – all spotlessly clean. It is vital when collecting **Trace Evidence** on which criminal proceedings may rely that there is no possibility of contamination which could render the evidence non-valid.

Specialist Kits
Police
Fingerprint kits: These have been available since the development of the science of **Fingerprinting** at the beginning of the last century. Today they are available in a wide range designed for every conceivable requirement. One of the most prolific suppliers of such items as the 'Basic Field Kit' and the 'Complete Field Kit' is the Faurot Company of New York. In 1904, Deputy Police Commissioner Joseph A. Faurot (a colleague of Thomas **Byrnes**) was the first American to travel to London to study the new fingerprinting technique at Scotland Yard, and on his return to the United States was the first detective to secure a conviction based on fingerprint identification.

Photographic hits: Always kept ready for the use of specialist scene-of-crime photographic teams and will contain all the equipment which might be required for recording the crime scene – facilities for colour photography, both indoor and out, close-up and wide-angle, 'instant' Polaroid, and these days video recording. In addition, the kits will contain spare films, tripods, filters, etc., and a number of tape rules and clearly marked rulers which are laid alongside objects and **Impressions** being photographed, as an indication of size and angle-distortion.

Vacuum kits: For the collection of micro-evidence special vacuum cleaners with an internal series of graded filters from coarse to very fine can be used for sucking contact trace material from the scene of crime, suspect's or victim's clothing, interiors of motor cars, etc. One American company, Sirchie, make a cased kit specifically for scene-of-crime use.

Medical

Mention has already been made of the doctor's 'little black bag', but this usually contains equipment and materials for the relief of suffering in the living. When a physician is called in by the police to the scene of a serious offence such as a possible homicide, suicide or rape he must have another set of paraphernalia. The final contents of the bag will vary according to the preferences of the individual physician, but as a general rule an official **Police Surgeon** will carry with him the following items over and above what he might carry as a general practitioner:

A bag that stands on a flat surface without falling over

Paper, pen, and outline diagrams for recording sites of wounds on body

Two thermometers, one at least wide range (0–100ºC)

Chinagraph pencil for marking glass (slides, etc.) and skin

Microscope slides

Disposable rubber/plastic gloves

Forceps: one pair broad ended, one pair rubber tipped

Clean plastic bags: most of which will be used to contain samples, but two must be large enough to cover the victim's hands to preserve clutched material or other contact traces; another to cover the head for the same reason

Paper envelopes

Test-tubes with rubber 'corks'

Specimen bottles

Pure cotton wool swabs in tubes

Hand magnifying glass

Tape measure

Chalk

String

Torch

Odontology

The forensic dentist (or **Odontologist**) in Britain is not expected to be quite as peripatetic as his counterpart in the United States, but the contents of a Forensic Dentistry Kit have been suggested by James A. Cottone, America's foremost forensic odontologist, whose work on the identification of victims of mass disasters is internationally renowned.

'CRIMINAL MAN'

There have been theories for centuries that certain individuals were 'born' to be criminals, though it was not until impetus was provided by Charles Darwin's theory of evolution (published as *The Origin of Species on the Basis of Natural Selection* in 1859) that anthropology as a science achieved popularity and was taken into the service of criminologists to help explain the bewildering conduct of habitual criminals.

Pioneers in the field were Lauvergne, the prison surgeon at Toulon, who made plaster casts of his patients' heads to demonstrate 'degenerate' features of the skull: and the psychologist Morel, who believed fervently in the 'spirit' of the habitual criminal. However, the acknowledged father of anthropometric criminology was Cesare Lombroso. Lombroso was born in Verona in 1836, and after studying at Padua, Vienna and Paris began his medical career as an army doctor, later being appointed Medical Superintendent of an asylum at Pesaro. Lombroso's studies had convinced him that a study of the *criminal* was more rewarding than a study of the *crime,* and in this he laid the foundation of modern criminology.

It also predisposed him to relate criminal behaviour to a distinct criminal 'type' (or more accurately, 'types') which could be identified by **Anthropometric** measurements. In 1876 Lombroso published his great study *L'Uomo Delinquente* (Criminal Man). In it he claimed that on the basis of a study of almost 7,000 criminals he had found that they 'reproduce in their persons the ferocious instincts of primitive humanity and the inferior animals'. By this Lombroso did not mean simply that a criminal behaved metaphorically 'like an animal', but that aspects of his very physique were close to the savage – which he took to be, among others, large jaws, high cheekbones, square ears of large dimension, and long arms.

So convinced were they that the key to identifying the criminal lay in his **Physiognomy**, that Cesare Lombroso and his adherents devised a whole range of bizarre measuring instruments the more easily to prove the theories. Anfossi invented the 'craniograph' which traced the profile of the cranium on to a piece of card; and Landolt devised the 'campimeter', an apparatus for testing Lombroso's contention that criminals suffered a restricted field of vision – a small ball was swung from side to side in front of the subject's eyes and his gaze as he followed it monitored.

LOMBROSO'S 'CRIMINAL TYPES'
Stature and Features

To sum up in a few words the results of a study of 6,304 living criminals, I found that the delinquent when a minor has a higher stature, and when an adult a lower stature than normal, and darker hair . . . *Swindlers, Bandits* and *Assassins* are apt to have a head of exaggerated size. Congenital criminals present frequent cranial and facial asymmetry; this is especially the case with *Ravishers* and *Thieves,* and yet less to them than the insane, although they exhibit more traumatic lesions of the head, and greater obliquity of the eyes. They less frequently have atheroma of the temporal arterius, abnormal position of the eyes, scantness of the beard, nystagmus, facial and cranial asymmetry, and mydriasis [excessive dilatation of the eye-pupils], and less frequently still, premature greyness or baldness; they have in about equal proportions with the insane, prognathism, inequality of the pupils, crookedness of the nose, and a retreating forehead; the face is apt to be longer than that of lunatics or of the sane, the cheek bones and jaws are more prominent; the eyes are a dark brown, the hair is thick and dark, particularly in *Highwaymen.* Humped backs, which are rare in *Murderers,* are more frequent among *Ravishers, Forgers* and *Incendiaries;* the latter, and *Thieves* to an even greater extent, often have a grey iris, and in stature, weight, and muscular force are inferior to *Highwaymen* and *Murderers.*

There are certain differential points in the various classes of criminals:

In *Assassins* we have prominent jaws, widely separated cheek bones, thick dark hair, scanty beard, and a pallid face.

Assailants have brachycephaly [a short, broad head] and long hands, but narrow foreheads are rare among them.

Ravishers have short hands, medium-sized brains, and narrow foreheads; there is a predominance of light hair, with abnormalities of the genital organs and of the nose.

In *Highwaymen,* as in *Thieves,* anomalies of cranial measurement and thick hair; scanty beards are rare.

Incendiaries have long extremities, a small atypical head, and weigh less than normal.

Swindlers may be distinguished by their large jaws and prominent cheek bones, heavy weight, and pale, frequently paretic faces.

Pickpockets have long hands, a high stature, black hair and scanty beards.

Criminal Anthropology, Cesare Lombroso, 1895

With the wisdom of hindsight it is clear that many of the theories of Lombroso and his followers were well off-track – sometimes to the point of fatuity. But the greater danger of these theories of 'criminal man' was that they militated against any attempt at social reform or the rehabilitation of the offender – after all, he was a *born* criminal.

However, it would be both unfair and inaccurate to treat the contribution of Cesare Lombroso himself so dismissively. He was a man of great scientific integrity, continually revising his ideas to take account of new information from others working in this new field of criminology. Towards the end of his professional life, when he was appointed successively Professor of Medical Jurisprudence and Professor of Psychiatry at the University of Turin, he had begun to take account of suggestions made by his disciples of the environmental and social contributions to criminality. The following table shows how exhaustive some anthropological investigations had become; it is based on the work of Tamburini, Strassmann, Berelli and Mario Carrara:

TABLE SHOWING THE ANTHROPOLOGICAL EXAMINATION OF INSANE AND CRIMINAL PATIENTS

I   ANAMNESIS

    A. Names
         Nationality/Domicile
         Profession
         Age
         Education
    B. *Economic and hygienic conditions of native place*
    C. *Family circumstances*
         Pre-natal conditions
         Infancy
         Puberty
    D. *Causes to which decease of parents may be attributed*
    E. *Causes of insaniiy*
         Neurosis
         Imbecility
         Perversity

Suicidal tendencies
Crime
Eccentricity in the family

F. *Progressive diseases or trauma in the subject*
G. *Offence and causes thereof*

II PHYSIQUE

A. *Sexual development*
B. *Height*
C. *Span of the arms*

III PHYSICAL EXAMINATION

A. *Muscular development*
B. *Colour of* **Hair** *and eyes*
C. *Distribution and quality of hair*
D. **Tattooing**
E. *Craniometry*

Antero-posterior diameter
Transverse diameter
Antero-posterior curve
Transverse curve
Cephalic index
Type and anomalies of the skull
Circumference
Semi-circumference (anterior, posterior)
Forehead
Length and diameter of face
Facial type
Facial index
Anomalies of conformation and development in:
Skull
Face
Ears
Teeth
Other parts

IV FUNCTIONS

V ANIMAL LIFE

A. *Sensibility*

Meteoric
Tactile
Thermal
Dolorific and Muscular
Visual
Auditory
Other senses

B. *Motivity*

Sensory left-handedness
Motory left-handedness
Voluntary and involuntary movements
Reflex action
   Tendinous or muscular
   Abnormal
   Chorea

VI VEGETATIVE LIFE
  A. *Muscular strength*
  B. *Circulation*
  C. *Respiration*
  D. *Thermo-genesis*
  E. *Digestion*
    Rumination
    Bulimy
    Vomiting
    Dyspepsia
    Constipation
    Diarrhoea
  F. *Secretions*
    Milk
    Saliva
    Perspiration
    Urine
    Menstruation
  G. *Dyscrasia:* poisoning

VII PSYCHIC EXAMINATION
  A. *Language*
    Written
    Slang
  B. *Memory (textural):* Reason
  C. *Attention:* Perception
    Excitability
    Passions
   Dreams
    Excitability
    Passions
  E. *Sentiments*
    Affection
    Morality
    Religion
  F. *Instincts and tendencies*
  G. *Moral character:* Industry
  H. *Physiognomical expression*
  I. *Education:* Aptitudes

VIII MORBID PHENOMENA
    A. *Illusions*
    B. *Hallucinations*
    C. *Delusions*
    D. *Susceptibility to suggestion*

IX   OFFENCES
    A. *Cause of first offence*
       Environment
       Occasion
       Spontaneous or premeditated
       Drunkenness
    B. *Conduct after the offence*
       Repentance
       Recidivation

That there is still an anthropometric contribution to be made in the analysis and prediction of deviant behaviour is shown by the recent study* by Dr Joel Norris, an American known internationally for his work on the profiling of serial killers. In a detailed list of twenty-one patterns of Episodic Aggressive Behaviour derived from data on people suffering such behaviour, Norris lists under Pattern Nineteen 'Evidence of Genetic Disorders':

1. Bulbous fingertips.
2. Fine or electric wire hair that will not comb down.
3. Very fine hair that is soon awry after combing.
4. Hair whorls.
5. Head circumference outside a normal range of 1.5cm or less.
6. Epicanthus: upper and lower eyelids join the nose (the point of union is either deeply covered or partially covered.
7. Hyperteliorism: larger than normal distance between tear ducts or lower than normal distance between tear ducts.
8. Low-seated ears: the point where the ear joins the head is not in line with the corner of the eye and the bridge of the nose; it is lower by .5cm or more.
9. Adherent ear-lobes: lower edge of ear is extended upward and backward towards the crown of the head.
10. Malformed ears.
11. Asymmetrical ears.
12. Very soft or very pliable ears.
13. High-steepled palate.

* *Serial Killers*, Dr Joel Norris, London, 1990.

14. Roof of mouth is definitely steepled or flat and narrow.
15. Forward tongue with deep ridges.
16. Speckled tongue with either smooth or rough spots.
17. Curved fifth finger: marked curve towards the other fingers or slightly curved inward towards other fingers.
18. Singular transverse palmar crease.
19. Third toe is longer than second toe or equal in length to it.
20. Partial syndactyly (see **Finger Abnormalities**) of two middle toes.
21. Larger than normal gap between first and second toes.
22. Abnormalities in teeth.
23. Abnormalities in dermatoglyphics.

CRUSH ASPHYXIA
(see Suffocation)

CYANIDE

To discourage grazing animals certain plants have developed a source of natural cyanide – this is commonly found in the stones of fruiting trees like cherry, plum and peach, but can also be detected in the pips of apples and pears; more significant quantities are found as a constituent of the leaves of the laurel and cherry laurel. In the human body no worse symptoms than mild heart palpitations accompanied by a headache will be experienced from ingesting a moderate amount of the natural substance; however, it was early discovered in the Middle East that distillation by evaporation from laurel-water resulted in a lethal concentration of the poison.

One of the earliest recorded misuses of concentrated laurel-water was the killing by Livia of her elderly husband Augustus in August of the year AD 14. The murder was effected by soaking the old man's figs in the poison.

When crushed, the laurel leaves give off hydrocyanic acid as they ferment, and it was once common for butterfly collectors to use them in their 'killing bottles'. Though the 'sweet, sickly smell of almonds' so beloved of detective fiction writers is a great exaggeration, one of the common features of poisoning by the cyanides is the faint odour of bitter almond on the breath or in the stomach. Other cyanide compounds bear different names, like prussic acid, oil of bitter almonds and Scheele's acid.

As poisons the cyanides are as brutal as they are lethal – fifty milligrams being sufficient to cause death within five minutes by an inhibition of the blood's capacity to absorb oxygen.

Case Study

JOHN TAWELL

The following extracts derive from a contemporary account of the trial, in 1845, of John Tawell for the murder of his mistress Sarah Hart. It provides a rare detailed account of early expert testimony by physician and analyst; the case also had the distinction of being the first occasion on which a murderer was apprehended with the aid of the newly invented electric telegraph.

History of the Case
The trial of John Tawell of Berkhamsted, Hertfordshire, attracted more than the usual attention on account of the cruelty of the act in poisoning the woman whom he had seduced, the position and character of the murderer as a benevolent and hospitable Quaker, and the novelty of the mode by which his detection was effected.

The Trial
At the trial at Aylesbury before Mr Baron Parke, Mary Ashley, a next-door neighbour of the deceased, was called. She had seen Tawell go to Sarah Hart's between four and five in the afternoon of 1 January [1845], and between six and seven the same evening. Hearing 'a sort of stifled scream' she had gone to her door with a candle and seen him leaving the cottage. Mrs Barrett, another witness, confirmed Mrs Ashley's account of the condition in which she found the deceased, but did not see any foam on her lips until she tried to pour some water down her throat.

Evidence was next given by William Williams: 'I am a sergeant of police on the Great Western Railway, at Paddington [London] Station. On the 1st of January, in consequence of a telegraphic communication* I observed the prisoner get out of a carriage and get into a New Road omnibus. I put on a private coat and acted as guard. He got out opposite Princes Street . . . and went towards the Jerusalem coffee-house, and

The communication was as follows:

Message: A murder has just been committed at Salt Hill [Slough], and the suspected murderer was seen to take a first-class ticket for London by the train which left Slough at 7.42 p.m. He is in the garb of a Quaker, with a brown great coat which reaches nearly down to his feet; he is in the last compartment of the second first-class carriage.

Reply: The up-train has arrived, and a person answering, in every respect, the description given by telegraph came out of the compartment mentioned. I pointed the man out to

Sergeant Williams. The man got into a New Road omnibus, and Sergeant Williams into
the same.

from thence to Scott's Yard where he lodged, and I left him. On
returning there the next morning he was gone, so with another officer I
went to the Jerusalem and took him into custody.'

Medical Evidence

H. Montague Champneys, surgeon at Salt Hill, who had been summoned a few minutes before 7.00 p.m. on 1 January testified: 'I ran, and
when I got there saw the deceased on the floor, felt her pulse but am not
certain whether I felt any pulsation. I put my hands under her clothes
over her heart, and could not discover any pulsation; considered her
dead, but still thought it best to open a vein in her arm, and obtained
about an ounce of blood. Next day I made a post-mortem examination
with Mr Norblad and Mr Pickering. Having previously examined the
external parts, we opened the body, when I smelt the odour of prussic
acid; the lungs were perfectly healthy, but the coverings had the appearance of inflammation. Examined stomach and contents. Rather more
mucus than there ought to be; the abdominal viscera perfectly healthy.
Put contents of stomach into a bottle, which I, with Messrs Norblad and
Pickering, took to Mr Cooper in London.'

Analytical Evidence [It is worth quoting the analyst's evidence in full as
an example of medical jurisprudence at its best.]

Mr Cooper, the Analytical Chemist and Lecturer on Medical
Jurisprudence, gave the following expert evidence: 'On the 3rd of
January Messrs Champneys, Norblad and Pickering called on me with
a carpet bag. The bag contained a bottle (an ordinary one such as olives
are usually sold in) full, or nearly so, with the contents of the stomach;
a portion of porter in an ordinary beer bottle, on which was a paper label
signifying that it contained Guinness's beer; a glass tumbler about half
full of what appeared to be a mixture of beer and water; a part of a plum
bun, and a phial containing a few drops (perhaps about half a drachm)
of a nearly colourless fluid; a small piece of pink paper, such as is
generally used by apothecaries for tying over the corks of medicine
phials, and had apparently been used for such a purpose; the stomach
and part of the intestines. The bottle which contained the contents of the
stomach was tied over with a piece of bladder and, I think, corked as
well; it was opened and smelt strongly of food in the process of

digestion, it had also the smell of beer. On the application of litmus paper to the surface of the contents it became red instantly, and so very red that I was disposed to consider Mr Norblad and the other gentlemen were right in their conjecture as to its containing oxalic acid. A portion was now taken out of this bottle and put into a porcelain evaporating basin, to which some distilled water was added, and stirred well together with a glass rod; the basin with its contents was then placed on the heated sand bath and kept stirring until it boiled, and even after it had boiled for some minutes. During the whole of this operation I was standing over it, and the vapour that escaped I smelt the whole time, but did not recognize the slightest odour of prussic acid; the odour was the same as that of the contents of the bottle, but it was more powerful. The contents of the basin were then put into a paper filter placed in a glass funnel, and that which passed through the filter was collected in a glass vessel placed for its reception. While this operation was going on I directed my attention to the contents of the beer bottle and the tumbler. I found them both to have an acid reaction on litmus paper, the contents of the bottle very decidediy so; but on the application of the usual tests employed for the detection of oxalic acid not a trace of it could be found.

'By this time a small quantity of clear liquid from the contents of the basin had passed through the filter; this was removed from the glass vessel employed to receive it into a test glass, and on the application of the tests for the detection of oxalic acid not the smallest trace was indicated. I then felt quite certain that oxalic acid had not been the cause of death.

'I was then shown the stomach and on examining its interior surface it did not appear to have been acted on by any corrosive substance: nevertheless I thought it advisable to search for sulphuric acid, and accordingly applied to a small portion of the liquid, filtered from that which had been boiled, the test for that substance, but none could be detected. In like manner I did also apply the tests for the detection of baryta, opium, arsenic, the salts of mercury, and other metallic poisons, and could find none of them. I then came to the conclusion that, if the person had died from the effects of poison, it could have been none other than prussic acid.

'A portion of the contents of the stomach was then taken from the bottle and put in a tabulated retort, to which was added a very small quantity of diluted sulphuric acid; the retort with its contents was placed on the sand bath, a receiver applied and a portion distilled off. When about two drachms of clear liquid had distilled over, it was removed from the receiver into a glass test, about a grain of green sulphate of iron was added, and when this was dissolved, a small quantity of solution of potassa. These were allowed to remain a short time together and stirred with a glass rod. Subsequently muriatic acid was added in sufficient quantity *when instantly Prussian blue appeared*, which could not have resulted unless cyanogen or hydrocyanic acid had been present. But it could not be recognized by the smell. Although I had no doubt in my own mind, from the gentle heat which had been employed in the above detailed process of distillation, that the prussic acid could not have resulted from any decomposition of the animal matters present in the contents of the stomach, yet I thought it prudent to conduct the process of distillation in such a manner as to preclude the possibility of such occurrence.

'Another and much larger portion of the contents of the stomach was put into another retort, to which a little dilute sulphuric acid was added as before, and the retort with its contents placed in a water bath to which some common salt was added. The salt-water bath was heated till it boiled; a receiver was put on to the retort, an adapter intervening so as to remove the receiver to a greater distance from the furnace, and the receiver was kept as cool as possible by folds of blotting paper kept constantly wet applied to its external surface. In this manner was the distillation slowly conducted, until about an ounce of clear liquid had distilled over.

'On the removal of the liquid from the receiver it had the same smell as that contained in the bottle had before distillation, and neither myself, Mr Norblad, Mr Champneys, nor my son could detect the smell of prussic acid in the slightest degree. In fact, the odour of beer and digesting food was so powerful as to cover or disguise the smell of the prussic acid in this weak state, but on applying the same tests as before Prussian blue was found in considerable quantity.

'The few drops of liquid which were in the phial before mentioned were now examined: they had no action on litmus paper, they smelt of camphor and acetate of ammonia. The test for prussic acid was applied, but it did not show the smallest quantity. The phial was then washed out, and the distilled liquid, with the precipitated Prussian blue obtained by the above-detailed processes, was put into it. It was corked and taken up by Messrs Norblad and Champneys, as was also some distilled water with the same tests applied, to which no prussic acid had been added, and which was colourless. As far as I can recollect this completed the first day's proceedings, it being now nearly dark.

'On the following day (Saturday) Mr Pickering came to me to request I would examine, by the coroner's desire, the contents of the glass tumbler, the beer bottle, and the remainder of the beer, to determine if prussic acid existed in any of them. On the Monday Messrs Norblad and Champneys came, bringing with them the whole of the things they took away with them on the Friday. The beer, the contents of the tumbler, the remains of the plum bun we each subjected separately to distillation in the salt-water bath, and to the liquor obtained by distillation the same results for detecting prussic acid were added, but not a trace could be found.

'I may here observe that, on the intervening Saturday, I continued the distillation of the larger portion before spoken of for the purpose of obtaining more of the distilled liquid, and in fact to continue the distillation until the whole of the prussic acid had been separated. A part of the distilled liquor had its Prussian blue precipitated, which was given to Messrs Norblad and Champneys, and to another part I added nitrate of silver for the purpose of separating the hydrocyanic acid, or rather the cyanogen it contained. I kept it safe from decomposition or change for the purpose of further experiments.

'Accordingly I put the cyanide of silver obtained by the above process, together with some very dilute muriatic acid, into a small retort to which a receiver was attached. The retort was placed over a lamp in order to be heated, and the receiver was surrounded by cold water. The distillation proceeded until about a drachm and a half had distilled over. *This liquor possessed* the *odour of prussic acid*, distinctly recognized by myself and also by two of my sons.

'It had occurred to me that as Messrs Norblad, Champneys and myself had distinctly seen among the contents of the stomach some undigested apple, the seeds or pips of the apple might give rise to the formation of prussic acid by distillation. I therefore determined on making an experiment to see if any and what quantity of prussic acid they were capable of producing. Accordingly the seeds from fifteen apples were bruised and put into a retort with some distilled water, and about an ounce of liquor was distilled off. On the application of the tests before spoken of, Prussian blue, in exceedingly small quantity was produce. On testing the last product of distillation, no Prussian blue was found. I have the whole of the Prussian blue thus prepared.

'About ten days ago I was applied to and requested to make more experiments for the purpose (if possible) of discovering the whole amount of prussic acid originally contained in the contents of the stomach, or at least of that portion brought to me. I stated that I had not the means in my possession of doing so, and that Mr Norblad or Mr Champneys possessed almost everything relating to the matter; but I thought it possible, if I had the remainder of the contents of the stomach, and if that were contained in the same bottle in which it was originally brought, I might be able to do so – having a distinct recollection of about the height at which the matter stood in the neck of the bottle. Mr Champneys delivered the remainder of the contents of the stomach which had not before been subjected to any operation of experiment, and which I had asked him to keep in a cool dark place in case such further experiments were required.

'The bottle was tightly corked and tied over with a piece of bladder. Before uncorking it I made a mark with a file on the outside of the bottle coincident with the surface of the contents in the interior. I then emptied the contents into a glass alembic, washed the bottle out with a little distilled water, and added this to the matter in the alembic. The head of the alembic was then put on, a condensing apparatus attached, the alembic placed as before on a salt-water bath, the bath brought to boiling point, and distillation conducted until the whole of the prussic acid was expelled. A solution of nitrate of silver was put into the recipient for the purpose of seizing hold of the hydrocyanic acid the moment it reached that vessel. By this process I succeeded in obtaining 1.455 grains of dry cyanide of silver, very slightly contaminated with chloride of silver. The latter did not amount to a quantity which could be collected and weighed. But if I allow 0.025 grains, and call the quantity of cyanide of silver produced in reality 1.43 on the quantity operated on in this instance, it must be very near the truth. But as the quantity operated on in this instance formed only 51 parts out of the 180 of the whole volume of the contents of the bottle as it was first brought to me, the following proportion will show how much was contained in the whole. For if 51 parts give 1.43 grains of cyanide of silver, 180 parts will give 5.047 grains of cyanide of silver. This quantity of cyanide of silver is equivalent to 1.002 grains of real hydrocyanic or prussic acid, which is equal to 50 grains of the prussic acid of the strength of the London Pharmacopoeia. The determination of the relative quantity operated on, and the original volume of the contents of the stomach, was ascertained by measuring, with water, the bottle filled – as near as possible to remember – to that part of the neck where the contents originally stood, which was 180 drachms, and to the mark made by the file 51 drachms. I may also remark that the contents of the stomach, after distillation, was still strongly acid, occasioned most probably by the acid in the beer, and also by the acid which is invariably produced during the process of digestion.'

During his testimony, Mr Cooper produced the bottles containing the Prussian blue derived from the stomach and from the apple pips – the former a dark blue in colour, the latter hardly more than tinged with it. When placed side by side on the front of the witness box the marked contrast caused much excitement in court.

Purchase of Prussic Acid

It was attested by a Mr Hughes, chemist of Bishopsgate Street, London, that: 'On the 1st of January the prisoner came to the shop dressed in a great coat and usual Quaker garb and asked for two drachms of Scheele's Prussic Acid . . . he said he wanted it for external application to varicose veins, paid four pence for it, which was entered in the book and produced. Next day he came in and asked for the same quantity. I had seen him frequently before and might have sold him prussic acid, I am not certain. He told me he had been a chemist and apothecary abroad [indeed, he had at one time been the principal druggist of Sydney, Australia].'

Verdict

At the conclusion of the judge's summing-up to the jury, they retired to consider the evidence, and in about half an hour returned a verdict of guilty. In a few impressive sentences in which he spoke of the prisoner's hypocrisy in adopting the garb of a virtuous, peaceful, benevolent and religious body of persons, the judge passed on the prisoner the dread sentence of the law, which he suffered on 28 March. Previously to his execution Tawell handed a written confession to the jail chaplain that he committed the murder for fear that his wife should discover his connection with the deceased Sarah Hart.

D

DECOMPOSITION
(see Putrefaction)

DENTAL IDENTIFICATION
Identification, by whatever means, for legal purposes, of an unknown body must be based on a comparison of ante-mortem records with post-mortem remains.

While visual identification is the customary procedure in cases of recent death without the complication of disfiguring trauma, other means must be found in the event of dismembered, decomposed, mummified or skeletal remains.

Fingerprinting is the most common secondary technique where sufficient tissue remains, but in the absence of fingerprints, 'oral structures' prove to be the next most scientifically reliable means of identification for the following reasons:

1. Human dentition tends to outlast all other body tissue after death.
2. Dental repairs, restorations, and prostheses (false teeth) are particularly resistant to chemical and physical degradation.
3. Given the infinite number of permutations of aspects of dentition, any given configuration is, for all practical purposes, unique.
4. Radiographic (X-ray) examination is capable of revealing even fuller data on structural features of teeth and jaws.

It must be emphasized, however, that for successful *positive* identification via dental patterns both ante- and post-mortem records must be available, and with a complete ante-mortem chart it may be possible to make an identification from as little as a single tooth.

The Post-Mortem Chart

Post-mortem dental records will be made using a combination of techniques including diagrammatic charts, radiographs, models, recorded commentary, etc. The fullest examination should always be made, recording as much information as possible. This is particularly important when it is not known how much material will be available on ante-mortem records. The main points of subsequent comparison will be:

1. *Number of teeth:* Keep in mind the distinct possibility of post-mortem loss in badly decomposed or skeletal subjects. Supernumery teeth, being rare, are worthy of particular note.
2. *Restoration and prostheses:* Dentures may prove valuable if they contain markings that will identify the dental practitioner, manufacturer or wearer. In America the customer's name and social security number may have been stamped into the base material.
3. *Dental caries*.
4. *Root cavity treatment:* As revealed by radiography.
5. *Occlusion:* Overjet and overbite details should be noted.
6. *Malposition:* Overlapping, crowding, unusual spacing, rotation, etc.
7. *Unusual formations:* Fused teeth, multiple cusps, etc.
8. *Oral pathology:* Record should be kept of any abnormal anatomical features, either in the tongue and soft tissues, if present, or the bony structures.
9. *Occupational disfigurement:* Those who are obliged to use their mouths as essential or useful 'tools' in trades or pastimes will frequently exhibit associated abnormalities or wearing of the teeth – musicians, for example, from clenching the mouthpieces of their instruments, or carpenters and upholsterers from holding nails between their teeth.

When all this information has been recorded, the forensic odontologist confronts the problems of determining, where relevant, the Age, Gender and Ethnic Origin of the subject.

Estimation of Age

Teeth represent the most reliable indicator of age in subjects from birth to fourteen years, when growth follows a remarkably consistent pattern;

from fourteen to twenty-odd the development and eruption of the third molars are a standard test. Beyond this age dental development is less predictable.

Gender
Determination not reliable by teeth alone, although it has proved possible to extract dental pulp cells and isolate the Y chromosomes of males – a reliable test up to five months post mortem.

Determination of Ethnic Origin
The determination of race is not most reliably achieved through odontology, and what little can be determined in this way is generally only supplementary to what has been learned from an examination of the skull and long bones. However, statistics lead one expert (Warren Harvey) to present the following common ethnic characteristics:

EUROPEAN
1. Narrow arch and crowding of teeth
2. Cusp of Carabelli

CHINESE
1. Wide arch
2. Enamel extension between roots of molars
3. Three rooted deciduous molars
4. Five cusped third molars

AUSTRALIAN ABORIGINES
1. Large arch and large teeth
2. Midline diastema
3. Marked attrition

NEGROID
1. Lower first premolar has two or three lingual cusps

MONGOLOID
1. Occlusal enamel pearls in premolars
2. Shovel-shaped incisors
3. Missing mandibular incisors

NORTH AMERICAN INDIANS
1. Marked attrition
2. Shovel-shaped incisory
3. Large teeth

Comparison of Records

As there is no internationally accepted standard for ante-mortem dental records it can be imagined that information retrieved – where it is retrieved at all – may be in all stages of completion and detail, and on all manner of designs of record card.

It has been conservatively estimated that there are over 150 different types of dental chart currently in use around the world, and symbols and designations are by no means standard. Add to this the frequently careless entries made on charts by overstretched dental practitioners (perhaps using a coding system all their own!), and further weight is added to the call to adopt a single international system.

The chart known as the 'Universal System', where teeth are numbered 1–32, seems to be the least confusing, but the 'Palmer Notation' and 'FDI' system also have their champions.

It is in the interest of clarity for the forensic odontologist (especially if he is expected to provide a written finding to be used in a court of law) to rationalize his ante- and post-mortem information on to similar documents.

Unlike fingerprints, there is no recommended number of 'positive points' of comparison – it will depend as much upon the quality of the identification as on quantity; indeed, a single tooth or fragment of jawbone can in certain cases be specific enough to establish positive identification.

Clearly, radiographs – particularly of the 'panoramic' kind – that accompany ante-mortem records will be usefully compared with post-mortem radiographs, and details revealed by sophisticated techniques such as Scanning Electron Microscopy (SEM) may add further strength to the forensic dental report.

Case Study

ANOTHER VICTIM OF THE WAR

A case that proved fundamental to the development of forensic dentistry was revealed in 1942 when Dr Keith Simpson was summoned to the ruins of a war-bombed Baptist chapel at Kennington in south-east London. A workman helping to make safe the building had prised up a stone slab in what had been the cellar and found beneath it a human body reduced almost to a skeleton. First appearances – that this was yet another victim of the Luftwaffe's Blitz on London – did not impress Simpson. War victims did not, in his experience at least, bury themselves under stone slabs. Nor did they dismember themselves and jump into a fire covered in quicklime!

The pathologist's estimate of the time of death was between one and one-and-a-half years before; a check of the police records for the area showed that a Mrs Rachel Dobkin, former wife of a fire-watcher, had been reported missing fifteen months previously. Harry Dobkin was employed to look out for fires by a company of solicitors whose offices had been located next to the Baptist chapel.

Although the corpse's lower jaw had become detached and was missing, the upper jaw showed evidence of extensive dental repair. An interview with Mrs Dobkin's sister, Polly, provided two vital clues – the first was that Rachel had been suffering from a fibroid tumour (evidence of which was found in the remains), and secondly that her regular dentist was a Dr Barnett Kopkin of Stoke Newington. Dr Kopkin, meticulous practitioner that he was, had kept records of the treatment undertaken on Mrs Dobkin's teeth and was able to draw a chart which corresponded exactly with that of the upper jaw of the corpse.

On 26 August 1942, Harry Dobkin was arrested and charged with the murder of his former wife. Three months later he was tried, convicted and sentenced to hang. It had been an unlucky day for Harry when Keith Simpson was assigned to the case; Simpson who went on to become one of the world's greatest authorities on dental identification.

Identification in Mass Disasters

Of all the undertakings of forensic medicine, perhaps the most harrowing is the analysis of mass disaster victims. Medical staff will be confronted with the problem of identifying vast numbers of bodies which have been burned, decomposed and fragmented beyond the capability of visual identification. Among the investigators will always be found the teams of dentists, for the teeth offer one of the most reliable, least degradable sources of personal information.

Although every mass disaster – even those of the same 'type', like air crashes – is unique, there are aspects common to each of them, not least multiple injury and loss of life. Medical procedures begin at the disaster site as soon as the area has been declared safe by fire officers. The first task is a sweep of the area to locate human remains and fragments which are marked with numbered tags; a grid chart is drawn up to plot the locations of the remains, which may help later to indicate injury patterns, family groupings, etc. As soon as this operation has been completed, no time is lost in removing the remains in body bags to the designated mortuary area of the 'disaster identification centre', where the process begins.

Although we are concentrating here on the role of the forensic dentist, a list of the different sections of expertise involved will give some indication of the scale of such an operation.

Disaster Identification Sections
1. Initial processing
2. Photography
3. Fingerprinting
4. Personal effects check
5. Pathology
6. Radiology
7. Anthropology
8. **Odontology**
9. Laboratory
10. Mortuary processing
11. Storage
12. Transportation to relatives, etc.

The remains are placed on trolleys and passed from section to section for treatment and processing.

Apart from a purely humanitarian requirement to identify disaster victims for the peace of mind of their family and friends, and to release the bodies for funeral arrangements to be made, positive proof of identity will be required in order to draw up death certificates for such local procedures as insurance claims and the execution of wills.

We have already seen in the paragraphs above how forensic odontology has proved vital in the identification of difficult homicide cases where visual identification is impossible. Exactly the same procedure – on a vastly larger scale – is followed in cases of mass disasters and no further explanation is required.

Recent Developments
Radiographic Techniques
Used in most disciplines of forensic science, but of particular relevance to pathology and odontology as a post-mortem technique for identification.

Post-Mortem Radiographs
This technique will reveal details unavailable by any other means – root structure, arrangement of sinus cavities, structure of bony areas, etc. The high degree of accuracy makes this one of the most reliable sources of identification on which to base a comparison with ante-mortem information.

In making estimates of age in the case of infants and children up to fourteen years, radiographs provide unique information on:

Root formation and degree of completion
Crown formation and degree of completion
Formation of tooth sockets
Clinical eruption of teeth
Degree of tooth mineralization

Xeroradiography
A new development in X-ray technology permitting the imaging of both soft and hard tissue on the same exposure. By this means also, non-metallic invading bodies such as plastics, glass and wood can be visualized. The fundamental principle is that charged selenium particles when exposed to the X-ray beam become photoconductive, producing an electrostatic image. The miniaturization of equipment has recently made this technique practical to forensic dentistry.

DENTISTRY
(See Bite-mark Analysis, Dental Identification, Odontology

DETECTION DYES
Detecting suspects by means of marking objects with indelible dyes has been used with greater or lesser degrees of sophistication for centuries, and is still encountered in situations where regular thefts from a particular place have been occurring over a period and it is

thought that a single suspect is responsible. The technique could not be simpler; the object – say a cash box, safe, drawer, money – is dusted with an inconspicuous powder which, if it is transferred to a suspect's hands, is sure proof that he handled the stolen goods – traces in his clothing pockets strengthen the case. Detective dyes are of three main types:

Visible Stains

These chemicals acts instantly when the dusting powder comes in contact with moisture, such as the fingers, staining the skin a particular colour. Although most dyes are fairly long-lasting, it is obvious that as soon as he sees the tell-tale stain, a thief will make every effort to wash it off – or at least keep out of sight until it has worn off. It is only in cases where speedy detection is anticipated that visible stains are useful. Dyes are available in a range of different coloured powders so that one of a suitably unobtrusive colour can be chosen to blend in with the colour of the object to be dusted.

The following is a list of the most commonly available visible detection dyes:

WORK-LOAD PASSING THROUGH FORENSIC SCIENCE SERVICE, 1984

Chemical	Normal colour	Wet colour
Chrysiodine	Maroon	Orange
Crystal Violet	Green	Violet
Gentian Violet	Violet	Violet
Malachite Blue	Dark Green	Blue
Malachite Green	Green	Green
Metylene Blue	Dark Green	Blue
Rhodamine B	Brown	Cherry

Invisible Stains

Work in very much the same way as visible dyes, except that the colour is only revealed under ultraviolet light. This has the advantage that a thief is quite unaware that his hands have become contaminated, though obviously washing in the normal course of events will eventually destroy the trace.

Radioactive Traces

Liquids in the form of isotopes which put a harmless trace in other liquids (petrol, for example) which can be detected by the use of a geiger counter.

DIATOMS
(see Drowning)

DIMINISHED RESPONSIBILITY

Enshrined in the British concept of Justice, and indeed the legal systems of most of the world, is the provision that a person cannot be punished for actions committed while in a state of mental incompetence or unbalance. This protection is encountered most frequently in a defendant's defence plea in court, and can take the form of Diminished Responsibility, **Insanity**, or **Automatism**.

In the case of Diminished Responsibility, the defendant will, through his legal representatives, assert that he was, at the time of his offence, suffering from such abnormality of mind that his responsibility was impaired. This comparatively new defence to the charge of murder was introduced into English (and Welsh) law by the Homicide Act of 1957 (Scotland has its own distinct legal system). A successful plea will result in an automatic conviction on a charge of manslaughter.

THE HOMICIDE BILL
(5 Eliz. 2)

A BILL
TO

Make for England and Wales (and for courts-martial wherever sitting) amendments of the law relating to homicide and the trial and punishment of murder, and for Scotland amendments of the law relating to the trial and punishments of murder and attempted murder.

Be it enacted by the Queen's most Excellent Majesty, by and with the advice and consent of the Lords Spiritual and Temporal, and Commons, in this present Parliament assembled, and by the authority of the same, as follows:

PART I
AMENDMENTS OF LAWS OF ENGLAND AND WALES
AS TO THE FACT OF MURDER . . .

. . . 2.–(1) Where a person kills or is a party to the killing of another, he shall not be convicted of murder if he was suffering from such abnormality of mind (whether arising from a condition of arrested or retarded development of mind or any inherent causes or induced by disease or injury) as substantially impaired his mental responsibility for his acts and omissions in doing or being a party to the killing.

(2) On a charge of murder, it shall be for the defence to prove that the person charged is by virtue of this section not liable to be convicted of murder.

(3) A person who but for this section would be liable, whether as principal or as accessory, to be convicted of murder shall be liable to be convicted of manslaughter.

(4) The fact that one party to a killing is by virtue of this section not liable to be convicted of murder shall not affect the question whether the killing amounted to murder in the case of another party to it . . .

Not surprisingly a finding of diminished responsibility accounts for some 20 per cent of the annual homicide figures for Great Britain.

In practical terms, the plea puts the burden of proof on the defence and, as in the case of Insanity, the proof need not be 'beyond reasonable doubt' but 'on a balance of probabilities'. Medical evidence must obviously be presented on the defendant's behalf as to his state of mind, but it is for the *jury* and not expert witnesses to decide, on the evidence offered, whether the abnormality amounts to diminished responsibility.

The defences of Diminished Responsibility and of Insanity are rarely encountered outside murder cases, because except in sentences for murder, indefinite and possibly life-long confinement to a secure hospital such as Broadmoor is infinitely worse than the standard punishment for the crime.

Case Study

MARY FLORA BELL

Mary was born on 26 May 1957, the illegitimate daughter of an emotionally unstable seventeen-year-old Scottish girl. Her parents married after the birth of Mary, though this was little compensation for a childhood characterized by instability and poverty. Indeed, Mary spent much of her early years being shuttled around various relatives and foster homes. Although she was a withdrawn child, Mary developed an outward exhibitionism and boisterousness that at times verged on the aggressive; school friends seemed to get 'hurt' more frequently when they played with Mary than they did playing with other children.

Playmates complained to their parents that Mary would squeeze their necks until they squealed.

Attributing it to nothing more than naughtiness, nobody took much notice of these childish scraps until 25 May 1968, when the body of four-year-old Martin Brown was found in a derelict house in the Scotswood area of Newcastle. There were no apparent signs of violence, and at first it was thought that Martin had died after eating the contents of a bottle of pills he found in the house; the inquest returned an open verdict.

On the following day a local nursery school was found broken in to, and when the police investigated they found a number of scribbled notes, obviously written by a child, one of which read: 'We did murder Martain brown Fuckof you bastard'. Five days later, the new alarm installed at the school rang at the police station and when a patrol car arrived at the building they found Mary Bell inside with Norma Joyce Bell (she was not a relative, but a close friend and neighbour). The girls denied the previous break-in, but they were charged, and their cases were due to be heard by the juvenile court when they were arrested for murder.

On 31 July, Brian Howe, three and a half years old, disappeared; his body was found later on a patch of waste ground. Brian had been strangled and his body pierced and scratched with the broken pair of scissors found beside him. Police conducted their questioning of the local schoolchildren by the novel means of a questionnaire, asking whether they had seen Brian Howe on the day of his disappearance, whether they had seen anything unusual or suspicious, and so on. Mary and her friend both made statements that seemed odd, and on fuller questioning they began to contradict themselves and each other. Then Norma insisted that she had seen Mary strangle Brian Howe, and Mary insisted it had been Norma who killed the child. Norma and Mary Bell were taken into custody and charged with the murders of Brian Howe and Martin Brown, whose cause of death had now been certified as strangulation.

The trial opened on 3 December 1968, and lasted two weeks. Predictably a great deal of the court's time was occupied with the reports of psychiatrists called as expert witnesses. Although he found no indication of mental abnormality, one forensic psychiatrist found Mary possessed of 'an unsocialized manipulative personality'. To another doctor she had seemed at times to display a complete lack of feeling for other human beings; 'Brian Howe had no mother,' Mary had said. 'So he won't be missed.' Later she added: 'If you're dead, you're dead. It doesn't matter then.'

Norma, although older by two years, had far less to say for herself, and the general impression was that it was upon her friend that Mary had exercised her 'manipulative personality'. Norma Joyce Bell was acquitted of the changes altogether, and Mary was found guilty only of the manslaughter of Brian Howe and Martin Brown on account of diminished responsibility. Before being sentenced, Mary Bell told a policewoman looking after her: 'Murder isn't that bad. We all die sometime . . .'

Although there was no shortage of adequate hospital facilities for maladjusted children, none was willing to take the risk of accepting such a potentially dangerous patient as Mary Bell. She was instead sentenced to be detained in a maximum security unit of an approved school.

In September 1977 after a transfer, Mary Bell escaped from Moor Court open prison, later claiming that she wanted an opportunity to prove she could look after herself in the outside world; Mary was recaptured after three days and finally released in 1980.

DISMEMBERMENT

It has been said that in 1726, when Mrs Catherine Hayes killed her husband and cut off his head to confound identification, she set a fashion in dismemberment which has continued in popularity to the present day. Of course, Mrs Hayes was not the first to decapitate her victim, but the case is the first of its kind to be so well documented, and illustrates perfectly the problems that arose in those days before police forces, and before an organized medico-legal profession. When John Hayes' head was recovered from the Thames by a startled boatman there was no other possible means of identification than visual recognition – in consequence, the grisly relic was impaled upon a pole and set to public view in St Margaret's churchyard, Westminster. To be fair, it worked – poor Hayes' features were indeed recognized by a horrified friend.

Although headless bodies still turn up periodically, the forensic sciences have developed to the stage where few corpses, intact or otherwise, remain unidentified for long. This, in combination with vastly more sophisticated murder investigation techniques, has helped the clear-up rate for murder – in Britain at least – to top ninety-five per cent. This despite the best efforts of a sometimes ingenious killer to cover his own tracks and to render his victim unidentifiable.

Frequently the dismemberment of a body is the result of a purely practical requirement to make a large heavy corpse more manageable – to make up into smaller parcels for disposal elsewhere – in rivers, rubbish bins, under bushes, in the fire . . . Or to make it fit better into some packing case or trunk to be deposited far from the scene of the crime. All have been tried, most have failed.

The present author is often asked which he believes to be the case that best sums up the triumph of the forensic sciences over crime. There is no hesitation; for sheer inspired dedication set against a ruthless killer, it is the case that was built up against Dr Buck Ruxton. Not that Ruxton was a particularly clever man – shrewd, yes; well versed in medicine and surgery, certainly. But for all that a killer who left clues behind him like the hare in a paper-chase. Everybody knew that Ruxton killed his wife and maid; the problem was proving it – proving even that the ghastly shambles of human remains scattered around the Gardenholme Linn *were* Mrs Ruxton and Mary Rogerson. It required all the skills of some of the country's most celebrated forensic scientists to undo Ruxton's fiendish attempts to remove all identifying features from his victims, and to restore to each of them an identity, as the law requires, beyond any possible doubt. To this end a great number of different techniques were employed, some of them, like photographic super-imposition, for the first time.

Case Study

DR BUCK RUXTON

On the morning of 29 September 1935, Susan Haines Johnson, a holiday visitor to the southern uplands of Scotland, passed over the old stone bridge which crossed the Gardenholme Linn, a tributary stream of the river Arran, some two miles north of the town of Moffat. As she looked idly over the bridge, Miss Johnson could scarcely believe her eyes; at the bottom of the steep gully a dismembered human arm was reaching up out of a large bundle. Susan Johnson lost no time in telling her brother Alfred, who lost no time in telling the police. By late that Sunday afternoon it had fallen the lot of Sergeant Sloane of the Dumfriesshire Constabulary to begin the official investigation; he was later joined by Inspector Strath, and between them the two officers began the grisly job of combing the tangled bankside of the Linn for pieces of flesh and bone. Such fragments as were found were removed to the tiny mortuary attached to Moffat Cemetery. The search was resumed on the following morning, when other portions were discovered, and on subsequent days until 7 October, when an unproductive use of bloodhounds convinced the police that nothing further was to be found in the immediate vicinity. On 28 October a left foot was found wrapped in newspaper on the Glasgow–Carlisle road nine miles south of Moffat, and on 4 November a young woman found a right forearm and hand lying by the roadside about a half mile south of the Gardenholme Linn.

During this time Professor John **Glaister** had been summoned from his duties at the head of Edinburgh University's Forensic Science Department; his initial inventory of the collection of human remains makes grim reading:

> Four bundles: the first was wrapped in a blouse and contained two upper arms and four pieces of flesh; the second comprised two thigh bones, two legs from which most of the flesh had been stripped, and nine pieces of flesh, all wrapped in a pillow-case; the third was a piece of cotton sheeting containing seventeen pieces of flesh; the fourth bundle was also wrapped in cotton sheeting and consisted of a human trunk, two legs with the feet tied with the hem of a cotton sheet and some wisps of straw and cotton wool.
>
> In addition, other parcels opened to reveal two heads, one of which was wrapped in child's rompers; a quantity of cotton wool and sections from the *Daily Herald* of 6 August 1935; one thigh; two forearms with hands attached but minus the top joints of the fingers and thumbs; and several pieces of skin and flesh. One part was wrapped in the *Sunday Graphic* dated 15 September which was subsequently to provide an important clue.

The remains were all badly decomposed and infested with maggots, so their immediate transfer to the Anatomy Department of Edinburgh University was ordered. Under the supervision of Dr Gilbert Millar the remains were first washed in a bath, treated with ether to destroy the maggots, and left in a preservative solution of formalin awaiting detailed examination and reconstruction. In all, seventy pieces of what appeared to be two bodies had been collected, and it was immediately clear that the extensive mutilation of the features was the result of a deliberate attempt to frustrate identification. The ears, eyes, nose, lips and skin of the faces had been removed, and some teeth extracted. The terminal joints of the fingers had been cut off, presumably to prevent identification by fingerprints. Even so, one of the heads could be confidently ascribed to a young woman, while the other after initially being thought to be male, was later identified as belonging to an older woman.

From this unsavoury shambles the medical experts were required to provide not only identification but legally acceptable proof of identification, plus such other details as time of death and cause of death, and any information that might point to a murder suspect.

Meanwhile, another team of experienced detectives were engaged in the detailed police investigation that necessarily accompanies a major murder hunt. Missing-persons inquiries were made over a large area around Moffat, though results were negative, as were inquiries into irregular movements by motorcars in the area of the Gardenholme Linn bridge. Officers examined closely the materials in which the dismembered remains were wrapped for any clue as to the origin of the victims. The first major breakthrough was in the sheet of the *Sunday Graphic* for 15 September 1935. This was recognized as what in the newspaper trade are called 'slip editions' – that is, issues celebrating an event of local importance, and circulated only in that area; this particular 'slip' contained features on the Morecambe festival and was sold only in the town, in Lancaster, and in the immediately surrounding district. Now, by happy coincidence the Chief Constable of Dumfries – under whose expert leadership the investigation was proceeding – saw an article in Glasgow's *Daily Record* which gave an account of the disappearance three weeks previously of a young woman named Mary Jane Rogerson, who had been employed as a nursemaid by the family of a Lancaster doctor named Buck Ruxton. Further investigation acquainted police with the fact that Mrs Ruxton had disappeared at the same time.

A distraught Mrs Jessie Rogerson, resident of Morecambe and stepmother of Mary Jane, was brought in to see if she could identift any of the material which had wrapped the grisly Moffat remains; to her great distress Mrs Rogerson immediately picked out the blouse which she had given to Mary after repairing it with a distinctive patch under the arm. Following a direct lead from Jessie Rogerson, the child's rompers were later identified by a Mrs Holme of Grange-over-Sands; she had passed on some children's clothing to the Ruxtons when they had stayed with her as boarders the previous summer.

So the connection between the dismembered bodies, the missing Lancaster women, and the family of Buck Ruxton was now established if not proved, and at this point the main thrust of the investigation was placed in the capable hands of Captain Henry Vann, Chief Constable of Lancaster. The Lancaster force had already had some contact with Ruxton – or rather he with them – on a couple of recent occasions he had exchanged some very excited dialogue with Captain Vann requesting that something be done regarding the spread of gossip linking him with the finds at Moffat. On the evening of 11 October, a distressed Ruxton again blustered into the police station at Lancaster demanding to see Captain Vann: 'My dear Vann, can't you do something about these newspaper reports? Look at this. This newspaper says that this woman has a full set of teeth in the lower jaw, and I know, of my own knowledge, that Mary Rogerson had at least four teeth missing in this jaw. Can't you publish it in the papers that there is no connection between the two and stop all this trouble?'

Dr Ruxton had been born in 1899 to a Parsee family living in Bombay. Originally given the names Bukhtyar Rustamji Ratanji Hakim, he abbreviated them first to Buck Hakim and later, in England, by deed pool to Buck Ruxton. Ruxton gained his Bachelor of Medicine and Bachelor of Surgery degrees at the University of Bombay, and subsequently served in the Indian medical service in Baghdad and Basra. It was to prove ironic that Ruxton also attended Edinburgh University where, although he failed to secure his fellowship of the Royal College of Surgeons, he did secure a life partner in the person of Isabella Kerr. Miss Kerr had been managing a café in the city, and was at the time married to a Dutchman named Van Ess. Ruxton and Isabella never married, though when he secured the practice at 2 Dalton Square, in Lancaster, they lived together as Mr and Mrs Ruxton, and she bore him three children. The household was completed by Mary Jane Rogerson, a cheerful girl of twenty whose duty it was to help with the children, and there were two live-out charladies, Agnes Oxley and Elizabeth Curwen, who shared the heavy work and much of the cooking.

The Ruxtons' was not an entirely harmonious relationship, characterized as it was by his insane – and quite groundless – jealousy. Although there was no doubt that a considerable affection existed between the couple, the quarrels became more violent as they became more frequent with Ruxton's growing obsession with his wife's imagined infidelity, occasioning at least two recorded visits from the local constable.

In 1934, two years after a desperate suicide attempt, Mrs Ruxton left her husband and fled to the comfort of her sister's home in Edinburgh.

She was finally persuaded by a hysterically sobbing Ruxton to go back to Lancaster, but it was clear that the relationship was nearing a crisis. A year after her return Isabella Ruxton was being wrongly accused of entertaining an affair with a young local man named Edmondson, the son of family friends. On 7 September 1935, Mrs Ruxton again escaped to Edinburgh, this time with her friends the Edmondsons. Although there was absolutely no foundation to his suspicions, Ruxton began a tirade of abuse on her return that was to last most of the following week until Mrs Ruxton took the family car up to Blackpool where it was a harmless annual custom for her to meet her two sisters for the day and enjoy the illuminations. To Buck Ruxton it was obvious that she had gone to meet a new lover.

Isabella Ruxton returned on that Saturday night, 14 September, as she had said she would. She was never seen alive outside 2 Dalton Square again; nor was Mary Rogerson.

Mrs Curwen was on duty on Friday, 13 September 1935 when Dr Ruxton told her that she could finish up now and go home and need not return till the following Monday. Mrs Oxley (who was expected on the Sunday) received a message via her husband that as Mrs Ruxton and Mary had gone on holiday to Edinburgh – an annual occurrence – there was no need to come. During the rest of that Sunday a succession of trades people came to the door about their errands, including the delivery of the *Sunday Graphic*. Shortly before midday Ruxton deposited his three children with the Andersons, close friends of the family with whom the children were familiar, and where they would spend the greater part of the next few days. When Ruxton arrived he complained of a cut hand – injured, he said, while opening a tin of fruit for the children's breakfast; he was to make much of this cut to everybody he met over the following days.

At four-thirty that afternoon Ruxton visited a Mrs Hampshire, one of his patients, and after relating the story of the cut hand persuaded her to return with him to Dalton Square to help 'prepare for the decorators' who were expected to arrive the following morning. He explained that Mrs Ruxton and Mary were away in Edinburgh.

In retrospect, this invitation to Mrs Hampshire (and later to her husband as well) was either grossly arrogant on Ruxton's part, or grossly stupid. This woman's evidence alone could have convicted the doctor at his trial – evidence of carpets soaked with blood taken up and rolled, strange stains on the bath, clothing so stained with blood that she could only burn it, and a similarly stained blue suit which Ruxton had the audacity to offer as a gift to Mr Hampshire.

Just a sample of the extraordinary trail of clues left about the scene of the crime by Ruxton, which were methodically welded into a completely watertight case by the police forensic laboratory. Scientific investigators, in collaboration with the police, established that other items of stained clothing and carpet had littered the yard at the side of the house, and that fires had been seen blazing at all hours of the day and night; charred fabric identified as having been Mary Rogerson's clothing was found in the ashes. An unwholesome smell had been noticed in the house by the charladies, and Ruxton had been obliged to spray with air freshener and eau-de-Cologne. Scraps of human tissue were found in the drains and waste pipes leading from the bath, and extensive bloodstaining was present on the stairs and stair carpets, bathroom walls and floor and various items of clothing.

Meanwhile, the forensic team at Edinburgh University (Ruxton's old Alma Mater) were performing minor miracles. Professor Glaister had enlisted the help of Professor James Couper Brash of Edinburgh University's Department of Anatomy, assisted by Dr E. Llewellyn Godfrey. The dental examination was entrusted to Dr A.C.W. Hutchinson, Dean of the Dental Hospital and School at Edinburgh and Mr A. Johnstone Brown. Later in the investigation (he was out of the country at the time of the discoveries) Professor Sydney **Smith** would lend the great weight of his experience.

Professor Brash had begun the painstakingly slow reconstruction of the remains. The collections of parts which until then had been roughly divided into boxes marked Body No. 1 and Body No. 2 were taking on separate identities. The size and shape of the heads were so dissimilar as to be differentiated at a glance and formed the basis of the identification. Some insight into the degree of determination on the killer's part to destroy the identity of his victims, and the consequent problems this raised for the pathologists, can be gauged by the mutilation of one of the heads alone:

Head No. 1: The head had been severed from the trunk immediately below the level of the chin, and had been much mutilated by removal of the skin and underlying tissues. The nose and both ears had been cut off, and both eyes removed. A large piece of the scalp was missing from the right side of the head, and most of the skin of the forehead and face had been removed. The lips had been almost entirely cut away, the two upper central incisor teeth had been drawn, and the tongue protruded slightly in the gap. Some skin remained on each cheek, down to the chin and below it . . .

Furthermore, the neat job that had been made of the dismemberment using only a surgical knife, clearly indicated a degree of anatomical knowledge. The removal of other parts of the bodies which would have more accurately revealed the cause of death suggested that the murderer was also in possession of extensive medical knowledge. Nevertheless, when news of the disappearance of Isabella Ruxton and Mary Jane Rogerson as communicated to Edinburgh along with their descriptions, it was possible to build convincing comparisons with Body No. 1 and Body No. 2 (see table on pp. 156–157).

Early in the examination it had been observed that Head No. 1 and Head No. 2 were markedly different in size and shape. Known photographic portraits of the two missing Lancaster women indicated that Head No. 1 could not be Mrs Ruxton, and Head No. 2 could not be Mary Rogerson. The 'positive' identification was achieved by means of a photographic comparison of the skulls with the portraits – a technique never before used in criminal investigation.

Two photographs of each of the women were used – a studio portrait of Mrs Ruxton (called Portrait A) and a snapshot showing the left-side view of the same woman (Portrait B). Of Mary Rogerson only two photographs could be found (Portraits C and D), both taken by an amateur and consequently losing some clarity of detail when enlarged to life-size. Then the two skulls, by now cleaned of their remaining tissue, were each photographed from four angles, matching as closely as possible the positions of the heads in the portraits. From the life-size prints of the skulls and the portraits, distinctive shapes and features were traced in ink on transparent paper; subsequent superimposition revealed that Portraits A and B (Mrs Ruxton) fitted well over the outline of Skull No. 2; similarly, Portraits C and D (Mary Rogerson) were found to fit Skull No. 1. Further elaborate photographic techniques were employed to provide the positive and negative images from the skulls and portraits which, when superimposed, also showed remarkable consistency. It should, however, be emphasized that impressive though this evidence was, it was not *conclusive* in the sense required by the court – indeed, defence counsel objected to the admission of the photographs at all, on the grounds that they were constructed evidence, so liable to error'.

	Mary Jane Rogerson	Body No. 1 – Female
Age	Twenty years (8 October) 1935).	Certainly between 18 and 25. Probably between 20 and 21
Stature	About 5ft.	4ft. 10in. to 4ft. 11½in. (without shoes)
Hair	Light brown.	Hair from scalp and body light brown.
Eyes	Blue. 'Gilde' in one.	Removed.
Complexion	Light. Freckles on nose cheeks.	Ears, nose, lips and most of skin on face removed; complexion of remainder of skin consistent.
Teeth	Old extraction of six teeth, four of them named.	Old extraction or loss of eight teeth, including the four named.
Neck	Short neck.	Very small larynx very highly situated.
Tonsils	Subject to tonsillitis.	Microscopic evidence consistent with recurrent tonsillitis.
Vaccination Marks	Four on left upper arm.	Four on left upper arm.
Fingernails	Maidservant.	Trimmed but not regularly manicured; scratches indicating some form of manual work.
Scars	1. Abdominal scar – appendix operation. 2. Operation for septic thumb which had left a mark.	1. Trunk missing 2. First segment of right thumb denuded of tissue; no scar on left thumb.
Identifying Peculiarity	Birth marks (red patches) on right forearm near elbow.	Skin and soft tissues removed from upper third of forearm, and lower two-thirds of front only.
Size and Shape of Feet	Left shoe as evidence.	Cast of left foot fitted shoe.
Form of Head and Face	Two photographs in different positions.	Outlines of photographs of skull in same positions fitted.
Fingerprints	Numerous imprints from house at 2 Dalton Square.	Positively identified as the finger-prints of both hands and palmar impressions of left hand.
Breasts	Age 20, unmarried.	Single breast, appearance and structure consistent.

	Isabella Ruxton	*Body No. 2 – Female*
Age	34 years 7 months (3 October 1935).	Certainly between 30 and 55. Probably between 35 and 45
Stature	About 5ft. 5in. to 5ft. 6in.	5ft. 3½in. (without shoes)
Hair	Soft texture, mid-brown with patch of grey slightly to right of top of head.	Scalp completely removed; a few adherent hairs to medium brown. Eyelashes dark brown. Available body hair mid-brown.
Eyes	Deep-set; grey-blue.	Removed.
Complexion	Fair.	Ears, nose, lips and skin on face removed.
Teeth	Denture replacing three named teeth in gap which would show during life; old extraction of one other named tooth.	Old extraction or loss of fifteen teeth, including the four named.
Fingers and Nails	Long fingers. Recognizable nails – bevelled, brittle, growing tight at corners, rounded at ends, regularly manicured.	Terminal segments of all fingers removed.
Legs and Ankles	Thick ankles. Legs of same thickness from knees to ankles.	Soft tissued removed from legs.
Left Foot	Inflamed bunion of left big toe.	Hallux valgus of left foot; tissues removed over metatarso-phalangeal joint down to bone and joint opened. X-rays showed exotosis of head of metatarsal.
Size and Shape of Feet	Left shoe as evidence.	Cast of left foot fitted shoe.
Nose	Bridge uneven.	Removed, but bone and cartilage arched.
Form of Head and Face	High forehead, high cheekbones, rather long jaw. Two photographs in different positions.	Corresponding features. Outlines of photographs of skull in same positions fitted.
Breasts	Pendulous breasts: three children.	Appearance and structure of pair of breasts consistent.
Uterus	Three children	Separate uterus. Could not be assigned but structure consistent.

Ascertaining cause of death presented predictable problems. In Body No. 1 (thought to be Mary Rogerson), the neck and trunk with its internal organs were never recovered, making cause of death impossible to establish, though swelling of the tongue was consistent with asphyxia. Body No. 2 (thought to be Mrs Ruxton) exhibited a congested state of the lungs and brain which, associated with the damaged condition of the hyoid bone in the throat indicated manual strangulation.

Establishing the time of death became the responsibility of Dr Alexander Mearns of the Institute of Hygiene at the University of Glasgow. In what was a pioneering piece of medical detection, Mearns was able, by studying the life cycle of the maggots that infested the remains in the Linn, to establish that the victims were killed at about the time Mrs Ruxton and Mary Rogerson were last seen alive (see **Insect Infestation of Corpses**).

Ruxton's trial opened at the High Court of Justice, Manchester, on Monday, 2 March 1936, before Mr Justice Singleton. Defending Ruxton was one of the greatest criminal advocates of his day, Mr Norman (later Lord) Birkett KC.

The proposition that was to be put so convincingly to the jury over the next eleven days was outlined by Mr J.C. Jackson KC, in his opening speech:

Now, it does not need much imagination to suggest what probably happened in that house. It is very probable that Mary Rogerson was a witness to the murder of Mrs Ruxton, and that is why she met her death. In that house the bedrooms are on the top floor; the back bedroom was occupied by Mary Rogerson, in one of the front slept Mrs Ruxton with her three children, and on the same floor was also the doctor's room. You will hear that Mrs Ruxton had received before her death violent blows in the face and that she was strangled. The suggestion of the prosecution is that her death and that of the girl Mary took place outside these rooms on the landing at the top of the staircase, outside the maid's bedroom, because from that point down the staircase right into the bathroom there are trails of enormous quantities of blood. I suggest that when she went up to bed a violent quarrel took place; that he strangled his wife, and that Mary Rogerson caught him in the act and so had to die also. Mary's skull was fractured: she had some blows on the top of the head which would render her unconscious, and then was killed by some other means, probably a knife, because of all the blood that was found down these stairs . . .

As had been expected, the medical evidence was presented with the same skill as that with which it had been gathered, and a faultless rendition of his findings by Professor John Glaister earned him this accolade from the judge:

No one could sit in this court and listen to the evidence of Professor Glaister, either in examination-in-chief or in cross-examination, without feeling that there is a man that is not only master of his profession, but who is scrupulously fair, and most anxious that his opinion, however strongly he may hold it, shall not be put unduly against the person on his trial.

It was nevertheless this unassailable scientific testimony that weighed so heavily against Ruxton, and there was very little that his counsel could do to shake the foundations of the prosecution case. In fairness, though, it must be emphasized that Norman Birkett's courageous championship of his client was nothing short of what might have been expected from so eminent a defender, and his attention to detail, to any hint in favour of his client, was untiring.

In the absence of any credible witnesses on the prisoner's behalf, Dr Ruxton himself stood sole testimony to his innocence. On the whole he displayed himself rather badly, being prone to outbursts of hysterical sobbing, and rambling, illogical accounts of his own behaviour, and his refusal to acknowledge the truth of even the clearest evidence in as much as it might incriminate him did much to emphasize the impression of a guilty man bluffing.

In accordance with British legal tradition, Norman Birkett, by calling Ruxton to the stand, had entitled himself to make his closing speech for the defence after the prosecution address instead of before it – in this way his words would be the last the jury would hear before his Lordship's summing-up:

It seems scarcely necessary to have to say to you that if you are satisfied of the fact that in the ravine on that day were those two bodies, identified beyond the shadow of a doubt, it does not prove this case. If, for example, the word of the prisoner was true, 'They left my house,' there is an end of the case. Even though their bodies were found in a ravine, dismembered, and even though those were the bodies, this does not prove the case against the prisoner. The Crown must prove the fact of murder, and you may have observed how much of this case has been mere conjecture. It is not for the defence to prove innocence; it is for the Crown to prove guilt, and it is the duty of the defence to propound a theory which would be satisfactory to your collective mind . . .

It is never incumbent upon the prosecution in a charge of murder to prove motive, but they say, 'We will show you the motive; here it is – jealousy because of infidelity.' I ask you to accept with the greatest reserve evidence spoken after the event, such as that which has been given in this court from the servants and others . . . The doctor is arrested for murder, and how it colours the mind. This is clear, and I do not seek to deny it, that there were intervals and periods of the greatest possible unhappiness. You will remember that phrase employed by Dr Ruxton, a phrase so revealing and so powerful – 'We were the kind of people who could neither live with each other, nor live without each other.' Unhappiness was no new thing . . . The Crown said this was a record of marital unhappiness, grievous quarrels; she had left him and under the persuasion of her sister had returned, and there in that family was this canker, this jealousy, and so he would kill her. I suggest to you it is fantastical, and to suggest that was the motive and that was the occasion is, in my submission, not to strengthen this case in any particular but on the contrary to weaken it. For years that unhappiness has subsisted, and there was nothing revealed to you upon the evidence which on that occasion should prompt him to do that which the Crown lay at his charge.

After an impeccably painstaking and impartial summing-up, the jury required just a little more than one hour to return a verdict of guilty against Buck Ruxton. An appeal was, of course, lodged on Ruxton's behalf, and heard before the Lord Chief Justice Lord Hewart, Mr Justice du Parcq and Mr Justice Goddard. Their Lordships, rightly, dismissed the appeal and Ruxton was left to face the hangman on 12 May 1936, at Strangeways Prison, Manchester.

There remains a curious postscript to the Ruxton case. On the Sunday following his death, a popular newspaper published what purported to be a sealed confession written by Dr Ruxton and left with instructions that it should be opened in the event of his execution.

However, in a letter received from his client by Mr Norman Birkett on the morning of the execution, Ruxton thanks his counsel for the efforts made to save his life, and concludes: 'I know that in a few hours I shall be going to meet my Maker. But I say to you, sir, I am entirely innocent of this crime.'

DISPUTED DOCUMENTS
Introduction

At its simplest, document analysis is one of the oldest of the forensic sciences; as far back as classical Rome the law made provision for evidence of handwriting comparison to be given in court. Indeed, there were handwriting experts whose testimony was regarded with the same credibility as today's document analyst. Curiously, the English were very backward in accepting handwriting evidence, and it was only in the nineteenth century with the development of what were regarded as more 'reliable', scientific methods of identification that it became adopted. In the United States the debate really opened at the turn of the century when courts began to make individual rulings, and by 1913 Congress had enacted a statute which read, in part: 'In any proceeding before a court or judicial officer of the United States where the genuineness of the handwriting of any person may be involved, any admitted or proved handwriting of such person shall be competent evidence as a basis for comparison by witnesses, or by the jury, court or officer conducting such proceeding, to prove or disprove such genuineness.' Since then, document analysis procedures have kept pace with science, and their practitioners are seen as contributing to the wider issue of forensic investigation.

For the purpose of this brief overview, a convenient definition of 'document' is something that contains *information* and is usually made of paper. In document examination the information contained occurs on two levels:

1. *The superficial level:* Where the document's information, or message, is expressed by such means as handwriting, typewriting or printing; and
2. *The hidden level:* Where the less obvious information can be found – evidence of fraud or forgery for example.

It is with the second level of inquiry that the document examiner is concerned. This information will be of vital importance first to the police investigators and subsequently, perhaps, in a court of law. Like other branches of the forensic sciences, document examination depends on identification and comparison.

The Love of Money . . .

Apart from carrying sufficient funds to make small purchases, most people in the modern developed world have all but eliminated the need for currency. The transfer of money between individuals, between individuals and institutions, and between institutions is now carried out by a wide range of transactions that transfer *figures* from one place to another. Cheques, credit and charge cards are today's main means of purchase, and few individuals do not rely on this means of transaction. The only means of identification normally required is a signature. Every time a cheque is written, a charge card used, the owner signs his name for comparison with the 'control' signature on his card. Not surprisingly the versatile forger has become responsible for frauds amounting to millions of pounds every year. The most common frauds are committed with cheques, closely followed by credit cards.

The fundamental principles of detecting frauds in these cases is common to all document examination – a comparison of the suspect, or 'disputed' document, with a known specimen of a person's signature/ handwriting. And for this reason, particular emphasis is placed on examination of handwriting.

Handwriting Analysis

An individual's handwriting depends for its character upon the inter-action of brain, eye and hand. It is affected by a person's physical and emotional well-being, the position in which he is writing, and circum-stances which might control speed. So in fact a person may have several handwritings, several signatures (indeed, two identical signatures could look suspicious!).

That said, there is, underlying these superficial deviations, an individual style which can be identified even though a person is *trying* to disguise his hand; the ways in which letters are started or ended for example, or the individual shapes such as whether or not the round letters like 'o' and 'a' are closed, the angle of the writing, its relation-ship to an imaginary straight line across the page, etc. The process of analysis and comparison is a long and painstaking one, and too complex to be encapsulated here.

In the matter of signatures, there is a basic technique which will indicate whether or not it has been forged.* Remember, no two signatures are *exactly* identical so it is useful for the analyst to have as many known examples of the *genuine* signature as possible for comparison – say, driving licence, marriage licence, etc.

Top-of-the-Letter Comparison
A tracing sheet is placed over the suspect signature (a photocopy should be used to avoid handling original evidence which may be required for fingerprint checks, etc.) and a small mark made at the highest point of the letters above an imaginary base line on which the signature sits. Each mark is then joined to the next, which will present a zig-zag line across the signature. The process is repeated for each of the known genuine signatures and the results compared.

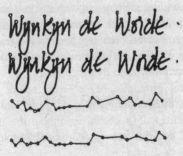

Bottom-of-the-Letter Comparison
This time the tracing paper is marked with a dot at the *bottom* of each letter, and the results compared as above.

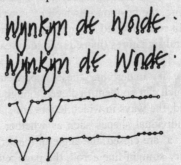

*Described in *Cross-check System for Forgery*, Doris Williamson, 1981.

Spaces

The procedure is repeated for each of the signature's spaces, both between words and, if there are any, between letters.

Slant Comparison

For this stage, the tracing paper is put over the suspect signature and an oblique line drawn through each of the letters that are *above* the base line. The lines are compared when this process has been repeated on the genuine signatures. Finally, the slants of the letters *below* the base line (the descenders) are plotted.

Further distinctive similarities and differences of letters will be noted for the final detailed report, but this simple procedure will give an almost immediate response to the fundamental question: Is the signature under consideration genuine or false?

Typewriting Comparison

Over the past one hundred years the typewriter has undergone many changes as manufacturers have absorbed new technology, and with the speed at which the miniaturization of computers and word processors is proceeding, lap-top electronics could make the old manual typewriter a machine of the past. For the moment, though, there are sufficient numbers of 'traditional' typewriters in use – albeit most of them at least electric, if not electronic – for the acquired knowledge of typewriting analysis and comparison to remain valid.

Typeface

Although adjustments and refinements have been made over the years, the general design of what we know as the 'typewriter' style of letters has remained fairly standard – its most noticeable difference from printing type being that with a typewriter all the characters are the same width. Of course, each manufacturer will have small variations, and within a single manufacturer's range of typewriters there may be differences of face. Some of the most common alternatives are the numbers 3 (with either a flat or curved top), 4 (with an open or closed triangle), the letters M and W (the centre point extending either the whole depth of the letter or only half-way), the cross-bar on the t, etc. Less common typewriter faces are available without serifs (sans serif) or in script.

Modern machines of a certain type print from a single moulded element – the familiar 'golf-ball' or 'daisy wheel'. With these, it is possible to interchange the elements which are available in a wide range of typefaces, sizes and weights. The printers attached to computers and word processors are often so sophisticated that they are able to produce *illustrations* as well as a vast range of existing and custom-created typefaces.

It is always useful to be able to identify the model of a typewriter responsible for 'writing' a particular document, as it will narrow the field when the original machine is being looked for. This information may also help to prove or disprove the supposed date of a typed document – for example, if it is a letter dated 27 July 1927, and the machine on which it was typed was not in production until 1937, then it is clearly very suspicious.

Most forensic laboratories with an active documents department will have access to specimens of most makes of typewriter, and in Britain there is available a computer-based sorting method that can be used from terminals nationwide. Interpol (International Criminal Police Organisation) has a vast card-based system in which the type styles are classified according to letter spacing and key features of numerals and letters.

Individual Comparisons

The most important evidence that can be deduced from a typewritten document, in the forensic sense, is which individual machine it was written on. This information may prove vital in cases where, for example, a kidnap ransom note or extortion letter has been typed.

In one of the most celebrated cases in American legal history, two young men, Nathan Leopold and Richard Loeb, the sons of wealthy Chicago families, kidnapped and murdered a fellow-student just to see whether it was possible to commit the perfect murder. As it turned out it was a most imperfect murder, for not only had Nathan Leopold left his spectacles on the ground where they dumped the body of Bobby Franks, but the ransom note sent to Bobby's millionaire father was typed on Leopold's typewriter. The killers were tried and convicted in 1924, and only an impassioned plea by the famous defence attorney Clarence Darrow saved them from the death penalty.

Although typewriters leaving the factory will to some degree carry minor imperfections, such as in the casting of the letters, or the fine alignment, by far the greater number of identifying 'fingerprints' will be imposed on a machine during its working life. The letters can become chipped and unevenly worn, alignments can be disturbed by frequent or heavy use causing a slant backwards or forwards, or at an angle, or it may produce an uneven printed image. The 'shift' key could become worn or damaged so that capital letters no longer align with the lower case.

Electric machines are prone to similar distinctive wear and tear, and in addition the pressure adjustments for some of the letters may become faulty and the characters consistently print more heavily or lightly.

Despite their more compact design, type-balls, or 'golf-balls', are liable to have letters chip, and the mechanism which rotates the ball can become slightly misaligned producing a characteristic unevenness of pressure or of alignment. The same is true of 'daisy wheels'.

The method of making a comparison is similar to comparing

handwriting. Typescript presented as evidence is matched against a control sample typed on the suspect machine and similarities (or differences) noted.

Where much finer comparison is required – for example, in the case of a new machine with no wear-and-tear features – it is possible to check the vertical and horizontal alignment of the letters with a sheet of clear plastic specially calibrated with a grid to match the line and letter spacing of a particular model of typewriter. When the grid is placed over a sample of typewriting, each letter should, in theory, be centrally placed in a small box. Very slight misalignments can thereby be checked and compared.

The Comparison Projector

This apparatus works, in effect, like a comparison microscope. Two documents are projected on to a screen (the degree of enlargement is largely a matter of choice) and can either be superimposed so that a check can be made for similarities and differences, or the documents can be flashed alternately so that they can be viewed in the same frame in quick succession. Obvious damage to the letters adequately identified with the naked eye will simply appear larger, but it is possible to locate and compare quite small imperfections and fine misalignments when the images are enlarged.

Carbon Papers and Ribbon

Mention must be made of the almost Sherlockian ruses employed to re-create a missing document. If carbon paper has been used to make a copy, the reversed image of the letter typed through it can be clearly seen and, viewed obliquely to the light in a mirror, read.

To give a clear, sharp image many modern typewriters take a one-use carbon ribbon. The plastic film carrier strip is coated with carbon and as each key is struck it transfers the character on to the paper before moving on. As each section of ribbon is used only once it is possible by unwinding it and writing down all the characters that have been punched out of the carbon, to re-create the document letter by letter.

Indented Writing

If one sheet of paper is directly under another being written on it will pick up an impression of the writing. Legibility will depend upon the thickness of the paper, whether the sheets were on a hard or soft surface, and the degree of pressure exerted by the writer. The significance of this effect is obvious in cases where an indented sheet is found which can be matched with a threatening letter, an attempt at blackmail or a ransom note. Another occasion on which indented impressions can disclose vital information to the document examiner is when pages have been torn from a book – a diary, say, or an accounts book.

Case Study

WILLIAM HENRY PODMORE

Although he had been missing since October the previous year, it was not until the morning of 10 January 1929, that the body of fifty-seven-year-old Vivian Messiter was found in a badly decomposed state at the Southampton depot of the Wolf's Head Oil Company. Messiter, the firm's local agent and a recently appointed director, appeared to have been shot through the head; in fact, it was not for some time that it was realized that the victim had been bludgeoned to death with a hammer which had pierced the skull giving the appearance of a bullet entry wound. Messiter had been robbed, but his business records had been left to provide the clue that eventually led to his killer.

Among the papers a receipt book was found from which the first nine pages had been torn leaving it blank; however, on the tenth page a blind impression was clearly visible of the writing on the previous receipt – 28 October 1928. Received from Wolf's Head Oil Company commission on Cromer and Bartlett, 5 gals at $6d = 2/6d$ W.F. Thomas.' Routine investigation showed that the firm against which the receipt had been issued was non-existent and the inevitable conclusion was that somebody was claiming commission on bogus sales. The signature on the receipt, 'W.F. Thomas', was compared with a letter signed 'William F. Thomas' found at Vivian Messiter's lodgings; it was an application for a job as a salesman with Wolf's Head. 'Thomas', predictably, had long since moved from the address on the letter and had been responsible for a further embezzlement in the Southampton area before transferring his attention to London where he was later arrested; one piece of information was forthcoming – Mr William Thomas was in reality Mr William Henry Podmore, a crook from Manchester in which city he was wanted for a number of car and motorcycle frauds.

While police in Southampton were hard at work establishing Podmore's link with the Messiter murder, their Midlands colleagues obligingly kept him safely under lock and key for the Manchester jobs.

On his release from Wandsworth Prison on 17 December 1929, he was immediately rearrested and charged with murder; later the same month William Podmore appeared at the Winchester Assizes. Despite a spirited insistence on his own innocence the case against Podmore was by now watertight – the fact of his dishonesty in charging Messiter commission on sales that he had not made was demonstrated to the court by means of photographs taken at an angle to the light which revealed the writing in the receipt book (a more sophisticated modern variation on this technique is Electrostatic imaging – see below). On top of this, two of Podmore's fellow-prisoners in Wandsworth gave evidence that he had confessed the murder to them. William Podmore was convicted by the jury and sentenced to death; he was hanged on 22 April 1930, aged twenty-nine.

More recently, in England, a particularly sinister spate of discoveries has centred around the misconduct of certain police officers who appear to have been involved in the manipulation of written statements with the result that a number of innocent people have been wrongly imprisoned. Subsequent examination of the statements using the ESDA process (see below) proved from the impressions that the order of pages had been changed and that other passages had been written at different times to those claimed.

Revealing Impressions

The simplest method of 'reading' impressions is to hold the sheet of paper in question at an oblique angle to a light source, which produces shadows in the depressions making them clearer. The document can be photographed in this light to create a permanent record.

Electrostatic Detection Apparatus (ESDA)

This machine, manufactured by the Foster and Freeman company of Worcestershire, England, is based on the curious and inexplicable phenomenon that impressions on a sheet of paper alter its dielectric properties. If an electrical current is applied to the surface, a different potential is created at the impressions but not on the surrounding area.

The apparatus comprises a flat bed made from the porous metal sintered bronze, below which is a vacuum suction, and above which runs a reel of transparent plastic called Mylar. A separate moveable box called a corona discharge unit has a thin wire stretched along its length capable of being charged to about eight kilovolts. The document is placed on the electrically earthed bed of the apparatus, covered with Mylar, and the resulting 'sandwich' held to the bed by vacuum suction. The corona discharge unit is switched on and passed over the Mylar several times, imparting an electrostatic charge. The bed of the ESDA is now tilted at an angle and a mixture of photocopy toner and fine glass beads is sprinkled over the surface. The greater potential created at the site of the impressions attracts the black toner. This enables the impressed images to be read with greater or lesser ease depending upon the depth of the indentation. ESDA has been used with success in cases where impressions were not visible to the eye.

One caution is that although the technique will still work several years after the first writing, treatment with any solvent will negate the effect. The test must consequently be carried out *before* any treatment to reveal latent fingerprints.

A method similar in principle to ESDA is the Electrostatic Mat used to enhance otherwise weak and incomplete **Shoe-Prints**.

Charred Documents

Whether the condition was caused by accident or malicious intent, one of the most difficult tasks for the document laboratory is handling charred paper. Often, however, with sufficient care and specialized treatment, the most unpromising debris can be 'read'. The care must start at the scene of the 'crime' – which may be a fire, or simply documents burned as part of a connected crime – embezzlement perhaps. After photographing at the scene, the charred remains must be handled with great care. They will frequently be fragile, twisted and warped, and can crumble with any attempt at flattening. Successful stabilization of charred paper has been achieved by spraying a three per cent solution of polyvinyl acetate in acetone which allows the sheet to be gently flattened and hand-delivered to the laboratory in a cotton-wool lined box.

Of the several methods of recovering information from charred papers, the simplest is to float the sheets in a large open dish containing either chloral hydrate (25 per cent) plus glycerin (10 per cent) in an alcohol solution, or glycerin (30 per cent) plus water (20 per cent) in 50 per cent alcohol solution. The evidence can then be photographed – either in black and white, or infra-red, and careful attention to lighting will reveal the original writing.

The most remarkable, and so it is claimed infallible, method of deciphering charred documents is to sandwich the sheet tightly between two unexposed photographic plates and place them in a lightproof container for about fifteen days. The plates are then developed in the normal way, producing negatives from which clear photographic prints can be made of the document 'as though it had never suffered burning'.

Inks and Paper

This section would become unnecessarily obscure if it included a history of inks and papermaking, but the following notes relate to their forensic importance.

Inks

There are four main types of 'modern' ink:

Ball-point ink: The early ball-point pens (they were first marketed in 1945) contained ink with an olein base with oil and soluble dye. The modern equivalent is polyethylene glycol with soluble synthetic dyes or insoluble pigments; the ink is about forty-five per cent dye, the rest solvent and additives.

Iron inks: Contain iron salts, dye material, gallic and tannic acid.

Carbon-black ink: Called Indian ink, a suspension of carbon in gum-arabic.

Dyestuff ink: These are the coloured inks generally labelled 'non-permanent'. They contain aniline (synthetic) dyes, gum-arabic, glycol, polyethylene, and sulphuric or hydrochloric acid.

There is a variety of laboratory techniques suitable for the analysis of ink samples, the most notable of which, when the possibilities of microscopic examination have been exhausted, are thin-layer **Chromatography**, **Spectrometry**, and ultraviolet/infra-red photography. For comparison purposes, the United States Bureau of Alcohol, Tobacco and Firearms has a reference collection of more than 3,000 ink chromatograms, and to overcome the impossibility of accurate dating of inks has suggested that manufacturers include a trace dye which is changed annually.

Paper

The bulk of the world's paper is now made from wood-pulp, though special papers still use linen and cotton, and various vegetable fibres. There are special additives to security papers (used, for example, in the printing of currency) which make forgeries easier to detect. A world price rise in the natural raw materials of paper, coupled with greater ecological awareness, has resulted in the development of a number of synthetic fibres for paper production. Fibres, whether natural or synthetic, are frequently 'filled' with a fine mineral chalk to give the paper greater opacity, less absorbency and more bulk. For fine colour printing the 'whiteness' can be enhanced by the addition of optical brighteners such as fluorocarbons. In addition, the surface of the paper may be treated by heat rolling, sizing, starching, or with synthetic resins.

All these separate distinctive products and processes combine to endow paper with, if not a 'fingerprint', then at least a set of reference standards to help in comparison. This analysis of 'type' will be the essential first step in deciding whether a document is genuine or whether it is a forgery. One would not, after all, expect to find a first folio of Shakespeare printed on synthetic paper, any more than one would trust one of the Bard's letters written with ball-point ink. Microscopic examination of the paper fibres will reveal information about the type of tree from which it was pulped and, as paper frequently uses more than one type of wood in its production, the area of similarities narrows.

Watermarks

Watermark patterns are moulded into the continuous roll of paper (or single sheet) during manufacture, and for centuries have identified the mill from which the paper originates as well as its type, or 'brand'. Watermarks change over the years, and even within the same type of paper from the same mill some type of rudimentary dating can be achieved by comparison with reference collections. Because it is put into the paper at an integral stage in its manufacture, the watermark is impossible to reproduce exactly. Attempts to rub through a stencil to remove the top layer of fibres are apparent even under low magnification, and fake marks 'printed' in oil from a woodcut can be distinguished from the original because the edges of the design are sharper. One method which can mislead the unwary is the technique of pressing damp paper between two plates, one bearing the raised design of the watermark. This has the effect of compressing the paper fibres beneath the area of the design giving a good likeness of an original. However, under magnification it can be seen as *compressed paper*, whereas the original mark is there because there are *fewer fibres* where the mark is.

DNA PROFILING

Background

Perhaps the most potentially important discovery in the recent scientific history of forensics has been the development of DNA profiling. There already exist biological tests which, although advanced to a high degree, have distinct disadvantages by comparison with DNA profiling for the same requirements. Blood grouping, for example, can exclude a putative father in a paternity dispute, but it cannot positively *prove* paternity. Immunological techniques are widely used in the forensic sciences – notably to identify the components of blood and the specific origin of tissue samples. With both these techniques problems can arise if the samples are old, impure, or insufficient in quantity for accurate analysis. These difficulties can be overcome with the use of DNA as the basic sample – it is so stable that DNA has been extracted from mummies millennia old. It is the basic unit of the human body, each individual's DNA is unique, and only minute samples are required for analysis.

It was in 1984 that Professor Alec Jeffreys, FRS, a Research Fellow at the Lister Institute, Leicester University, achieved the breakthrough that made DNA a practical tool to identify positively any individual from the minutest body trace. Professor Jeffreys discovered that within the DNA molecule a particular sequence of information exists which varies greatly in unrelated individuals. These sequences can be 'visualized' in the laboratory as prints from X-ray film which are as unique to an individual as a conventional fingerprint – hence the colloquial term 'DNA finger-printing'. A UK patent was granted in 1987, and through a commercial agreement with the Lister Institute, a branch of ICI – Cellmark Diagnostics – hold exclusive rights to the technology.

Technique

Every human cell contains within it all the information required to create a whole human body – in other words, the 'blueprint for life'. This information is carried in the chromosomes. Chromosomes are found in the nuclei of all human cells; each nucleus contains coded information in the form of DNA (deoxyribonucleic acid) arranged into groups called genes. These in turn are arranged on entwined strands of DNA which are chromosomes. The four building blocks, called 'bases', which make up DNA are Adenine, Cytosine, Guanine and Thymine – known by their initial letters ACGT.

The ribbon of DNA has been compared to a zip fastener with the bases ACGT forming the teeth. The difference is that in order to join the two strands of DNA, A must pair with T, and G must pair with C. (See illustration below.)

There are an enormous number of these bases in a chromosome, though as far as can be determined only about forty-five per cent are required for cell operation – the function of the remaining fifty-five per cent is not yet known.

The forty-five per cent functional units are distributed throughout the length of the chromosome, interspersed with the unexplained fifty-five per cent. Along the length at random intervals bases in certain combinations of six occur and are called 'restriction sites'; the sites are palindromic, that is, the order of bases on the top strand is the exact reverse of the order of bases on the bottom strand:

A   A   G   C   T   T
T   T   C   G   A   A

Natural defence systems known as 'restriction enzymes' can be found in certain bacteria and they are capable of recognizing and cutting DNA at its palindromic sequences. The fragments are then separated from each other by gel electrophoresis. The technique is basically this: the DNA sample is put in a slit at one end of a 10 × 14 × 0.5cm block of gel; a high-voltage electrical current is applied across the gel causing the DNA fragments to move through it, the distance each fragment moves being determined by its size. The separated fragments can be lifted from the gel on to a nylon membrane, rather as blotting paper will lift ink (in fact, the process is known as 'Southern blotting' after its inventor, Professor Ed Southern). It should be added that at this stage the characteristic 'bands' are invisible to the eye.

Besides the palindromic restriction sites the chromosome chain also has sections along its length where base sequences are repeated again and again; it is this feature which allows the DNA fragments to match and rejoin. The membrane is incubated overnight with what is called a radioactive 'probe' – a solution consisting of fragments of DNA containing repeated sequences which have been 'labelled' with radioactivity so that they can be detected by matching repeat sequences on the membrane which will unite, or 'hybridize', with them. For example, if the membrane contains a strand with the sequence AGCCTGCTCTTA and the probe a complementary sequence TCGGACGAGAAT they will bind to form a double strand.

The next stage is to wash the membrane clean of any unbound probe material and place it in contact with X-ray film. The radioactivity of the sections where the probe has bound to the DNA will produce dark bands on the film. The X-ray film is printed out revealing a pattern of bands not unlike supermarket bar-codes, and with the exception of genetically identical twins every individual has a unique pattern.

Keeping It in the Family

Although the news concerning this remarkable discovery has tended to centre around the more spectacular cases of trapping killers and rapists, by far the greatest number of tests is conducted routinely to establish the identity of a father in a paternity dispute, and to prove or disprove family links in applications for immigration.

A child inherits half its chromosomes (and hence DNA) from each of its parents. In cases of disputed paternity DNA fingerprints are obtained from the mother, the child and the two (or more) putative fathers. Each band on the child's chart must match one on either its mother's or its father's chart; so by lining up all four charts it is possible to identify the father absolutely.

This could have serious repercussions for fathers attempting to avoid supporting their illegitimate children by denying paternity. In June 1991 for the first time, an English judge ordered a man whose blood-test was inconclusive (it determined only that he could not be excluded) to submit to DNA profiling.

Criminal Matters

The application of DNA profiling to criminal investigations has revolutionized the whole concept of 'positive identification'. For example, a blood or semen stain found at the scene of a crime – even if it is minute in size and of considerable age – can be analysed and a DNA profile obtained. In due course this can be compared with the DNA profile derived from a suspect or suspects. The importance of the technique lies in its certainty – either the profiles match and the suspect is guilty, or they do not and he can be eliminated from the police inquiry.*

*An anomaly of the British legal system at present under investigation by the Royal Commission on Criminal Justice is that a suspect can legally refuse to give a sample of his blood if he feels disinclined. It has been pointed out that alleged drink-drivers *are* obliged to give samples, but alleged murderers and rapists are not. It is expected that the Commission will ask for police to be given powers to ask a court to demand a sample, with heavy penalties for defiance of the order.

Recent Advances

The technique of DNA profiling has advanced so rapidly since its discovery that profiles can be obtained from *any* sample of human tissue – in June 1989 a rapist was convicted in St Albans Crown Court on the evidence of a DNA profile derived from one of his hairs.

This is not to say that the brief history of genetic profiling has been a one hundred per cent success. It has, like all new techniques, been subject to a number of shortcomings – not least the length of time that it takes to derive a conventional profile (up to six weeks). However, in 1991, Doctor (later Sir) Alec Jeffreys announced another major break-through: digital DNA profiling. This more efficient use of computers in analysing and categorizing DNA samples cut the time it took to process a DNA profile to just two days.

Subsequent breakthroughs – including the further enhancement of computer techniques and the completion of the Genome Project (the precise mapping of the entire human DNA double-helix) – have meant that criminals will soon have to wear sealed environment suits if they wish to avoid all possibility of DNA identification at the scene of the crime. Police forces around the world are enthusiastically building-up DNA profile indexes, just as their forbears did with early fingerprint evidence.

Calls for a **Universal Index** – in which every citizen's DNA profile is stored – have so far been blocked by understandable fears over damage to civil liberties. Yet, given the enormous potential of DNA identification – the virtually automatic capture of rapists, for example – the probability of a universal index some time in the future seems undeniable.

DOCUMENTS
(see Disputed Documents)

DRINK/DRIVING
(see Alcohol)

DROWNING

Death by drowning is by no means as rare as one might think – though few such deaths are the result of homicidal foul-play. The majority occur in connection with shipping and boating accidents, or to small children falling into rivers and ponds while at play; drunks falling into water also account for a number of incidents every year.

Drowning is one of the kinds of death by **Asphyxia**, and results from a combination of the effects of water on the blood, and when air is prevented from entering the air passages and lungs by water. It can be stated with certainty that although the severity of the post-mortem signs of anoxia will depend on how much the victim struggled while in the water, if *no* signs of anoxia are present then cause of death was *not* drowning, even though the body was taken from the water.

Finally, it is not necessary for the body, or even the whole head, to be submerged; it requires only the mouth and nostrils to be under water for anoxia to result – it has been recorded more than once that an intoxicated person has fallen and drowned in a puddle only inches deep.

The Process of Drowning

In a typical case, the victim will begin to panic from the first ingestion of water into the air passages, and in the subsequent struggle will take enough water into the lungs to mix with the air and mucus to produce a choking froth. At the same time the lungs will become water-logged and heavy making it difficult to remain afloat. Struggling will cease for a short time before a final burst of convulsions leads to death.

There is the likelihood that if a person is suddenly and unexpectedly plunged into cold water cardiac inhibition will cause the condition known as 'reflex cardiac arrest', in which case the signs of *drowning* will not be present. Such sudden death may also be induced in people who are heavily intoxicated when they enter the water.

Post-Mortem Appearances

There are few external symptoms of drowning, the main one being the fine white foam created by the mixture of air, water and mucus, which appears at the nostrils and mouth. Other signs will be a wrinkling of the skin on the palms of the hands and soles of the feet (so-called 'washer-woman's hands') if the victim has been in the water for any length of time.

In cases of suspected drowning, the pathologist will look for the presence of objects such as stones and water-weeds which have been grabbed at during the pre-death struggle and become locked into the clenched hand by **Cadaveric Spasm** – a sure indication of death by drowning.

Autopsy will reveal the lungs pale and distended so that when the thoracic cavity is opened they will tend to 'balloon' out. Lungs will be wet and heavy so that pressure from a finger will leave a clear indentation. Trachea and bronchi will be found to contain foam, and so will the lungs when sectioned.

Water is usually present in the stomach and oesophagus, and may contain debris from its source – weeds, algae, etc.

In most true cases of drowning conspicuous haemorrhaging will be found in the middle ear caused, it is thought, by barometric pressure. The same effect cannot be found in cases of, for example, submersion resulting from reflex cardiac arrest.

Tests will be made to ascertain the presence of any factors which may have contributed to the drowning – not only disease and illness, but the presence of alcohol and drugs. One authority puts apparent domestic drownings in a bath which in reality resulted from drug overdoses as high as fifty per cent.

Although all injuries on the body must be carefully recorded and closely examined, their presence does not necessarily prove homicide. A body in water is prey to all manner of hazards – striking submerged rocks, being struck by boats, chewed by fish, and so on. Furthermore, the appearance of wounds can be misleading because of changes in the blood caused by water, making it difficult to ascertain with confidence whether injuries were received before or after death.

Finally, it must be borne in mind that many of the signs described above will be destroyed or masked as the body becomes putrefied (see entry on **Putrefaction** for a time-table of post-mortem changes in water).

Diatom Tests

When death is caused by drowning in 'natural' water such as lakes and rivers, the water entering the body will contain microscopic organisms called diatoms; while the blood is still circulating these diatoms will be distributed around the body, finding their way into the organs and even bone marrow. Thus if a body is already dead when it enters the water diatoms will not be found (with the exception of a few which may gravitate into the lungs). In order to isolate the diatoms, parts of the organs removed at autopsy are dissolved with strong mineral acid leaving the acid-resistant silica shells of the diatoms observable with a microscope.

The diatom phenomenon is of use in investigations where a body was found in a different location to where it was drowned. It has been recognized that diatoms can be identified with their area of origin with considerable accuracy due to the fact that any combination of the more than 15,000 species is likely to be unique.

Blood Tests

Specific-gravity tests will be made of the heart blood to confirm whether drowning occurred in fresh or salt water. Fresh water (rivers, canals, ponds, etc.) is termed *hypotonic* to plasma, and will enter the heart through the pulmonary capillaries and dilute the blood. As much as two litres can be absorbed in this way, at the same time reducing the concentration of chloride. Salt water is *hypertonic* and will have the effect of extracting water *from* the blood and increasing the chloride concentration. Blood tests should be carried out within twenty-four hours of death, before putrefaction begins to alter the chemistry of the blood.

DRUGS

Introduction

An inevitable consequence of the progress of medicine has been the development of natural and, more recently, chemical substances for the treatment of sickness and disease and the alleviation of pain. Many of the naturally occurring preparations have been known and valued for thousands of years. The juice of the white opium poppy, for example, was used as a pain-killer and soporific by the Sumerians more than six thousand years ago, and cannabis was used in China and Asia as early as 3000 BC.

But the capacity of drugs to alter the mental state of their user has been recognized for as long, and humankind throughout history has used substances of various kinds to induce a sense of euphoria and well-being both as part of religious ritual and for personal gratification; and has continued to do so until the present day. It should also be borne in mind in any discussion of the contemporary drug problem that until comparatively recently (that is, the late nineteenth century) **Opium** could be bought as easily as alcohol can today, and was used for many of the same reasons. A growing awareness of the problems of drug addiction finally led to some restrictions being imposed in the 1890s, and at the time of World War I opium and cocaine were made illegal lest their use should impair the ability of soldiers to carry out their duty.

It was not until the explosion of 'youth culture' during the decades of the 1950s and 1960s – both in the United States and Europe – that the widespread misuse of drugs became a fashionable problem. Young people were rebelling against the attitudes of authority, and along with revolutionary art, music and politics came experimentation with 'mind-expanding' hallucinogenic drugs such as cannabis and LSD. In Britain in 1964, the Dangerous Drugs Act made it illegal to grow cannabis, and two years later the Act was extended to include the manufacture and possession of LSD and mescaline. Against a seeming flood of new dependence problems the Misuse of Drugs Act, 1971, sought to classify drugs, according to their strength and potential danger, into three categories:

Class A: e.g. morphine, cocaine, heroin
Class B: e.g. amphetamines
Class C: e.g. cannabis, methaqualone

These relate to maximum penalties incurred for drug offences:

Class A: Life imprisonment for both trafficking and possession
Class B: 14 years for trafficking; 5 years for possession
Class C: 5 years for trafficking; 2 years for possession

International cooperation on the restriction of physically addictive drugs has resulted in the more recent Misuse of Drugs Regulations, 1985. These regulations impose additional classification of drugs into schedules:

Schedule 1: High potential for abuse. In the United States they have no currently accepted medical use; in Britain the drugs can only be used under special licence from the Home Office. Includes: cannabis, heroin, LSD, methaqualone.

Schedule 2: High potential for abuse. Medical use with severe restriction – in Britain may be administered only by doctors and dentists. Includes: opium (and opium derivatives not covered by Schedule 1), cocaine, methadone, most amphetamines, barbiturates containing amobarbital, secobarbital and pentobarbital. Phencycladine was transferred from Schedule 3 in 1978.

Schedule 3: Less potential for abuse than 1 and 2. Currently acceptable use in medicine both in the United States and, under restriction, Britain. Low to moderate physical dependence or high psychological dependence. Includes: all barbiturates not in 2 (except phenobarbital), certain codeines.

Schedule 4: Relatively low potential for abuse. Current medical use in the United States, in Britain subject to POM (Prescription Only Medicine) regulations. May lead to limited dependence. Includes: diazepam (Valium), chiordiazepoxide (Librium), meprobamate (Miltown), phenobarbital, tranquillizers.

Schedule 5: Low potential for abuse. Current medical use in United States, some subject to POM regulations in Britain. Includes: some opiate mixtures containing non-narcotic ingredients.

Drug Dependence

Over the past decade or so drug abuse in the United States and Britain has risen alarmingly, the more worrying for Britain where this is a comparatively new phenomenon. For example, the number of people addicted to one or another of the opiates rose from 10,716 in 1987 to 17,715 in 1990; the same source quotes the unofficial figure of 100,000 heroin addicts. As for cannabis, the Institute for the Study of Drug Dependence estimates that at least one million people in Britain use the drug every year.

It is comforting to think of this 'abuse' of scheduled drugs as being an illegal activity engaged in by a twilight world of 'junkies' unlikely to encroach upon the lives of decent citizens – but this takes no account of the dangerous misuse of *legal* drugs. The organisation Alcohol Concern is on record with an estimate that more than one and a half million Britons drink **Alcohol** at levels which seriously damage their health, and there is no shortage of studies which link excessive use of alcohol with violence and crime. Prescribed drugs such as tranquillizers and barbiturates have devastating effects on the many people whose lives have become dependent upon them after perfectly legal prescribed use to alleviate stress and depression. Warnings against tobacco smoking have become so familiar that it is often overlooked that its constituent drug, nicotine, is one of the most deadly poisons (see **Poisons** 'Nicotine').

Although some of the substances are subject to legal restriction (as is alcohol) glues containing volatile solvents have become another deadly form of pleasure-seeking, particularly among children and young adults.

The capacity of a drug to build addiction – or dependence – has varied patterns and degrees of intensity. It depends upon the type of drug, the level of the dose, frequency of administration, metabolic rate of the user, and so on. Factors such as 'normal' behaviour of the user will help determine the likelihood of dependence, as will the motive for drug use – whether the user is *escaping* from psychological pain or *pursuing* pleasure.

There are, however, two distinct and identifiable patterns of dependency – *psychological* and *physical:*

Psychological dependence (or habituation), where the dependence is on the desire to repeat the use of the drug because of the sense of pleasure that it gives. The frequency with which a substance will be used depends to some extent on the nature of the drug. Alcohol, heroin and the barbiturates, for example, frequently lead to high usage, while marijuana and codeine have a lower potential for dependence.

Physical dependence: Once dependence upon emotional self-gratification has been achieved through a drug and maintained or repeated by intensive use, there are some substances capable of effecting physiological changes which encourage continued use and produce severe physical symptoms of withdrawal. One specialist described the problem like this: 'For the addict who is accustomed to receiving large doses of heroin, the thought of abstaining and encountering body chills, vomiting, stomach cramps, convulsions, insomnia, pain and hallucinations serves as a powerful inducement for continued drug use.'

The Drugs

Almost every substance that produces a pleasurable (or at least interesting) alteration of the mental and physical state is open to misuse by somebody, and the number of substances finding their way out of the laboratory and on to the streets is too hopelessly large to review in an entry as restricted for space as this.

However, it is useful to give one representative example of this ever-increasing pharmacopoeia of potentially lethal thrills. A report arrived from New York in February 1991 of squads of police cars being sent on to the streets of the Bronx delivering loudhailer warnings about a deadly new concoction of heroin that had already killed twelve people and hospitalized a further one hundred in the previous forty-eight hours. This 'designer' cocktail was on the streets under the name 'Tango and Cash' (after a film of the same name starring Sylvester Stallone) and was apparently twenty-five times more powerful than heroin. The warning was also being broadcast around the drug centres of New Jersey, New York State and Connecticut. The deadly addition to the heroin was methyl fentanyl, a powerful tranquilizer developed for surgical use by Jaanssen Pharmaceutical of Belgium, and supplied as a liquid. For the illegal market, dealers were converting the liquid to a powder and combining it with heroin. According to one expert: 'You could put enough fentanyl on the head of a pin to kill fifty people. A handful of flour could contain two million doses. There would be enough in two shoe-boxes to satisfy every heroin addict in this country for six months, with some left over.' There are currently 500,000 *registered* heroin addicts in the United States.

This entry will confine itself to a description of the more commonly abused drugs and the ways in which they are treated in the forensic science laboratory. As an indication of the forensic importance of drugs it was estimated that in the United States more than seventy-five per cent of evidence being analysed in the laboratories is drug-related. The picture is less gloomy around Britain's laboratories, but for how long is anybody's guess.

Drugs can be divided into four main categories:

1. Narcotics
2. Depressants
3. Stimulants
4. Hallucinogens

Narcotics
The word derives from *narkotikos,* the Greek description of a state of lethargy, and adequately demonstrates the effects of the opiates in relieving pain and inducing sleep. The problem is that the word 'narcotic' has been incorrectly used to describe a whole range of popularly misused drugs, so giving a misleading impression of their effects – even to the extent of confounding drug legislation. For example, in the United States until the 1970s marijuana was classed as a 'narcotic', and even today it is common to find cocaine in the same bracket as morphine.

The opiates are drugs which derive from the gummy juice exuded by the unripe seed-pod of the white opium poppy, and comprise opium itself, morphine, heroin and codeine; the term also covers a wide range of synthetic substances that are opiate-like in their effects, such as methadone and pethidine.

Opium was once the fashionable drug of pleasure and escape, and the classic tales of Sherlock Holmes and his contemporaries abound with 'opium-dens' where both high-born and low squander their lives and fortunes seeking dreams and oblivion. It is now a deeply unfashionable drug, having had its popularity stolen by a derivative, heroin. Quite why morphine never attracted attention is an enduring mystery, for morphine has to be extracted from opium before it is converted into heroin by reacting with acetic anhydride or acetyl chloride. The powdered drug is then diluted ('cut') with another substance, such as starch, glucose or lactose, to as much as ninety-five per cent before it finds its way on to the street. Heroin is prepared for intravenous injection by dissolving it in a small quantity of water in a spoon (the process is often hastened by heating over a candle or matches) and using a syringe to inject the liquid into a vein. Other methods of absorbing heroin are to heat the solid substance on a piece of metal foil or a spoon and breathe the resulting smoke up the nose, often with the help of a short paper tube – this method is called 'chasing the dragon'. The drug can also be powdered and sniffed up the nostrils like tobacco snuff. Because these two methods seem so far removed from the 'junkie' stigma of mainlining, many young people coming to heroin for the first time underestimate the dangers of its strength and its ability to produce dependence.

The sense of well-being lasts for a relatively short time – three or four hours – but heroin 'highs' produce none of the impairments of the faculties associated with alcohol or barbiturates.

Codeine, which is synthetically prepared from morphine, is only about one-sixth the strength and finds little favour with serious addicts.

Of the synthetic opiates, methadone is probably the best known since it is the drug used to wean addicts off the more dangerous heroin. It does this by being taken orally in liquid form which eliminates the addict's need for heroin, while itself producing few undesirable side-effects. The starter doses of about 120 milligrams are gradually reduced, and although there is a high rate of reversion the treatment has proved successful.

Depressants
This category of drugs works by depressing the central nervous system, instilling in the subject a mild sense of euphoria and inducing sleep. In misuse, the larger dose causes a kind of intoxication and an impairment of both the mental faculties and physical coordination. The most familiar of the depressant drugs is **Alcohol**; it is also one of the most

dangerous, causing irreparable damage to the liver and brain. In fact, alcohol and barbiturates are both considered in many ways more dangerous than heroin.

The most dangerous of the depressants are barbiturates (see also page 377), commonly called 'downers' because they relax the body and replace anxiety with a sense of calm well-being. They are also very addictive and easy to overdose on, particularly if used in combination with alcohol. The most potentially lethal means of administering barbiturates is by intravenous injection. This is because the drug is manufactured to be taken orally in capsule form and intended for slow absorption into the bloodstream through the walls of the small intestine; injection forces the drug directly into the bloodstream, often causing irreparable physical damage. Barbiturate preparations have many different forms, the most dangerous of which are phenobarbitone, Nembutal, Seconal, Amytal, Sodium Amytal, Soneryl, Tuinal and Pentothal. In prescribed doses over short periods, the drugs are relatively safe, but danger lies in prolonged use, where the body builds up a resistance requiring larger and larger doses until physical dependence develops.

Tranquillizers (benzodiazepines) can come in the form of sleeping pills – such as Mogadon – or sedative pills – such as Librium, Valium and Ativan. Their effects are similar to those of barbiturates, but without many of the harmful side-effects. They do not, for example, impair the mental faculties, and they produce dependence only in repeated high levels of dosage. Unlike with barbiturates, it requires a very large quantity of the benzodiazepines to cause death, though the risk is multiplied by combination use with other drugs such as alcohol or opiates.

The sniffing of various materials containing volatile substances – often given the umbrella term 'glue-sniffing' – originated in the United States in the early 1960s and reached Britain in the 1970s. The substances sniffed range from solvents in impact adhesives, through vaporous liquids like petrol and nail varnish, to compressed gases such as lighter fuel and aerosols containing fluorocarbon propellants. For maximum effect the substance is usually inhaled from inside a plastic bag where the vapours can build up, except compressed gases which are sprayed directly into the mouth. Most of the vapours act primarily as depressants on the central nervous system and have an effect rather like alcohol – a mild feeling of exhilaration sometimes accompanied by hallucinations, slurred speech and impaired faculties. Unlike with alcohol, the effects last only about half an hour. Although glue-sniffing is nowhere near as harmful as the media scare-stories report, deaths have occurred and sniffers do expose themselves to the hazard of liver, heart and brain damage. In the United States a significant number of deaths has resulted from the inhalation of halogenated hydrocarbons. However, short of banning whole ranges of household products there is no way that legislation can adequately deal with the problem (though some adhesives containing volatile solvents are on restricted sale). Education and the search for alternative vehicles for the most abused products seem to be the only realistic answer.

Stimulants

This range of drugs has the opposite effect of depressants, serving to stimulate the central nervous system and induce sensations of alertness and confidence. As distinct from the previous categories, stimulants are not *physically* addictive, though frequent high-level users are susceptible to a psychological dependence on the good feelings the drugs give.

Amphetamines – the 'uppers' or 'speed' of the drug subculture – are prescribed in therapeutic doses of between five and twenty milligrams per day, and for short periods are not especially harmful. However, the body quickly builds up a tolerance, and ever increased doses are needed to achieve the same effect; side-effects include impaired sleep pattern, loss of appetite leading to undernourishment, uncomfortable itching of the skin, and a growing sense of apprehension and paranoia.

The other popular stimulant drug of misuse is cocaine, a white powder extracted from the leaves of the South American *Erythroxylon coca,* which is sniffed up the nostrils and absorbed into the bloodstream through the mucous membranes; its effects are similar to those of amphetamines. More dangerous than cocaine is the fashionable derivative called 'crack', manufactured by heating a mixture of cocaine, baking soda and water. The resulting material is dried and broken into tiny 'crack rocks'. This free-base cocaine is sufficiently volatile to be smoked and produces an instant effect far more intense than untreated cocaine. In the United States cocaine abuse is increasing, and attempts to stem the illegal flow from South America – notably Colombia – have so far met with mixed success.

Hallucionogens

A category of drugs which is characterized by creating marked alteration of moods and perception accompanied by hallucination.

The most commonly used hallucinogen (indeed, the most commonly used illicit drug) is marijuana, a preparation derived from the plant *Cannabis sativa L.* Cannabis is usually encountered in the form of a herbal mixture of shredded parts of the cannabis plant, or in the form of a solid brownish resin (hashish) extracted from the plant. Less often cannabis is found in the form of an oily liquid. In any of these forms, cannabis is usually smoked – the herb mixed with tobacco, the resin heated and crumbled into tobacco, and the liquid dropped on to the end of a cigarette or into the tobacco in a pipe. Cannabis can also be baked into cakes and mixed with other foodstuffs, and brewed as a herbal 'tea'. The effects of the drug were eloquently described in a report of the US Government's National Commission on Marijuana and Drug Abuse:

> At low, usual 'social' doses the user may experience an increased sense of well-being, initial restlessness and hilarity followed by a dreamy, carefree state of relaxation. Alteration of sensory perceptions including expansion of space and time, and a more vivid sense of touch, sight, smell, taste and sound. A feeling of hunger, especially a craving for sweets, and subtle changes in thought formation and expression. To an unknowing observer, an individual in this state of consciousness would not appear noticeably different from his normal state.
>
> At higher, moderate doses these same reactions are intensified but the changes in the individual would still be scarcely noticeable to an observer . . . At very high doses, psychotomimetic phenomena may be experienced. These include distortion of body image, loss of personal identity, sensory and mental illusions, fantasies and hallucinations.

A number of chemical hallucinogens are available, the most powerful of which is LSD (lysergic acid diethylamide). LSD is sythesized from lysergic acid which itself is derived from ergot, a poisonous fungus which affects certain grasses and cereal grain (see **Fungi**). As well as inducing the oft-described 'mystical experience', it also causes drastic mood changes, often accompanied by feelings of anxiety.

The greatest hazard with LSD is the possibility that the 'mystical experience' might develop into the proverbial 'bad trip', a journey of nightmare and horror which could result in distress and depression when the effects of the drug wear off. Other chemical compositions classed as hallucinogens include mescaline, phencycladine (PCP) which in some forms is called 'Angel Dust', psilocybin, and dimethyltryptamine (DMT).

There is no medical evidence that hallucinogens (with the exception of PCP) are either addictive or pose a threat to health. For this reason there have been increasingly loud demands over the past twenty or thirty years for marijuana to be legalized. Nevertheless, the smoking of cannabis still carries with it the same health dangers as smoking tobacco – respiratory diseases and lung cancer.

Drug Identification

The identification of drugs gives toxicologists some of their biggest headaches, for not only is the bewildering list of drugs and hybrids rising by the month, but each separate incident must be treated as painstakingly as any piece of evidence in a major homicide inquiry. Like the bloodstain left at the scene of a crime, the suspect substance must be subjected to a rigorous laboratory testing that allows no margin of error. Once his report has been made the chemist must be prepared to stand in the witness box and defend the validity of his results.

As the drug abuse problem has grown, so has the sophistication risen in laboratory techniques available for analysis; and this too has compounded the toxicologist's dilemma. Faced with the task of *positively* identifying a substance of unknown origin and composition he must devise a set of screening tests to at least eliminate some of the thousand or more possibilities. It would clearly be impractical in view of the size of the workload to subject each separate case to the vast range of analytical tests available until the correct result was achieved. To avoid this a system known as 'presumptive testing' is used, whereby the test itself is not necessarily sufficient to identify a drug positively, but will narrow the options sufficiently to pin-point the most appropriate test to be used for more detailed analysis.

Colour Testing

Usually the first screening technique will be one of the main colour tests. Simply, when a drug is put into contact with a specific chemical reagent the reagent will change colour.

Dillie-Koppanyi Test: Turns violet-blue in the presence of barbiturates.

Duquenois-Levine Test: Three-part reagent which shows final purple when added to marijuana.

Marquis Test: In the presence of most opium derivatives, but especially morphine and heroin, the reagent will turn purple. As well as for opiates, the test is specific for amphetamines, which turns the reagent an orange-brown.

Scott Test: Three-part test for cocaine. Solution A is composed of 2 per cent cobalt thiocyanate in one part each of water and glycerine; Solution B is concentrated hydrochloric acid; Solution C, chloroform. Solution A is added to the suspect substance which, if it contains cocaine, will turn it blue. Confirmation is provided by the addition of Solution B which will turn the blue colour pink, and with the addition of solution C the blue colour will reappear in the chloroform layer.

Van Urk Test: Specific for LSD; turns reagent blue-purple.

Microcrystalline Testing

A suspect substance is brought into contact with a drop of chemical reagent on a glass microscope slide and left until the chemical reaction produces a crystalline precipitate. Under the microscope the crystal structure will be specific and identifiable for a wide range of drugs. The analysis is more specific than colour testing, and several hundred individual crystal tests are now available.

Chromatography

Both thin-layer and gas chromatography are well suited to drug analysis, though somewhat unspecific; it is customary to subject a substance to preliminary colour or crystalline tests (for a description of the process see **Chromatography**).

Spectrometry

Spectrometry is a useful technique which though inconclusive in the ultraviolet spectrum is specific enough to reduce the possibilities considerably. However, in the infra-red spectrum each pattern is unique and it is possible to identify a substance positively. In practice it is normal to screen a sample first with UV spectrometry, and then make the positive identification with IR. Although the technique sounds ideal, there is the drawback that the drug must be in as pure a state as possible for analysis, which usually means that to be of any use it may be necessary to subject a sample to extensive purification before using the spectograph.

Mass Spectrometry

Typical of the imaginative advances made in analytical techniques is the link between gas chromatograph and mass spectrometer. On its own the chromatograph is not specific enough in its analysis to identify a substance positively. However, if the gas chromatograph is connected to a mass spectrometer, as the sample emerges from the chromatograph and enters the spectrometer it is bombarded with high-energy electrons which break up the sample's molecules. The principle is that no two substances will break up in quite the same way, thus giving each substance a unique pattern that can be compared with a 'control'. Thus every component of the substance under test can be positively identified.

DUST ANALYSIS

Definitions of words such as dust, debris and soil are so subjective and so interchangeable that for the present purpose it is simpler to collect all three together and attempt some common definition. Dust may be described as any fine dry deposit left by a crumbled surface material. This includes mud, which is dust mixed with water, and grime, which is dust mingled with body secretions such as sweat. The justification in both instances is that the dry dust can be recovered from mud and grime.

Dust usually comprises substances of animal, vegetable or mineral origin, though increasingly, synthetic substances such as plastics will be found, particularly in the form of industrial and occupational dusts.

In most instances the source will show direct derivation, while some will be of indirect derivation (usually following human intervention), such as brick dust, paper and earthenware.

Dust is a valuable, and common, contact trace which is easily carried from the scene of a crime embedded in the soles of shoes, picked up on clothing, or in the hair or on the skin. Because the composition of dust from a particular location will tend to be clearly identifiable it can prove to be very strong evidence in linking a person with a location. Although its composition may traverse several disciplines in the forensic laboratory – biology, mineralogy and chemistry – the analysis of dust will, like so much forensic work, be mainly a matter of comparison with a 'control' sample. However, it is possible that a sufficiently large deposit of material readily identifed as 'soil' could be associated by a geologist with a special knowledge of local soil composition with a particular location.

The blue mini-car from which heiress Janie Shepherd disappeared was discovered in a London street on 9 February 1977. Miss Shepherd had been missing since the 5th, and the car was proved to have travelled roughly seventy-five miles; this meant that the body could have been dumped anywhere within a thirty-five-mile radius of where the car was abandoned. From the thick deposits of mud on the lower parts of the vehicle it had clearly been driven along some fairly rough tracks, and samples of the soil were sent for forensic examination. This revealed that the soil could have come from any one of four counties, and more than fifty police officers were employed in intensive searches of locations which were consistent with the samples; it was the first time in a British murder inquiry that dogs specially trained to sniff out dead bodies were used in the ground search. In the end it was not the police but a couple of schoolboys who found the victim's remains on a muddy patch of open land in Hertfordshire – the local soil was a match for that thrown up on the car during that last fatal trip.

In many instances laboratory examination will require only a visual comparison of colour, texture, etc., which can be achieved by simple **Microscopy** or with the use of a **Comparison Microscope** – it has been estimated that there are as many as one thousand identifiable soil colours alone. Magnification will also reveal the specific contents of the sample such as biological material and man-made debris. Material that needs finer analysis can be tested successfully by **Chromatography** and **Spectrometry**.

Any hard and fast classification of 'dust' is impossible, but for convenience four main types can be identified according to their place of origin:

Road and Footpath Dust
Caused by wear and tear of the surface by traffic and pedestrians, mixed dust, and soil carried by the wind and rain from the countryside. Modern road-building practices have tended to make road surfacing materials fairly uniform, but differences may be apparent from the depositing of debris from distinctive local sources – such as industrial or agricultural material. These types of footpath dust will be picked up by cars and in the treads of their tyres, on shoes and clothing, and may be sufficiently distinctive to be useful in comparison tests.

Soil
Originates from open land, gardens, unmade tracks, wooded areas, etc. This type of debris is of the greatest use to forensic science as it will

comprise many identifying micro-organisms, minute insect life, vegetable traces, pollens and spores, as well as locally distinctive mineral traces.

One remarkable case in Australia was solved by a comparison of airborne fungus spores. On 7 July 1960, eight-year-old Graeme Thorne – whose parents had recently won the Sydney lottery – was abducted on his way to school; the kidnapper later demanded a ransom of $A24,000. On 16 August Graeme's body was found on waste ground ten miles from his home. The boy's killer, Stephen Bradley, was trapped by the ingenuity of forensic botanists who proved that fungus spores found in the victim's lungs came from a rare combination of trees growing in Bradley's garden.

Dust from the Air
Fine airborne particles have so many possible origins and are so difficult to retrieve that they constitute no very significant part of the laboratory's work.

Industrial Dusts
Although dusts with industrial origin will help put a unique 'fingerprint' on the general composition of particulate material, they are more important if they can prove identity through contact trace. Examples are the product of cement works, flour mills and pigment grinders.

Occupational Dust
Picked up on the clothing and footwear of employees as well as in their hair and under their fingernails. Most occupations have their own type of 'dirt' which will identify individuals who work in them, and which may later be deposited at the scene of a crime. The traces may also be picked up by people who are on the premises with felonious intent and link them with the crime. Examples are coal dust, brick dust, cement and sand from construction sites, flour and yeast from bakeries, paper fibres, stone dust from masonry, and so on.

Case Study

THE BLUE SERGE SUIT
It was in 1931 that Leslie Stone and Ruby Anne Keen met and began walking out together. Ruby was living with her widowed mother, her

elder sister and brother in Leighton Buzzard, and was well aware of the attention that her attractive looks and pleasing personality earned her, and was never backward in accepting the invitations of her admirers; in short, Stone was merely one more pebble on the beach.

Nevertheless, it was assumed by their families that sooner or later Leslie and Ruby would become Mr and Mrs Stone. Leslie was an engaging enough young man; twenty-four years old, and a building labourer.

And married they might have been had Leslie Stone not been posted to Hong Kong in 1932 on service with the Royal Artillery. Ruby was not the sort of girl to sit at home pining, and it was not long before the space in her life so recently occupied by Leslie had been filled by other admirers – among them two constables in the Bedfordshire police force. In the middle of 1936 one of them was elevated from the position of suitor to that of fiancé.

Shortly after this – in December 1936 Leslie Stone was discharged from the Army on medical grounds and returned to his native Leighton Buzzard. Though Ruby's letters had long since ceased to brighten his life, Stone was still anxious for some kind of reconciliation. On 4 April 1937, the couple were seen drinking in the *Golden Bell*. The following week they had another date, in honour of which Stone had bought a new blue serge suit, which he was wearing for the first time. Indirectly, it was to hang him.

After the rendezvous in the *Golden Bell*, Stone and Ruby Keen moved on to the *Cross Keys* and from there to the *Stag Hotel* where Stone was overheard earnestly entreating his companion to forsake her new fiancé and marry him; his ardour was no doubt fired by the six or more pints of mild ale that he had consumed. Around closing time at ten o'clock they left the *Stag* and were seen to walk past Ruby's home in Plantation Road and into a 'lovers' lane' called The Firs.

At seven o'clock the following morning, 12 April, a railway worker named Cox was on his way to work when he found Ruby Keen's almost naked body, wet with dew, lying where it had fell in The Firs. Ruby had been strangled with her own silk scarf, though despite the disarray of her clothing there was no evidence of sexual assault.

The scene that presented itself to Scotland Yard's Chief Inspector William Barker gave testimony to the valiant struggle that the unlucky victim had put up to protect herself. However, the ground was not so scuffled that the experienced eye of the detective could not glean at least one set of clear footprints and two impressions in the sandy soil, which were consistent with the killer kneeling by his victim while strangling her.

There were three immediate suspects; three men known to have had an emotional attachment to Ruby Keen. Two of them were policemen, the other was the man seen drinking with her on the night she died.

When Leslie Stone's blue serge suit was taken from him for forensic examination by Sir Bernard **Spilsbury**, it presented the odd fact that, though new, the knees had been brushed so vigorously that the nap of the cloth had been rubbed away. Even so, it took no time for Sir Bernard and his microscope to find the minute traces of sandy soil embedded deep in the fibres of the suit and in the turn-ups of the trousers. If that soil could be matched to the soil on which poor Ruby had been murdered, then Leslie Stone must have been there – not only that, but he must have been there on the night that she died, because on his own admission it was the first time that he had worn the suit; the soil particles were a perfect match. Furthermore, the microscopic examination of Stone's jacket had also revealed a single silk **Fibre** matching exactly the dress in which Ruby Keen had been killed.

Which is how Leslie George Stone came to be charged with murder. And how two months later, on Monday 28 June 1937, he came to be standing in the dock of the Old Bailey. In the witness box Leslie Stone, who had at first denied being anywhere near The Firs on the night of the murder, told his new story. In this version of the events he and Ruby had quarrelled; she had taunted him and eventually struck him on the head with the palm of her hand: 'It made me jump at her. I caught hold of her scarf I think, and pulled it. I think I knotted it again after that . . . I was in a kind of rage.' He described Ruby's near-nakedness as being caused when he tried to prevent her falling, and when she did – despite his best efforts to keep her upright – the clothing ripped apart. He had then knelt down beside her, decided that she was only stunned, and strolled away leaving the luckless girl to come, quite literally, to her senses.

The jury were not out for long – just twenty-five minutes – and it surprised nobody that they returned with a verdict of guilty. Leslie Stone was hanged at Pentonville prison on 13 August 1937; it was a Friday.

E

EAR IDENTIFICATION

Although the unique nature of the human ear, as well as its tendency to remain the same basic shape from birth, was recognized by **Bertillon** and **Lacassagne**, its use as a means of criminal identification has never been extensive. True, Jacques Penry, the man who devised Photo-FIT, was enthusiastic in his praise of the feature which was 'as unique to every face as a fingerprint is unique . . .', but only one person has devoted painstaking research to the development of a qualitative and quantitative system of ear identification capable of taking its place among the tools of forensics. Alfred Iannarelli does not often appear indexed in books on forensic science and criminalistics, nor have the conclusions of his study been widely broadcast:

1. The human ear has highly individual morphological characteristics.
2. The ear assumes a permanent shape in the embryo then, after possible changes in the first nine months after birth, retains the same basic shape until death.
3. The ear grows in proportion to the rest of the body, with growth most noticeable in the lobe. This change in size does not affect the basic anthropometric shape.
4. No two ears are identical (however, children of the same parents share similar characteristics).
5. The ear has individuality on a level with that of fingerprints.

Identification and Comparison

The ear (Iannarelli specifies the right ear) is divided into eight basic

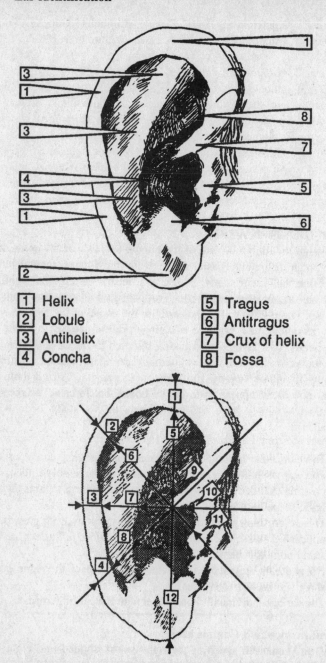

1	Helix	5	Tragus
2	Lobule	6	Antitragus
3	Antihelix	7	Crux of helix
4	Concha	8	Fossa

external characteristics: Helix, Lobule, Antihelix, Concha, Tragus, Antitragus, Crux of Helix, and Fossa (see diagram on p.196).

Primary Classification
For identification a photographic enlargement of the ear is overlaid by a clear plastic sheet which is marked with horizontal, vertical and diagonal lines, dividing the area into eight sectors; the point at which the lines cross is aligned on the 'crux of the helix'.

Before commencing measurement, the outside contour of the ear is marked where it cuts the lines (▲ on the diagram). The first measurement (1) is of the breadth of the uppermost edge of the helix, then in a counterclockwise direction around the helix (2, 3, 4). Measurement 5 is the lower edge of helix to inside of antihelix, and 6, 7, 8 follow, still counterclockwise. Measurement 9 is the lower extent of fossa to centre, 10 crux to centre, 11 tragus to centre, 12 antitragus to lobule.

For some unfathomable reason these measurements are then charted against gender – M (male), F (female) – and race – W (white), N (negroid), A (Asian). The odd measurements 1–11 are plotted alongside gender, the even measurements alongside race:

F 1* 3 5 7 9 11
W 2 4 6 8 10 12

Secondary Classification
Allowing for the possibility of more than one person sharing these statistics, Iannarelli provides for a second classification:

1. Join horizontal and vertical lines.
2. Construct diagonals 1–6.
3. Derive measurements:
      1. Helix ridge to antihelix
      2. Helix ridge to antihelix to concha
      3. Helix ridge to concha
      4. Helix ridge to concha
      5. Antratigus to helix ridge
      6. Concha to tragus
4. Insert measurements on formula:
      1 3 5
      2 4 6

*On an actual chart these would, of course, be measurements.

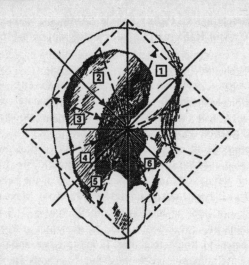

This adds up to a total of eighteen measurements taken from a single ear, which should provide enough points of reference for positive comparison.

It would be easy to regard ear identification lightly, but just as Bertillon taught observation of the ears as part of his training in **Portrait Parlé**, so it may now be possible to use ear identification in those cases where other forms of identification are impossible – for example, in badly mutilated victims, or in the case of a robbery where the thieves are masked but for their ears.

EMBOLISM

Embolism is a pathological condition in which the bloodstream becomes polluted with some substance, such as fat or air, which circulates for a distance before becoming wedged and blocking the blood vessels feeding some crucial organ, such as the heart or brain, causing death.

Air Embolism

There is a great deal of mythology surrounding the matter of air embolism, and a belief has entered the popular imagination that the injection of a bubble of air from a syringe into a vein will cause death. Of course it will do no such thing; as much as 10cc – a whole syringe full – is unlikely to have any lasting effect on a normal healthy person, and the debate over the size of a fatal injection ranges between 50cc and 300cc. Indeed, crime scientist Dr John Thompson is of the opinion that a more realistic instrument than a syringe might be a bicycle pump!

The wide debate on air embolism came into the international arena in the wake of what came to be known as 'The Mercy Killing Case'. In 1949 a forty-one-year-old physician named Hermann Sander of New Hampshire, USA, had a terminally ill cancer patient named Mrs Abbie Borroto. Mrs Borroto was beyond any hope of medical treatment save the pain-killing drugs which made life at least comfortable. The patient's husband had quite understandably begun to get accustomed to the inevitable and asked, not insistently but frequently, how much longer his wife was going to live.

In early December Dr Sander confided to Mr Borroto that he doubted his patient would live through the night. Sander had good reason for his doubts – that night he prescribed a massive dose of Mrs Borroto's pain-killing drugs. To his surprise she was still alive when he visited her room the following morning. Then Sander ordered the nurse to get a syringe, and after putting a tourniquet round Mrs Borroto's arm, injected a full 10cc of air into her bloodstream; then another 10cc, another, and another – 40cc in all. The nurse was, to say the least, mystified at the scene which was going on; every time the doctor injected, the patient gave a sort of groan. Then she didn't move or make a sound any more.

The death certificate was prepared stating cause of death as 'carcinoma of the large bowel with metastases', and Mrs Borroto was embalmed and buried. Ten days later Dr Sander completed her medical record, giving full details of the drug overdose and the injections of air to cause embolism. The file was read by the records clerk, who alerted the hospital's medical administrator, who suggested that Sander was 'temporarily unbalanced' when he wrote the report. Sander, nevertheless, refused to retract a single word of it. Quite how, one can never be entirely sure, but such matters have a way of unerringly finding their way on to newspaper front pages; and from thence to a court of law. Which is how one modest New Hampshire physician became a world-wide celebrity in 'The Mercy Killing Trial'.

Although the patient's body had been embalmed before burial, effectively making proof of embolism impossible, Sander's defence counsel insisted on an autopsy, and it was carried out by Dr Richard Ford of the Department of Legal Medicine at Harvard Medical School. Representing the Attorney General as an observer at the autopsy was

America's leading Medical Examiner, Dr Milton Helpern. Facts were elucidated with difficulty, and though there was no way of making a positive diagnosis of death by air embolism, there was no proof against it – and Dr Sander had already admitted culpability in his report.

The trial opened in February 1950, and by this time Sander had been persuaded to reconsider his position and was now claiming that Mrs Borroto was already dead when he injected her arm with air. In answer to the obvious question of why he should have done that, Sander explained that he wanted to make sure she was dead. The issue before the court was simple – if Abbie Borroto was alive, Sander had killed her; if she was dead then he couldn't have.

It fell to Milt Helpern's lot to explain to the jury, with the help of a blackboard and chalk, what air embolism was: 'Air pushed into a vein in the arm can travel through the bloodstream until it reaches the right side of the heart, then the pulmonary artery in the lung. At a certain critical volume of air (which is different for various people and in different circumstances) the injected air forms bubbles and froth in the heart which results in an air-lock – the air also is suddenly released through the lungs to form bubbles in other vital organs, especially the brain.'

The biggest source of contention was the *amount* of air necessary to induce embolism. Richard Ford suggested it would be around 200–300cc; Helpern believed much less – indeed, if the prosecution was alleging that it *was* air embolism that killed Mrs Borroto, then it would obviously, in this case at least, have required only 40cc.

To general public approbation, the jury finally brought in a verdict of 'not guilty', and Dr Hermann Sander – seen as a champion of euthanasia – became a hero.

Accidental air embolism has been reported as a consequence of surgical operations (and wounds) of the neck, where an incision allowed air to enter the veins. There have also been cases of air embolism resulting from criminal abortion procured with the use of a Higginson-type syringe.

Fat Embolism

Following severe injury to the bones, or damage to the subcutaneous fat through **Burning** or injury, fat particles can be released into the circulation which will eventually block the passage of blood to the vital organs and cause death.

DVT

Over the late 1990's a third form of embolism greatly impinged on the public mind, although it has yet to be proved to be linked with any deliberate criminal act. Economy Flight Syndrome, or deep vein thrombosis (DVT) to give it its medical name, is a clotting of the blood in a victim's outer limbs (especially the lower legs) that when dislodged into the bloodstream can lodge in the pulmonary artery that feeds the lungs, blocking effective air transference and fatally starving the brain of oxygen.

DVT most often strikes down passengers on or, more typically, leaving long-distance flights. The relatives of victims claim that the airlines have shown criminal negligence in making economy seating so cramped that movement of passengers' legs and arms is over-restricted, allowing the clots to form on long flights. The airlines have, so far, successfully fought off all claims concerning DVT cases, denying any connection with their services, but it is also noticeable that airline stewards now invariably advise passengers to exercise their arms and legs as often as possible on long-haul flights.

EPILEPSY
(see Automatism)

ERGOT
(see Fungi, Drugs)

ESDA (ELECTROSTATIC DETECTION APPARATUS)
(see Disputed Documents)

EXHUMATION

Exhumation – digging up a body that has been buried – is an extreme measure confined to the need either to resite a burial or, more rarely, to establish the presence of injuries or toxic substances in cases where hindsight has made cause of death seem suspicious. Exhumation for any purpose must be authorized by the office of the Home Secretary, most often at the formal request of the police or a coroner.

It is obviously vital that the site of the burial is correctly identified, not only from the headstone, but also with reference to the cemetery superintendent's groundplans.

The coffin is disinterred under police supervision and identified; in this matter it is helpful if the original undertaker is available to confirm the identity of the coffin and coffin-plate.

Although it is not uncommon for a mechanical digger to be used to remove the greater depth of soil, in cases where poisoning is suspected it is important that soil samples are collected during excavation from:

1. Surface ground above the coffin
2. Six inches above the coffin
3. Each side of the coffin
4. Beneath the coffin
5. Control samples from other parts of the cemetery*

The coffin is then removed to the mortuary for post-mortem examination, though advantage may be taken of the open air to raise the lid of the coffin slightly and allow gases to escape.

Once at the mortuary the coffin is opened and positive identification established by any means appropriate to the state of decomposition of the remains. If the body was recently buried visual identification by a relative or acquaintance may be possible; otherwise, fingerprints or dental records should be compared.

Subsequent post-mortem examination of the remains will be for the purpose of determining the cause of death, and according to Professor Francis Camps should follow this procedure:

1. X-ray taken of body.
2. Photographs taken of body.
3. Full autopsy carried out and tissues removed for histology and preservation (usually in alcohol).
4. Tissue samples should be made available to the analyst, plus samples of hair, skin, finger- and toe-nails, and any fluid in the coffin.
5. Samples should also be taken for analysis of any other materials that have been in contact with the body – wood from the coffin, coffin lining, shroud, etc.

*This is crucial in cases of suspected arsenic poisoning as soil may naturally contain high concentrations of the poison; a phenomenon which has led to conflict and confusion in medical evidence (see **Arsenic**).

If the body is particularly badly decomposed, the brain may be in too liquid a state for removal and examination. However, it is reported that Belgian pathologists employ the procedure of removing the head and solidifying it in a deep-freeze cabinet. The frozen head is then cut laterally through the scalp, skull and brain, and the two halves fixed in formalin to harden the brain tissue which can then be removed.

Following **Post-mortem** examination the remains are reburied.

EXPLOSIVES

Because of their capacity to inflict maximum damage for their size, and the randomness of their destruction, bombs have always been the favoured weapon of the terrorist. Unfortunately, with readily available information on simple bomb chemistry any single-issue fanatic with a grievance can become a bomb-wielding terrorist.

More specifically, bombing campaigns have been the spearhead of groups such as the IRA and the Red Brigade, for whom the fear and disruption generated by even the *threat* of bombs have as great an importance as the death and destruction caused by the weapons themselves.

Although a group calling themselves the Angry Brigade went on a bombing foray in London during the late 1960s, and isolated instances of letter and parcel bombs have punctuated the last couple of decades, the main threat of bombing in Britain has come from the IRA, whose elaborate cell network on mainland Britain has ensured regular disruption in the capital. In the main, the bombs contain fairly small amounts of explosive and are deposited in confined spaces such as public houses. Injuries and deaths are usually the result of flying glass and debris and the collapse of the building's fabric. In Northern Ireland, where the greater force of the IRA terror campaign is directed, the situation is very different. The bombs tend to be much larger, between 600–700lbs (270–330kg) in weight, deposited outdoors, often in cars, and intended to wreak the maximum destruction and disorder. With these explosions many deaths are directly attributable to the effects of the explosion itself, the blast dismembering victims, tearing bodies open and scattering viscera over a great area. One **Police Surgeon** serving in Northern Ireland recalled: 'One recent explosion in which I was involved showed the presence of three mutilated bodies. An extra heart, four or five thoracic vertebrae, and rib remains were also discovered. Further search revealed only a small amount of other human remains, none of which could be related to any particular person.'

Case Study

THE CASE OF THE MAGUIRES

In 1976 six members of the Maguire family and one of their friends were given prison sentences of between four and fourteen years for possessing firearms; it was alleged that they were running an IRA bomb factory. The sole evidence against them was a scientific test which showed results consistent with traces of nitroglycerine being on their hands. The jury had been told that this test was conclusive; it was not, because the same result would have been obtained if, for example, the defendants had been handling angina tablets containing another explosive called PETN.

Despite considerable disquiet over the convictions, and vociferous protests by the family and their supporters, it was not until 1990 that the case was referred to the Court of Appeal, and then only as a side-issue to the discovery of police malpractice in the case of other convicted 'terrorists', the Guildford Four.

At best the scientific evidence given at the original trial could be described as 'badly presented', at worst there have been accusations of malpractice. The tests on swabs and rubber gloves taken from the Maguires were carried out at the Royal Armament Research and Development Establishment; the method was thin-layer **Chromatography**. The fact that the jury were not informed of other possible interpretations of the laboratory results was bad enough, but it was subsequently discovered that another series of tests carried out while the trial was in progress and which supported the defence were never revealed; also that information on yet another series of tests to identify the explosive – which proved negative – was not properly conveyed to the defence. There were also allegations that the evidence was contaminated *after* it arrived at the laboratory. In the end the Maguires were acquitted of any guilt – far too late for one of the seven, Guiseppe Conlon, who died in prison in 1980.

The tragedy has only partly to do with the conviction of seven innocent people and their incarceration for as many as fourteen years; the greater implication is for the future of the forensic sciences. So great has been public and legal alarm in recent times over the unreliability of evidence such as **Identification**, confessions and alibis, that increasingly the interests of justice must be served by scientific evidence to prove guilt or innocence. With the increasing sophistication of forensic techniques, notably the refinement of **DNA Profiling,** this is the way the future lies – the way in which we can ensure fewer miscarriages of justice. The difficulty, in the light of incidents like the Maguire case, is retaining the *credibility* of forensic scientists.

The Chemistry of Explosives

An explosion is produced by combustion accompanied by the creation of heat and gas, and it is the sudden build-up of expanding gas pressure that causes the violent blast at the centre of the explosion. When it is detonated the explosive substance creates huge volumes of gases and heat energy inside its container, forcing the walls outwards under enormous pressure so that they blast and fragment, pieces flying in every direction – the so-called shrapnel. The gases, released from pressure, suddenly expand and force the surrounding air outwards from the centre of the explosion in a blast of gas that can be as strong as 7,000 miles per hour, sufficient to topple buildings and lift vehicles.

Explosives are classified as either high or low. High explosives, such as TNT, dynamite and PETN are so called because they detonate almost instantaneously at a rate of between 1,000–8,500 metres per second, *shattering* their target.

Low explosives include black powder and smokeless powder used in gun cartridges (see **Firearms**), natural gas, and mixtures of air and a gaseous fuel such as petrol. Low explosive will normally just burn unless it is contained, when it can be very devastating indeed. Explosions are characterized by being slow burning, creating a *throwing* action as distinct from a shattering one.

Unlike low explosives, high explosive devices need to be started by a separate, 'detonating' explosion, such as a blasting cap activated either by a safety fuse or by an electric current (in portable bombs usually a battery). In addition, many terrorist devices require to be timed, and many ingenious switching-mechanisms have been designed – from clocks to mercury switches.

Scene of Crime

Special skills and experience are needed in the identification and collection of evidence from the scene of an explosion, and officers must be aware of the items and substances that will be needed for analysis in the chemistry laboratory. Clearly the most important task is to recover any undetonated samples of the explosive from the debris, and the most likely place to look will be the site of the explosion. It is normal to collect all the soft and porous material from the area where the blast originated – soil, wood, furnishings – which will more easily have been penetrated by explosive residues.

Because of the nature of the event, clues to the origin of an explosion will be blown over a wide area, and a painstaking search of the whole area is necessary in order to recover any trace of a detonating device or shrapnel from the bomb. Every scrap of debris must be sifted, often through a fine wire-mesh, in the search for clues. Like all scene-of-crime evidence, it is vital that material remains uncontaminated on its journey to the laboratory, and is properly labelled.

Analysis

The debris delivered to the forensic laboratory will first be subjected to examination with a microscope in order to separate out the different categories of evidence, and to search for unconsumed explosive traces. Once the useful material has been removed the debris can be 'washed' with acetone which absorbs most explosives and can be used for chemical testing. There is a range of **Instrumentation** suitable for the analysis and identification of explosives, the most usual being thin-layer **Chromatography**, where the resulting chromatograph can be matched with the 'control' chromatograph for a known explosive. Water-soluble substances (such as nitrates and chlorates) can be 'washed out' with water instead of acetone and tested in the same way.

Colour spot testing is useful for simple screening of both water- and acetone-soluble explosives (as it is for **Drugs**); a drop of a specified reagent being introduced to a suspect substance and the resulting colour change compared with a reference chart.

Confirmation tests are generally carried out by infra-red **Spectrometry**, which will provide a unique pattern for each substance.

'Taggants'

The US Treasury Department has advanced a suggestion for including in all commercially manufactured explosives a quantity of tiny colour-coded elements about the size of a grain of sand which could be used to identify the substance in the event of its criminal use. To help identify them at the scene of crime and in the laboratory, the chips would be made fluorescent and magnetic so that they could be recovered by a magnet or seen in ultraviolet light. The markers, called 'taggants', consist of layers of colours in an identifiable sequence which can be 'read' under a microscope for details of when, where, and by whom they were made. The manufacturer is routinely obliged to keep detailed records of where his explosives are distributed, and so the last *legal* owner of a particular batch of explosive can easily be identified. Although several European manufacturers have shown interest, it looks like being a slow process to introduce taggants.

As of this writing (September 2003) the development of taggants has been largely blocked in the United States by the pro-gun lobby. Groups like the National Rifle Association (NRA) have claimed that taggants are unsafe (potentially causing the accidental detonation of explosives) and unworkable (because tagged chemicals would pass through so many forms as they are combined into different types of ammunition and explosive). Critics of the NRA suggest their real reason for opposition is their fear that *any* weaponry control law, no matter how sensible, is one step closer to the repeal of the Second Amendment (the 'right to bear arms'). As they are the biggest arms market in the world, nobody is going to manufacture taggant bearing chemicals as long as they are unsellable in the United States.

Criminal Intent

By no means all explosions are caused by terrorists, though the felonious use of explosives in Britain is rare because of the restricted availability of the materials (in the United States, on the other hand, low explosives like black powder and smokeless powder are on sale in any gun-shop). Among the better known English explosives crimes is the murder of his tyrannical father by Eric Brown. The family were living in Rayleigh, and since a motorcycling accident some years before, Archibald Brown had become gradually less mobile due to paralysis of the spine. By 1942 he could not walk unaided and was regularly perambulated around in a wheelchair by his nurse. On 23 July 1943, Nurse Mitchell helped the old man into his mobile chair and they set off on their afternoon trip. About a mile from home Brown demanded a cigarette, and as the nurse walked around to the back of the wheelchair there was a huge explosion. Miss Mitchell was thankfully just thrown to the ground, while Mr Brown was scattered over a large area of rural Essex. It did not take long to identify the murder weapon; it was a Hawkins No. 75 anti-tank grenade mine, which had been strapped beneath Archibald Brown's wheelchair. And it did not take long to identify the killer – Eric Brown had nursed a resentment against his father's bullying ways for years; he was also a soldier who had recently been inducted into the destructive powers of the Hawkins No. 75 grenade mine. Eric, who claimed only the desire to make his mother's life happier, was found guilty of murder, but insane.

In the same decade, Albert Guay in collaboration with two other people blew up a Quebec Airways DC-3 killing all twenty-three passengers and crew. While they were checking the passenger list, police came to the name of Rita Guay, whose husband was a known offender who at the time was known to be involved in a romantic liaison with a woman named Pitre. Pitre was identified as having delivered a package to be transported aboard the fatal flight. Albert Guay was arrested and made a confession implicating his accomplices. All three were tried, found guilty of murder and, in 1951, hanged.

The South African Huibrecht de Leeuw was one of those individuals whose ambitious needs are always frustrated by their slender purses; however, he was disgraced not by his lack of funds, but by the unworthy means by which he sought to increase them. De Leeuw was the town clerk of Dewetsdorp, in the Orange Free State, and had for some time been attempting to juggle the cash kept in the exchequer safe and the record kept in the accounts books to his own financial advantage. It was clearly not a state of affairs that could pass unnoticed for ever, and time was already running out. In brief, the books were in a mess, and the mayor himself was demanding that a tally be made. Unable to raise any tangible gesture of sympathy from his friends, de Leeuw turned – as so many have done before him – to more desperate solutions. On 8 April 1927, Mayor P.J. von Maltitz, accompanied by two representatives of the town's finance committee, arrived to conduct their own inspection of the accounts. As they pored with increasing anxiety over the colunms of incomplete and misleading figures, a tremendous explosion ripped through the building, tearing off the roof and setting the fabric ablaze, during which conflagration the mayor perished instantly and his financial advisers received fatal injuries. An arrest was made not long after, when a local tradesman told police how the improvident de Leeuw had been obliged to borrow a match from him to ignite the home-made contraption of dynamite and petrol. With the message 'I am prepared to meet my Creator', de Leeuw was hanged on 30 September 1927.

F

FACIAL RECONSTRUCTION

A great deal of information about the living appearance of an individual can be gleaned from a specialized study of the skeleton – this is work which has always been included in the job of the forensic pathologist, who may be called upon to substantiate a victim's identity from partial or skeletal remains as part of **Post-Mortem Procedures**. More recently – particularly in the United States – the last resort in cases of difficult identification has been forensic **Anthropologists**, whose special knowledge and experience of osteology can reveal information that often seems little short of miraculous.

The Work of Richard Neave

A man who has been creating apparent miracles for some time is Richard Neave, a leading medical illustrator with the Department of Anatomy at Manchester's University Medical School. Neave has been following in the footsteps of the Russian Mikhail Gerasimov (see below) in reconstructing the facial tissues of long-dead historical figures from their skulls – he has enjoyed great success with the head of Philip II, father of Alexander the Great, and in collaboration with his colleague at Manchester Dr John Prag, keeper of Archaeology at the Museum, the head of King Midas, whose fabulous wealth inspired the legend that everything he touched turned to gold.

But Richard Neave has more recently enjoyed a different kind of celebrity, outside the cloistered atmosphere of academe on the touch-lines of tragedy. One does not have to be famous or rich to be dead, nor indeed does one have to be a king to benefit from the skills of Manchester's Department of Anatomy. In 1987 a horrific fire broke out on the London underground railway system at King's Cross station; it claimed the lives of thirty-one people. A year later there was still one victim who had not been identified; a man burned beyond visual recognition and apparently unmissed. The **Pathologists** and **Odontologists** had provided all the information that their combined skills could – the man was white, aged between forty and sixty but nearer the latter, and between 5ft and 5ft 4in tall. He was wearing an old pair of dentures, tobacco stained, with the initials EH or FH on them; he had undergone a brain operation during the past ten years which necessitated the removal of a piece of the right side of his skull, and there were early signs of coronary disease which would have resulted in chest pains. In November 1988 a plaster cast of the skull was sent to Richard Neave; three days later he had re-created the 'good, strong English face' of the last victim of the King's Cross inferno.

Not surprisingly the very special talent of Richard Neave and his team has been used by police attempting to put identities to skeletal remains of possible murder victims, and in 1990 he enjoyed remarkable success in the case of Karen Price, until then known simply as 'Little Miss Nobody', and for whose brutal killing two men were later jailed for life.

Technique

The technique of facial reconstruction is disarmingly simple – its tools consist of clay, modelling tools and a packet of cocktail sticks. It also requires the eyes and hands of an artist and the specialized knowledge of an anatomist.

The process starts with a cast of the skull made in a compound called Algenate. First the gaping eye sockets are fitted with polystyrene 'eyeballs' and the gaps around them filled; it is strange how the head already looks more 'human'. The next, vitally important stage is to drill small holes at significant anatomical points on the skull into which pieces of cocktail stick are pushed to a depth predetermined from a table showing the estimated thickness of body tissue at that point. The muscles are then gradually built up over the face with modelling clay to the height of the pegs. First the jaw and neck are constructed, followed by the cheeks and temples, the mouth and the eyes. The nose is always slightly problematical because the skull gives only very basic information, leaving it to the experience and inspiration of the sculptor to determine the finer shaping. The cheeks and jaw muscles then get filled out, and the thin layer of tissue over the forehead and scalp is put on in strips. By now the skull has been covered with clay and its surface is smoothed to give a semblance of skin. Ears and facial hair such as eyebrows are also problem areas relying on experience. Occasionally scalp hair has been found with the remains and this gives a general indication of the length of the subject's hair, but rarely the style in which it was worn. In the end, although no more is claimed for the face than that it is of the same *type* as the victim, the reconstructions produced at Manchester have produced some remarkable results.

The Work of Mikhail Gerasimov

The father of the technique of facial reconstruction was the Russian palaeontologist Mikhail Gerasimov. It was in the early 1920s that Gerasimov began to explore the correlation between the skull and the face based on previous work by Professor A.D. Grigoriev, holder of the chair in forensic medicine at the Third Medical University College in Moscow. Gerasimov worked under Grigoriev for two years, and finally developed a repetitive system of measurement of the thickness of the soft tissues of the heads of corpses awaiting dissection at the college; eventually sufficient reliable data had been assembled to attempt a reconstruction.

In 1925 Gerasimov was appointed scientific technical assistant at the Irkutsk Museum, and from 1927–30 was put in overall charge of the Department of Archaeology. During these years Gerasimov worked to reconstruct the faces of the earliest known fossil men – Neanderthaloid and Pithecanthropus. There followed a period while Gerasimov perfected his still infant art of facial reconstruction which culminated in his being awarded the unique degree of Doctor of Facial Science.

Despite considerable prejudice shown by criminologists, Mikhail Gerasimov was given the first opportunity to exercise his skills in the solution of a murder case – two years later he began one of the crowning achievements of his work when he led a team of Russian scientists into the tomb of the Mongol warrior king Tamerlane the Great; later he completed his celebrated reconstruction of the king's head. Like most tombs of the ancient kings, Tamerlane's had a curse on it – and among the superstitious it did not go unnoticed that the very day after Gerasimov opened the grave – 21 June 1941 – the Nazis launched their invasion of the Soviet Union.

In 1950, Professor Mikhail Gerasimov saw his dreams fulfilled with the founding of the Laboratory for Plastic Reconstruction at the Ethnographical Institute of the USSR Academy of Sciences.

Laser Facial Reconstruction

An exciting new technique was unveiled to the press and public in April 1991, when the world was introduced to Eymund the Viking, a fisherman from the tenth century. The project had been initiated by the Jorvik Viking Centre in the English city of York, once a Viking stronghold. A cemetery had been discovered in Fishergate and excavated in 1986, during the course of which some 68 burials were located. One of the interments was of a man, 5ft 6in tall and slightly built; **Anthropologists** set his age at late twenties to early thirties.

The lesson of facial reconstruction is that the appearance of an individual's face is determined largely by the skull underneath it, making it possible with the application of certain rules to rebuild a face with some accuracy. As part of a programme to create an authentic Viking setting in the town, the York Archaeological Trust (in the person of Dr Dominic Tweddle) entered into an ambitious and imaginative collaboration with Dr Robin Richards and his team at the Medical Physics Department of University College Hospital, London. The department had created a laser/computer technique for predicting the results of delicate facial surgery and it was this technology that would allow Tweddle to step back one thousand years and put flesh back on to the skull of the man he called Eymund.

The first stage was to clean the skull and repair any damage with plaster of Paris. It was then set on a turntable with a low power laser beam directed at it. As the skull rotates the laser beam is reflected back from the contours and picked up by a video camera which in turn passes the information on to a computer for reassembly. The second stage is to select a living person whose general appearance matches that of the skeletal remains – in this case a slightly built male. The man's head is laser-scanned in exactly the same way as the skull. When both sets of information have been put together in the computer they are amalgamated; the modern muscle tissue fills out the ancient skull, as that is what determines facial appearance. Finally, the computer information is fed to a milling machine which cuts an accurate three-dimensional portrait of the re-creation in hard foam. The final touches are added by a sculptor. The technique can be equally successful in putting features on to the skull of a possible homicide victim.

FIBRES

Like **Hairs**, fibres are among the most common transfer **Trace Evidence** between two individuals in close contact; and like hairs they are capable of accurate identification and comparison, not only by the ubiquitous **Comparison Microscope,** but by a whole range of sophisticated new techniques such as **Chromatography**, **Spectrometry**, and birefringence (see below).

In cases of serious crimes such as homicide the search for minute traces like fibres which had begun at the **Scene-of-Crime** will continue with the pathologist's **Post-Mortem** examination of the victim's body. Once a suspect has been identified, it is possible that samples will be taken from *all* his clothes for potential matching with scene-of-crime fibre traces. In the case of John Duffy, the notorious 'Railway Killer' who murdered three women on the outskirts of London in 1985–6, police removed no fewer than seventy items of clothing from the suspect's home, of which samples were taken from thirty. From among the two thousand individual fibres put under the microscope the Metropolitan Police laboratory was able to make a convincing thirteen positive identifications.

Identification and Comparison

Fibres can be divided into two main classes – Natural and Man-made. In turn natural fibres can be classified as having animal, vegetable or mineral origin.

Natural Fibres

Animal fibres: The structure of animal **Hairs** and the methods for their identification have been covered in a separate entry, but the following is a list of those most commonly found in fabrics, furnishings and floor coverings:

Wool	Mohair	Cashmere
Goat hair	Camel hair	Alpaca
Vicuna	Llama	Wild Silk
Horse	Rabbit	Cultivated Silk
Cow	Beaver	

Vegetable fibres: Like those of animal origin, vegetable fibres are easily identifiable under a microscope and can be compared with the collection of control samples kept in the biology laboratory. The composition of vegetable fibre is plant cells, made up of cellulose, fats and waxes, and colouring materials. They are classified according to their position on the growing plant:

1. Seed: The fibres, such as cotton and kapok, are attached to the plant's seed.
2. Fruit: Comprises the coarse fibres, such as coir which grows around the husk of the coconut.
3. Leaf: Fibres obtained from the fibrovascular bundles in the leaves of plants – manila and sisal are examples.
4. Stem (sometimes called the 'bast'): Main fibres are hemp, flax and jute: derived from the fibrous layers within plant stems.

Cotton	Kapok	Coir
Abaca	Alfa	Sisal
Henequen	Magney	Flax
Hemp	Jute	Kenal
Ramie	Sunn	

Mineral fibres: Asbestos, which is crushed from serpentine (hydrated magnesium silicate) and other rocks which are formed by their fibres running parallel.

Man-made Fibres

Until the nineteenth century the only sources of fibres for textile manufacture were either animal or vegetable. However, nearly half the fabrics used today have been manufactured using man-made fibres created from a wide range of materials from the commonly encountered polyester and nylon (organic polymers deriving from petrochemicals) to glass and metal.

Synthetic fibres are manufactured from a polymeric substance which has been made viscous through melting or dissolving in a solvent; this liquid is extruded under pressure through minute holes in a spinnerette (sometimes 'spinneret'). The resulting continuous fibres are then solidified either by immersion in hardening chemicals (viscose is produced by this process), evaporation of the solvent (cellulose acetate process), or air-cooling of melt-spun substances (nylon).

Each of a wide range of man-made fibres has been developed for its specific properties and uses, but there are a number of broad observations that can help initial identification:

1. Fibres are usually solid, though if a hollow fibre is required this can be induced at the spinning stage;
2. By altering the shape of the holes in the spinnerette fibres of different cross-section can be extruded;
3. Fibres normally consist of a single component but it is possible to create fibres for special purposes by bonding two polymers – e.g. sheath/core, side-by-side.

Natural Polymers	Synthetic polymers	Inorganic fibres
Viscose	Nylon	Glass
Hollow Viscose	Aramid ('Nomex'	Carbon
Modal	and 'Kelvar')	Rock Wool
Paper	Polyester	Aluminium Oxide
Cupro	Hollow Polyester	Aluminium Silicate
Acetate	Acrylic	Metallic Fibre
Triacetate	Modacrylic	
Alginate	Chlorofibre	
Protein	Fluorofibre	
Rubber	Vinylal	
	Polyethylene	
	Polypropylene	
	Polyurethane	
	Elastane	

Microscopy

The **Microscope** is the first instrument used in the laboratory in the identification and comparison of fibres. It has already been stated that most natural fibres can be identified solely by this means; however, owing to the similarity between different groups, man-made fibres can present a problem, and may need analysis by sophisticated instrumentation.

Birefringence

One of the optical properties of man-made fibres is double refraction, or birefringence. When the viscous liquid polymer is forced through the spinnerette it emerges with the molecules aligned parallel to the length of the fibre, causing a crystalline effect which is what makes the fibre strong. It also splits polarized light into two components causing it to emerge either parallel to or perpendicular to the length of the fibre. These two components, the two **Refractive Indexes** (see page 271) are each measured and the birefringence is the difference between the two resulting values. In this way different fibre types can be identified by their birefringence values compared with a specifications list or with a 'control' sample.

Fibre	REFRACTIVE INDEX		Birefringence
	Parallel	*Perpendicular*	
Acetate	1.478	1.477	0.001
Acrylic	1.524	1.520	0.004
Nylon 6	1.568	1.515	0.053
Polyester (Dacron)	1.710	1.535	0.175

Infra-red Spectromety
Like any other organic substance the polymer that comprises man-made fibres will selectively absorb infra-red light in a characteristic pattern, making infra-red the most suitable means of identifying fibres by **Spectrometry.**

Pyrolysis Gas Chromatography
Polymers such as plastics, paints and synthetic fibres are suited to the method of analysis known as Pyrolysis Gas **Chromatography**. Because of the difficulty of dissolving these polymers for injection into the gas chromatograph they are heated (or 'pyrolized') to a very high temperature so that they decompose into the gases which *can* be used (see page 109 for a description of the process).

Analysing Fibre Dyes
Methods suitable for the analysis and comparison of fibre dyes include **Spectrometry** and thin-layer **Chromatography.**

FINGER ABNORMALITIES

Every system is subject to exceptions, and in the **Fingerprint** system physical abnormalities of the fingers are encountered which make classification – and even the taking of prints – difficult:

Polydactyly
Supernumerary fingers which, though normally existing as an ill-formed appendage to the thumb or little finger, can occasionally manifest as six or more fully formed fingers.

Macrodactyly
Fingers that are abnormally long.

Syndactyly
Commonly called 'webbed fingers', where the digits are joined together with skin; the condition can be found in only the lower one or two joints, or as fusing the whole length of the finger. Cases have been recorded where all four fingers have been joined together in this way. A rarer abnormality occurs when the fingers are fused together not by skin but by the bones.

Brachydactyly
Fingers that are abnormally short.

Ectrodactyly
Where one or more digits have been absent from birth.

FINGERPRINTS

The Early History
Marcello Malpighi (1628–94)
Italian anatomist and microscopist who described the patterns on the tips of the fingers as part of an overall study of the skin; his contribution is immortalized by the lower epidermis being named the 'Malpighian layer'.

Dr Nehemiah Grew (1641–1712)
British contemporary of Malpighi, Fellow of the Royal Society and of the College of Physicians, described the 'innumerable little ridges' in *Philosophical Transactions for 1684*:

> For if anyone will but take the pains, with an indifferent glass to survey the palm of his hand, he may perceive . . . innumerable little ridges, of equal bigness and distance, and everywhere running

parallel one with another. And especially, upon the hands and first joints of the fingers and thumb. They are very regularly disposed into spherical triangles and elliptics.

Jan Evangelista Purkinje (1787–1869)
Czechoslovakian physiologist who, in 1823, recognized and described the basic patterns of fingerprints – 'whorls', 'ellipses', 'triangles', etc. in his *Commentatio de examine physiologico organi visus et systematis cutanei*:

After innumerable observations, I have found nine important varieties of patterns of rugae and sulci, though the lines of demarcation between the types are often obscure:

1. Transverse curve
2. Central longitudinal stria
3. Oblique stripe
4. Oblique loop
5. Almond whorl
6. Spiral whorl
7. Ellipse
8. Circle
9. Double whorl

William Herschel (1833–1917)
As a young administrative clerk in colonial India, Herschel began, around 1858, to be aware of the different shapes and patterns of fingerprints which illiterate workers had become accustomed to use in place of a signature. Several years later, he was able to find a practical application for this observation. Herschel was engaged in paying the government pensions to retired Bengali soldiers, when he gradually became conscious that the wily old Indians were collecting their pay, scribbling their mark, and joining the end of the queue again. By requiring all claimants to register their fingerprints on both their pay-book and their receipt it was possible to check them against each other for fraud. After many more years' interest in the wonders of the fingerprint, Herschel was able to prove one of the fundamentally important features of the marks – *that they did not change with age* (in fact, from the sixth month of inter-uterine life until death). It was, therefore, a bitter disappointment when the Inspector General of Prisons in Bengal dismissed Herschel's suggestion for a system of fingerprint classification and analysis, and in the later months of 1879 William Herschel returned to England.

Dr Henry Faulds (1843–1930)

This Scottish physiologist and medical missionary attached to the Tsuki Hospital, Tokyo, observed that in certain underdeveloped areas handprints served as signatures which, he discovered, were totally different each from the others. Faulds is credited with the first documented crime solved by the use of what he designated 'dactylography' or finger-writing. In the summer of 1879 a Tokyo sneak-thief had made his escape over a whitewashed garden wall leaving behind a dirty handprint. Inspecting this print and comparing it with that of a suspect Faulds was able to say with confidence that the luckless man under arrest was not the thief. The mirth with which this new tool of criminal detection was greeted by the Japanese police was silenced when three days later a felon was held who confessed to the robbery and whose handprint exactly matched that left on the wall. This convinced Faulds that he was on to a new breakthrough, and he communicated his news to that venerable London organ of gentlemen scientists, *Nature*:

> When bloody finger marks or impressions on clay, glass, etc. exist, they may lead to the scientific identification of criminals. Already I have had experience in two such cases . . . There can be no doubt as to the advance of having, besides their photographs, a nature-copy of the forever unchangeable finger furrows of important criminals. (October 1880)

This coincided with the arrival back in England of William Herschel – to find that his 'discovery' had been pre-empted. Herschel was understandably chagrined and there followed an acrimonious exchange of letters through *Nature's* correspondence columns before the controversy fizzled out and everybody forgot about finger-writing.

Sir Francis Galton (1822–1911)

The one man on whom the possibilities hinted at by Herschel and Faulds were not wasted, Galton was one of the most gifted and eclectic 'gentleman scientists' of his day, and was to make several important contributions in the field of meteorology. One of his more eccentric and least successful experiments was an attempt to estimate scientifically the efficacy of prayer. It was in the late 1880s, during his collaboration with Alphonse **Bertillon** into the possibility of an accurate system for the identification of criminals, that Galton recollected the 'dactylography' controversy, and sought the acquaintance of William Herschel. To Galton must go the full credit for moulding the process of fingerprint identification into a manageable science. From the ostensibly bewildering millions of different patterns Galton began to see basic recurring shapes and configurations of lines and that almost every print featured a 'triangle' where the ridges ran together. These triangles, or 'deltas' fell into four basic patterns:

1. No triangle
2. Triangle on the left
3. Triangle on the right
4. More than one triangle

Juan Vucetich (1858–1925)

An article by Galton published in the *Revue Scientifique* was read by a young officer in the Buenos Aires police department, Juan Vucetich. Vucetich had already begun researching methods of 'anthropomorphic measurement', and had discovered Galton's 'triangles' independently. He had developed, over a period of many years and without official finance, a remarkable ten-finger classification system of his own. As an 'unrecognized' fingerprint expert, Juan Vucetich was to play a leading role in the very first murder case in which fingerprint evidence was decisive. However, his recommendation for a national fingerprint record proved so violently unpopular (see **'Universal' Registers**) that Vucetich became disillusioned to the point of abandoning all further scientific research.

Edward Henry (1859–1931)

As Inspector General of the Bengal police, Henry read with professional interest Galton's book *Finger Prints* (1892). Fascinated by the potential of the system, Henry met and consulted with Galton and with his enthusiastic cooperation began work on developing the as yet incomplete classification system. Edward Henry was soon able to lay down the five discernible patterns which formed the basis of the system: Arches, Tented Arches, Radial Loops, Ulna Loops and Whorls. These were subsequently divided further into sub-patterns. In 1898 Henry published *The Classification and Uses of Finger Prints,* which remained the definitive police textbook on the subject of practical fingerprinting for many decades.

Landmarks
Great Britain
   1900

By now disquiet was already being felt at the prevailing method of keeping criminal records by a combination of Bertillon's 'anthropometry' and the infant science of 'dactylography'. A committee of inquiry under the chairmanship of Lord Belper was established to look into 'the working of the method of Identification of Criminals by Measurement and Fingerprints'. One of the experts to give evidence was Edward Henry, and in December 1900 the Belper Committee recommended that the current method be superseded by 'Mr Henry's system'.

   1901

On 1 July, Edward Henry was put in charge of Scotland Yard's new Fingerprint Branch. The previous requirement to take prints only of habitual criminals (that is, re-offenders) widened to include all prisoners whose sentence was more than one month.

   1902

June saw the first felon convicted through fingerprints found at the scene of the crime. A burglar named Harry Jackson left his thumbprint on the paintwork of a house he entered in South London, and despite the intimidating task of comparing thousands of prints Detective-Sergeant Charles Stockley Collins and his colleagues at the Branch identified it with Jackson's record card. In September the burglar was sentenced to seven years, and fingerprinting as a means of identification had been vindicated in the English courts.

   1905

The Stratton brothers appear before Mr Justice Channell at the Old Bailey; the first murder trial in which the prosecution relied on fingerprint evidence.

   1906

Edward Richard Henry knighted.

   1921

Now a Detective Superintendent, Charles Collins publishes his research on sending fingerprints by wireless telegraph, *A Telegraphic Code for Fingerprint Formulae*. Collins saw in his 'code' the basis for a 'single-fingerprint' identification system; this important work was continued by Detective Chief Inspector Harry Battley when he took charge of the department on Collins' retirement in 1926. Battley, in collaboration with another great pioneer, Frederick Cherrill, published *Single Fingerprints* (1930).

1931

First palmprint case to be brought before an English court. Due to the prisoner's plea of guilty, however, Detective Inspector Cherrill was not required to present his evidence.

1937

Mr Rupert de la Bere asked the Home Secretary in a Commons question whether he would consider a scheme for a 'national registration of fingerprints' to assist the identification of people 'suffering loss of memory'. The idea was rejected.

1942

The first case of a palmprint found at the scene of a crime being matched to one of Scotland Yard's small but growing collection. Sam Dashwood was consequently hanged by the print that he had left on a safe door when he committed robbery and murder.

1948

Mass fingerprinting for the first time in Britain in an attempt to identify the brutal killer of three-year-old June Anne Devaney.

1953

A meeting between the Home Office and experts from five of the major fingerprint bureaux reached agreement on a national standard for fingerprint identification evidence given in court.

1955

First mass palmprinting takes place around Potters Bar, London, in an attempt to identify the killer of Mrs Elizabeth Currell.

1964

Gerald Lambourne, as head of Scotland Yard's Fingerprint Bureau, begins work on the computerization of the nation's almost two million sets of fingerprints.

1970

The technique of 'lifting' prints becomes acceptable practice in the British police for the first time.

1973

Importation of the Videofile system, designed by the Ampex Corporation of Redwood City, California, to transfer all the fingerprint records currently being computerized on to videotape. The custom-designed system was installed in 1975.

1978

Further innovations are always under test at the Police Scientific Development Branch, and by 1978 it had become possible to look realistically at automatic fingerprint recognition. After a laboratory test period the Automatic Fingerprint Recognition System (AFR) was installed for working tests.

United States of America
1904

In May the World's Fair was hosted by the town of St Louis, Missouri, and while the British sent six representatives of the Metropolitan Police Force to guard the Royal Pavilion, the American International Association of Chiefs of Police moved its bureau from Washington DC, to St Louis for the duration of the exhibition. Here John Ferrier of Scotland Yard's Fingerprint Branch was able to lecture the International Association on the advantages of finger-printing over 'Bertillonage'. In the same year Detective-Sergeant Joseph A. Faurot of the New York police visited London to study fingerprinting under Charles Collins at Scotland Yard, and encouraged by British successes it was not long before fingerprinting became established in the United States as the main system of criminal identification.

1911

The People V. Jennings. In the same year, the case of the burglar Caesar Cella who was convicted on the fingerprint evidence of Faurot becomes national news.

1915

Foundation, in California, of the International Association for

Criminal Identification (IAI), an organization which continues to flourish to this day.

1918

State V. Kuhl, heard in the American Appeal Court, a crucial case challenging the admissibility of palmprint evidence.

1924

Foundation of the FBI Identification Division. Records of the National Bureau of Crirnnal Investigation housed at Leavenworth Penitentiary removed to Washington – among them the core collection of 810,000 fingerprint cards.

1928

Fingerprinting of *all* criminals introduced in New York State.

1971

Computerized Criminal History file added to the National Crime Information Center (NCIC) containing personal descriptions of people arrested for serious crime, including a computer-based fingerprint classification.

1977

Kodak introduces the 'Miracode Retrieval System'.

Case Study

FIRST MURDER CONVICTIONS ON FINGERPRINT EVIDENCE

FRANCESCA ROJAS (Argentina, 1892)

In 1892, the work of Argentinian fingerprint expert Juan Vucetich was responsible for securing the first ever 'fingerprint conviction' for murder.

The victims of this cynical crime were the two illegitimate children of Francesca Rojas, who lived in Necochea, outside Buenos Aires. The children, aged four and six, were found bludgeoned to death in their shack home, and the mother, too, was slightly wounded. Suspicion inevitably fell on a man-friend of Francesca's, a farmer named

Velasquez; indeed, she herself accused him. It was a lucky day for Velasquez when a disciple of Juan Vucetich was assigned to his case. Fingerprints in blood found on the shanty door were later matched with those of Francesca Rojas herself. Whether, at this stage in the development of fingerprinting, it would have been accepted as evidence in court is debatable, but Señora Rojas was so impressed that she broke down and confessed to the murders and to hurting herself superficially to reinforce her story.

It transpired that a new amour had proposed marriage – if only she were not encumbered by children . . .

HENRI-LEON SCHEFFER (France, 1902)
Paris, 1902: Europe is about to witness its first important fingerprint case. The scene of the crime is the luxury apartment of dentist-surgeon Monsieur Alaux, the victim his valet, Joseph Reibel. On 17 October, Alphonse **Bertillion** was summoned to the scene, where he found the rooms ransacked, though so little had been stolen as to make robbery unlikely.

As Bertillon began the business of photographing the scene, he observed a pane of glass broken out of a wall cabinet, lying splintered on the carpet. It was obvious from the blood that the intruder had cut himself and obligingly left behind a set of bloody fingerprints. It was Bertillon's lack of enthusiasm for fingerprints that was nearly his undoing, for although he routinely included prints on his anthropometric record cards, there existed no logical classification – thousands of cards had to be checked with a glass, and if Joseph Reibel's assassin had never been arrested, never been 'Bertillonized', the search would be wasted.

Fate was surely smiling that grey winter's day when Bertillon, with a shout of triumph, held aloft the record card of Henri-Leon Scheffer, convicted swindler recently of Marseilles. The good policemen of that port were spared the need to root Scheffer out when, burdened with guilt and remorse, he gave himself up.

As Bertillon had suspected, it was not a case of burglary; Reibel and Scheffer had been homosexual lovers who fell out, and Scheffer had killed in a moment of passion and attempted to fake a robbery.

For Alphonse Bertillon it was one more accolade. One might have hoped he would reassess his attitude towards a fingerprint classification system for the Sûreté. But he did not; and it was only after Bertillon's death that his anthropometric records were scrapped in favour of dactylography.

ALFRED AND ALBERT STRATTON (England, 1905)

William Jones arrived for work at the Deptford oil and colour shop in the rain; it was before eight, but the boy was familiar with Mr Farrow's habit of opening up early, and was surprised to find the door locked. Unable to rouse anybody he set off for Greenwich where George Chapman, who owned the shop, had his own business. Chapman sent an assistant back with Jones, and together they forced an entry. It was a badly shaken pair of lads who, minutes later, were running to the nearby police station.

Officers found seventy-year-old Thomas Farrow first – beaten to death in the back parlour. Upstairs they found his wife, still alive, but with such dreadful injuries that she died three days later.

Meanwhile, Scotland Yard's Chief Inspector Fox took command of the scene-of-crime search, which yielded a vital clue. One which would change the course of British criminal identification procedure, and would elevate this sordid crime into national celebrity. More important, it would introduce a completely new feature to crime investigation. Close to the body of Thomas Farrow the police found a cashbox, which had been forced open and robbed of its contents; in the process a right thumbprint was left on the metal tray. When comparison had eliminated persons known to have handled the box, it was clear that the print belonged to the murderer. A simple deduction, but this was 1905, and the Yard's Fingerprint Department was only four years old. Besides, there was no precedent for such evidence being acceptable in a capital case. It had been difficult enough to convince scientists of the unique characteristics of fingerprints – what chance with a jury of twelve ordinary people?

Before long a pair of vicious petty crooks, Alfred and Albert Stratton, were picked up and taken to Tower Bridge police station where Detective Inspector Charles Collins took their fingerprints. This established beyond doubt that the thumbprint on the cash box belonged to Alfred Stratton. It remained to convince a court, and when the case opened at the Old Bailey in May 1905, it was not only the brothers Stratton who were on trial, but the credibility of fingerprint identification. Sir Richard Muir, for the Crown, in partnership with Charles Collins in the witness box, patiently inducted the jury in the technicalities of fingerprinting. With the aid of giant enlargements, they showed how comparisons were made between Alfred's thumbprint and the impression left on the cash box. Clearly impressed with this new information, the jury had one of their own members fingerprinted in order to test the theory.

The judge seemed quite unconvinced by this new-fangled system. Nevertheless, he acknowledged a strong resemblance between the two fingerprints, and the jury, after a brief retirement, announced a verdict of guilty. Thus the end of Alfred and Albert Stratton – hanged by a fingerprint – was the beginning of a new era in the fight against crime.

THOMAS JENNINGS (USA, 1911)

It was not until 1911 that fingerprint evidence was admitted in a criminal case in a United States court. The case began in Chicago on 19 September 1910. At 2 a.m. Clarence Hiller went to investigate a strange noise in the house and came face to face with an intruder. They struggled, then both men fell to the bottom of the stairs. Two shots rang out, followed by the slamming of the front door. Mrs Hiller ran down to the lifeless body of her husband and screamed.

Meanwhile, a mile away, two officers about to go off duty had their suspicions aroused by a man coming towards them. He was cautioned and searched, which revealed a loaded revolver and bloodstains on his clothing – enough to earn an invitation to the station. There, officers learned his name was Thomas Jennings, recently released from Joliet Penitentiary.

Scene-of-crime detectives had by now found perfect impressions of four fingers of a left hand on a newly painted window frame at the Hillers' house, prints that matched Jennings' prison record in every detail.

After a trial that was to make US legal history, Jennings was sentenced to death for the murder of Clarence Hiller; his lawyers lodged an appeal claiming the unreliability of fingerprint evidence. It was fifteen months before the Supreme Court of Illinois reached its historic decision. On 21 December 1911, it ruled:

When photography was first introduced it was seriously questioned whether pictures thus created could properly be introduced in evidence, but this method of proof, as well as by means of X-rays and the microscope, is now admitted without question . . . We are disposed to hold from the evidence of the four witnesses who testified, and from the writings we have referred to on this subject, that there is a scientific basis for the system of fingerprint identification, and that the courts are justified in admitting this class of evidence . . . The general rule is that whatever tends to prove any material fact is relevant and competent.

The Value of Fingerprints as Evidence

The enormous significance of fingerprints in establishing personal identity has been recognized for more than a century, and their use can be divided into three main categories:

1. *The confirmation of the identity of a known criminal already in custody*. A comparatively simple task as fingerprints both from the suspect and criminal records will be complete and only require cross-checking through classificanon.
2. *The identification of a suspect in custody by comparison with prints left at the crime scene*.
3. *Matching prints left at the scene of a crime with those of a known criminal on record*. The ease with which this will be possible depends upon the state of the marks left.

Characteristics

Any system of identification and classification relies on being able to observe variations on a series of known features. In fingerprinting these 'features' are the shapes and configurations of the papillary ridges and furrows. The following is a list of the standard ridge variations:

1. Bifurcation
2. Hook
3. Scar
4. Downthrust ridge ending
5. Upthrust ridge ending
6. Ridge crossing
7. Enclosure (or Eye)
8. Island (or Short Ridge)

Fixed, or 'Focal' Points
For the purpose of classification, Loop. Whorl and Composite impressions (see below) have two fixed points:

Delta – Called the Outer Terminus

A delta may be formed in two ways:

1. Where the upper and lower sides of the delta are formed by the bifurcation of a single ridge, and the point of bifurcation is the 'outer terminus' (where there is more than one bifurcation the outer terminus is that nearest the 'core'):

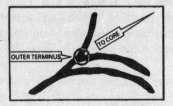 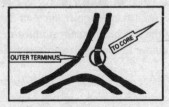

2. Where the upper and lower sides of the delta are formed by the abrupt divergence of two ridges that had previously been running side by side. The nearest ridge in front of the point where divergence begins is the outer terminus:

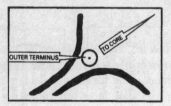 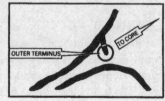

Core – Called the Inner Terminus:

A core will consist of:

1. An even or uneven number of ridges which are *not* joined together:

In the case of an even number, the ridge *farthest from the delta* is the 'point' of the core; in the case of an uneven number, the top of the middle ridge is the point:

  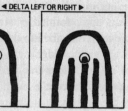

2. Two ridges joined at the top (sometimes called a 'staple'). The shoulder of the staple *furthest from the delta* is the point of the core:

Various types of cores

The Four Main Divisions

All fingerprint impressions can be divided into four main 'types' and some variations of these types:

Loops

Types of Loops – classification according to the formula below as either Radial or Ulnar

. Wide range of variations where some of the ridges make a backward turn; there is one delta. Loops are divided into two groups important to the technique of classification:

1. Where ridges around the core have a downward slope towards the *left* and the delta on the right.
2. Where the ridges around the core have a downward slope to the *right* and the delta on the left.

If group 1. appears on a finger of the right hand it is called a *Radial Loop*.

If group 2. appears on a finger of the left hand it is called a *Radial Loop*.

If group 1. appears on a finger of the left hand it is called an *Ulnar Loop*.

If group 2. appears on a finger of the right hand it is called an *Ulnar Loop*.

In classifying right-hand prints: the symbol \ is used for Ulnar
the symbol / is used for Radial

In classifying left-hand prints: the symbol / is used for Ulnar
the symbol \ is used for Radial

This is best seen on a hypothetical diagram:

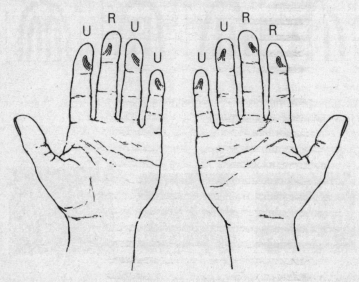

Arches

Where the ridges run from one side of the finger to the other making no backward turn. There is no delta as such.

Tented Arches

As above, except that near the middle of the pattern there is an upward thrust which gives the effect of an axis or 'spine' towards which the ridges converge.

Whorls

In this wide category some of the ridges complete a turn through at least one complete circuit, and there are two deltas.

Compounds

These include patterns which combine two or more of the above types in the same print.

Central Pockets

  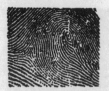

Sometimes, for convenience, included under 'Whorls', the pattern has several ridges about the core of the Whorl type, while the rest of the pattern conforms to the 'Loop' type. (In the United States commonly included under Loops.)

Lateral Pockets

Two Loops; two deltas which are on the *same side* as the ascending Loop.

Twinned Loops

Two well-defined Loops intertwined; with two deltas on *either side* of the ascending Loop.

Composites

Comparatively uncommon patterns which comprise complex Whorls possessing three, four, and even five deltas.

Accidentals

Rare patterns too irregular to group under any other 'Compound' category. Comprise complex Whorls possessing three, four, and even five deltas.

The 'Henry' System

Introduction
A full description of the 'Henry' system of fingerprint classification (incorporating, as it now does, so many modifications) is too large an undertaking for a general overview such as this. However, the following explanation of classification and retrieval will give readers a working understanding of the basic principles.

The system depends upon the fact that all prints fall into one of four main types:

    Arches
    Loops
    Whorls
    Compounds

and statistics indicate that

    60 per cent of prints are Loops
     5 per cent of prints are Arches
    35 per cent of prints are Whorls and Compounds

Primary Classification
For Primary Classification purposes, Arches are combined with Loops (L) and Compounds with Whorls (W).

The hands are viewed together, and grouped into five pairs of fingers:

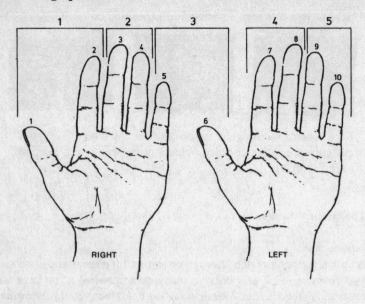

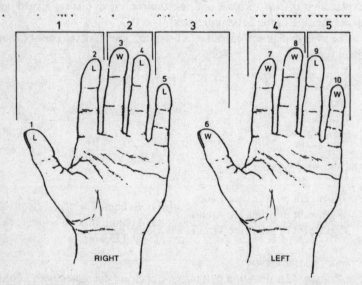

Mathematically, the possible combinations for a second pair would be the same, making the available combinations for two pairs together 16 [4×4], for three pairs 64[4×16], for four pairs 256 [4×64], and for all five pairs 1,024 [4×256] = 32^2. By allocating a different numerical value to a print with a Whorl, according to its position on the hand, we can establish a formula for every combination, and any print with a Whorl (W) can be given a value according to the adjoining pair (reading from left to right):

Fingers 1–2 = 16, Fingers 3–4 = 8, Fingers 5–6 = 4
Fingers 7–8 = 2, Fingers 9–10 = 1

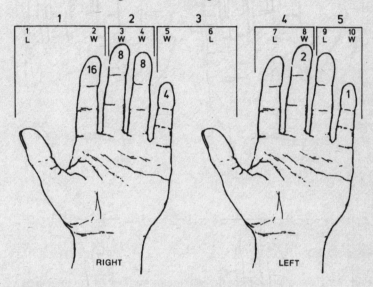

Each pair of fingers can now be written as a fraction:

Numerators	0	8	0	2	0		10
	–	–	–	–	–	adding to	—
Denominators	0	0	4	2	1		7

(It should be noted that hands with no Whorls equal $\frac{0}{0}$ which is given the value $\frac{1}{1}$ in order to satisfy the mathematical requirement for all pairs to equal 32^2, and 1 is added to the Numerator and Denominator of the sum of all other cases.)

For example:

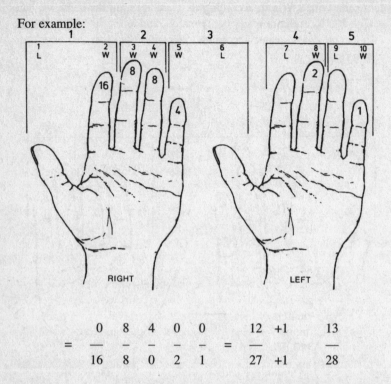

$$= \frac{0}{16} \quad \frac{8}{8} \quad \frac{4}{0} \quad \frac{0}{2} \quad \frac{0}{1} = \frac{12}{27} \quad \frac{+1}{+1} \quad \frac{13}{28}$$

Following these principles, the maximum number of combinations of Whorls and Loops (including Arches) is 1,024, with fractions between $\frac{1}{1}$ (all Loops) and $\frac{32}{32}$ (all Whorls).

In practice, groupings do not occur in equal proportions (for example, the group in which no Whorls at all appear, $\frac{1}{1}$, is by far the largest). Clearly in these cases further sub-division is essential.

*Secondary Classification**

In this sub-division, the Index finger of each hand is taken as a 'fulcrum', symbolized by a capital letter. The Thumb takes a small (lower case) letter to the left of the fulcrum, the remaining fingers (all small letters) are placed to the right of the fulcrum in the equation.

As they occur comparatively infrequently, only Arches (*A* or *a*), Tented Arches (*T* or *t*) and Radial Loops (*R* or *r*) are used (either capital or small letters).

*In the United States this is called 'Small-letter Grouping'.

Take the previous primary classification formula $\frac{1}{1}$ (no Whorls) and add Secondary Classification:

Numerator (R.H.)	1	a A r	*a*rch	Arch	*r*ad. Loop
Denominator (L.H.)	1	r R A	*r*adial Loop	*R*ad. Loop	*a*rch

This, of course, can be done with any primary numerical formula.

Sub-classes: Can be formed when Whorls *(W or w)* and Ulnar Loops *(U or u)* are added as possible ingredients to Secondary Classification:

1	a	U	a	–	t
1	–	R	–	u	w

Ridge Counting

In the paragraphs on characteristics of fingerprints above, the terms *Outer Terminus* (delta) and *Inner Terminus* (core) were explained. One of the finer degrees of classification and retrieval is determined by counting the number of ridges between the outer and inner termini on the Index and Middle fingers.

An imaginary line is drawn between the two points and the ridges that the line crosses (excepting the termini) are counted:

On the Index Finger

Counts between 1–9 ridges are termed Inner (*I*); Counts of 10 or more are termed Outer *(O)*.

On the Middle Finger

Counts between 1–10 ridges are termed Inner (*I*); Counts of 11 or more are termed Outer *(O)*.

The formula may now read:

Num. (R.H.)	1	a A r	IO	Index = 10 ridges; middle = 11
Den. (L.H.)	1	r R a	I I	Index = 9 ridges; middle = 8

Ridge Counting (Final)

A sub-classification called 'Final' (although it is not by any means) takes the ridge-count of the *Right Little Finger* and adds it to the existing formula:

Num. (R.H.) 1   a A r   10
  —   ———   —
                                7 [Right Little Finger = 7]
Den. (L.H.) 1   r R a   11

Conclusion

There are further sub-division and sub-classification systems in use in many parts of the world, notably the United States and Great Britain.

At best, this traditional classification system is cumbersome, and advances in micro-technology have enabled significant strides forward to be made in classifying, retrieving and comparing fingerprint information by computer.

Identification Standards

When a print found at the scene of a crime is matched with an example in the Criminal Records Office it must show a convincing enough resemblance to establish a common origin. Different countries' legal systems make greater or lesser demands for these 'Identification Standards'. In 1953 a meeting between Britain's Home Office, the Director of Public Prosecutions and experts from five of the major regional fingerprint bureaux – Scotland Yard, Lancashire, Manchester, West Riding and Birmingham – reached agreement on a national standard of sixteen points of resemblance. These points (in the case of a *complete* single print) are considered to be irrefutable evidence of identity in a court of law.

The following partial table of international requirements illustrates just how exacting the British standard is:

France	17 points of reference
Great Britain	16
Greece	
Switzerland	
Yugoslavia	12
Spain	
Sweden	10
Turkey	8
India	6–12 (depending on State)
USA	No longer has a standard

It was in 1973 that the US Standardization Committee of the International Association for Identification recommended abandoning a formal standard. Their report stated that a minimum requirement had no scientific validity.

Developing Latent Prints

Fingerprints encountered during the course of a criminal investigation are likely to have been deposited in one of three ways:

1. As an impression in some soft substance, such as wax, putty, soap, wet paint, etc.
2. A print made by a deposit on the finger – dirt, oil, blood, paint, etc.
3. The deposit of secretions from the skin. This will include varying amounts of natural substances, such as amino acids, oils, urea, salts, etc.

In the first two cases the print is usually obvious, and can be photographed, 'lifted', or carried away to the laboratory. As a matter of course all prints that can be made visible before treatment for example, by angling against the light – must first be photographed.

With deposits left by the skin (called 'latent' prints), these are often barely visible and require some means of 'enhancement' to reveal them. At its simplest the technique may be the brushing on of fine powder, though a vast range of more or less sophisticated procedures has been devised by forensic laboratories to meet every eventuality, including techniques for revealing fingerprints left on human skin.

The following annotated list covers basic techniques and procedures, and a supplementary table presents 'state-of-the-art' information on new advances as recommended by the British Home Office.

Powders

1. Fine carbon powder (vegetable black) for latent prints on smooth, firm, light-coloured surfaces.
2. Aluminium powder or Lanconide (white) for latent prints on smooth, firm, dark-coloured surfaces.

Advantages: Powders are quick and inexpensive, and can be used immediately at the scene of the crime.

Disadvantages: Messy and may interfere with other forensic traces. Should not be used on wet or sticky surfaces.

Iodine Vapour

A technique developed for enhancing prints on rough, absorbent, light-coloured surfaces, such as paper and cloth. The print is exposed to the vapour from iodine crystals in an enclosed fume cabinet, and as the oil in the fingerprint secretion absorbs the iodine the print develops as a brown image.

Advantage: Quick and simple to carry out on small objects.

Disadvantages: Comparatively short time in which the image fades thus requiring fixing, and insensitivity to fingerprints more than a few days old. Unsuitable on metal, which it corrodes.

Ninhydrin

A simple general purpose reagent, ideal for paper and some other porous surfaces, such as raw wood and plasterboard. Ninhydrin reacts with amino acids and other components of the fingerprint to produce a purple image.

Advantages: Simplicity of use, and ability to detect fingerprints months, even years old.

Disadvantages: Because of the metabolic composition of some prints they may not be detected by this method. Stubborn fingerprints may take several weeks to develop, and may require retreatment.

Gentian Violet

Used to treat fingerprints on sticky surfaces, such as adhesive tapes and films, and other surfaces contaminated by grease and oil. Working solution comprises Gentian Violet + Phenol + Alcohol, the dye staining the fatty constituents of the print an intense violet, the phenol removing stickiness.

Advantages: Simple, cheap process ideal for its purpose.

Disadvantages: Very toxic and must be applied in a fume cupboard, making it unsuitable for treating large surfaces. Not suitable on porous surfaces.

Amido Black

Specifically for the enhancement of faint blood prints, Amido Black is a dye which stains the protein present in blood blue-black.

Advantages: A simple, inexpensive process.

Disadvantages: Will only stain blood. Will not develop prints containing only the usual constituents of sweat.

Development of Fingerprints on Skin

While fingerprints contaminated with, say, grease may be routinely developed on dry skin with powders, or blood prints examined under ultraviolet or laser light, there is as yet no convincing body of research into the various experimental methods of developing *latent* fingerprints on skin. The difficulty lies mainly in the shrinking of the skin after death, causing prints to distort or disappear.

Techniques under trial are:

1. Transfer of print to Kromecote (glazed art paper) then dusting with powder.
2. Magnetic powder transferred on to Dacty-foil.
3. Iodine transferred on to silver plate.
4. Lead dust followed by X-ray imaging.

In this last case, the process was developed in Scotland at the Glasgow Victoria Infirmary by two radiographers named Daniel Graham and Hugh Gray. The technique is that of Electron Autography, where a high-energy primary beam of X-rays, hardened by being passed through copper, irradiates the emitting material (in this case lead powder) and releases electrons to form an image. Lead is chosen because its high atomic number permits a large emission of electrons which give a strong image on film.

Lifting Prints

To those accustomed to reading detective fiction it may come as a surprise to learn that the technique of 'lifting' fingerprints only became acceptable practice in the British police forces in 1970. Prior to this the photographic team were required to record fingerprints *in situ* – not always either easy or effective; or worse, manhandle cumbersome objects back to the laboratory for treatment. It was firmly believed (against all evidence from abroad) that lifting prints would damage the evidence to such a degree that it would be disallowed in court.

Lifting takes place after the latent print has been dusted, and is effected by the simple technique of laying a strip of low-adhesive tape over the developed print, rubbing the back gently but firmly to 'lift' the impression, then carefully removing the tape. Finally, the tape is placed

	Fluorescence examination	Amido Black	Gentian Violet	Iodine	Ninhydrin	Physical developer	Powders	Radioactive Sulphur Dioxide	Silver Nitrate	Small Particle Reagent (dish development)	Small Particle Reagent (spray development)	Sudan Black	Superglue	Vacuum metal deposition
Blood	●	⊙			●	●	○							
Fabric								○						
Wax/waxed surfaces	●						○			◄		●	●	●
Raw wood (untreated)	●				⊙	○	○		○					
Untreated metal	●		◁				○			◄		●	●	◄
Adhesive coated *paper*	●				●	⊙								◄
Adhesive coated surfaces	●	⊙						●						
Vinyl/Rubber/Leather	●						○			◄	●		●	○
Plastic packaging	●						○			◄◁		○	○	⊙
Paper + board	●					⊙	●	○						
Rough/non-porous surfaces	●	◄					○			◄		●	●	◄
Smooth/non-porous surfaces	●	◄				⊙				◄		●	●	○

Legend:

- ⊙ Most Effective Method
- ● Effective
- ○ Not Most Effective Method
- ◄ Small Articles Only
- ◁

(adhesive side down) on to a suitable piece of clean white card which is marked with details, such as case number, date, location, name of fingerprint officer, etc. The lifted print can now be removed to the laboratory for photographing.

In the United States an alternative method uses a rubber 'lifter pad'. The thin, transparent celluloid cover is removed from the adhesive side of the patch which is then used to lift the print in the same way as tape. The lifted print is re-covered with the celluloid for storage and transportation.

The Technique of Taking Prints

Taking Fingerprints

The following procedures derive from the British Home Office manual *Methods of Taking Fingerprints,* and the US Department of Justice's *Science of Fingerprints:*

1. Place a small amount of ink on the surface provided and roll out to a fine, even coating.
2. Roll each finger in the ink, from one side of the nail to the other, starting with the right thumb. Be sure to ink to just below the first joint of the finger.
3. Roll the finger on to the appropriate section of the standard form (they do not vary greatly around the world). It is essential to roll from nail edge to nail edge in order to include any 'deltas' which fall to either side of the 'pattern'. Only a slight pressure is required so as not to blur or clog the ridge marks.
4. Continue with the right forefinger, and so on through the right and then the left hand.
5. When the ten fingers have been individually recorded, the four fingers of the right hand are printed simultaneously, then the left four. This provides a check that the individual prints have been recorded in their correct sequence.
6. Finally, the two thumb prints are taken simultaneously in their respective boxes.

Taking Palm Prints

Success in taking palmars relies on care and a steady technique. United States and British practices tend to differ; the American variant is given first:

1. Around a cylinder of about 7.5cm in diameter and 12.5cm wide, roll a sheet of blank white paper and secure at either end with an elastic band.
2. Load the roller (preferably just wider than a hand) with ink, transfer it across the palm in a light manner, but sufficient to cover all areas; start at the fingertips and work towards the wrist.
3. Placing the paper-wrapped cylinder under the fingertips, get the subject to roll the cylinder gently, so depositing the print.
4. The finished print should be dated and signed by both the subject and the officer taking it. In British practice an impression of the right forefinger is taken alongside the palm.

British Variation

Stage 3, according to *Methods of Taking Fingerprints,* should be carried out as follows:

A sheet of paper is laid over a round ruler about one inch in diameter and one foot long (a section from a broom handle is suggested in an emergency). The inked hand is slowly and evenly rolled forward, the operator's hand controlling the movement. Rolling continues until the heel of the hand has passed over the ruler.

Fingerprinting the Dead

In most cases of suspicious death, fingerprinting will form part of the post-mortem identification procedure. However, due to the potential importance of other forensic traces on the hands or under the finger-nails, fingerprinting should be left until last; then both finger- and palm-prints should be taken.

Methods

The Recently Dead

With the corpses of the recently dead, it is not necessary to observe any special procedures save to recognize that fingerprinting is more easily effected when *rigor mortis* has passed off, and if the body has been in cold storage, when it has thawed.

For practical reasons it is advisable to cut the fingerprint forms so that each finger can be printed separately (more than one attempt may be needed for some digits) and the complete 'good' set pasted back on to a complete form.

Difficult Cases

In the case of hands in a difficult state of decomposition or mummi-fication, application should be made to the coroner to have the hands surgically removed from the body for fingerprinting. In some extreme cases it may be necessary for the individual digits to be removed – in which case they must be put into separate, clearly labelled containers.

Hardened and contracted flesh: In instances where a body has become 'mummified', it is essential to soften the finger tissues before attempting to take prints. Soaking in a solution of glycol, lactic acid and distilled water is the usual procedure, though in some extreme cases the process may take several weeks.

Skin wrinkled by damp: There are three reliable ways of treating this condition:

1. With a hypodermic syringe, injecting glycerine or liquified paraffin wax into the bulb of the finger from below the joint.
2. Gently manipulating the tips of the fingers between the operator's thumb and forefinger.
3. Removing the skin from the fingertip, scraping off the surplus flesh, and mounting.

Skin peeling after long immersion in water: By cutting around the joint below the bulb, the skin may be removed like the finger of a glove; slipped over the operator's own finger (over a thin surgical glove), it may be printed in the usual way.

Where the skin has peeled off flat, carefully ink the underside of the skin where a reverse image of the ridges may still be intact. The ink will enable the 'print' to be photographed.

A similar method is to take a cast in silicon rubber of the underside of the skin which can be mounted and printed.

In some cases where the ridges seem to have disappeared with bloating, it is possible to suspend the dermis in hot Neatsfoot oil, which shrinks the skin to reveal the pattern.

Case Study

THE ROCHDALE MUMMY

On Tuesday 15 March 1977, the mortal remains of James Finley were found unceremoniously bundled up in a shopping trolley in the garbage bay of a municipal housing complex in Rochdale.

Not that anybody knew it was Finley at the time; the head had been enclosed by a plastic bag inside which millions of maggots had picked the face clean of any identifying features. The skin of the trunk had been mummified, though the comparatively good state of preservation of the internal organs made it possible to identify barbiturate poisoning.

The hands were in a particularly advanced stage of decay, and with the deterioration of the skin any hope of fingerprint identification appeared lost. However, Detective Chief Inspector Tony Fletcher was able to reappraise them with the advantage of some very special experience. Not long before the finding of the 'Rochdale Mummy', Fletcher had been involved with Manchester Museum's Department of

Egyptology on a scientific analysis of its mummies. The problem he now faced was essentially similar, and Fletcher decided to use the technique he had developed at the museum on the one finger of this corpse that might yield a print.

A special quick-drying, fine-grain dental putty was gently applied to the tip of the finger and left to set. The 'mould' was then carefully peeled off and the inside treated with several coats of acrylic paint; when the paint was dry and had been removed it reproduced an accurate cast of the fingerprint which could be printed by the usual ink-and-roll method. It showed a remarkable sixteen points of similarity with those of James Edward Finley, whose prints were already on file.

Eventually, Mrs Eileen Finley admitted that, eighteen months previously, she and her husband had been having one of their frequent squabbles, during which she found herself on the receiving end of James's fists. In a fit of anger he threatened to kill himself and Eileen obligingly threw him a bottle of sodium amytal tablets, and with a parting 'Bloody well get on with it, then!' stalked out. Returning several hours and many drinks later, Eileen Finlay found her husband lying dead on the sofa.

Tying a bag over his head so she could not see his face, Eileen Finley pushed the body into a cupboard where it remained until March 1977 when eviction made its removal necessary. Where more appropriate than the rubbish bay of the flats?

Despite a suspicion that Mrs Finley might have been more than a passive participant she was tried and convicted only of two obscure criminal charges – concealing a death, and not giving James a decent Christian burial.

Mass Fingerprinting

Case Study

PETER GRIFFITHS

At 1.20 a.m., Saturday 15 May 1948, nurse Gwendoline Humphreys was making her routine round of children's ward CH3 at Queen's Park Hospital, Blackburn. Of the twelve cots only six had occupants, and the oldest was three-year-old June Anne Devaney. Nurse Humphreys' heart-beat stopped momentarily as she looked into the empty cot, where

June had been sleeping. With help from the Night Sister, Gwen Humphreys searched the immediate area, noticing a vitally important piece of evidence – beneath June's bed was a large 'Winchester' bottle of the type commonly found in hospitals. Having failed to locate the child, the local police were alerted, and officers began a systematic search of the grounds. Ninety minutes later June Devaney's body was found; she had been sexually assaulted and suffered terrible injuries to the head.

Detective Chief Inspector Colin Campbell, head of the Lancashire Fingerprint Bureau, arrived at the hospital later in the morning and began collecting evidence, including fingerprints on the bottle which had inexplicably been placed by June Devaney's cot.

It became the task of detectives from the Lancashire Constabulary to trace and fingerprint every person who in the past two years could have had a legitimate reason to be in the ward. In one month they made 642 sets of prints. On the bottle, Campbell had eliminated all but one set; these, he declared, were the marks of June's killer. But fingerprints are only useful where there is a suspect with whose prints they can be compared, or when a match can be found in police files. In this case there was no suspect, and whoever killed June Devaney had no previous record.

The situation demanded desperate measures, and Yard commanders took the unprecedented step of fingerprinting every male over sixteen who had been in Blackburn on the 14th and 15th of May; the Chief Constable gave his solemn assurance that all prints taken would later be destroyed or, if preferred, returned to the donor. Using twenty officers and the electoral register, Inspector Barton began a trawl of more than 35,000 homes. Colin Campbell designed special compact cards for the convenience of the 'mobile' fingerprint squad, with spaces on one side for name, address, National Registration number (a wartime require-ment), and the left thumb and forefinger prints; on the reverse other fingers of the left hand (to match with the prints on the Winchester bottle).

Towards the end of July the fingerprinting had been all but completed but revealed no apparent lead; it began to look as though June Devaney's killer had slipped through the net. Then a procedure was tried that would be impossible today. In the immediate post-war years, rationing persisted, and records were kept of the issue of ration books and the Registration Number by which they and their owners were identified. It was a simple if time-consuming operation to check the local registration file against the numbers on the fingerprint cards, the shortfall being those individuals who had been missed.

In the event some 200 sets were missing; one of them belonged to Peter Griffiths, a twenty-two year-old former soldier then living in Blackburn. At 3 p.m. on Thursday 12 August Chief Inspector Campbell confirmed that Griffiths was the owner of the prints on the Winchester bottle.

On 3 November the police honoured their pledge to the citizens of Blackburn; about 46,500 fingerprint records were publicly pulped. Two weeks later Griffiths was hanged at Liverpool prison.

New Developments

Advances in fingerprint techniques, in common with other forensic sciences, tend to reflect developments made by science and technology in general. For example, the study of weak or damaged prints has been greatly advanced by Laser Image Enhancement.

Other advances have been made in finding appropriate methods of developing latent prints on difficult surfaces – such as enhancement with radioactive sulphur dioxide.

Computerized Fingerprint Systems

However, it is with computer science that the greatest strides forward have been made. Since the 1960s the enormous potential of computerization in handling the world's tens of millions of fingerprint files has been recognized, and urgent research programmes carried out into means of automating classification and search procedures.

As early as 1973 Canada's Mounted Police completed conversion of its massive files on to computer, and Sweden's automatic reading system became fully operational in 1975. In West Germany, the Bundeskriminalamt began using a system in 1976 to handle its 17 million records.

The systems used in the United States and Great Britain during the 1970s and 1980s were based on an electronic spot scanner that measures light reflected from the fingerprint image and converts the information into digital data which can be transferred to, classified, and stored by the computer until required for comparison.

Like previous manual systems, the computer matches prints by seeking points of similarity (in encoded form) and narrows the field down to a very small number which may require final visual comparison. In order to make this visual comparison fast and automatic, a system called Videofile was developed which combined all the information stored by the computer on to tape replayable on a video display unit. More recently, the so-called 'second generation' computers enable more than 60,000 comparisons per second to be made.

Another advantage of coded information is the speed and accuracy with which 'fingerprints' can be sent via telephone lines between police forces. (See also **Radio Transmission of Fingerprints**.)

Encoding Systems

There are many codes available for processing fingerprints on to computer. The example given is in use by the FBI's National Crime Information Center, and is based on the Henry system of classification. Its advantage over Henry is that it does not require expert knowledge of the visual 'language' of fingerprints in order to identify a pattern – it is a simple matter of comparing code numbers and letters.

The system recognizes three basic patterns: Loops, Arches and Whorls, and the fingers are coded in the same order as that on a fingerprint record card: 1. Right Thumb, 2. Right Forefinger, and so on to 10. Left Little Finger.

Each finger is followed by two letters or numerals as follows:

NCIC FINGERPRINT CLASSIFICATION CODING

Pattern Type	Pattern Subgroup	NCIC Fingerprint Code
Arch	Plain Arch	AA
	Tented Arch	TT
Loop	Radial Loop	Ridge count number to which 50 is added (e.g. ridge count count = 14 + 50 = Code 64).
	Ulnar Loop	Actual ridge count; if less than ten, add 0 in front (e.g. ridge count 9 = 09)
Whorl	Plain Whorl	
	Inner	P1
	Meeting	PM
	Outer	PO
	Central Pocket Loop Whorl	
	Inner	CI
	Meeting	CM
	Outer	CO
	Double Loop Whorl	

Pattern Type	Pattern Subgroup	NCIC Fingerprint Code
	Inner	DI
	Meeting	DM
	Outer	DO
	Accidental Whorl	
	Inner	XI
	Meeting	XM
	Outer	XO
Missing/Amputated Finger	Only use if finger is completely amputated or entire first joint is missing	XX
Scarred/Mutilated Pattern	Only use if finger cannot be accurately classified.	SR

Discouraging Reports from Britain
1988

Despite the increasing sophistication of fingerprint techniques, a report prepared by the Parliamentary Audit Commission criticized Britain's police forces for making insufficient use of facilities at their disposal. Although 40,000 fingerprint identifications were made in the previous year (1987), they only represented 2 per cent of cases: 'In many cases, the offender will have left no mark, but the proportion of crimes where identification might be made using fingerprints is certainly greater than this.'

The audit team found that in one police force burglaries were not investigated by scenes-of-crime officers because of a shortage of vehicles; another force had a backlog of uncatalogued prints going back four years.

1990

Reports originating at the Home Office confirmed that the long-promised British system of automatic fingerprint matching had been abandoned. Instead, ministers invited three commercial concerns – Morpho/IBM, De La Rue, and NEC – to install trial systems in six key police forces.

Any system adopted would be linked to the second generation police national computer, itself linked to prison and court records. The ill-fated 'British initiative', which had been underway for almost twenty years, never, it was claimed, managed to achieve significantly better than an experienced human eye. Nevertheless, a spokesman for the Police Scientific Research and Development Branch expressed disappointment and undisguised annoyance: 'This Government is either cynically disregarding the potential impact that research and development in crime detection can and is having, or is naïvely assuming that commerce will provide . . .'

FIRE
(see Arson, Burning)

FIREARMS
Types of Firearms
Firearms, or small arms as they are generally encountered in the subject of forensic ballistics, are of two main types: Smooth Bore and Rifled.

Smooth Bore Aims
Those in which the inside surface of the barrel – called the Bore – is perfectly smooth, and circular in cross-section:

BORE
(Calibre)

Rifled Arms
Which have grooves, parallel to each other but in a spiral, cut longitudinally down the inside of the barrel from breech to muzzle. In cross-section the bore displays the characteristic 'grooves' and 'lands':

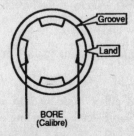

Groove

Land

BORE
(Calibre)

Both types of firearms are classified according to the 'calibre' of their bore – i.e. the internal diameter of their barrel.

Calibre of Smooth Bore Arms

One exception is the case of the larger smooth bores which are measured by the quaint method of adding up the number of spherical balls of pure lead, each exactly fitting the bore, which equal one pound weight. Thus a 12-bore (or 12-gauge) is one in which the bore would need to contain 12 spherical shots in order to make up one pound.

Calibre of Rifled Arms

In both the United States and Britain the calibre of rifled arms is denoted as a decimal of one inch, e.g. .250, .303, .455, etc. On the Continent these measurements are given in millimetres: 6.35, 6.5, 7.9, etc.

CATEGORIES OF SMALL ARMS

Smooth Bore

SHOTGUNS

For all practical purposes, arms with a smooth bore comprise variations on the Shotgun, or sporting gun; firing charges consist of multiple small shot. (Single bullets can be fired by smooth bores, but their limited accuracy makes them unsuitable for criminal purposes.)

1. *Single-Barrelled Guns*

   Simple, single-shot mechanism, usually with external firing hammer.

   Slide- or Pump-Action Guns

   Single-barrel, magazine repeaters with a 'slide' under the barrel which when moved backward, then forward, positions another cartridge in the chamber and closes the breech.

   'Automatic' Shotgun

   A single repeater gun originating in the United States.

2. *Double-Barrelled Guns*

   Barrels constructed either 'Side-by-Side' or 'Over-and-Under'. Either 'Ejector' or 'Non-Ejector' depending on whether the empty cartridge case is, or not, automatically ejected when the gun is re-loaded.

Sawn-Off Shotguns

Weapons in which the barrels have been cut down to about 12 inches, and the stock shaved down, enabling it to be carried more discreetly – a facility which compensates for the resulting reduction in accuracy. At one time much favoured by gangsters, and a variation was used by 'Doc' Holliday at the OK Corral.

3. Shot Pistols

Either single- or double-barrelled, looking like small shotguns but with pistol stocks.

Rifled
HANDGUNS
1. Revolvers

Derive their name from the characteristic cylindrical magazine containing several chambers (usually five or six), each chamber holding one cartridge.

Single Action

Where the hammer must be 'cocked' each time to revolve the cylinder and present a new cartridge to the firing pin.

Double Action

Although the hammer *can* be cocked by hand, it can also be cocked by exerting prolonged pressure on the trigger.

Hammerless

A variation on the double-action gun, where the hammer is incorporated in the action and not on view.

2. Pistols

Comprise the category called 'automatics', though this is a misnomer. A true automatic is one which will go on firing as long as the trigger is held back; these require the trigger to be pulled for each shot and are more properly called 'self-loaders', or 'semi-automatics'. Pistols generally carry their cartridges (six or seven) in a vertical magazine which clips into the weapon's stock.

Single-Shot Pistols
Require to be manually loaded each time the gun is to be fired. The Derringer is a variant, having two barrels which are loaded and fired separately.

RIFLES
Divided into several general categories:

1. *Sporting Rifles*
2. *Military Rifles*
3. *Target Rifles*
4. *Small-Bore Target Rifles*

Then sub-divided according to their mechanical method of re-loading:

A. Single-shot (requires loading each shot)
B. Lever-Action
C. Bolt-Action
D. Slide- or Pump-Action (see SHOTGUNS above)
E. 'Automatics' (not, in fact, true automatics, but self-loaders – see note on 'automatic' pistols).

SUB-MACHINE GUNS
Sometimes called 'machine pistols', and capable of being used as semi-automatics or as true automatics. Sub-machine guns fire pistol cartridges.

Ejection/Extraction
In forensic ballistics, the means by which a specified class or individual weapon disposes of its spent cartridges may be of the greatest importance in identification. Broadly, there are two methods, the mechanics of which will leave marks or traces on the cartridge case: those in which the breech opens automatically and the case is *ejected;* and those where the case is merely unseated from the chamber and requires to be *extracted* by hand.

Types of Cartridges
Modern cartridges, although they come in a bewildering variety of shapes and sizes, share the same components and overall construction. They comprise four main parts:

1. Cartridge Case
2. Primer, or Cap
3. Propellant, or Powder
4. Bullet

Cartridge Cases
Usually made of brass, or a combination of brass and paper or plastic (in the case of shotgun shells), it is the purpose of the case to contain the other components. There are three overall shapes:

> Straight
> Bottleneck
> Tapered (now rare)

classified into five sub-divisions according to the shape of their base, 'rim':

1. Belted
2. Rimmed
3. Semi-rimmed
4. Rimless
5. Rebated

(It can be observed that revolver cartridges are always rimmed, and self-loading pistol cartridges are always rimless.)

A large percentage of cartridge cases bear what are called 'Head Stamps' on their base – a sequence of letters, numbers and symbols identifying the manufacturer and the calibre. Military cartridges also carry the last two numerals of the year in which they were manu-factured.

Primers, or Caps
Depending upon the location of the primer, a cartridge is termed either
> Centre-fire, or
> Rim-fire

In both types the discharge is effected when the cap is struck by the firing pin (in the case of centre-fire in the middle of the primer cap, and in the case of rim-fire on the rim of the cartridge).

When a weapon is fired, the firing pin strikes the primer cap forcing the primer compound against the anvil which causes it to explode. Holes in the anvil allow the flame into the cartridge case igniting the propellant.

In rim-fired ammunition the primer is packed into the rim of the cartridge case, and is ignited when a firing pin strikes the rim.

The composition of primer compound varies. In the United States all primers use chemical ingredients, usually barium nitrate, lead styphnate and antimony sulphide. Virtually all manufactured cartridges contain combinations of these three compounds, and in determining whether a suspect has fired a gun it is usual first to test for traces of these substances.

Propellants, or Powder

Up to the beginning of the twentieth century all cartridges were loaded with what was called 'Black Powder' or gunpowder – a mixture of potassium nitrate, sulphur and charcoal. The disagreeable characteristic of black powder was that it produced a dense white smoke.

Towards the end of the nineteenth century experiments were afoot to develop a smokeless powder. In 1884, a French chemist named Vieille reduced nitrocellulose to a gelatinous colloid with alcohol and ether, and the resulting compound was reduced to flakes. Three years later Alfred Nobel improved the technique using nitroglycerine. These two smokeless powders are called, respectively, 'Single-Base' and 'Double-Base'. Grain shapes vary among flakes, discs and cylinders. In 1933, Winchester produced a form of ball-grain powder from dissolved nitrocellulose.

Bullets

The bullet can be described, at its simplest, as the part of the cartridge that is propelled along the barrel of the gun. Modern bullets are of two main types:

Lead, and Metal-jacketed

Lead bullets are cast from an alloy of lead, tin and antimony (to increase hardness). Although shape varies, most are grooved with 'Cannelures' into which the cartridge case is crimped during assembly.

There are four basic shapes:

1. Round-nose
2. Wadcutter – designed primarily for use on target ranges

3. Semi-wadcutter
4. Hollow-point – the cavity in the nose allows the bullet to expand on impact.

Unjacketed lead bullets are seldom used in high-velocity centre-fire rifles as the speed of travel down the barrel would melt or fragment them; most usually they are associated with revolvers.

Metal-jacketed bullets are designed for use in automatic pistols and high-velocity rifles. Bullets may be either full- or partially-jacketed (though all military ammunition is full metal-jacketed in accordance with the Geneva Convention's requirements for the most 'humane' type of missile).

Jacketed bullets have either a lead or steel core with a skin of:

Gilding metal (copper and zinc)
Cupro-nickel (copper and nickel), or
Alumimum

In the late 1990's there was much media hysteria in the United States over so-called 'cop-killer bullets'. As the tabloid invented name implies, these Teflon coated bullets are capable of penetrating police-issue armoured vests and helmets, but the Teflon has nothing to do with their penetration ability. The bullets consist of a steel core, jacketed with first a layer of brass, then an outer layer of Teflon. In fact, 'cop-killers' are little more dangerous that any other type of steel-cored bullet (or, indeed, the vast majority of normal, lead rifle bullets). The Teflon is not added to 'slip through armour plating', but to reduce the wear on gun barrels.

Military Bullets
There are four types of military bullet:

1. Ball ammunition (full metal-jacketed lead or mild steel)
2. Armour-piercing ammunition (full metal-jacketed hard steel)
3. Tracer bullets (full metal-jacket housing lead core and tracer compound)
4. Incendiary bullets (full metal-jacket housing steel core and incendiary compound)

Case Study

THE SILENT ASSASSIN

Because there are exceptions to every rule of identification, account must be taken of the assassin who rejects the ready-made and goes into the small arms business on his own account.

In 1934 Bashall Eaves, in Lancashire, was as medieval in its outlook as it was in its appearance; no more than an isolated hamlet, it had absorbed none of the surface sophistication of its larger neighbour Clitheroe. John Dawson lived at Bashall Hall with his sisters Annie, Lily and Polly and Polly's son Albert Pickles. He also had a live-in stockhand with whom he shared the credit for his modest prosperity from dealing in the local livestock auctions.

On Monday 19 March, forty-six-year-old Dawson was on his way home from an evening's drinking, leaving the comforts of the Edisford Bridge Hotel at an uncommonly early hour for him. Shortly before 9 p.m., cap down and collar up against the wild seasonal winds, John Dawson strode off into the night at the start of his twenty-minute hike home. It was as he passed the entrance to Tommy Simpson's farm that things took on a sinister cast.

Passing the Simpson gate John Dawson experienced what he described as a light tap on the back following a faint click. Apparently unconcerned, he made the rest of the way to Bashall Hall without incident, arriving at around 9.20 p.m. According to the visible evidence on the table, he had then eaten a hearty supper before Tommy Kenyon, the stockhand, returned at about 11 p.m. from his outing to Clitheroe. Dawson was basking in the warmth of the kitchen fire now, the oil lamp casting a flickering light around the room as Kenyon entered. After a brief, rather surly exchange of words, young Tommy joined the rest of the household in sleep.

Like all land-workers, Tom Kenyon and Albert Pickles were accustomed to be awake and up long before dawn on milking duties; Dawson's sister Annie was also on early-morning detail in the kitchen preparing the men's breakfasts. 'I don't like the look of our John,' she armounced. 'When I took him in his tea he asked me to look at his back where he had a bit of pain. He's covered with blood, Tommy! There's a wound in his back and everything's covered with blood!' Dawson's chair in the kitchen was soaked in his gore as well, and a trail of dried blood led upstairs to his bedroom.

John Dawson had always been a stubborn, cantankerous man, and his obstinacy manifested itself this morning in his absolute refusal to see a doctor; fortunately, Annie was just as stubborn and called one anyway, who with patience beyond the call of his duty persuaded Dawson to go with him to the hospital for an X-ray. The print revealed a foreign body about the size and shape of a small bird's egg lodged just below John Dawson's liver; it was obvious that it had entered through the gaping wound below his shoulder blade. It required another day of what must have been unbearable pain before the patient consented to have the object removed. It was found to be a strange kind of home-made bullet: fashioned from a short length of hard steel rod, about half an inch in diameter, the missile had been rounded at both ends with a file. Discharging himself, Dawson returned home where he refused all further medication and succumbed to gangrene and septicaemia on Thursday afternoon, 23 March. To the end he said no more than that he didn't know who had shot him.

When Detective Chief Superintendent Wilf Blacker arrived in Bashall Eaves he found a deep mistrust and an even more profound silence; it was made quite obvious that any information he got he would have to hunt for himself: the villagers 'knew nothing'. Blacker observed afterwards, 'It was like talking to a brick wall.' He may have been on his own, but veteran policeman Wilf Blacker was far from beaten yet. He had three important leads to start off with:

1. Dawson had felt the 'light tap' on his back (in reality a chunk of hardened steel embedding itself in his body!) at the gate to Tom Simpson's farm.
2. The victim had heard a click – presumably made by a gun.
3. Blacker had the singular home-made 'bullet'.

Why was John Dawson killed, and who killed him? It would help if he could understand the extraordinary behaviour of Dawson after the incident – was it really possible that his evening drinks had sufficiently anaesthetized him to the searing pain that any normal human being would have suffered after receiving such a wound; to pursue his everyday activities for the next fifteen hours with a hole in his back and a steel slug in his body? To show almost disdain for any attempt to help him or to solve the crime? Did John Dawson know his assassin and plan to exact his own retribution when he had recovered?

DCS Blacker lost no time in summoning the legendary London

gunsmith Robert Churchill, consultant in some of the most celebrated shootings in the history of crime investigation.

Blacker and Churchill kicked off by calling in all local guns of whatever type or age for expert examination; garages and workshops were systematically searched for any trace of the materials or tools used to make the missile; and the scene of the crime was checked and rechecked for the slightest clue.

But what was anyone to make of the clue of the dead dog – the poor creature that had been found shot on Tommy Simpson's farm with no bullet in the carcase? Then there were the Simpsons themselves; for all the tight-lipped secrecy, a few tongues had moved if not wagged. Who had made seventeen-year-old Nancy Simpson pregnant? Tommy Kenyon? Was that why he and Simpson had been seen brawling in the lane outside the Simpson farm? Was the bullet then meant for Kenyon? Was Dawson the father of Nancy's child? Was revenge the motive? And why did Tommy Simpson hang himself ten days after John Dawson died? All these questions remain unanswered to this day.

Only one further piece of information ever came out of the case, and that simply served to deepen the mystery: many years later Tom Kenyon revealed that shortly after the shooting of Dawson a man known as Henry – supposed to be a relative of the Simpsons – removed a bag from the Simpson farm. Kenyon himself had seen both man and bag in the local pub afterwards, and was convinced that this bag was in some way connected with the murder. Did it contain a gun? If this information had been available to Wilf Blacker in March 1934 this case might well have had a very different conclusion. But then again, it was obvious that a lot more people could have given a lot more information. The code of silence had successfully protected somebody; but who?

Airguns

Although no gun was ever identified as the murder weapon in the case of the killing of John Dawson, Robert Churchill was able, on the basis of available evidence, to advance the suggestion that the victim had been shot with a type of airgun called a 'poacher's arm'. This would account for the click heard by Dawson just before he felt the 'tap' on his back, but not the kind of loud report that would have accompanied the firing of a percussion weapon. The fact that, at its crudest, the air-cane is little more than two metal tubes that fit together would also have made it harder to identify it for what it was in the police search.

The principle of the air-cane is simple: one sealed metal tube acts as 'reservoir' for the compressed air and is charged by means of a hand-pump. A second tube (either rifled to fire a slug or smooth to fire shot) is screwed into the cylinder and acts as the barrel. When a 'trigger' is pulled, a valve opens to allow enough of the air out to force the projectile with great velocity down the barrel.

Although such weapons subsequently became a tool of the trade for poachers – for obvious reasons – it was the common principle behind many types of English sporting gun in the early part of the nineteenth century. Like the sword-stick, air-canes were also popular weapons of self-defence; and a type known as a Girandoni even found its place on the field of battle in the hands of Austrian infantrymen at the end of the eighteenth century.

FITNESS TO PLEAD
(see Competence to Stand Trial)

FOOTPRINTS
(see Barefoot Prints, Impressions, Shoe-Prints)

FORGERY
(see Disputed Documents)

FRAUD
(see Arson, Disputed Documents)

FUNGI
Poison mushrooms are more the stuff of detective fiction than forensic fact, and their victims are more likely to be careless mycologists than unwanted spouses. However, no reference work that deals with poisons can entirely ignore the subject of poisonous fungi, beloved as they were of murderers in classical Rome.

The likelihood of encountering truly poisonous mushrooms by mistake is very slim – partly because there are so few species (no more than ten among more than 3,500 in the British Isles), and partly because their reliance upon specific host trees rarely produces conditions conducive to growth.

The symptoms of mushroom poisoning are fairly typical of other plant poisons, beginning with sickness, diarrhoea and stomach pains. Most poison fungi will already have signalled that it is best not to eat them by their bitter and acrid taste, and a sensation of burning in the mouth and throat. There follows what might be compared to an 'incubation' period, while the toxin spreads through the body. This is the danger of poison fungi, that by the time the symptoms become alarming enough to really worry the victim, the poison has spread. Manifestations may continue with giddiness and a tendency to sweat; often there are hallucinations and a general feeling of anxiety and mental distress. As the heart-rate increases with growing panic, so the poison is pumped more rapidly around the body system. Without immediate treatment the subject may fall into a coma from which death by respiratory failure follows.

This is the pattern of symptoms at their worst, which would be brought on mainly by the most poisonous mushrooms, the *Amanitas*.

The Amanita Group

The most deadly of the group are *Amanita phalloides,* called Death Cap, and *Amonita virosa,* the Destroying Angel, a deceptive pure-white fungus. They contain what are known as alpha and beta amanita toxins, which act stealthily, almost without causing discomfort for the twelve hours during which the poison spreads, in the end attacking and destroying the nuclei of the body cells.

The best-known of the *Amanita* is *mustarina,* the mystical fly agaric with its bright-red cap spotted with white, and familiar for providing the most popular dwellings for pixies. The fungus has been known down the centuries as an hallucinogen, and has played a major role in many religions. It was believed by the Koryak tribe of eastern Siberia that the fly agaric was inhabited by spirits they knew as Wapag Men, and the wisdom of the spirits would be revealed by eating the fungus. Which is similar to the belief held by the hippie cults inhabiting London and San Francisco in the 1960s that the 'Magic Mushroom' was the doorway to another spiritual world.

Other poisonous fungi which are less toxic are the Ink Caps (Common and Glistening varieties) and *Gyromitra esculenta,* the Helvellic acids derived from which cause haemolysis, a breaking down of the red blood cells, and the ergot group.

Ergot

Ergot is a parasitic fungus which grows on rye and other cereals and grasses and which, until the advent of crop spraying and genetically engineered seed, was the scourge of bread eaters as the fungi were milled into the flour. There are horrific tales told of the effects of gangrenous ergotism which resulted in a swelling of the arms and legs accompanied by great pain. Slowly the limbs became numb, blue and cold to the touch. Then quite suddenly the whole limb would turn black, and the only remedy was amputation. The uncomfortable tingling in the hands and feet that characterized less serious cases of ergot poisoning was popularly known as 'St Anthony's fire'.

Chemically, the fungus contains a group of drugs one of which, ergotamine, is closely related to LSD (see Drugs) and has been blamed for outbreaks of mass hallucination.

G

GAS
(see Carbon Monoxide Poisoning, Poisons)

GLAISTER, JOHN (1892–1971)

Son of Glasgow University's Regius Professor of Forensic Medicine, John Glaister succeeded him, and between them the Glaisters held the chair for sixty-five years. John Glaister junior was among the first to set the general table of times for the development of decomposition of the human body, and to suggest a formula for the estimation of **Time of Death**; he was also a pioneer in the identification of **Hairs** and **Fibres** using the comparison microscope.

John Glaister was born in May 1892, at Townhead, Glasgow, where he later attended the High School. Despite having a father who was already Regius Professor of Forensic Medicine at the University of Glasgow, young John was inclined to a career on the stage; or if not, that other great opportunity for the aspiring actor – law. His father, not unsurprisingly, had a future in medicine mapped out for him.

In the end it was to be law *and* medicine. In 1916, John Glaister graduated, and was commissioned into the Royal Army Medical Corps with which he served in Egypt. Between 1919 and 1925 he worked as Assistant in the Department of Forensic Medicine at Glasgow University, and was called to the Bar at the Inner Temple in 1926. The following year Professor Sydney Smith resigned his chair at Cairo and returned to Edinburgh; at the same time Glaister took over Smith's official and academic posts in Egypt, consolidating the high reputation of Scotland's medico-legal experts abroad. Glaister had always had an interest in the analysis and comparison of hair, and in 1931 published *Hairs of Mammalia from the Medico-Legal Aspect,* which remained for many years the standard reference on the subject. When John Glaister senior gave up his chair at Glasgow it was only fitting that his son should take over, and from 1937 he occupied the chair until he retired with the honour of Professor Emeritus thirty-two years later.

Professor Glaister's autobiography was published in 1964 under the title *Final Diagnosis,* in which, among other things, he strongly emphasized the importance to forensic science of **Trace Evidence**, or 'contact traces', reinforcing the theories of his illustrious predecessor Edmond **Locard**: 'It is almost impossible for anyone to go to the scene of a crime without either leaving some trace of his visit behind him or carrying away, all unsuspectingly, some trace which links him with the place.'

Surviving his great rival at Edinburgh, Sir Sydney Smith, by two years, Glaister died on 4 October 1971, aged eighty.

Celebrated Cases

1934. *Jeannie Donald* A combination of Glaister's special knowledge of hairs and fibres and Sydney Smith's expertise with the comparison microscope sent Mrs Donald to prison for life (see page 284).

1935. *Dr Buck Ruxton* One of the most remarkable achievements in the history of forensic pathology brought together the three Scottish medico-legal giants: Glaister, Smith and James Couper Brash (see page 149).

1947. *Stanislaw Myszka* Using his expert knowledge in the classification and identification of animal hairs, Glaister was able to match hairs taken from Myszka's razor-blade used while in custody with those found on a blade in the hide-out associated with the killer of Mrs Catherine McIntyre.

GLASS

Glass is one of the most frequently encountered substances submitted to the forensic laboratory as transfer fragments. This can be explained in part by the window being the commonest point of felonious entry into buildings, and in part because large quantities of broken glass are produced by automobile accidents, hit-and-run incidents, and so on.

Evidence that can be supplied by glass fractures is also of importance

to the scenes-of-crime officer at the site of a break-in or in an incident
where shots have been fired through a window.

Glass Fractures

The type of information which might be derived by scene-of-crime
experts from a visual examination of broken window glass are: the side
from which the force was exerted, the angle of shot, if a gun caused the
fracture (the presence and position of flaking on the exit side of the
glass will indicate this), sequence of penetrations, etc.

Cone Fractures

When pressure is exerted on one side of a sheet of glass the molecules
directly in front of the point of impact push forward and create a
'snooker-break' effect, each molecule dislodging the one adjacent to it,
forming a coneshaped hole; the entry side has the smaller hole, the exit
side the larger. Most of the glass displaced from the 'cone' will fall on
the exit side. The clearest examples of cone fractures will be found
where a high-velocity shot has been fired through plate glass (such as a
shop window):

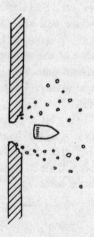

Radial Fractures

The commonest causes of radial fractures are either low-velocity shots
or larger missiles, such as stones thrown through a pane of glass. As the
object penetrates, the glass 'bends' in the direction of the force, causing
uneven pressure on the opposite (exit) side. This results in star-like

fractures that radiate out from the point of contact (hence 'radial'). As the missile continues its course it takes with it some of the finer points of glass from the inside of the 'star:

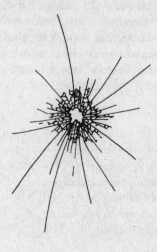

Spiral Fractures

These fractures present as circular fracturing in arcs around and through the radial fracture lines, but originate on the opposite side of the glass (that is, on the side where force was applied). Because of this, resulting spicules of glass tend to spray back towards the person exerting the force, with the possibility that they will adhere to clothing as contact traces:

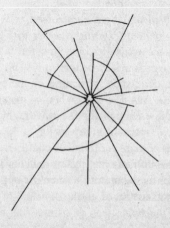

Sequence of Penetrations

When more than one projectile has penetrated a pane of glass it is often useful to know the sequence. It was explained above that as a missile penetrates glass, fractures will radiate outwards from the point of impact; the same effect will result from a second penetration, except that the fractures will only run through the glass to the point where they meet a fracture caused by the first penetration. When a fracture line terminates at another fracture line, the blow causing the terminated fracture was second in the sequence:

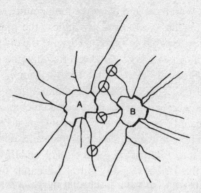

Fracture terminations (circled) reveal shot B to have followed shot A

Analysis and Comparison

'Jigsaw'

The simplest method of making a comparison between two pieces of glass is the 'jigsaw' method – testing whether they fit together or not. The reliability of this technique lies in the fact that when glass is broken the stress fractures the broken surface unevenly. This breaking produces tiny shell-shaped, or 'conchoidal', fractures on the opposite side of the glass to which force was exerted. When a match is found, these fractures are compatible enough for the two fragments to 'lock into' each other and be quite resistant to separation.

When tiny spicules of glass are found as contact traces on a suspect's clothing or person it is unlikely that jigsaw matching will be a practical option. In these cases the laboratory's scientific apparatus is turned to the very special characteristics of glass.

Refractive Index

Glass is possessed of a property known as 'refraction', which means that it bends rays of light as they pass through it; this is because light travels more slowly through glass than it does through air. The ratio of the speed of light travelling through air (or more properly a vacuum) and through glass (or any other transparent material) is called the 'refractive index'.

Measurement of the refractive index of a sample is carried out on a **Microscope** with a heated platform and sample carrier in which the glass fragment is mounted in a drop of silicon oil. The refractive index of the oil changes with heat, and when the temperature is reached where oil and glass share the same refractive index, the glass is no longer visible. From a pre-prepared calibration curve of the oil, the temperature at which the match was made can be converted into the refractive index of the glass sample. If the test is repeated for samples of glass taken from the scene of the crime it can be ascertained from their respective refractive indexes whether they could have had a common origin.

Whether this match if it is positive – is of any great value as evidence will depend upon how common glass with the same refractive index is. It is possible to test to a fine degree of accuracy, and there is a computer file available at the Home Office Central Research Establishment of data on all forensic tests of glass samples. Reference to this information will give some indication of the comparative rarity of a sample's refractive index.

Emission Spectrometry

Spectrometry is an extremely accurate technique for matching glass samples, but because of its destructive nature it is not always the most suitable. The material must first be burned (thus destroying its further use as evidence) and the emitted spectra will demonstrate common origin by comparing the composition of their trace elements. Although the spectrograph can measure the minutest quantity of elements, caution must be observed in the testing of common glass, such as is used in windows, which is so impure that its elemental ingredients will be variable.

GLOVE PRINTS

Under the leadership of Gerald Lambourne, Commander of the Fingerprint Department 1975–80, Scotland Yard's interest in 'non-finger' fingerprints was expanded to a separate section. This reflected

Lambourne's own long-standing preoccupation with glove prints, and his firm conviction that they were capable of positive identification. Like many officers before him, Gerald Lambourne had felt frustrated by criminals who wore gloves in an attempt to defeat justice. After all, gloves are only covers for hands, and would pick up and deposit grease and dirt just like fingers.

The individuality of a glove is determined by many factors, among them the material from which it is made, its construction – knitted, sewn, moulded, etc. – the natural landscape of the glove as it is worn, and the creases and scars imposed by use.

In the case of latex kitchen gloves, research proved that, due to the nature of plastics moulding processes, each pair of gloves is capable of its own individual 'fingerprint', caused by microscopic imperfections, such as air bubbles or foreign bodies on the surface of the glove.

This new weapon in the arsenal of law and order was given its first practical test in 1971, when officers summoned to a building in south-west London in response to a burglar alarm picked up a man running from the scene. He naturally denied committing any crime, but fingerprint experts examining the scene of the attempted break-in found a glove print which was subsequently identified as the mark made by a left-hand suede-finish glove with some surface imperfections – in fact, a perfect match for the sample prints taken from the suspect's glove. On 6 May 1971, Gerald Lambourne successfully presented the first glove-print evidence heard in a court of law.

A curious 'glove' case is recalled by another leading expert in fingerprinting, Detective Chief Inspector Tony Fletcher, head of the Fingerprint Bureau at Greater Manchester.

It involved a safe-blowing on the outskirts of the city, where the burglar had lowered himself on a rope through a post-office roof and wired the safe to the electric light switch with gelignite. Amid the resulting debris, police found a pair of rubber gloves which, when routinely turned inside-out, displayed a complete set of fingerprints; the burglar had obviously put the gloves on (or put them on again) after his hands had picked up a sooty deposit from the explosion. The prints were so clear that their owner was identified and in custody within hours.

GRANT, JULIUS (1901–91)

Born in east London in the first year of the nineteenth century, Julius Grant first gained a part-time degree in chemistry from Queen Mary's College, and then continued his research at King's College, London, until joining the John Dickinson Paper Company in 1931. It was here that he specialized in the field of paper technology, acquiring skills which he later applied with such success to the field of forensic document examination.

During the war Grant applied his ingenuity to a range of 'patriotic' endeavours such as the production of forgery-proof ration books; this he achieved through the simple expedient of mixing the finely chopped hair from cows' tails into the furnish of the paper which smelt awful when the genuine article was subjected to fire. Edible paper for spies, and paper which retained 'invisible' writing for prisoners of war contributed to making Julius Grant's war read like a chapter from *Boys' Own*; but it was an excellent background to his future career as one of the country's most inventive forensic scientists.

One criminal who entertained the highest respect for Julius Grant was the safe-breaker and master escaper Alfred Hinds. It was in great part Grant's expert evidence which put Hinds behind bars – and there is an affectionate story told that every time 'Alfie' escaped, he would always telephone his former adversary to talk over old crimes.

In 1963, Grant was called to inspect the evidence left at Leatherslade Farm, the premises occupied by the Great Train Robbers while they divided their spoils. Six years later he was at another notorious farm – Rooks Farm, Stocking Pelham – where Arthur and Nizamodeen Hosein took the kidnapped Mrs Muriel McKay and subsequently killed her. Grant's examination of the ransom notes and a notebook taken from the Hosein's farmhouse proved a common origin – evidence which helped put two murderers in prison for 'life'.

In 1967, Julius Grant was responsible for debunking the first of two bogus wartime documents that made international news, and put the seal on his international reputation. Despite endorsement by some of the world's leading authorities, including the 'author's son', diaries which had been attributed to the Italian Fascist dictator Benito Mussolini were proved by Grant to be forgeries – with the most conclusive proof that it was possible to offer. Julius Grant found that the paper on which the documents were written was made eleven years *after* the diary dates.

It was almost two decades later when Julius Grant made world headlines again. It appeared that manuscript books claimed to be the wartime diaries of Adolf Hitler were found in Germany. Already reputations and millions of dollars had been invested in their authenticity. It was Julius Grant who was chosen to make a physical examination of the diaries. No sooner had he laid eyes on them than Grant, with one simple experiment, proved the diaries false. The paper had fluoresced under untraviolet light, betraying the presence of optical dyes – additions which were not made to paper until after the war.

It was his unrivalled knowledge of the dating information that lies hidden in paper and inks that led Grant to the unmasking of the modern master forger Tom Keating, whose remarkable copies and pastiches of the work of the nineteenth-century visionary painter Samuel Palmer had fooled the dealers and academics for years.

Julius Grant was in turn President of the Medico-Legal Society and the Forensic Science Society, and until his death in July 1991 was still actively involved in the conundrums of document analysis.

GROSS, HANS (1847–1915)

Born in Austria in 1847, Hans Gross became one of the most influential figures in the history of criminal detection. He was trained as a lawyer and rose to the position of examining magistrate, but although he was untrained in the sciences Gross's true interest always lay in the application of academic and scientific disciplines to the solution of crime. Subsequently he was honoured with the chair in Criminology at the University of Prague and was Professor of Penal Law at the University of Graz, a popular lecturer who had the ability to transmit his evident enthusiasm for the subject to his students. Gross's contemporary, the Professor of Criminal Law at Nancy named Gardeil, wrote that he was: 'An indefatigable observer; a far-seeing psychologist; a magistrate full of ardour to unearth the truth, whether in favour of the accused or against him; a clever craftsman; in turn draughtsman, photographer, modeller, armourer; having acquired by long experience a profound knowledge of the practices of criminals, robbers, tramps, gipsies, cheats, he opens to us the researches and experiences of many years.'

Hans Gross's outstanding didactic contribution to forensic science was the publication in 1893 of his *System der Kriminalistik* (translated into English as *Criminal Investigation* in 1907). The work is based entirely on the practical application of scientific techniques such as **Microscopy**, **Serology** and **Fingerprints**. One of Gross's specialties became **Ballistics**, and in this study he was inspired by the autopsy performed on his own grandfather in 1845. While serving in the Austrian Army in 1799, the elder Gross had been shot in the head and the ball lodged behind his eye in such a position that it was more dangerous to remove than to leave alone. When it was removed after death the missile was passed on to Hans who noted a series of 'identifying' marks on the surface to which traces of powder were still adhering. One day, Gross remarked, such details would solve crimes!

The 'father of criminalistics' lived until 1915, by which time his classic *Criminal Investigation* had already been reprinted many times and had become a truly international standard on the subject, being translated into, among other languages, French, Spanish, Danish, Russian, Hungarian, Serbian and Japanese. A fitting tribute to Gross himself was Gardeil's description of this work: 'It is a living book, because it has been lived.' More wryly, a later reviser (Ronald Martin Howe, MC, 1949) commented in his preface: 'When noticing the formidable list of qualities demanded of a detective by Dr Gross, plus the unnumbered obstacles that may stand in his path, a reader may wonder by what means such a mortal can exist and remain sane.

GUNSHOT WOUNDS
Classification of Gunshot Wounds
Contact Wounds

In which the muzzle of the weapon is held against the surface of the body.

1. *Hard contact:* Weapon held tightly against the body so that the skin envelops the muzzle; in this case the edges of the wound will be burned by the combustion gases and blacked with soot which becomes indelibly embedded in the surrounding skin.
2. *Loose contact:* Weapon held lightly against the body so that when it is fired the gases preceding the projectile create a gap between skin and muzzle allowing soot to be carried outwards by the gas and forming a band around the entrance wound; soot is not embedded.
3. *Angled contact:* Barrel held at an acute angle to the body allowing gas and soot to radiate outwards from the muzzle forming an oval wound and an extended pattern of soot.

In all contact wounds traces of soot, powder and vaporized metals are deposited along the bullet's path through the wound tract.

Intermediate-Range Wounds

Where the muzzle of the weapon is away from the surface of the body, but close enough for expelled powder grains to mark the skin with a charcteristic tattooing'.

Tatooing: Consists of numerous tiny orange-brown lesions around the entry wound and is an *ante-mortem* phenomenon proving that the victim was alive when he received the wound. If the wound was inflicted post-mortem, powder marks may still occur but will be characteristically grey-yellow in colour.

Soot: Soot will also be discharged as a result of the combustion of the powder. Soot is carbon containing traces of vapourized metal from the primer, cartridge case and bullet. The size, intensity and general pattern of the soot deposit on the body will indicate the range from which the shot was fired, although this will itself be modified by considerations such as barrel length, calibre and type of weapon. As the range increases, so the area of soot blackening will increase with an associated *decrease* in the density of the blackening. At a certain distance the soot will be so faint through dispersion that it can offer no accurate information on range.

Long-Range Wounds

No powder or soot deposits on the victim's body, the only marks will be those caused by the entry of the bullet.

Entrance and Exit Wounds

Entrance Wounds

Regardless of range, most entrance wounds will be surrounded by an inflamed ring of abraded skin. This condition is caused when the bullet in flight indents the skin as it punches a hole through, abrading the skin around the wound as it does so. The abrasion ring varies in width depending upon the calibre of the projectile and the location of the wound on the body. Even where there is no evidence of an abrasion ring, it will, nevertheless, be obvious which is the entry wound as it presents a circular to oval punched-out hole.

Exit Wounds

Again regardless of range, exit wounds share common characteristics, being larger and more irregular in shape than entry wounds and lacking an abrasion ring. The shapes vary, and can be slit-like, circular, crescent, star-shaped or completely irregular.

Shotgun Wounds

Shot has little penetrating power, and most of the discharge, including the wads, will be found embedded in the soft flesh.

The pattern of a shotgun wound will be markedly different depending on the range from which the gun was fired. The discharge of a shotgun between contact and a few inches does not allow the shot to scatter, resulting in a solid mass of metal and wadding ripping into the body causing extensive destruction of bone and tissue, the hot gases burning and the powder particles tattooing the skin. In cases of suicide where a shotgun muzzle has been applied to the forehead or the roof of the mouth, the greater part of the head may be destroyed.

At close range, between two and three feet, the shot creates a ragged wound between one and one-and-a-half inches in diameter with scorching and tattooing. Beyond a range of three feet the shot begins to spread and at four feet the central wound is surrounded by small perforations; there is no powder marking. Further than about four feet the chances of fatality are markedly less (unless a major artery is severed), the shot spreading to cause extensive, painful perforations of the skin.

Although a lot depends on the 'choke' of the individual weapon, a rough guide to the range of discharge with a shotgun is to measure in inches the diameter of the wound between the furthest pellet marks, subtract one, and the result will indicate the distance in yards. Thus a six-inch wound would result from a range of five yards.

Interpreting Injuries

When a body is found shot, there are three alternatives – accident, suicide or homicide.

Accident

There are surprisingly few accidental fatalities with guns, particularly among the sporting fraternity where strict rules of safety are practised and enforced and weapons are well maintained. The familiar fictional scenario in which we find the colonel shooting himself through the head while cleaning his guns is rarely encountered in true life – few people who handle guns regularly are silly enough either to leave them loaded or to fiddle about with them before checking that they *are* unloaded.

An accidental shooting could, of course, have been committed by some person other than the deceased, although in the early stages of an investigation this cannot be distinguished from homicide unless the person who fired the shot volunteers the information. For all practical purposes there are no distinctive features of accidental shooting, and only the elimination of homicide and suicide plus the individual circumstances of the incident will determine the means as accidental.

Suicide

Although it seems obvious to make the point, in the case of suicide the resulting wound *must be capable of being self-inflicted*. For example, if the body has a bullet hole in the forehead and another at the back of the head it is only likely to have been a suicide if the entry wound is at the front; if the entry wound is at the back of the head the position is more consistent with homicide. Likewise, if the fatal shot was fired from a shotgun at a range of three feet there is very little chance of its being suicide. Other determining factors such as trajectory will be investigated at post-mortem stage, and may reveal that the angle at which a bullet entered the victim is inconsistent with its being self-inflicted.

One popular misconception that should be addressed is the 'suicide note'; it is in reality only left in something like one quarter of all suicides, and the absence of such a note should not immediately be taken as an indication of homicide.

In the United States, with the ready availability of firearms, the most common method of suicide (and the great majority of male suicides) is shooting. The following table indicates the favoured sites on the body for self-inflicted gunshot wounds according to the types of firearm:

Sites of suicides/Type of weapon – USA

Site	Handgun	Rifle	Shotgun
Head (incl. neck)	83*	81	51
Chest	16	14	35
Ahdomen	1	5	13
Total	100	100	99

*Percentages

Homicide

Shooting is by far the most common method of homicide in the United States, and the fifth most common (after knifing, bludgeoning, etc.) in Britain. It is generally easier to identify homicides from gunshot wounds than suicides – such factors as range of shot, site of wound, trajectory, number of shots and general circumstances of the incident (armed robbery, etc.) will clearly point to homicide. The police investigation team and the post-mortem pathologist will both submit all material recovered – weapons, spent cartridges, bullets removed from the body, etc. – to the **Ballistics** section of the laboratory for analysis and report.

Case Study

THE TELL-TALE CARTRIDGE

On 10 November 1976, a heavily diguised man walked up to till number three at the Upper Ham Road branch of Barclays Bank at Richmond, Surrey. He levelled a sawn-off shotgun at the clerk behind the safety screen and without raising his voice simply said: 'Give me some money.'

As the terrified girl pushed money from the till across the counter the man's finger tightened on the gun's trigger, the safety glass shattered into a million fragments and Angela Wooliscroft was thrown from her stool by the impact of burning shot ripping through her hand and chest. She died in the ambulance before reaching hospital.

An experienced team from Scotland Yard led by Detective Chief Superintendent James Sewell lost no time in issuing a description of the armed robber compiled from the recollections of shocked bank staff. Scenes-of-crime officers painstakingly collected the glass and debris from the gun's discharge, and bagged for forensic examination a woman's yellow raincoat in which the killer had concealed his weapon, and an empty plastic bag which had once contained chemical fertilizer. The pockets on the raincoat were found to contain two scraps of paper – one of which was to prove a vital clue in the hunt for Angela Wooliscroft's killer. It was part of an entry form for a wine-making competition which had been signed 'Grahame', and on the reverse side used as a shopping list. In response to police publicity Mr Grahame James Marshall laid claim to the wine-club entry, and his sister to the shopping list. On the day of the shooting Miss Marshall had driven her car to Kingston and left it in the car-park at Bentall's department store. When she returned after shopping Miss Marshall noticed that the car was in a slightly different position and a pair of sunglasses and her yellow raincoat were missing from inside. The maroon Austin A40 had already been described by observers as the raider's escape car.

Meanwhile, Home Office pathologist Professor Keith Mant had examined the body of the victim and drawn certain conclusions regarding the shooting that would prove vital in the case against the murderer. Material recovered from the body and the scene of the shooting was passed on to the ballistics team which immediately identified the weapon as a twelve-bore shotgun.

Chief Superintendent Sewell's next break came not from the police investigation, but from an informant who claimed to have seen a known criminal named Michael Hart putting a shotgun into the back of a car in Basingstoke. Although Hart initially provided a convincing alibi for his whereabouts at the time of the shooting, and a general search of his house revealed nothing incriminating, James Sewell felt that Hart's previous record was sufficient reason to keep him under supervision. It was the hunch that solved the crime, because on 22 November Hart's car, which had been involved in an accident, was picked up by the crew of a police patrol car; a search of the vehicle turned up a Hendal .22 automatic pistol with ammunition. During a more intensive search of Hart's home, a box of 'Eley' No. 7 trapshooting cartridges was found; these, together with the Hendal and its ammunition and a double-barrelled Reilly shotgun were part of a haul stolen from a Reading gun dealer on 4 November.

But it was at this point that an alarming discrepancy began to show in relation to the ballistics evidence. The pellets removed from the body of the victim were No. 7 *gameshot;* the cartridges found in Hart's possession were No. 7 *trapshot* (which is gameshot containing more of the hardening agent antimzyne). However, when the laboratory removed the contents from Hart's trapshot cartridges they were found to be gameshot. The enigma was quickly cleared up by the manufacturers, Eley Kynoch of Birmingham; it transpired that, through simple human error, the wrong label had been put on a small batch of cartridges – the batch that was supplied to the raided gun-shop. Furthermore, the wads – the compressed board discs used to pack the shot – were both of a type unique to Eley, made from cardboard impregnated with paraffin wax and only in use since March 1976. The wads found in the victim's wound and those in Hart's cartridges were identical.

Even so, it was not until 20 January 1977 that Michael George Hart was taken into custody, and a further ten months before he appeared in court. In the meantime he had attempted to hang himself in his cell, and then confessed to killing Angela Wooliscroft 'by accident'. He had, so he said, tapped on the glass screen with the gun as Miss Wooliscroft had leant over to the right to fish money out of the drawer, and it had simply gone off. But it was too late for this kind of cynical deception; the scientists had done their job too well – the wounds were just not consistent with such an explanation. When Michael Hart finally led police officers to the stretch of river from which they dragged the abandoned shotgun, the last piece of indelible evidence was slotted into its place.

On 3 November 1977, almost a full year after he had deliberately blasted away a young woman's life at close range, thirty-year-old Michael Hart was convicted of murder and sentenced to serve not less than twenty-five years in prison.

Discharge Traces

When a gun is fired some of the chemical discharge will blow back on to the hand holding it, and swabbing the hands of a person suspected of having fired a weapon should be carried out as soon as possible to secure the residues before they can be cleaned off. The presence of gunshot residue is also useful in helping to confirm a suicidal death.

Gunshot Residue Collection Procedure

1. Technician should wear plastic gloves (or at least scrupulously wash his own hands before taking samples).
2. Moisten a 100 per cent cotton swab with two or three drops of five per cent dilute nitric acid solution.
3. Swab the region of the back of the left index finger, thumb and web. Place swab in a *plastic* envelope, seal and label.
4. Repeat for back of right hand with separate swab.
5. Similarly swab the area of the palm side of the left index finger and thumb, seal and label.
6. Repeat for right palm.
7. A fifth specimen, a swab simply moistened with the acid solution, is sealed as a 'control' sample.

H

HAIR

Analysis of Hair

Although inferior in accuracy to fingerprint or blood identification, hair can prove of great assistance in forensic investigation. Besides some indication as to age, sex and race, microscopic examination of hair can often result in placing a suspect at the scene of a crime or in physical contact with a victim.

Human hair is categorized according to its place of origin on the body and divides into six types, each with its characteristics:

Head: Generally circular in cross-section, the ends often 'split'.
Eyebrows and Eyelashes: Also circular in section, but tapering tips.
Beard: Generally triangular in section.
Axillary (underarm): Oval in cross-section.
Body: Oval or triangular in section, often curly.
Pubic: Oval or triangular in section, tends usually to curl. Identification of pubic hair is often instrumental in identifying attackers in rape cases – particularly as the hairs, with their shorter roots, are more easily deposited.

Hair is an appendage of the skin, growing from a 'follicle'; the roots, or 'bulb' of the hair is embedded in the follicle and the 'shaft' of hair grows from it ending at the 'tip'. Under a powerful microscope hair can be seen to consist of three layers:

Medulla

The central core, consisting of a collection of cells running through the hair. Individuals may vary in the appearance of their hair medulla, which can be classified into three groups:

Continuous   Interrupted   Fragmented

Or there may be no medulla at all. However, human head hairs generally exhibit no medulla or fragmented ones (with the exception of Mongoloids where the medulla is continuous). Many animals display differing and complex medullary structure.

Cuticle

The outer sheath of overlapping scales (which, incidentally, always point towards the tip of the hair).

Cortex

It is formed of keratin and contains the pigment granules that determine the hair's natural colour. The colour and distribution of these pigment granules (called melanin) are useful in identifying differences between the hair of individuals.

It is the cuticle that mainly identifies the animal origin of the hair, and can be classified so as to attribute it to human or animal, and to differentiate between different species of animal. This can be useful in, for example, placing a suspect or victim by a comparison of animal hairs found on clothing with those found at the scene of a crime.

One of the most useful characteristics of hair is its virtual indestructibility. Apart from burning with fire or acid, hair will outlast all but the skeleton, providing useful clues to the fate of even the long-dead. It will, for example, retain traces of poison (notably **Arsenic**) almost indefinitely, and in cases of slow poisoning with arsenic the hair – which grows at a constant rate (approximately 0.44mm per day) – and the contamination of the poison, also at a constant rate, provide a calendar of 'dates' on which the toxin was administered.

Trace hairs will also be routinely tested for chemical treatments, such as tinting and dying, curling or straightening, lacquering, etc.

Identification and Comparison

The first step in any laboratory examination of hair evidence is to determine whether or not it is human. Although this is a relatively simple exercise (only some other apes have similar hair) it must always be borne in mind that even with human hair (indeed, even among the hairs of the same person) there are sometimes big morphological differences.

The hair of different species of animals also differs very markedly, and most biology laboratories will have access to extensive reference standards for comparison, if they are required to be specific; it may, for instance, be significant that a suspect's clothing carries sheep hairs if he denies sheep rustling.

Most often the laboratory will be asked to confirm whether or not a hair recovered from the scene of a crime matches that of a suspect. In this respect it is true to say that forensic scientists rarely have to deal with other than head and pubic hairs (the latter usually only in cases of sexual assault and rape). A **Comparison Microscope** is a perfect instrument for allowing the examiner to view the two hairs beside each other, noting the points of similarity. Features looked for are colour, length, diameter, distribution of pigment granules, type of medulla, etc. Cosmetic treatment, such as dying or bleaching, can serve as an indicator, as can abnormalities of structure associated with disease.

Although it is not possible by microscopic examination alone to associate a hair with a particular individual to the exclusion of all others (see below, Recent Developments), a study carried out by the forensic laboratory of the Royal Canadian Mounted Police estimated that it could offer odds of about 4,500 to one against a head hair originating from somebody other than the stated subject; the study of pubic hair comparisons gave odds of 800 to one.

Case Study

A STUDY OF HAIRS

The victim, eight-year-old Helen Priestly, lived with her parents in a flat on the first floor of a tenement at 61 Urquhart Road, Aberdeen. Below them on the ground floor lived the Donalds, thirty-eighty-year-old Jeannie and her husband Alexander. As the result of some long-forgotten grievance, Mrs Donald and Mrs Priestly had not spoken to each other for five years.

On 20 April 1934, Helen arrived home from school for lunch and afterwards rushed round to visit a friend, Mrs Robertson. She returned home at about ten minutes past one o'clock, and was sent out again to buy her mother a loaf of bread. Helen was seen by several people walking back from the shop with her purchase – it was around one-thirty. Helen Priestly was never seen alive again.

When her daughter failed to return home, Mrs Priestly alerted the neighbours to her fears, and during the rest of that day and through the night, police searchers were assisted by parties of local people anxious to offer their support in the Priestlys' hour of crisis. At five in the morning, one volunteer who had been home for a few hours' sleep, entered 61 Urquhart Road to tell Mr Priestly he was ready to resume the hunt for missing Helen. Here, in the half-light of the communal lobby, his search ended; in a recess under the stairs was a brown sack, and as his eyes became accustomed to the gloom, he saw the hand and foot of a child protruding from it.

At first sight it appeared that Helen had been strangled and sexually assaulted, and a great deal of time was wasted hunting for a mysterious man. However, a post-mortem established that although some instrument had been intruded into her body, there were no signs consistent with rape or attempted rape; the most logical conclusion was that Helen had been slain by a woman who faked the abuse in order to deflect suspicion. Death had occurred at around two o'clock on the afternoon of her disappearance, and the cause of death was asphyxia, possibly from manual strangulation, although vomited particles were found in the windpipe and smaller air tubes.

By the middle of the week following Helen Priestly's death, gossip had reached the ears of the police about the long-standing feud between Mrs Donald and the Priestlys (Helen had often taunted Mrs Donald with the nickname 'Coconut'), and on 25 April, after lengthy questioning at Urquhart Road, both Jeannie Donald and her husband Alexander were taken into custody. Two weeks later, his alibi having checked out, Alexander Donald was released; Jeannie was committed for trial, and on 16 July 1934, she stood arraigned before Lord Justice Clerk Aitchison at Edinburgh.

The evidence against Jeannie Donald proved to be a damaging jigsaw of interlocking facts collated from the reports of pathologists, chemists and bacteriologists. Bloodstains and bacteria found on the child's garments matched those on articles in the Donalds' flat. Some idea of the detail of the lengthy scientific evidence can be seen from Professor

Glaister's report below on the hair samples found at the scene of the crime.

Mrs Donald had already protested her innocence, and saw no reason to go into the witness box to repeat it. The trial occupied six days, but at the end of it the jury required no more than eighteen minutes to return a majority verdict of thirteen 'guilty' and two 'not proven' (a uniquely Scottish verdict). Jeannie Donald was sentenced to death, although that grim sentence was subsequently commuted to life imprisonment; she was released on special licence on 26 June 1944.

No motive ever emerged at the trial – though in fairness it must be said that it is not required of a prosecuting counsel to prove motive. But if the late Wllliam Roughead, lawyer and crime historian was right, Jeannie Donald was not guilty of murder at all:

Helen Priestly used to call Mrs Donald 'Coconut', and plainly held her in low esteem. It may be that by a fatal chance on that Friday they met at the Donalds' door. The child may have done something to rouse the woman's wrath: kicked at the door, put out her tongue at her, or otherwise annoyed or mocked her. She lost her temper, seized the child by the throat, and shook her. Such a shock, owing to the child's physical defect [she had an enlarged thymus gland], would result in a sudden collapse, passing into coma. [If she vomited during this period of unconsciousness she could easily have choked on her own vomit, which would have been consistent with the post-mortem finding of asphyxia.]

The woman, horrified, thought she had killed her. She carried her into the kitchen and frantically strove to revive her, but without avail. What was she to do? There was bad blood between them; doubtless she would be accused of deliberate murder. Then to her, panic-stricken and distraught, the very Devil suggested as the sole means of safety the vile expedient of simulated rape . . .

MEDICAL REPORT BY PROFESSOR GLAISTER
In the Case of Jeannie Donald

Acting on instructions received from the Lord Advocate I made examination of the undermentioned productions relating to the above case:

1. A mass of debris which was obtained from ashes, Label No. 41, taken from the fireplace of the accused.
2. Test-tube containing hair taken from the body of Helen Priestly, from scalp, partly cut and partly pulled out by the roots.
3. A hair, Label No. 43, found in a bucket under the sink in the kitchen of the accused.
4. Label No. 124, a hair taken from the brush found in the house of the accused.
5. Label No. 198, sample of hair taken from the brush used by the accused in prison.
6. Label No. 15, hairs removed from the sack in which the body of the deceased child was found.

All the productions were suitably treated and were thereafter examined with the following results:

Production 1. Debris, Label No. 41
Some 50 to 60 individual specimens of hairs were carefully examined and were thereafter relegated into the following groups:
   a. Light coloured hairs without a core.
   b. Dark coloured hairs with a core.
   c. Dark coloured hairs with a broken core.
   d. Light coloured hairs with a broken core.
It should be noted that a number of these hairs showed an irregularity of calibre with a degree of curling.

Production 2. Test-tube containing hair
The hairs were relegated to the following categories:
   a. Those without a core and of light colour.
   b. Those with a core and of dark colour.
   c. Those with a broken core and of dark colour.

Production 3. Hair found in bucket, Label No. 43
This was fine hair without a core and without any obvious colour.

Production 4. Hairs from brush found in house of accused, Label No. 124
Certain of the hairs from this brush were without core and devoid of appreciable pigment.

Production 5. Hairs from brush used by accused in prison, Label No. 198

Hair specimens examined were relegated to three groups:

   a. Hairs devoid of core and of medium dark colour.
   b. Hairs with absence of core and medium light colour.
   c. Hairs showing a faint core and of medium darkness.

It should be noted that the general character of all these hairs was a lack of uniformity of calibre. On examination of the cross-sections of these hairs the contour was inclined to be angular.

Production 6. Hairs from sack, Label No. 15

These hairs showed the following character:

   a. Hairs with slightly irregular core and a medium darkness and showing some irregularity of calibre.
   b. Similar hairs but revealing a much heavier core. A characteristic of these hairs was their irregular calibre.

Comparisons of the various hair samples was made with the following results:

Some of the hair retrieved from debris, No. 41, showed identical characteristics to the hairs of the accused, No. 198, both in their general characters and in their special peculiarities. Other hairs revealed strong similarity to hairs taken from the head of the deceased but showed equally close resemblance to a hair which was taken from the brush found in the house of the accused, No. 124

The hair found in the bucket, No. 43, showed characteristics which were practically identical with the non-pigmented hairs taken from the head of the child. This hair also bears strong resemblance to a hair taken from the brush of the accused, No. 124.

The hairs from the sack were compared with the head hair of the deceased (Tube A), and also with the hairs of the accused, No. 198, and it was found that no similarity existed between these hairs and those from the head of the deceased, but revealed similar characteristics to the hair of the accused, No. 198, the most outstanding feature being the existence of marked irregularity of calibre in both the areas of bulging in both cases.

As the result of my examination of the above-mentioned productions I am of the opinion that:

1. Some of the hairs from the debris, No. 41, were identical in character with certain of the hairs of the accused woman while others

were identical in character with certain of the head hairs of the deceased.

2. Some of the hairs from the sack, No. 15, were identical in character with certain hairs of the accused.

3. A hair found in a bucket under the sink, No. 43, was similar in all respects to certain of the hairs from the head of the deceased child, but since a hair showing similar characters was obtained from the brush taken from the house of the accused, no significance can be attached to the similarity.

These are attested on soul and conscience.

Signed, John Glaister, MD, DSc, etc.
Regius Professor of Forensic Medicine, Glasgow
30th June, 1934

Racial Origin

It was noted above that the scalp hairs of Mongoloid peoples showed a continuous medulla. Other features that provide an indication of racial origin are that Caucasians have the greatest variety of colour types – blond, red, brown and black; and that the Chinese, Japanese, Mongoloid and American Indian races share straight black hair.

The differences between Negroid and Caucasian hair are easily identifiable, the former tending to be kinky with dense, unevenly distributed pigment, while the latter is usually straight or wavy with finer granules of more evenly distributed pigments. Cross-sections show Caucasian hair to be oval to round in shape, Negroid hair flat to oval.

That said, the examiner must be continually aware of the many inconsistencies in these generalizations, not least because of increasing racial intermarriage.

Recent Developments

As the forensic laboratory becomes better equipped with modern scientific **Instrumentation**, so its staff will adapt new processes to solve old problems. This has been particularly noticeable in the possibilities offered of making increasingly reliable comparisons with less and less trace material.

Neutron Activation Analysis

It is possible with the use of **Neutron Activation Analysis** to identify at least fourteen different elements in a single inch (25.4mm) of a single human hair, both quantitatively and qualitatively: antimony, argon, bromine, copper, gold, iridium, lanthanum, manganese, mercury, selenium, silver, sodium, strontium and zinc. It is claimed for the process that the likelihood of two individuals having the same concentration of nine different elements is about one in a million.

The advantage of NAA over analysis by **Spectrography** – a technique formerly used – is that NAA is a non-destructive process while with spectrography it is necessary to destroy the sample of evidence.

Blood Factors

When a head hair is *pulled* from the scalp (as distinct from cut or broken off or naturally fallen out) it will have follicular tissue adhering to the bulbous root – cells from the sheath of the root. It is now possible to derive blood factors from an analysis of this tissue which will increase the chances of identifying a hair as belonging to a specific individual.

Eminent American criminalist Richard Saferstein has cited this example of a case analysed in his own laboratory:

White and brown head hairs were found adhering to the vehicle of an individual believed to have been involved in a hit-and-run fatality. The brown hair compared microscopically to the victim's brown hair control. The white hair offered minimal physical characteristics; however, sufficient follicular tissue was present on the hair root to identify the following blood factors: EsD 1, PMG2-1 and GLOI-1. These factors, present in approximately four per cent of the population, were also found in the victim's control hair tissue.

DNA Profiling

With the impressive advances in technique achieved with the process of **DNA Profiling** since its discovery in 1984, it has become possible to use live cell tissue from the root of a human hair in the same way, and with equally reliable results, as was previously applied to blood and other body secretions.

In June 1989, for the first time in British legal history, a rapist was convicted on DNA evidence derived from his hair. After the rape of two elderly women, a combined Metropolitan and Hertfordshire police operation code-named 'Vulcan' uncovered Lawrence Connors as a strong suspect. Although Connors refused to supply a blood sample (as was his right), he agreed to hair samples being taken (as these are considered 'non-intimate' samples he could not have refused anyway). Cells from the hair roots matched genetically the samples taken from the scene of the first rape and this, supported by other forensic transfer evidence, was sufficient to win the conviction.

HANDWRITING ANALYSIS
(See Disputed Documents)

HANGING
Generally described as death due to compression of the neck (commonly by a ligature) in which the constricting force is the weight of the body itself. The proximate **Cause of Death** is **Asphyxia**.

Fixed and Running Nooses
The pattern of the groove cut into the neck by suspension from a ligature will depend upon whether the noose is fixed or running. In the case of a fixed noose, the side nearest the suspending cord will be pulled upwards by the weight of the body, forming an inverted 'V' shape (because the head will tend to loll *away* from the suspending cord, there may be a patch of unmarked skin at the apex of the V). In the case of a running noose, the weight of the body causes the noose to tighten into an almost horizontal position.

Complete Suspension of Body
When the victim is fully suspended with feet clear of the ground, the body weight will cause compression of the neck and completely close the blood vessels – most importantly the carotid arteries – and also the air passages. The result is cerebral anoxia followed by loss of consciousness and death may be expected to result within a very few minutes. Such pressure as the weight of the body exerts will furrow deeply into the skin of the neck, the pattern of the groove depending on whether a fixed or running noose has been used.

However, initial damage to the neck will be comparatively slight – the sternomastoid muscles may be ruptured, the thyroid may be damaged, and the fragile hyoid bone is often broken as in cases of manual **Strangulation**. Where a body has suffered a drop of some feet before the ligature tightens there may be dislocation of the spine at the atlanto-axial joint.

Partial Suspension of Body

Hanging can as easily, though less rapidly, be achieved if a greater part of the body weight is supported by the ground – for example, suspension from a door-handle, bed-head or wall-hook, where the victim is in a crouching position. If the ligature is not tight, death will ensure mainly from the effects of coma produced by pressure closing off the cerebral circulation; as little constrictive force as 10lbs (4.5kg) is required to cause eventual death. The subject may exhibit the characteristics of slow asphyxia – swollen, purplish face and considerable petechial haemorrhaging.

Post-Mortem Appearances

The face is usually pale, the pupils of the eyes dilated. The lips and tongue (which may protrude slightly between the teeth) may be cyanosed – a blue discoloration of the skin caused by deoxygenated blood – and considerable petechial haemorrhaging will be found under the conjunctivae.

The phenomenon of penile erection has been greatly exaggerated by popular mythology. Nevertheless, slight degrees of engorgement – with or without the presence of semen – can be observed in cases of death by hanging, as with other forms of death. It is thought that the effect is due to hypostasis, or perhaps rigor mortis.

In hanging, as in death by other means, the sphincters lose control, resulting in vacuation of the bowel and bladder.

A great deal of information may be derived from the pattern and position of the furrows made by the ligature. In cases of suicide, the ligature mark will generally follow the line of the lower jaw before going upwards behind the ear – though clearly this will be modified by whether a fixed or running noose has been used. Particular attention should be paid to the areas around the ligature marks, where injuries not consistent with hanging may indicate that an apparent suicide has been fatally attacked before suspension.

The internal post-mortem appearances are those for asphyxia; the brain shows considerable congestion, and petechial haemorrhages may be found in the trachea and larynx and on the epiglottis. The hyoid bone may be fractured, the sternomastoid muscles damaged, and the thyroid cartilage broken.

Accident? Suicide? Homicide?

Although hanging can result from all three, it is suicide which accounts for the greatest percentage of deaths. Certain signs will point to suicide at the scene of the incident, such as finding a suicide note. Suicides tend to hang themselves with some part of the body touching the ground – in many cases this is a purely practical consideration in that most domestic ceilings are not high enough to allow any alternative, and there are rarely any means of suspension. In cases where a suicide has allowed himself a 'drop', the overturned chair or step-ladder will be close by.

The discovery of wounds on a subject's body that seem unconnected with the hanging will obviously arouse the suspicions of the investigating officers and the pathologist; however, it is not unknown for a suicide to make other attempts by various means before succeeding at hanging.

Accidental hanging has been recorded, though its incidence is rare, and there are usually other contributory factors such as drunkenness or frail old age. In short, it is not easy to become accidentally hanged.

Due to the relative difficulty of the procedure, there are few instances of homicidal hanging, and then the act is usually carried out by more than one person. More common, and in many ways more interesting to the criminologist, are cases where homicide is made to look like suicidal hanging.

One scenes-of-crime investigator recalls the case of a man who telephoned the police after his wife, so he claimed, had hanged herself at home. He described finding his wife suspended from a rope, which she had first tied to a door-handle and then passed over the top of the door to the other side before putting her head in the noose. He had cut her down, tried in vain to revive her, and then called the police. To somebody unaccustomed to judging heights and distances this would seem a reasonable explanation of the scenario. However, to the experienced officer it was quite obvious that the rope was simply too short to have covered the distance required. Thus an 'obvious' case of suicide became a matter of murder.

In the celebrated case of Norman Thorne, the Sussex chicken farmer, he claimed to have found his fiancée swinging from a roof-beam in the hut in which he lived. Thorne told the police that he had cut poor Elsie Cameron down and tried to revive her; when it was obvious she was dead he panicked, dismembered the body, and interred the neatly parcelled pieces beneath the chicken runs. Norman Thorne's insistence that Miss Cameron had been the instrument of her own death was undermined when it was pointed out by detectives that not only were there no rope-marks on the beam in question – which might reasonably be expected if a heavy weight had been suspended from it – but it was quite clear that the thick layer of dust on the top surface of the beam had not been disturbed in a very long time. Nor, Sir Bernard **Spilsbury** was prepared to say, was there any evidence on the victim's neck to suggest that she had hanged herself; but judging from the extensive bruising, there was very good reason to suppose that Elsie Cameron had been battered to death. Norman Thorne was executed at Wandsworth Prison on 22 April 1925.

Judicial Hanging

Hanging, as an instrument of judicial execution, entered England by way of the Anglo-Saxons, who had inherited the method from their German ancestors. It became the established punishment for a great many crimes when Henry II instituted trial-by-jury and the assize courts in the twelfth century. By the Middle Ages, the power to try, sentence and hang felons was vested in every town, abbey and manorial lord. Hangings until the present century were extremely crude affairs – carried out publicly and often preceded and succeeded by additional barbaric torture. Elaborations like hanging, drawing and quartering became popular spectator events.

But even at best, a simple hanging was little better than slow strangulation – sometimes lingering on for hours; indeed, it was considered a great act of kindness on the part of the executioner to allow some relative or well-wisher to pull on the victim's legs, and so hasten death.

With the last public hanging in 1868, and the confinement of such practices to the execution shed of prisons, a more enlightened and humane procedure was developed to dispatch the prisoner with the greatest speed and least pain. The act of hanging became a science based on the accurate relationship of weight to distance, and the hangman became its craftsman.

By means of an accurate assessment of the 'drop' required and the crucial positioning of the thick leather washer behind the prisoner's ear, it was in most cases a quick – if not always instantaneous – death.

Unlike other more 'private' methods of hanging, the procedure of judicial execution is designed to cause death by dislocation of the upper cervical vertebrae, thus causing severance of the spinal cord close to the junction with the brain.

Sexual Asphyxia

An entry on hanging would be incomplete without reference to the phenomenon of self-induced asphyxia for the purpose of sexual gratification. It is by no means rare, and is an almost exclusively male activity.

The manner in which asphyxia is induced varies, but is typically strangulation by a ligature. There is some evidence that the restriction of oxygen to the brain can, in some instances, effect orgasm. It also causes loss of consciousness and, if the supply is not restored in time, asphyxia results. Acts of sexual asphyxia can usually be distinguished by the general appearance of the scene of the incident: the presence of pornographic literature close to the body; evidence of masturbation; mirrors positioned so that the subject can watch himself 'hang'; In addition, the subject may be in some stage of nakedness, wearing women's clothing, leather, rubber, etc. To prevent marking the body, there is sometimes soft padding – a handkerchief, for example – between the neck and the ligature.

HYOSCINE

> '. . . Upon my secure hour thy uncle stole,
> With juice of cursed hebenon in a vial,
> And in the porches of mine ears did pour
> The leprous distilment . . .'
>
> *Hamlet*, Act I, Scene 5

Hyoscine is a vegetable drug occurring naturally in several plants: in deadly nightshade where it is mixed with atropine (belladonna), in thorn apple (called Jimson Weed), and in henbane (Shakespeare's 'hebenon'). It is commonly called 'scopolamine' to distinguish it from another drug, hyoscyamine.

All the effects of hyoscine relate to depression of the central nervous system, and characteristics depend on the size of the dose administered. Very tiny amounts can be effective in the treatment of anxiety-related problems, and it is sometimes prescribed against travel-sickness. Larger doses begin to break down the patient's ability to discriminate and make reasoned judgements, which has led to its use as a so-called 'truth drug'.

Still larger amounts cause hallucinations, and in particular the sensation of floating – it was this effect which so endeared henbane to witches and sorcerers of former times for use in 'flying' ointments; the ability to be as toxic administered externally as internally renders it a doubly useful substance for both physician and poisoner. Unfortunately, hyoscine is unpredictable in its effect on different people, making it hazardous to administer even the smallest of doses. Death occurs when the nerves of the heart become affected and that organ ceases to function.

Hyoscine as a murder weapon was introduced to the world in 1910 by Dr Crippen, who used it to dispose of his wife.

HYPNOSIS

Hypnosis is still one of the great 'unknowns', and psychological research has so far failed to establish the precise nature of this altered state of consciousness. In effect, it is a 'waking sleep' where the mind appears to be at rest while the motor reactions, such as walking and talking, remain active, and the subject becomes susceptible to suggestion.

The phenomenon was certainly known in the last quarter of the eighteenth century when Franz Anton Mesmer (1734–1815), an Austrian physician, put his subjects into a trance state by what he called 'animal magnetism', so that they became subject to his will. This activity was viewed with such official disapproval that Mesmer was exiled from Vienna and subsequently earned some considerable reputation in Paris. Here Mesmer became celebrated for his 'healing' sessions, at which he appeared clothed in purple silk brandishing an iron rod with the help of which he would put the 'magnetic field' of his patients' bodies under the influence of the planets. Popular entertainment or not, this mumbo jumbo did not impress the gentlemen of the Academie des Sciences which utterly rejected his theories. It is symptomatic of hypnotism's indefinable quality that Mesmer was able to induce it in his subjects without having the least idea what it was that he was doing.

Like ordinary sleep, hynposis is very much a matter of auto-suggestion, and in most cases it is impossible to hypnotize a person against their will. There appear to be three stages of hypnosis which merge into each other. The first is *flexibilitas cerea*, in which the limbs become rigid, there is marked anaesthesia of parts of the body, and the subject is extremely susceptible to suggestion. The second stage is one of 'lethargy', where the body is flaccid and the subject gives the appearance of unconsciousness.

The third stage is akin to a state of somnambulism. The subject is again extremely susceptible, and it is necessary for the operator merely to make a suggestion for the subject to perform actions which may be quite impossible for him in a waking state. More important, the hypnotized subject is capable of remembering incidents which he cannot recall in a normal state, and by this method it is possible to reach into the subconscious in order to uncover hidden memories. This factor is of potentially great value to the criminal investigator in dealing with victims or witnesses suffering post-traumatic amnesia.

As one of the techniques of the forensic psychologist (as distinct from the forensic psychiatrist, whose specialism is the diagnosis and treatment of abnormal offenders), hypnosis has only recently been viewed as a serious technique with a valuable contribution to make to legal medicine.

Hypnotism can presently be encountered in two main areas:

1. The induction of relaxation in witnesses whose testimony might otherwise be impaired by the anxiety and stress provoked by the legal process.
2. Receiving information from victims/witnesses that is not available by any other means.

Hypnotherapy

The first of these areas is self-explanatory and is readily acceptable in the light of 'alternative' therapy techniques being increasingly used in the fight against stress-related disorders.

Investigative Hypnosis

A more contentious practice altogether, broadly covering those occasions when a victim – say, of rape or other violent assault – may be suffering from repressive amnesia; similarly, with witnesses of some particularly shocking event, such as a murder or serious accident. In both these cases, however, it is obvious that only the most qualified practitioners should be trusted to hypnotize patients for whom accompanying emotional abreaction is a frequent danger.

The problems faced by practitioners of hypnosis in having their findings accepted as 'new evidence' result both from its admissibility in court, and fears that the future independence of witnesses subjected to hypnosis may be impaired.

In regard to the first objection, it is a fact that, as yet, no overall ruling on the admissibility of evidence derived from hypnosis exists, and the few cases in which such evidence has been introduced have been devalued by the unprofessional circumstances of the original interview. In the second objection – what solicitors term the 'hypnotic tampering' with witnesses – there is always in any set of circumstances the danger of malpractice, and where there exists the slightest possibility of 'tampering' with witnesses in *any* way then it must be strenuously resisted. However, if current safeguards that are applied to regular interview techniques, such as the use of video-film and audio-tape recordings, are extended to the retrieval of information by hypnosis, and as long as the presence of qualified practitioners and independent observers is assured, there is no reason to suspect interference with potential 'evidence'.

As part of its guidelines for the use of hypnosis as an investigative technique, the British Home Office emphasizes that:

1. Hypnosis induces relaxation, in which state there is a tendency for a subject to recall past experiences in greater detail.
2. Hypnosis does *not* deprive the subject of control or awareness, nor cause them to lose consciousness.
3. Under the strict control of a qualified hypnotist, the experience is safe and free from after-effects.
4. A subject is assured that no attempt will be made during hypnosis to seek information not directly relevant to the investigation, or that will cause the subject to incriminate himself.

Conclusions

It has been shown that new and accurate information can be obtained by means of hypnosis. Criticisms that hypnosis increases a susceptibility to 'leading questions' have, as stated above, begun to be addressed by improvements in practical interview techniques.

However, one eminent expert* is led to conclude that: 'The lack of empirical evidence that hypnosis facilitates the remembering of eye-witness materials makes it questionable whether the time and expense involved in the hypnotizing of witnesses can be justified. Furthermore, the overestimation by many police officers of the effectiveness of forensic hypnosis, and the evidence that hypnosis increases suscepti-bility to leading questions, suggests that hypnotizing a witness can harm the quality of the police investigation into crime.'

*D. Mingay, 'Hypnosis and Eye-Witness Testimony', in *Hypnosis,* ed. Michael Heap, London, 1987.

Crime Committed Under Hypnosis

The reverse of the forensic use of hypnosis is its criminal use. Although the number of reliably documented cases of crimes committed under hypnosis is small, it does validate the theory that it is *possible* to hypnotize a person into committing actions which, in the general order of things, they would abhor.

In the United States in 1981, the case arose of an eighteen-year-old woman who admitted shooting and seriously wounding two United States marshals while attempting to assist her husband to escape from custody; she pleaded the unusual defence that hypnosis had *prevented her from forming the requisite intent to kill. In* other words, diminished responsibility. At the young woman's trial her husband gave evidence that he had been hypnotizing her for about three years, sometimes more than a dozen times a day. He had, under hypnosis, coerced her into believing that he was, variously, her mother, her father, and God. It was he, so he claimed, who instructed her to bring the gun and use it to help him escape. The defence plea was based on the fact that, as the defendant believed that it was God instructing her, she could not have thought that what he said could be wrong: 'If God tells you to do something you think it's right.' The result of the trial was that the woman was acquitted of the charge of assault with intent to commit murder.

HYPOSTASIS

Sometimes called post-mortem lividity and *livor mortis,* the process of hypostasis sets in immediately following death, and although it is no longer considered reliable, was once regarded as an indicator of time of death.

When the blood ceases to circulate around the body it follows the law of gravity and sinks to the blood vessels in the lowest part of the body. As the red corpuscles settle first the affected parts exhibit a livid colour (hence 'lividity'). The phenomenon becomes discernible between one and three hours after death when the discoloration is patchy and a bluish-pink colour; at around six or eight hours the patches have fused together into larger purplish areas, and if pressed the skin will blanch. When the blood coagulates in the vessels after ten to twelve hours the purple stain becomes fixed and will not blanch under pressure.

These characteristic stains cannot form where the pressure of either tight clothing or ligatures, or contact with a firm surface, prevent the capillaries from filling with blood. Thus a body that was lying on its back on the floor after death will show marked lividity on the back of the neck, the small of the back and the thighs. The back of the head, shoulders, buttocks and calves which have been in contact with the floor will show as white patches. This observation is of vital importance in determining whether a body has been moved to a different location or position after death, and where the previously 'fixed' marks of lividity are inconsistent with the present position.

Case Study

EDITH DAISY CHUBB

Edith Daisy Chubb was a drudge. She had not been born so, but at the age of forty-six she found herself with sole responsibility for an inconsiderate, ill-tempered husband, an elderly mother, five children, and a domineering sister-in-law. In addition to her seemingly endless domestic commitments, Edith Chubb kept the family just this side of poverty by working a gruelling twelve-hour, three-day-a-week shift as a cleaner in the Haine Hospital near her home in Broadstairs. Edith was constantly tired, constantly in debt and, like too many women forced into this position, an eternally silent martyr.

Sister-in-law Lily was a maiden lady of a type popularly characterized on the English comedy stage – that is to say, she was middle-aged, prim, opinionated and overbearing. Miss Chubb was employed as a sales assistant in the ladies wear department of a big store, and in perfect keeping with the rest of her character, she left home on the dot of 8.40 every morning, and left work on the dot of six every evening.

The morning of 6 February 1958 was the one time that she varied the habit – but it was hardly the result of a temporarily wayward spirit. This was the day that Edith's mind chose to seize up. Her husband had left for work, the children for school; the two women were alone in the house. 'I felt irritated by the way she put her teacup down,' recalled Mrs Chubb; 'I followed her down the stairs, and pulled hard on her scarf . . . I didn't meant to hurt her . . . just to shake her up. She fell backwards on to the floor, striking her head on the banister.' Outside the front door, the milkman could be heard making his daily delivery; inside, Lilian made a low, groaning sound, and Edith put her hand over her mouth to stop it . . .

That evening there was great surprise in the Chubb household – Lilian was late home! Consternation set in when she did not come home at all; and it was Edith Chubb who next morning went to the Broadstairs police station to report her missing. That was at around 10 a.m. One hour later the police returned her visit; Lilian Chubb had been found in a hedge. She was dead; the doctor said it was strangulation. Edith could hardly believe her ears: 'I just can't imagine anything like this happening; we are a very happy, united family.'

It was only after Miss Lily had been given the questionable privilege of a post-mortem by one of the country's leading forensic pathologists, that Edith Chubb's story was seriously doubted. Professor Francis Camps confirmed that Lily Chubb had died from strangulation, and he also identified the probable cause of the strangely situated patches of lividity on the body. The state of lividity, or hypostasis, is simply the result of the blood in the body – no longer circulating after death – finding its own level and coagulating in the vessels; thus, those parts of the corpse that are in contact with a hard surface, such as the floor, will not show the characteristic livid patches where the blood lies. On this principle, it was Camps' contention that the body of Lilian Chubb had been sat in a chair shortly after death and left for some time before disposal.

It had already been established that Lilian Chubb had not reported for work on the morning of the 6th; what is more, none of the neighbours, who were familiar with her punctual nature, had seen Miss Chubb leave at her customary time that morning. So she must have died in the house!

The forlorn, long-suffering Mrs Chubb stepped into the witness box at her trial, and with the help of her defence counsel began the long recitation of depressing events in a deeply depressing life: 'Lily was so smug; nobody knows what she was like . . .' Poor Lilian, she became the focus, rightly or wrongly, for all Edith's discontent. Then finally: 'Something came over me. I pulled the scarf tightly round Lily's neck. She didn't struggle . . . When I realized she was dead I was horror-struck.' Edith Chubb put her victim in the old invalid chair that was in the garden shed, and pushed it back into the shed. Early next morning she covered the corpse with a rug and wheeled it down to Reading Street Road where she dumped it: 'It didn't take me long.'

And it didn't take the jury long to reach their verdict. They had heard medical evidence from Edith's doctor, Gordon Marshall, who testified that she was a woman close to breaking-point, and they found her guilty of manslaughter. The next four years, during which

Edith Chubb was a guest of Her Majesty, were probably the most comfortable of her life.

The marks of post-mortem lividity closely resemble bruises, and this confusion has periodically led to conflict between expert witnesses at a trial for murder. It was at the base of the dispute over the 'disappearing bruise' between the eminent pathologist Sir Bernard Spilsbury and his equally celebrated adversary Sir Sydney Smith. At the trial of Sidney Harry Fox for the murder of his mother in Kent in 1929, it was Spilsbury's contention that what he identified as a bruise on Mrs Rosalie Fox's larynx indicated manual strangulation. Appearing as an expert witness for the defence, Smith declared that the 'bruise', which had faded completely by the time he examined the pathological specimen, was simply a patch of discoloration from post-mortem staining:

Sir William Jowett (cross-examining Smith for the prosecution): You said yesterday that in training assistants you had to be careful in distinguishing in post-mortem examination between bruises and discoloration marks; do you put Sir Bernard Spilsbury on a par with one of your assistants? Do you suggest Sir Bernard would not know the difference between the two? – *Sir Sydney Smith:* Nobody can tell merely by looking; I do not think anyone should say a bruise is a bruise until it has been proved that it is.

Do you say that you would not say a bruise was a bruise until you put it under the microscope? – No, I should cut into it.

If you saw a fellow with a black eye would you say: 'Let me put it under a microscope before I say it is a black eye?' Sir Bernard says there can be no two opinions about it. – It is very obvious there can be.

You are bound to accept the evidence of the man who saw the bruise? – I do not think so.

How can you say there was not a bruise there? – Because if there was a bruise there it should be there now. It should be there for ever.

The jury chose either to accept Sir Bernard's 'bruise' or to ignore this piece of unresolved evidence altogether, for they convicted Sidney Fox, and he was later hanged for matricide. The exercise did, however, emphasize the care that needs to be taken in interpreting marks on a dead body.

The basic difference in this case is that in hypostasis the discoloration is the result of filling of the vessels with blood after death; with a bruise, impact will force blood *out* of the vessels into the surrounding tissue – conditions which can be distinguished without difficulty under a microscope.

I

IDENTIFICATION

In the very broadest terms, of course, all forensic science is about identification – of people, substances, physical conditions, states of guilt . . . But in a more practical sense, 'identification' here is understood as the marking of a suspect as the result of some visually descriptive information – a photo-FIT, an artist's impression, a witness description.

It might logically be expected that a person who has just witnessed an incident is the perfect source of identification. In reality this proves to be far from the truth – quite often, sometimes with alarming consequences, an eye-witness proves *counter-productive* to the investigation. This is because, excluding the professional observers such as police officers, we tend to imagine our powers of recall and description to be better than they really are, and those powers are likely to be confused by any number of physical and psychological factors. For instance, alarm or fright at being so close to a serious crime or accident can momentarily 'paralyse' the mind as it might the body; and elements such as distance and light and shadow can give deceptive impressions of size.

Frederick Porter Wensley, the great detective and one-time Chief Constable of Scotland Yard's CID, wrote:

> Another line of thought that, to me, seems muddled is in regard to methods of identification. I do not believe that anything can prevent an honestly mistaken identification. There are people who unquestionably have doubles in appearance, action and speech. They might be wrongly recognized in any circumstances, under any precautions.

In practical detective work what happens is this. A man who has been responsible for a crime has been seen by one or more people who say they would know him again, and can give some sort of description. It is very difficult for the ordinary person to give a description of someone he may only have seen once, and one has to consider how far a particular witness has been likely to observe and remember, and is capable of conveying an impression.

Detective Days, 1931

In fact, the current tendency is to accept eye-witness identification only when supported by other, scientific, evidence. This was tentatively endorsed by the English court of appeal in 1977 in the case of Turnbull, leading to what became known as the 'Turnbull Rules', requiring that a judge warn a jury of the dangers of identification evidence and direct them' to 'examine closely' the circumstances in which the identification was made. Lord Devlin, the former Law Lord, has observed: 'The highly reputable, absolutely sincere, perfectly coherent and apparently convincing witness may, as experience has quite often shown, be mistaken.'

Certainly research carried out into the subject so far (notably by Shepherd, Haydn and Ellis) supports his Lordship's misgivings. Findings indicate that juries are as likely to give credence to an inaccurate eye-witness as to one whose testimony is accurate. Race can play a negative part, and in particular white people are bad at identifying blacks – a problem which is serious in a society in which whites predominate and blacks occupy a disproportionate place in court and in prison (e.g. Britain and the United States). There is growing evidence to support the accusation that the identification of the offender is the largest single cause of miscarriages of justice.

Identification Parades

When an accused person faces criminal proceedings as the result of positive identification in a police line-up there is a cynical suggestion that he has all but been convicted – after all, the police must have had strong enough suspicions to place him in custody in the first place, mustn't they? Positive identification is seen merely as corroboration. A further danger is that a witness may simply pick out the person who most approximates his recollection of the offender and then, unwittingly, transfer this new image back into his visual memory where it becomes fixed as 'fact'; this is the type of problem that renders the identification parade unreliable, rather than any inherent 'unfairness 'in the way it is conducted.

In fact, a suspect cannot be forced to take part in a line-up; however, as it can be arranged for him to be seen among a group of other people by the witness with a view to identification, it is probably safer to allow it to happen in a formal atmosphere; at any rate a suspect is wise to take legal advice before agreeing, and in many cases, where identification may be crucial at trial, an accused may wish to *insist* on an identification parade.

In 1978 the Home Office issued a set of strict guidelines to be observed in conducting ID parades, the most important of which are:

1. The suspect should be given a leaflet outlining, and have explained to him, his rights.
2. He should, provided it does not cause 'unreasonable delay', be allowed to have a solicitor or a friend present.
3. The witness must not be allowed to see the suspect before the parade takes place.
4. The suspect should be placed among persons (at least eight, preferably more) who are as far as practical of the same age, height, general appearance (including dress and 'grooming') and social position as the suspect. Members of a homogeneous group, such as soldiers or policemen, should not be used as participants unless the suspect himself belongs to the police or armed forces. Only one suspect must be included in the parade (unless there are two suspects of *similar appearance* in which case they must be assembled with at least *twelve* other participants).
5. The suspect should be allowed to select his own position in the line and should be expressly asked if he has any objection to the arrangements or any other participants in the group. Objections should be noted by the officer in charge of the parade and, as far as possible, steps taken to remove the grounds for objection.
6. The line should be visited by only one witness at a time; the witness should be informed that the suspect may or may not be in the line.
7. If a witness requests to hear members of the line-up speak or see them move, he should first be asked if it has been possible to make an identification by appearance only; it must be explained that the participants in the line were chosen only because of similar visual appearance (not, for example, for their similar voices).

8. When one witness has left, the suspect must be told that he has a right to alter his place in the line before the next witness enters.
9. When the parade is finished, the suspect may, if he wishes, record his comments on the proceedings.

Photographic Identification

The Home Office has laid down similar guidelines covering witness identification from photographs:

1. If an identification parade can be organized it must take precedence over identification from photographs.
2. The witness should be shown no fewer than twelve photographs at a time, the photographs being as far as possible of a similar type (e.g. a studio portrait should not be included in a collection of mug-shots). As in the parade, all photographs should bear a close resemblance to the suspect.
3. The witness should be told that the photograph of the suspect may or may not be among the collection.
4. If a firm identification is made from the photographs, a witness must then be asked to attend an identification parade.

Case Study

THE BROUGHTY FERRY MYSTERY

Few people have been judicially executed in error (though enough to make capital punishment a questionable tool of justice), but there is an uncomfortable number of cases in which, but for the intervention of luck, an innocent party could have lost their liberty . . . or worse. This is the story of one such man, and his unwitting involvement in a crime which remains unsolved to this day.

On Sunday 3 November 1912, the battered body of Jean Milne was discovered in the hallway of her fourteen-roomed mansion at Broughty Ferry, close to Dundee. Miss Milne was sixty-five years old, wealthy, and considered rather eccentric in her habits, though much of this local 'reputation' rested on the fact that she chose to live alone and enjoyed wearing flamboyant clothes. It was estimated from the state of decomposition of the body that Miss Milne had been killed – with the poker which lay beside her – on the 15th–16th of the previous month. Her ankles had been tied together with curtain cord and, a bizarre feature never explained, she appeared to have been pricked on the body with some kind of two-pronged fork. Robbery was immediately ruled out as a motive, as Miss Milne's diamond rings were still on her fingers, and her purse containing £17 in gold was untouched. Furthermore, it was apparent that whoever put such a cruel end to her life had been known to the victim – there were no signs of forcible entry, and the dining-room table was laid for tea for two persons. If her anticipated guest had *not* been her killer, it seems certain that they would subsequently have informed the police of the abortive visit.

It did not take detectives long to collect together a body of useful information from the local residents; after all, Miss Milne being something of a village curiosity, her movements tended to be monitored by gossip-hungry neighbours. Margaret Campbell, a servant employed in the house next door, recalled seeing a tall, handsome stranger walking in the grounds of Elmsgrove House around the date on which its occupant was killed. This seemed to confirm the local belief that, despite her advancing years, Jean Milne had far from forsaken romance. Indeed, she had encouraged such speculation. After one of her lengthy sojourns in London in the spring of that year, she confided to a friend that she had met a 'gentleman' at her hotel (the Strand Palace), who had 'taken her about' and paid her much attention; Miss Milne had even gone so far as to suggest that this might prove to be the beginning of a partnership for life.

There was a further sighting of the mysterious stranger in the early hours of the morning of 16 October. James Don, a scavenger about his cleaning duties, had seen a man in a bowler hat and dark overcoat walk out of the gate to Elmsgrove House and turn down the lane. Then John Wood, a gardener employed by Miss Milne, remembered a gentleman calling at the house while he was there the previous September. His recollection was that Miss Milne 'skipped along the passage just like a lassie' to greet her visitor.

On the basis of these observations, Detective-Lieutenant Trench issued a description of the man they wished to interview in connection with Miss Milne's murder. Among the recipients of this document were the prison authorities at Maidstone Gaol, Kent, who connected it with one of their guests – a Canadian by the name of Charles Warner. Warner had been convicted of defrauding an innkeeper in Tonbridge, and was currently serving his sentence. Consequently, a party of witnesses was transported from Broughty Ferry to inspect the hapless Canadian in his cell.

James Don identified Warner immediately as the man he had seen leaving Elmsgrove House; James Wood was convinced that he was Miss Milne's welcome guest, and two sisters named McIntosh swore that Charles Warner was the man they saw leaving the mansion on 9 October. Margaret Campbell was less certain until she saw Warner's eyes – 'I cannot forget his eyes.'

All this clearly came as a great surprise to Charles Warner, not least because, he said, he had never been to Scotland. In fact, at the time of Miss Milne's murder he had been in Antwerp, where he had arrived via Paris, London, Liverpool and Amsterdam, which would have been a perfect alibi had Warner been able to prove it. What hotel was he staying at? – None, he had been so completely out of funds that he had slept rough in the park. Was there anybody who could vouch for his being in the city? – No, he had wandered friendless, penniless and anonymous.

In fact, if his recent past had been bleak, Charles Warner's future looked even bleaker. With no supportable alibi, and five witnesses who placed him at the scene of a murder, he now stood a chance of losing a great deal more than his freedom.

It was luck that literally saved Charles Warner's neck. He suddenly remembered that on the very day of the incident at Broughty Ferry he had been constrained by circumstances to exchange his overcoat for a few guilders in an Antwerp pawnshop. And this time he could prove it.

When Detective-Lieutenant Trench arrived in Belgium, he had with him a pawn-ticket; a crumpled scrap of paper that for no good reason had remained in a corner of Warner's jacket pocket. It was the scrap of paper that drew Charles Warner out from the shadow of the gallows. More important, and more disturbing, it prevented a gross, and possibly irreversible, miscarriage of justice.

IDENTIKIT

It was in 1940 that Hugh C. McDonald, chief of the civilian division of the Los Angeles Police Department, devised the first working Identikit system, based on the principles of **Bertillon**'s earlier **Portrait Parlé**. In every respect it was a matter of necessity being the mother of invention. McDonald was on a mission in Europe tracking down the rag-bag of crooks and con-men who had been exploiting the confusion of war in order to carry on their various misdeeds, and Hugh McDonald was acquiring so many vague and partial descriptions from witnesses that he found himself composing rough sketches of his suspects. To save time McDonald drew up a set of transparent sheets of different eyes, noses, face shapes, and so on, which he could use in collaboration with his sources. Back home in the United States the detective took his project to the Townsend Company of Santa Ana, California.

Development by the Townsend Company resulted – some years later and after considerable consultation with neighbouring police forces – in the first Identikit field pack. It consisted of around 525 coded and numbered transparencies, each 4.5 × 7 × 10 inches, and bearing a drawing of a single facial feature; there were 102 pairs of eyes, 32 noses, 33 lips, 52 chins, and 25 moustaches and beards. Hugh McDonald claimed that it was possible to compile as many as 62 *billion* different combinations. It is interesting that there were no ears on these kits because: 'From our first experience, many victims of crime – especially crimes of violence such as rape, or a coshing – are usually facing the criminal at the all important moment, and never see his ears properly. Special marks like big or deformed ears, or scars and moles, can be drawn in afterwards on the slides with a wax pencil.'

One of the advantages of this coded system in the days when fax was not an option, was that an officer in one city could transmit Identikit pictures to an officer in another city, simply by passing on the number/letter code of the individual sheets.

By 1960, the Identikit system was in use by many of the world's police forces; among the first was Great Britain.

Case Study One

SUCCESS

It was in 1961 that the Metropolitan police enjoyed their first Identikit success in a case of murder. On 3 March, Mrs Elsie Batten was brutally stabbed to death while working alone in a curio shop just off London's busy Charing Cross Road. A young half-caste Indian had visited the shop on the previous day inquiring the price of a dress-sword; it was £15. He then went across the road to the shop of a gunsmith named Roberts and asked whether he bought such things as dress-swords; he did. On the following morning the youth revisited the curio shop, stabbed Mrs Batten and stole the sword, taking it immediately to Mr Roberts with whose son he left it for appraisal.

It so happened that on that very day Detective Sergeant Dagg of

London's CID had completed his Identikit training course, and based on the statements of Roberts and son built a likeness of a lean-jawed Anglo-Indian man. The portrait was circulated to all the police stations in the area, and five days later, on 8 March, Police Constable Cole was walking his beat down Old Compton Street, not half a mile from the scene of the crime, when towards him walked the face that had been staring down at him from the station notice board.

Edwin Bush was taken into custody and later made a confession; he had needed the money to buy his girl-friend an engagement ring. He also had blood on his clothing, had left an identifiable shoe-print at the shop, and two fingerprints and a palm print on the paper he used to wrap the sword. Unsurprisingly Edwin Bush was convicted of murder, sentenced to death and later hanged. After pronouncing sentence, Mr Justice Stevenson addressed PC Cole: 'You deserve the congratulations and gratitude of the community for the great efficiency you displayed in recognizing Bush. You have been the direct instrument of his being brought to justice. Your vigilance deserves the highest praise, and I hope it will be clearly recognized by the highest authority.'

Identikit, it seemed, had a bright and illustrious future in the unending war against crime.

Case Study

FAILURE

Before long Britain learned that however much help the Identikit system was in polarizing the recollections of witnesses into a single graphic image, it was not a magic wand. As one critic put it: 'Slight shifts in memory can produce marked differences between pictures produced and the hunted man.'

On the evening of 22 August 1961, Michael Gregsten sat in his parked car by a field in Slough, Buckinghamshire. Beside him sat his mistress, Valerie Stone. Suddenly a man appeared at the door of the car, climbed in, and with a gun to Gregsten's head forced him to drive along the A6 to the appropriately named Deadman's Hill. Here he ordered Gregsten to pull into a lay-by, shot him dead and raped and shot Valerie Stone. By a miracle she survived, though paralyzed for life.

Detective Sergeant Jock Mackle, Scotland Yard's Identikit expert, made up Valerie Stone's image of her attacker at her hospital bedside.

On 29 August two Identikit pictures were released to the press – Valerie Stone's and another compiled from the recollections of three 'witnesses'. The Identikits looked like two entirely different people – the only common feature were the deep-set brown eyes which Valerie Stone had so positively remembered.

Meanwhile, investigations had turned up two suspects; a man named James Hanratty in whose hotel room were found two cartridge cases from the murder weapon, and Peter Louis Alphon who had occupied the same hotel room on the previous night.

Not only did the two Identikit pictures look nothing like each other, but they did not look like James Hanratty either – not least because he had clear pale blue eyes. Hanratty's hair was neither dark, nor was it brushed back – an impossibility anyway because he had a pronounced 'widow's peak'. One man who did fit Valerie Stone's Identikit almost perfectly was Peter Alphon.

For reasons never satisfactorily explained, Valerie Stone subsequently retracted her description of her attacker's eyes, which became 'icy-blue' and 'saucer-like', as well as of other important features. She did not pick Peter Alphon out of a special identity parade arranged at the hospital on 24 September, but on 14 October she picked Hanratty out of a parade staged at Stoke Mandeville hospital. Hanratty was arrested on the spot.

When James Hanratty was put on trial his defence was one of alibi – though he refused to name the friends with whom he claimed to have been in Liverpool on the night of the shooting – and they did not volunteer themselves as witnesses. Hanratty then made the fatal mistake of changing his alibi – no matter that it was almost certainly the truth. Now he insisted he had been in Rhyl on the day the murder took place; but this also remained unsupported by witnesses.

Hanratty was found guilty of murder and hanged at Bedford Prison on 4 April 1962; but not before enormous doubt had been expressed as to the safety of that verdict. It was partly that witnesses had been found who thought they remembered seeing Hanratty in Rhyl, but mostly because Peter Alphon began to make a sequence of extraordinary statements in which it became clear that it was he, 'hired by an interested party' to break up the Gregsten/Storie romance, who had committed the murder and framed Hanratty.

Hanratty's family have long petitioned for a posthumous pardon for him, but in 2001, newly discovered DNA evidence seemed to prove that Hanratty was guilty. The Pardon Hanratty campaign, however, claims that this DNA evidence is the result of cross-contamination over the forty years since the murder and rape took place. As of this writing, (September 2003) conclusive proof has yet to be offered by either side.

IMPRESSIONS

Casts of impressions taken at the **Scene-of-Crime** will be useful in connecting the person or tool which fits the impression with the offence. Perhaps the best-known types of impressions are footprints (or more correctly, **Shoeprints** and tyre-prints (tyre impressions).

When an object such as a shoe is impressed into a soft material such as soil, it will leave behind a negative 'mould' of itself and any marks and imperfections that it may bear – signs of wear, maker's details, etc. By carefully filling the mould with a suitable substance, such as plaster of Paris or one of the many modern quick-set materials now available, an exact reproduction of the surface of the original object (sole of the shoe, say) is made. This will be sent to the laboratory where it is analysed and compared with any suspect object.

The first practical step in preserving an impression is to photograph it from as many angles as necessary to present the maximum information. A clearly marked ruler should always be laid alongside the subject as a future guide if the prints are enlarged to life-size; photographs taken with oblique lighting give the best contrast.

Casting Large Impressions

When the photographer has finished his work a frame, usually of card or wood, is built around the impression to contain the casting mixture. Before pouring in the plaster, it helps to bind the surface if a few layers of shellac or hair lacquer are carefully sprayed on, followed by a fine mist of talc to assist removal of the cast from the mould. In the case of a large impression it may be necessary to pour the cast in two stages with a reinforcement of wire mesh, or even small twigs, between the stages. While the plaster is not quite set, details such as date and identifying information can be scratched into the surface. When the cast is *completely* hardened it is carefully lifted from the impression – it is a wise officer who remembers that he gets no second chance – and gently brushed clean of any unwanted material before packing and labelling.

Casting Small Impressions

The process for casting small impressions, such as **Tool Marks**, is identical but reduced in scale; due to the finer detail to be recovered from the impression, a fast-setting plastic or silicone rubber casting material – such as 'Silastic' – replaces the coarser plaster of Paris.

INSANITY (AS A DEFENCE)

There are in fact two 'insanity' defences:

1. That, because of a disease of the mind, an offender does not know the nature and quality of his act; and
2. That even if he did know the nature and quality of his act, because of a disease of the mind he did not know it was 'wrong'.

As in pleas of diminished responsibility, it is for the defence to establish a defendant's insanity 'on a balance of probabilities'. It is for the jury to decide, and the guidelines for their use are embodied in the McNaghten Rules which, in part, state: 'Every man is presumed to be sane, and to possess a sufficient degree of reason to be responsible for his crimes, until the contrary be proved to their [the jury's] satisfaction'.

The McNaghten Rules

On 20 January 1843, in Downing Street, a Glasgow wood-worker named Daniel McNaghten drew a pistol and shot and killed Edward Drummond, secretary to Prime Minister Sir Robert Peel (ironically the founder of the Metropolitan police force). The ball had been intended for Sir Robert himself, but McNaghten seems to have been unfamiliar with the PM's appearance and to have shot the first likely candidate.

At McNaghten's subsequent trial before judge and jury at the Old Bailey, it transpired that he had had, with no apparent justification, an unreasoning suspicion that 'Tories' were persecuting him. The matter was a serious one – not only in that murder had been committed on the open street, but that Her Majesty's Prime Minister could so easily have been the victim. There was, then, a certain tinge of self-interest in the disquiet voiced by Parliament when the jury returned a verdict that McNaghten was insane and should therefore be merely confined to hospital. Great, too, was the public discomfort at this verdict, and it was contested in the House of Lords.

Their Lordships decided to require Her Majesty's judges to advise them on the matter – an ancient right of the House, though seldom exercised. The joint answer given by the fourteen judges formed what became the McNaghten Rules, and reads in essence as follows:

> Jurors ought to be told in all cases that a man is presumed to be sane, and to possess a sufficient degree of reason to be responsible for his crimes, until the contrary be proved to their satisfaction; and that to establish a defence on the ground of insanity, it must be clearly proved that –
>
> At the time of committing the act, the party accused was labouring under such defect of reason, from disease of the mind, as not to know:
>
> a) The nature and quality of the act he was doing; or if he did know it
>
> b) That he did not know what he was doing was wrong.
>
> c) That if the accused labours under partial delusion only, and is not in other respects insane, we think he must be considered in the sane situation as to responsibility as if the facts with respect to which the delusion exists were real. (For example: if under the influence of his delusion he supposes another man to be in the act of attempting to take away his life, and he kills that man, as he supposes, in self-defence, he would be exempt from punishment. If his delusion was that the deceased had inflicted a serious injury to his character and fortune, and he killed in revenge for such supposed injury, he would be liable to punishment.)

These compact, simple guidelines, neatly parcelled into English law, sufficed only until medicine began to advance beyond law. Revolutions were occurring in the understanding of the mind and its disorders; doctors were beginning to beat tracks through the uncharted regions of the human brain; inevitably, the McNaghten Rules were left hopelessly lacking, absurdly narrow. Were it not for the fact that they were loose enough to allow for imaginative interpretation by the learned judges, and a willingness to cooperate on the part of expert psychiatric witnesses, there could have been many miscarriages of justice.

But this is not to say that there were no active attempts at reform; there were at least three major landmarks on the route to the Homicide Act of 1957:

1922: The Lord Chancellor set up a *Committee on Insanity and Crime;* their report recommended: '[that] it should be recognized that a person charged criminally with an offence is irresponsible for his act when the act is committed under an impulse which the prisoner may be, by mental disease, deprived of any power to resist'. On the subject of Irresistible Impulse the government decided not to act.

1924: Lord (previously Mr Justice) Denning's *Criminal Responsibility (Trials) Bill* failed to secure a second reading.

1949–53: The Royal Commission on Capital Punishment, with expert evidence from the British Medical Association, reported that the McNaghten Rules were thoroughly defective and in need of amendment along lines suggested by the BMA; i.e. that encompassed 'a disorder of emotion such that, while appreciating the nature and quality of the act, and that it was wrong, [an accused] did not possess sufficient power to prevent himself committing it'. No immediate action was taken on the commission's recommendations.

Only in 1957 did Parliament take action, which in effect drew English law into line with provisions that already existed in Scotland in allowing the defence of **Diminished Responsibility** (Homicide Act, 1957).

The defence of insanity is notoriously difficult to establish, and some forensic psychiatrists, such as the American Dr Ronald Markman, believe that it is impossible to find a method for objectively evaluating criminal insanity that is acceptable to all psychiatrists.

It is a dilemma that is further complicated when a cunning killer attempts to fake insanity; though this is less likely now that the supreme penalty for murder is not death. One outstanding example from the past is the case of John George Haigh, the English 'Acid Bath Murderer' who attempted, in 1949, to establish a defence of insanity with preposterous confessions to drinking the blood of his victims. This was a particularly transparent piece of guile in the light of previous conversations Haigh had with police officers during which he pointedly asked: 'What are the chances of anyone being released from Broadmoor?'

An unusual situation arose in the case of Peter Sutcliffe, the English serial killer called 'The Yorkshire Ripper'. Sutcliffe claimed that his murderous attacks on women whom he believed to be prostitutes were in direct response to instructions from God, which he had heard emanating from a grave in Bingley cemetery. In an unusual collaboration, the Ripper's defence attorney, the Crown prosecutor, and the Attorney-General agreed that Sutcliffe was suffering from paranoid schizophrenia and sought to have the trial averted by placing him immediately in a special hospital. It was the trial judge, Mr Justice Boreham, who insisted that the trial proceed, that the jury be the final arbiters of Peter Sutcliffe's sanity. In fact, the jury found him sane and guilty of thirteen murders and seven attempted murders. Ironically, just three years after his life sentence began, Sutcliffe had to be moved from the top-security wing at Parkhurst Prison on the Isle of Wight to Broadmoor – his mental stability had deteriorated to such a degree that psychiatric treatment was imperative. The Yorkshire Ripper is now, if he was not at his trial, legally insane.

In Britain the success of an insanity defence will require the special verdict 'not guilty by reason of insanity', and the prisoner will be committed to hospital until such time as the Home Secretary directs otherwise.

INSECT INFESTATION OF CORPSES

It is a well-known fact that dead animal flesh is a haven for all manner of insects, notably flies, which feed and lay their eggs on the body.

It follows that an examination of the remains, and the identification of the maggots found, may be useful in estimating the time of death. If the life-cycle of the insect is known it is possible to ascertain the stage reached in its development and establish the time which has passed since the laying of the eggs. This is properly the province of the entomologist whose expert opinion may be sought by the pathologist.

The three maggots usually encountered on decaying flesh are from the common blue-bottle, the green-bottle and the common house-fly:

The common blue-bottle (Calliphora erythrocephalus): Eggs are laid on fresh, in preference to putrefied flesh. The maximum number of eggs laid by a single female is 2,000 in groups of about 150. The eggs hatch between eight and fourteen hours later depending upon environmental temperature (cold weather delays hatching). After a further eight to fourteen hours the first skin is shed and a larger larval instar* emerges. The second larval instar emerges after two to three days, and the third stage emerges within seven to eight days and remains feeding for a further five days. When it is fully grown the maggot leaves the

*'Instar' is simply the name given to the stages of growth in the life-cycle between two successive sheddings of the outer skins of the growing larvae.

body at night and travels some distance where it buries itself in the soil and pupates. The pupal stage lasts approximately twelve days, and the flies of *Calliphora* are found in the early spring to late autumn.

The green-bottle (Lucilia caesar) has a life-cycle entirely similar to *Calliphora*.

The common house-fly (Musca domestica): The female lays about 150 eggs, which hatch in between eight and fourteen hours, the first larval stage lasting thirty-six hours. Second instar, one to two days; third instar, three to four days depending upon conditions (temperature, moisture). Pupal stage generally seven days, again depending upon conditions – warm temperature will hasten the process. As with *Calliphera* the full-grown larvae leave the food at night and pupate beneath the soil.

Differentiation

It was during the extensive medical investigations carried out during the Ruxton case (see page 149) that Dr Alexander Mearns of the Institute of Hygiene at the University of Glasgow was engaged in pioneering work on the study of the maggots that infested the dismembered remains of Mrs Ruxton and her maid Mary Rogerson. Dr Mearns identified the larvae as those of *Calliphora*, and his estimation of the development times in the Ruxton case was:

Stage of Development	Time (outside limits)
Egg	8–14 hours
First Instar	8–14 hours
Second Instar	2–3 days
Third Instar	7–8 days
Total	10–12 days

Mearns added: 'The total life of the largest larvae taken from the remains could not have exceeded twelve days but was probably less. It was considered unlikely that the eggs had been laid more than a day or two after the deposit of the remains in the ravine. It is accepted that *Calliphores* having laid their eggs do not as a rule return to the same material. It was not practicable to search for pupae in the soil as some time had elapsed before the investigation of the maggots was undertaken. The possibility of a laying of eggs by the progeny of the first generation of blue-bottles could be eliminated. That would have required a period of a month, which was quite irreconcilable with the state of putrefaction of the remains.'

Case Study

WILLIAM BRITTLE

It was maggots that they were looking for on that June day in 1964. Two thirteen-year-olds scouting through Bracknell woods in the hope of finding a dead pigeon or squirrel, any dead meat that might be home to the fat white maggots that they needed for fishing bait. Then they found them; thousands of the things. The excitement ended as soon as the boys saw what the maggots were feeding on, as soon as they saw the arm. Terry King and Paul Fay, bright lads, went to the police: 'There's a dead body buried in the woods!'

For pathologist Keith **Simpson** the call-out was routine – a body discovered in suspicious circumstances. Beneath the covering of moss and leaves was the body of a man, lying on his back, his head wrapped in towelling. The corpse was too far decomposed for any normal **Time of Death** tests – in fact, the police thought it might have been there for up to two months. But they had reckoned without a very special study that Keith Simpson had made his own. Simpson put the time of death as at least nine or ten *days* – 'but probably not more than twelve; it's astonishing how quickly maggots will eat up flesh'.

The pathologist had routinely collected samples of the insect infestation and identified the maggots as those of the common blue-bottle *(Calliphora eiythrocephalus):* 'The larvae I was looking at were mature, indeed elderly, fat, indolent, third-stage maggots, but they were not in pupa cases. Therefore I estimated that the eggs had been laid nine or ten days earlier. Adding a little more time to allow for the blue-bottles getting to the dead body, I reckoned death had occurred on 16 or 17 June.'*

Post-mortem examination revealed that the bones of the larynx had been crushed, and death had resulted from blood seeping into the windpipe. Identifiable features indicated that the victim was Peter Thomas, reported missing from his home at Lyndney on 16 June. It was also learned that Thomas had lent the sum of £2,000 to a man named Brittle. Under questioning William Brittle admitted that he had met Thomas at Lyndney on 16 June – in fact, he had gone there specifically to repay the loan, so he claimed.

* *Forty Years of Murder,* Professor Keith Simpson, Harrap, 1978.

Now it came to light that Brittle had been trained in unarmed combat while serving in the Army; information which was not lost on Professor Simpson, whose report on Thomas's throat injuries were entirely consistent with a blow such as a karate-chop. It was the firm belief of the police that Brittle *had* visited Peter Thomas on 16 June, not to repay £2,000, but to dispose of his debt rather more decisively; he had then transported Thomas's body in the boot of a car to Bracknell woods.

Unfortunately, the police had an independent witness who adamantly insisted that he had seen Peter Thomas, alive and well, in Gloucester on 20 June.

In the end William Brittle was committed for trial and the main scientific evidence was offered by Professor Simpson. Simpson testified that he had found maggots of the common blue-bottle on the corpse, and that they had not yet pupated; this put the time since death at nine or ten days. Though he was appearing as an expert witness for the defence, the eminent entomologist Professor McKenny-Hughes corroborated Simpson's findings, and William Brittle was convicted of murder and sentenced to life imprisonment.

INSTRUMENTATION

The main techniques of scientific forensic analysis and comparison are treated in separate entries throughout this book, and cross-references to techniques are found where appropriate. Some techniques are found to be more suitable than others for testing individual substances, and some techniques will be wholly inappropriate. There are also techniques that require the destruction of the sample in order to analyse its components, so if there is only a small sample and it is important that it remains intact for presentation as evidence, then some non-destructive method of analysis must be found. The table below lists the techniques described throughout the text with an indication of their suitability for use with individual substances.

INSTRUMENTATION MARKS
(see Tool Marks)

Technique* Sample/Crime	Microscopy	Gas Chromatography	Thin Layer Chromatography	Infra-red Spectrometry	Ultraviolet Spectrometry	X-ray Spectrometry	Emission Spectrometry	Neutron Activation Analysis	Atomic Absorption
Arson		•		•					
Blood		•		•					
Bullets	•						•	•	•
Cartridge cases	•								
Documents	•			•	•		•	•	•
Drugs	•	•	•	•	•	•	•	•	•
Explosives	•	•	•	•		•	•	•	•
Fibres	•	•		•	•	•			
Fingerprints	•					•			
Glass	•					•	•	•	•
Hair	•							•	•
Inks	•		•	•	•		•		
Metal	•					•	•	•	•
Paint	•	•	•	•	•	•	•	•	•
Soil	•					•	•	•	•
Tool marks	•								

K

KNIFE WOUNDS

In Great Britain, the majority of its 600-odd homicides every year are committed with knives – victims dying of stab wounds or complications arising from stab wounds. In the United States, murderous attacks with knives come second to those with guns. In both countries, the carrying of knives has become part of the gangland subculture, often regarded as much a young man's accessory as his comb and wallet. Unlike the situation with guns, legislation is powerless against knives. Although Britain has outlawed the manufacture, import and sale of 'semi-automatic' knives like switch-blades and flick-knives, the majority of stabbings are carried out with perfectly legal chef's knives. A vicious modern trend is the use of Stanley-type handyman knives.

It is entirely consistent with this cultural background that knives are 'contact' weapons – the victim and attacker have to be within touching distance and it is almost impossible for the attacker to escape being soiled with his victim's blood. Thus most fatal stabbings are committed either in the home during a domestic dispute, or during brawls in public houses, clubs, street corners, football grounds, etc. where there is anyway an expectancy of interpersonal violence.

Knife wounds are classified either as *incised wounds,* where the edge of the blade makes cutting gashes to the body, often during a struggle and frequently on the arms of a victim trying to protect himself; or *stab wounds,* where the point of the knife goes into the body followed by the length of the blade. While incised wounds tend to generate a great deal of blood, there will be little external haemorrhaging from stab wounds, the danger in this case being damage to the internal organs, causing internal bleeding from which death will result. This presupposes that the wound has been inflicted in an area where it can cause this kind of damage – usually the chest or abdomen. Stab wounds need not, of course, be inflicted with a knife, but with instruments such as a pair of scissors, a tool like a bradawl, even a sturdy hat-pin.

Although in theory the shape of a stab wound should provide the pathologist with information about the weapon used, the interpretation of such injuries is very imprecise. For example, when a knife is pushed into the body there is a certain amount of stretching of the skin before it is pierced, so when the blade is withdrawn the skin will spring back naturally to the original position leaving a hole apparently smaller than the blade which caused it. Sometimes – though less frequently than fiction might have us believe – the type of knife can be determined by the *shape* of the wound. A knife with two sharp edges leaves a wound with two acute angles one at each end; a sheath-knife type of blade with one sharp edge will produce a wound with one acute angle cut and the other blunt.

Visual appearances will be further complicated by the degree of rocking back and forth of the knife in the wound or by twisting the blade.

Suicide or Homicide?

There is little likelihood of a fatal stabbing being accidental, and in those few unfortunate instances the cause will be obvious. However, it is not always easy to distinguish between stabbings with a suicidal and those with a homicidal intent. As a general rule the comparatively ready access to poisonous drugs these days has resulted in a dramatic reduction in the number of suicides by violent means, such as **Hanging** and stabbing.

The site of the wound provides the clearest clue, because apart from the fact that the site has to be accessible, a suicide will generally choose to inflict his wound through the chest just over where he believes the heart to be; the other site is the stomach. Unlike homicidal stabbings, the suicide will usually strike once, or occasionally twice, and it is common for clothing to be removed from the spot first. Thus when a body is found with multiple stab wounds, through the clothing, at various points on the body, homicide should be suspected.

After homicidal struggles involving knives it is common to find extensive cuts on the hands and arms of the victim where he has tried to grab the knife or fend it off – these will obviously not be present in cases of suicide.

Throat-Cutting

Throat-cutting is a class of incised wound which belongs more to the gaslight era of that quintessential cut-throat, Jack the Ripper. It is still occasionally encountered, but as a homicide it has almost ritualistic qualities, and because of the difficulty of cutting the throat of a struggling person, it is usually carried out while the victim is helplessly bound or unconscious.

'Cutting one's own throat' is still a means of suicide, and can usually be recognized by the direction of the cut. If the subject is right-handed, the cut will start quite high on the left side of the neck and slash down at an oblique angle across the voice-box; and vice versa for a left-handed suicide. The number of slash marks is also significant because a suicide almost invariably makes one or two 'practice' cuts while summoning the courage for the final act. A homicidal throat cut is more forcibly and positively delivered, usually at the side of the neck. One point about suicidal throat-cutting is that there is a temptation, while baring his neck, for the subject to throw back his head – a counter-productive action which allows the main arteries to slip back and be protected by the windpipe. In such cases death will be by a combination of bleeding from the cut tissues and perhaps **Asphyxia** if blood clogs the windpipe. It is not unknown for a failed cut-throat to achieve suicide by some other method immediately afterwards.

Case Study

THE DEATH OF ESSEX

A classic cut-throat case which involved the suicide/homicide debate predated even Jack the Ripper, and is a rare example of lucid forensic analysis in the seventeenth century.

At the end of June 1683, Arthur Capel, Earl of Essex was arrested on a charge of high treason, accused of conspiring to assassinate King Charles II and the Duke of York as part of the Rye House Plot. Prior to his trial Essex was, according to custom, confined to the Tower of London. On 13 July his servant, Paul Bromeny, found Essex dead in the lavatory adjoining his bed-chamber, lying in a pool of blood. Beside him lay an open razor and subsequent examination showed his throat to have been so savagely slashed that it had almost decapitated him. As he was one of the most prominent men of his day, this was clearly a huge embarrassment to Essex's Whig cause, and political dynamite that he should be found apparently a victim of his own hand – a clear admission, his opponents crowed, of treacherous guilt. The politics need not concern us here, but there was bound to be a counter-accusation by Essex's loyal followers that he had been assassinated in such a manner as to make it look like suicide. The following pamphlet, explaining the reasons, was published in 1689:

> '*MURDER WILL OUT:* or, a clear and full Discovery that the EARL of ESSEX did not MURDER himself, but was MURDERED by others; both by undeniable Circumstances, and positive Proofs.

[After providing ample evidence that Essex had, far from contemplating self-destruction, taken many steps to preserve himself *against* murder – like having his food and drink prepared by his own followers – the tract then outlines the proofs that the Earl *could not* have taken his own life.]

1. Because it was impossible that he at one Cut (as the verdict saith) could cut four Inches in Depth, and eight in Length, because none can manage his Hand to guide a Razor so to do at once, viz. from the left Side of the Neck-bone to the right.
2. Because it is impossible that with that *French* razor, which was but four Inches and an Half long, and Without a Tongue (necessitating taking two Inches and an Half at least in his Hand) that he could, with two Inches of such an Instrument, cut four or five Inches in Depth, and eight or nine in Length.
3. Because it is impossible in Nature that when he had cut the left Jugular and Windpipe to the Neck-bone, which let out so much of the Blood and Vitals, that he should have neither Life nor Strength to proceed to cut the other also, as all skilful surgeons and Anatomists can demonstrate.
4. Because it was utterly impossible that after he had locked himself into the Closet, he could so cut his Throat as it was, and then open the Closet-door, and fling the bloody Razor out of the Chamber-window at such a Distance from the closet, and then get the Razor up again and keep it in his Hand (as some) or fling it by him (as others) and all this after he was dead, for he instantly died saith the Inquest, and none but himself in the Room say their Witnesses, therefore it was impossible he could with that Razor so murder himself. And that

the bloody Razor was flung out of the Chamber-window is made good by no less than ten Witnesses.

Thus you have some Grounds and Reasons (from the Improbability and Impossibility of the Thing) to clear his Innocency from the horrid Fact so impudently charged upon him, and consequently the Guilt of others, and which may be sufficient to all wise Men to detect the Murder . . .'

L

LACASSAGNE, ALEXANDRE (1844–1921)

Jean Alexandre Eugene Lacassagne was born at Cahors in 1844 and attended the Military Academy at Strasbourg before qualifying as a surgeon. It was during his commission in North Africa that Lacassagne came into contact with a great number and variety of **Gunshot Wounds**, and at the end of his service in 1878 this experience was brought together in his treatise *Précis de médecine*.

It was largely as a result of the book's success that in 1880 Lacassagne was invited to occupy the newly founded chair in Forensic Medicine at the University of Lyons. Although he spent a lifetime making new contributions to the growing battery of forensic techniques, there is one phrase coined by Professor Lacassagne which underlays the whole of his research and which he was at pains to instill in his students: 'One must,' he emphasized, 'know how to doubt.'

In the spring of 1889, Alexandre Lacassagne was the first person to recognize the significance of the striations etched on the surface of a bullet that had been extracted from a murder victim, and suggested that they might be identified with the gun from which it was fired. He was right, and in this could be said to have founded the science of **Ballistics**. In November of the same year, Lacassagne had the opportunity to exhibit his Sherlockian talents for reading evidence during an investigation into the identity of a partly decomposed murder victim which had been found in a sack, dumped by a river about ten miles from Lyons. The police were of the opinion that it was the body of a Parisian bailiff named Gouffe whose relatives had reported his disappearance. To add to the mystery, a decaying wooden travelling trunk had been found close to the corpse and judging from the unhealthy smell it had once contained the sack of remains; the trunk bore a label indicating that it had been sent by rail from Paris to Lyons. During his autopsy, Lacassagne remarked that the condition of the skeleton's right leg and ankle suggested that the muscles of that limb had been weaker during life than those of the left leg – possibly as the result of some tissue-wasting disease. In addition, the knee-cap of the same leg was deformed, almost certainly the result of inflammation of the joint during life. In short, Lacassague's post-mortem diagnosis was that the victim had suffered a tubercular disease of the right leg causing a pronounced limp. Which, the Sûreté discovered, described bailiff Gouffe exactly. It transpired that a man named Eyraud and his mistress Gabrielle Bompard had ended the unfortunate man's life in order to prevent his disclosure of some illegal business they were transacting. For Monsieur Lacassagne it was another triumph of forensic detection; for Monsieur Eyraud it was an appointment with the guillotine.

Alexandre Lacassagne turned his experience of the criminal mind to good account in 1898 when he was asked to make a study of the 'French Ripper', a degenerate named Joseph Vacher who had committed a series of horrific sex murders on children of both sexes, which were characterized by mutilation and dismemberment of a most awful kind. When Vacher was brought to trial he pleaded insanity and it was Lacassagne's task to prepare the psychological report. After an exhaustive five-month examination, he concluded that Vacher was feigning madness; the butcher was guillotined on the last day of 1898.

The man who could truly be described as the founder of modern forensic science, who had been the first to study the relationship between an attack on a victim and the shape and configuration of **Bloodstains**, who had first recognized the need for an adequate means of identifying criminals through a police filing system (later taken up by **Bertillon**), died in 1921.

LASER FACIAL RECONSTRUCTION
(see Facial Reconstruction)

LAUDANUM
(see Opium)

LAUREL-WATER
(see Cyanide)

LIVIDITY
(see Hypostasis)

LIVOR MORTIS
(see Time of Death, Hypostasis)

LOCARD, EDMOND (1877–1966)
Locard was born in France in 1877, and after preliminary schooling at the Dominican College at Ouillins he attended the University of Lyons from which he graduated as Doctor of Medicine and also Licentiate in Law. Locard was fortunate in being taken under the wing of criminology's great pioneer Alexandre **Lacassagne**, who was at the time Professor of Forensic Medicine at Lyons, and whose assistant Locard became. Locard held this post until 1910, when he resigned in order to establish the influential Police Laboratory.

Locard began to expand the ideas Lacassagne applied to forensic medicine to cover other scientific disciplines and methods, and in time his laboratory became the official laboratory of the Technical Police for the Prefecture of the Rhône. It was Locard who advanced the theory upon which most forensic science is founded, the theory that 'every contact leaves a trace' (see **Trace Evidence**), a principle which he was able to prove very effectively in his investigation of the case of Emile Gourbin in 1912. Gourbin, a bank clerk of Lyons, had been accused of the murder of his lady-friend in a fit of anger, but had set up an apparently unshakeable alibi. Enter Edmond Locard and the contact trace theory. Locard examined the body of the dead young woman and it was clear from the marks around her throat that she had succumbed to manual strangulation; he then took scrapings from under the fingernails of the suspect and examined the debris beneath a microscope – there were, as he had anticipated, flakes of skin that could have come from the victim's neck – but there was even more damaging evidence, the flakes of skin were coated with a fine pink powder – the same cosmetic powder with which Gourbin's victim made up her face and neck. Emile Gourbin made a full confession and was later convicted of murder.

With the assistance of a regular flow of visiting researchers, Locard was able to pioneer new laboratory techniques to expand the scope of the newly invented **Fingerprint** system, adding his own rather eccentric contribution, **Poroscopy**, a study of comparative pore patterns. He also made contributions in the field of investigating **Disputed Documents**, including handwriting analysis and micro-chemical methods of ink examination.

Edmond Locard was a natural teacher, and his knowledge and lucid presentation ensured that he was a popular lecturer, becoming attached to the Department of Criminalistics of the Faculty of Law, and later the founding director of the Institute of Criminalistics. Locard also added greatly to the literature on his subject, and in 1940 published the seventh and last volume of his formidable classic, *Traité de criminalistique*. In the first volume, published in 1912, he had written: 'To write the history of identification is to write the history of criminology.' Edmond Locard was active in his researches until his death in 1966.

LOMBROSO, CESARE
(see 'Criminal Man')

M

McNAGHTEN RULES
(see Insanity)

MARSH TEST
(see Arsenic)

MEDICAL EXAMINER
(see Coroner)

MERCURY
(see Poisons)

MICROSCOPY

Although it has passed somewhat into detective fiction, the Sherlockian hand-held magnifying lens is in real-life one of the most useful pieces of scientific 'apparatus' available to the scene-of-crime detective, and also at the first stage of examination in the laboratory.

The larger, multi-lens microscope is the most commonly used instrument of analysis and comparison in the forensic laboratory, and owing to its flexibility, most types of work are capable of being done with the microscope alone.

There are several types of microscopes in service to forensic science, listed here in order of complexity:

Simple
Compound
Stereoscopic
Comparison
Polarizing
Electron
Infra-red

Simple Microscope

With usually one, but sometimes two or three lenses, this is the basic 'fingerprint viewer'. The magnification is about 12× (the magnification of any lens is described by the number of diameters the object can be enlarged in front of the symbol ×).

Compound Microscope

Sometimes called the 'medical' microscope, it is the instrument which most people have at one time or another used in a school science class. Its enlargement is commonly between 100–400×. The essential parts comprise the occular lens (eyepiece), the objective lens, a mirror to reflect light, a condenser to control the light coming from the mirror, and the stand which holds all the parts in alignment and carries the 'stage' on which the glass slide is put for examination.

The most important lens on the microscope is the objective, and it is common to find a set of three having different numerical apertures and magnification mounted on a revolving block, or 'nosepiece'. This disposes of the need to change lenses and renders the instrument more flexible. The overall magnification of the microscope is worked out by multiplying the magnification of the occular lens (say 10×) by that of the objective lens (say 10×) which gives 100×.

Compound microscopes are perfectly adequate – indeed perfectly suited – to the examination of most biological samples like blood and semen, and also hairs and fibres. The magnification 100–400× also makes the apparatus useful in the microscopic study of drugs and poisons.

Stereoscopic Microscope

With magnification between 100–150×, the stereoscopic microscope is made by combining two compound microscopes which, by the use of prisms, allow an image to be 'three-dimensional'. This makes the instrument ideal for the examination of three-dimensional objects – for example, a chip of automobile **Paint** mounted vertically in order to examine the sequence of colour layers; also for checking murder weapons for blood, hair and tissue traces, and analysing and comparing soil samples.

Comparison Microscope

Although it is best known for the comparison of bullet rifling and cartridge marks in **Ballistics** works, the comparison microscope is invaluable for the comparison of any two samples – **Hair**, **Fibres**, **Tool Marks**, etc. Magnification tends to be in the relatively low range 5–35×. By means of a double tube whose separate images are brought together by a pair of mirrors and a pair of prisms into a comparison eyepiece the images can be viewed simultaneously.

Other Laboratory Microscopes

In addition to the essential instruments described above, other more specialized microscopes have been developed to suit specific requirements. The *Polarizing Microscope* uses, as its name suggests, polarized light – light that is forced to vibrate in only one direction. This situation is created by dividing light through a prism housed in the microscope's substage into a polarized ray and a non-polarized ray which is reflected out of the prism. A second polarizing prism is located above the stage in either the microscope tube or the eypiece. When the prisms are positioned so that they cross, no light will reach the eye until a sample which is optically active is placed on the stage. Suitable subjects are crystalline materials and some fibres.

Infra-red microscopes provide magnification in cases where infra-red 'visualizing' needs to be enlarged – such as in the examination of **Disputed Documents**, for the study of suspected forged signatures and clearing obliterated writing.

Because the whole scientific principle is different – in that it makes use not of light beams but of beams of electrons – **Scanning Electron Microscopy** is explained in a separate entry.

MUMMIFICATION

The whole structure is desiccated, shrivelled, brownish-black in colour, and the anatomical features are well preserved. The skin, which clings closely to the shrunken framework of the body, the hair on the scalp, and the skeletonized features of the face are well preserved. A body in this condition is practically odourless.

Glaister, *Medical Jurisprudence*

The process of mummification comes about when the natural onset of **Putrefaction** of the body is by some means, either natural or artificial, prevented from dissolving the tissues. In hot climates such as Egypt, the drying effect of the hot sand in which bodies were interred led to the preservation of the dead with a 'life-like' appearance. Such climatic conditions do not prevail in the temperate zones and natural mummification is a rare occurrence.

According to what few statistics there are, the commonest incidences of mummification are the concealed deaths of new-born babies. The reason that these infants are so suitable for the process is that at birth a baby's body contains few bacteria, which eliminates the main cause of putrefaction. In addition, the child will normally be well wrapped up and hidden in a warm, dry place – a drawer, or the back of a cupboard – where, given a moderate circulation of air and the relatively small size of the body, dehydration will take place.

Examples of adult mummification are seldom encountered, the best-known being the desiccated corpse found in the hall cupboard at an address in Rhyl, North Wales in 1960. The Harvey family had always lived in the house in Kinmel Street, and when her husband Alfred died in 1938, Mrs Sarah Harvey took paying guests to help make ends meet. In 1960, at the age of sixty-five, Mrs Harvey was admitted to hospital for a routine check-up, and in her absence her son Leslie, now married and living in nearby Abergele, decided to redecorate the house as a 'welcome home' present.

As they made their way up the stairs making a note of jobs to be done, Leslie Harvey and his wife found themselves facing the large wooden cupboard on the first-floor landing. In Leslie's recollection it had always been locked and strictly out-of-bounds when he was a child; he had been told that it contained some things belonging to Mrs Frances Knight, a former lodger who had long since moved on. With renewed curiosity Leslie Harvey prised open the double doors with a screwdriver, prepared at worst for the task of clearing out some dusty old suitcases. With an understandable revulsion he stood speechless as the contents of the cupboard were revealed by the invading light. These were not somebody's possessions – they were somebody's remains; and they had obviously been there for a very long time . . .

The Chief Constable of Flint, Reginald Atkins, and coroner Dr Rhys Llewellyn Jones peered closely at the grim bundle that had until so recently occupied the landing cupboard. The body was in a doubled-up position, clothed in a now-faded and cobweb-encrusted nightdress and dressing gown. The skin was shrunken and leathery, what flesh remained was hard as stone – the whole corpse had been mummified by the natural process of warm, dry air rising and circulating around the cupboard, slowly drying out the body tissues. Atmospheric conditions which had made it possible to conceal a corpse for many years without the tell-tale stench of putrefaction. Quite obviously Mrs Harvey had some explaining to do; it is not every day that a twenty-year-old corpse is found in your cupboard. She admitted hiding the body of Mrs Knight when she died some time in April 1940, and she admitted claiming her former lodger's maintenance grant every week since then, but Sarah Harvey emphatically denied that she had murdered the woman. The Crown put up a half-hearted case at best, and mainly in deference to her advanced years and declining health, Mrs Harvey was found guilty only of the lesser charge of fraud and sentenced to a token fifteen months imprisonment.

The Bog People

Over the past two hundred years in Denmark the peat-bogs common in certain areas have been yielding up the almost perfectly preserved bodies of men and women who died between 1,500 and 2,000, even sometimes 5,000 years ago. The remarkable state of preservation is due to acids in the peaty soil.

The name of Professor P.V. Glob, Director of the National Museum at Copenhagen, has become synonymous with the Danish bog people, and he has documented their strange history in scores of articles, books and pamphlets. The most intriguing fact to emerge is that a significant number of these ancient people died by unnatural means – that is, when their remains have been subjected to examination using forensic techniques they have exhibited evidence of murderous attack. Glob suggests that some of the victims may have been criminals (or at any rate offended against the gods), who were executed and thrown ignominiously into a bog. Others may, he supposes, be the victims of ritual murder: . . . it emerges clearly that the circumstances of the bog people's deposition show nothing in common with normal burial customs, but on the contrary have many of the characteristics of the sacrificial deposits. Probably, then, the bog people were offered to the

same powers as the other bog finds, and belong to the gods . . .
Naturally we must except from this interpretation those who ended their
days in the bog by accident, such as those who went astray in fog or rain
and were drowned one dark autumn day. We must also except those
who were murdered and hidden in bogs, away from the beaten track.
Several such are known amongst the bog people; but by far the greatest
number of the bog people, where proper observations are recorded, bear
the stamp of sacrificial offerings.'

The soil conditions which have created the unusual state of preservation in the Danish finds also prevail in certain other northern countries,
including Britain.

On 1 August 1984, Andy Mould and Eddie Slack were standing by
the elevator to a peat-shredding mill at Lindow Moss, a bleak scrub-
covered peat marsh in Cheshire. Mould casually threw off the conveyor
what he thought was a block of wood; its fall to the ground knocked off
a covering of peat, and the block of wood was revealed as a human foot.
By 6 August archaeologists had recovered the rest of the body, and it
had been established that this was no ordinary victim of violence or
accident, but a prehistoric corpse preserved over centuries by the
chemical action of the peat. The rare find was taken to Macclesfield
District Hospital mortuary, where it was subjected to the eager attentions of a bevy of scientists including the forensic specialist Dr Ian
West. As the peat was carefully removed from around the body, it
became apparent that Lindow Man (who had been affectionately
christened Pete Marsh after his place of origin) had been the victim of
a violent death. There was evidence of a multiplicity of deliberate
injuries any one of which could have been responsible for the bog man's
death:

1. *Stab wound to the chest:* Forensic examination was unable to
confirm absolutely that this was a deliberately inflicted wound, though
its straight and clean cut was consistent with the appearance of a
stabbing.
2. *Bludgeonings:* After the peat had been cleared from the head,
wounds were apparent that indicated a severe battering. Blows from
some blunt instrument had split the scalp in two places and had been
delivered with enough force to shatter the skull, driving fragments of
bone into the brain.
3. *Asphyxia due to strangulation:* The most intriguing evidence of
foul play could be seen when the area around the neck was cleaned

and examined. What at first was thought to be a length of root fibre caught in the folds of skin proved to be a ligature made from two twisted and knotted strands of sinew. Rather than a decorative necklace, it was clear from the way in which the thong had bitten into the flesh of the neck that it had been used in the manner of a garrotte. Additionally, the abnormal angle at which the neck had set, and the two broken cervical vertebrae seemed to lend credence to the strangulation theory.

4. *Throat cut:* During the examination of the neck region and the thong associated with it, another potentially fatal wound was discovered on the right side of the throat. Certainly there was every evidence to suggest a human agency behind the cut, though whether the intention had been to kill or merely to bleed the victim is uncertain.

It is likely that the bog victim was a man of some importance judging by the neat appearance of his trimmed beard – this kind of shaping is not known on other bog people – and examination with an electron scanning microscope revealed a rudimentary manicure. Incongruously, Lindow Man was naked but for a fox fur armband.

That he was murdered is certain, but assuming that he was not the victim of Iron Age footpads, each of whom tried to kill him in a different way and then robbed him even of his clothes, what explanation could fit the bizarre facts?

One plausible theory fitting the known facts is that Pete Marsh was the subject of an elaborate ritual sacrifice; this provides the most reasonable explanation of the list of potentially fatal wounds which he suffered and concurs with the earlier theories of Professor Glob. Don Brothwell (see also **Anthropology**) in his excellent account of the investigation of Lindow Man compares the evidence of injuries sustained by other bodies recovered from peat bogs in Denmark and the rest of Europe with the Lindow find:

	Tollund Man	Borre Fen Man	Graubelle Man	Rendswühren Fen Man	Osterby Man	Borre Fen Woman (II)	Borre Fen Woman (III)	Elling Woman	Lykkegard Man	Stidsholt Fen Woman	Werdingerveen Man	LINDOW MAN
Chest Wound	•			•							•	•?
Other Fractures			•			•						
Skull Injuries		•	•	•	•	•	•					•
Throat Cut			•									•
Asphyxia (Hanging and Strangulation)	•	•						•	•			•
Beheading					•					•		

Lindow Man is now on permanent display at the British Museum, though ownership has been contested by Manchester University Museum.

MUTILATION AS A MEANS OF IDENTIFICATION

For millennia the value of being able to identify convicted felons has been appreciated, and has resulted in sophisticated computer-controlled Criminal Records Bureaux becoming essential to the efficient operation of the world's law enforcement agencies.

It was not always quite so civilized, and methods were adapted to the requirements of their times – the most economical and efficient way to mark a criminal for future identification was to mutilate his body in some conspicious way. This had the added advantage that the pain caused served as an additional incentive to future good behaviour. It is often difficult to distinguish between mutilation as a means of identification and mutilation as a punishment, though one clear-cut example of the former was branding, as the following extract from *The Chronicles of Newgate* shows:

Branding was often carried out with circumstances of atrocious barbarity. Vagabonds were marked with a letter V, idlers and masterless men with the letter S betokening a condemnation to slavery; any church brawler lost his ears and for a second offence might be branded with the letter F as a fraymaker and fighter. Sometimes the penalty was to bore a hole of the compass of an inch through the gristle of the right ear. Branding was the commutation of a capital sentence on clerk convicts, or persons allowed benefit of clergy [see below), and it was inflicted upon the brawn of the left thumb, the letter M being used in murder cases, the letter T in others.

Arthur Griffiths, HM Inspector of Prisons, 1883

Benefit of Clergy
This remarkable loophole in English law resulted from the separation, in the Middle Ages, of the ecclesiastical and secular courts, which enabled the clergy to exempt themselves from secular jurisdiction. Thus, persons in Holy Orders accused of a crime were sent before the Bishop's Court, a feature of which was that it could not pass sentence of death.

[It was to reverse such encroachments by the Church courts upon secular law that Henry II appointed Thomas Becket archbishop of Canterbury in 1162. Becket proved less compliant than his former friend had supposed, and the archbishop – as much a victim of his own arrogance as of Henry's displeasure – was assassinated in Canterbury Cathedral in 1170.)

This Benefit of Clergy was subsequently extended to all persons who were eligible for ordination into the Church – effectively anybody who could read. So corrupt, however, were the courts that in order to 'Plead' it was necessary only to learn by heart the first verse of the 51st Psalm, which became known as the 'neck-verse':

Have mercy upon me, O God, according to thy loving kindness; according unto the multitude of thy tender mercies blot out my transgressions.

The judge would ask: 'Legit aut non legit?' ('Can he read or not?') The chaplain replied: 'Legit ut clericus' ('He reads like a clerk'). Sentence would then be reduced to some other form of physical punishment, like flogging, or imprisonment or fining. Nor was it entirely necessary to learn the saving verse by heart; a few coins in the chaplain's hand would ensure a few promptings in the felon's ear.

By a statute of 1490 it became possible for secular prisoners only to plead benefit of clergy once. To ensure this laymen were marked by branding on the ball of the thumb (colourfully described as 'glymming in the paw', or 'burning in the hand'). There always having been 'one law for the rich and another for the poor', it comes as no surprise that many judges were prepared, either for money or favour, to allow the use of a cold iron.

In the reign of William and Mary, when the privilege of Benefit of Clergy was found to be greatly abused, an Act was passed by which the culprit was branded or 'burned in the most visible part of the left cheek nearest the nose'.

Benefit of Clergy was abolished in England in 1827, but is said to have been successfully invoked in the state of Carolina, USA, in 1855.

N

NARCOTICS
(see Drugs)

NEUTRON ACTIVATION ANALYSIS

Nuclear energy, made practical by the discovery that it is possible to alter the number of sub-atomic particles in the nucleus of an atom, has had both alarming and beneficial repercussions for the continued welfare of humankind. On the one hand, controlling the urge to use its destructive powers has at times seemed perilously close to failing; on the other, the process seems to offer an alternative source of power to the world's dwindling stocks of fossil fuels. It has also offered new possibilities to forensic science for the chemical identification of unknown substances.

Of the naturally occurring radioactive elements the best known are uranium and radium, and they emit 'radiation' rays of three main types – alpha rays (helium atoms), beta rays (electrons), and gamma rays (X-rays). The kind of radiation emitted, and its exact energy, is unique to an element and it can be identified by making precise measurements with a device called a scintillation counter.

If a material is not naturally radioactive it can be made so by bombarding it with sub-atomic particles called neutrons. The newly radioactive substance will then give off gamma rays and a detector will identify the radioactive atoms by measuring the energies and intensities of the rays.

Although neutron activation analysis has proved a vitally important tool in forensic chemistry, and can be used to identify microscopic (somewhere in the region of one-billionth of a gram) traces in substances like metals, paint, glass, hair, soil, etc., it does require the laboratory to have access to a nuclear reactor, for it is in the core of the reactor that neutrons are produced. The sample is placed in a capsule and inserted into the reactor where it becomes radioactive. The analysis may reveal traces of several elements, all of which are measured precisely so that substances having apparently identical composition as far as their ingredients are concerned will be found to differ in their trace elements.

NICOTINE
(see Drugs, Poisons)

O

ODONTOLOGY (FORENSIC DENTISTRY)

Introduction

Forensic Odontology, both as an aid to identification and in the analysis of **Bite-Mark** evidence, relies on comparison.

In the former case, the comparison of ante- and post-mortem dental charts, in the latter matching teeth with the marks that they make in soft substances.

To understand the functioning, and therefore the importance of this branch of forensic medicine, it is useful to have some rudimentary understanding of the physical structure of dentition, and the methods of recording it.

The permanent teeth of an adult human number thirty-two, which comprise, when set out in their usual elipsoid pattern, four symmetrical portions, each containing

Two Incisors;
One Canine (also called 'eye' or 'dog' tooth);
Two Pre-molars; and
Three Molars (including one 'wisdom' tooth).

For convenience of recording the teeth, simplified charts have been devised which vary from one part of the world to another. The British standard system is attributed to the Austrian chemist Richard Zsigmondy.

The teeth in each quarter, or 'quadrant', of the mouth are numbered from the front centre-line outwards; thus the first molar tooth in the left lower jaw becomes 'lower left six' or ⌐6, the upper right canine tooth becomes 'upper right three' or 3⌐, and so on.

An alternative, less quirky, notation is called 'Viohl's Two Digit System', and substitutes the square bracketing with the following numerical equivalents:

    Upper right   = 1
    Upper left   = 2
    Lower left   = 3
    Lower right   = 4

In which our examples become ⌐6 = 36, and 3⌐ = 13.

The standard US chart is very different, more detailed, and numbers from the upper right third molar = 1, round the mouth to the lower right third molar = 32.

For the purpose of description and record, the individual teeth are simplified as a cube with five sides (the sixth, or bottom, being the jaw).

The upper surface is referred to as the Occlusal surface (O), though this clearly does not apply to the incisors or canines which are sharp.

Surface contacting the cheek = Buccal (B)

Inner surface = Palatal (P) in the upper jaw

                 = Lingual (L) in the lower jaw

Surface nearest centre-line = Mesial (M)

Surface furthest away = Distal (D)

This 'shorthand' enables the dental practitioner to record quickly and accurately the existing configuration of his patient's teeth and any work that he performs on them in the future.

As there are few people who have not at one stage or another in their lives sought treatment from a dentist, it can be seen how – in the context of identification – a post-mortem dental comparison chart may be more useful than post-mortem comparison fingerprinting – not only known criminals have dental records!

Furthermore, in cases of bodies unsuitable for visual identification, such as through fire or extended immersion in water, the teeth may be the *only* possibility of identification. It must be said, however, that while fingerprints remain unchanged from birth, dentition becomes unique only through natural or acquired 'abnormalities'.

Some Landmarks in Forensic Odontology

45–70 AD (Rome)

There are three variants on the theme of dental identification associated with the Emperor Claudius and his son Nero. Poisoning among the Roman nobility was commonplace, and any or all of the stories could be true:

1. Nero's mistress Sabina persuades him to murder his mother, Agrippa, whose body is identified by two maxillary canine teeth.
2. Sabina persuades Nero to kill his first wife, who is identified by either a discoloured tooth or a malocclusion.
3. Agrippina orders the death of Lollia, mistress of her husband the Emperor Claudius; her decapitated head is presented for identification by a discoloured tooth or a malocclusion.

1066 (England)

There is a legend that William the Conqueror, King William the First, having an unusual malocclusion, 'signed' the official seal of England by biting into the wax.

1477 (France)

The body of Charles, Duke of Burgundy (called 'the Bold') was identified, after his death at the hands of the Swiss in Nancy, by the absence of some anterior teeth.

1776 (USA)

Identification of the body of General Joseph Warren of the Massachusetts militia, who had been buried by the British after falling in the battle of Bunker Hill. Warren was disinterred by his countrymen and identified by the piece of walrus tusk that replaced a missing maxillary canine tooth.

1813 (Scotland)

A number of medical students stood accused of 'snatching' the body of a Mrs McAllister from her grave for the purpose of dissection. The good lady's denture was produced and found to be a perfect fit to the toothless maxilla of the corpse and identification was considered settled. However, after some delay in the trial the denture was discovered not to articulate properly with the remaining teeth, nor did it any longer fit the maxilla. It is assumed that substitution of the corpse had taken place.

1837 (England)
Dr Edwin Saunders established the criterion of determining the ages of children from the eruption pattern of their teeth.

1850 (USA)
The case of John White Webster provides the US with its first murder conviction on dental evidence.

1897 (France)
After the tragic fire at the Bazaar de Charité ball in Paris, many of the 126 victims were identified from their records by Dr Amoedo and two dentist colleagues.

1906 (England)
Bite-mark evidence was first used in a court of law to convict two burglars, one of whom had been foolish enough to take a bite out of a piece of cheese, leaving the imprint of his teeth in the remaining portion.

1925 (USA)
In an attempt to defraud an insurance company, a chemist named Schwartz set fire to his laboratory leaving behind an unrecognizably charred corpse which his 'widow' identified by two missing teeth. Closer inspection revealed that the teeth in question had been recently removed, the cavities not having healed, while Schwartz had lost his years before.

1948 (England)
First bite-mark evidence to convict a murderer, in the Gorringe case (see **Bite-Mark Analysis** Case Study).

1967 (England)
Gordon Hay convicted of murder in a pivotal case of bite-mark analysis (see **Bite-Mark Analysis** Case Study).

1973 (USA)
Extensive dental identification involved in naming the twenty-seven

victims of mass murderers Dean Corll and Elmer Wayne Henry in Houston, Texas.

1973 (USA)

Two of the United States leading forensic odontologists, Dr Lester Luntz of Connecticut and Dr Lowell Levine of New York, oppose each other in the case of the People v. Milone. Milone was eventually convicted of rape/murder on the strength of a bite mark on the victim's thigh.

1974 (USA)

Los Angeles police shoot dead six members of the so-called Symbionese Liberation Army, who are later identified from dental evidence.

1975 (England)

Mass disaster on the London underground at Moorgate station. Due to the frightful state of trauma of the victims, the City of London coroner orders that dental identification should take preference over other visual methods.

1976 (USA)

First use of a computer in the analysis of dental identification data in a mass disaster; the 139 victims had been recovered from the Big Thompson Canyon Flood.

1979 (USA)

Bite-mark evidence plays a large part in convicting Theodore 'Ted' Bundy, notorious serial killer of up to 40 young women in Washington and Florida States.

1979 (USA)

American Airlines Flight 191 crashes near Chicago with the loss of 274 lives. Identification carried out by two teams of ten dentists comparing ante- and post-mortem records.

1979 (Guyana)

Use of computers vital to sort the massive forensic data involved in identifying the 913 victims of the mass cult suicide/murder master-minded by James Warren Jones in the People's Temple at Jonestown.

1981 (USA)

The body of Lee Harvey Oswald, supposed assassin of President John F. Kennedy, disinterred in order to establish identity after the spread of rumours that a Soviet spy had been impersonating Oswald. Leading American forensic dentist Dr James A. Cottone made a positive identification based on Oswald's military dental record.

ODOUR IDENTIFICATION

The tracking down of criminals – and in particular escaped convicts – by means of sniffer dogs is a method of identification so antique as to have entered the classic tales of Dickens and Conan Doyle, and the folklore of American slavery. Indeed, the term 'bloodhound' has frequently been applied to the dogs' human counterpart, the pertinacious – or 'dogged' – detective.

Dogs are well known for their superior sense of smell, and the bloodhound was developed especially for tracking human beings. This depends, of course, on the fact that every person leaves behind them an invisible odour trail that is as unique in its way as a fingerprint, and the dog only needs a whiff of a 'control' object, such as an item of clothing worn by the fugitive, to pick an unerring path to its quarry.

The curiously old-fashioned concept of man's best friend as an arm of the law has recently been revised, and the hound's remarkable powers of scent have been specially trained to assist customs officers and drug enforcement agencies to sniff out narcotics, and in the ceaseless battle against terrorism to locate explosives and firearms. Dogs have even been trained to search for dead bodies, and although the animals are often brought in to assist in murder hunts where a body has not been found, their greater use is in the location of victims of earthquakes and transport disasters.

In his classic work *System der Kriminalistik* (1893), one of the fathers of forensic science, Dr Hans Gross, suggests:

> There is one possible expedient when the object is to discover a corpse [in open country] – to make use of a good bloodhound . . . We have mentioned that a considerable number of murdered people are buried in rather deserted places; a great number of these are often dug out by animals who easily scent out such spots. When a corpse is not completely covered, it is of course easy for dogs or even men to find it.

However, there are other ways in which smell can be used to trap a criminal – not by tracking him (after all in the modern world a scent will be lost as soon as the fugitive drives off in his car) but by identifying him much as one would with a fingerprint. But unlike the fingerprint, which can be masked with the use of gloves, or the use of a disguise to defeat visual identification, nothing can be done to hide smell. It follows that if some means could be devised of storing and analysing the smell left at the scene of the crime for future comparison it would be a most useful addition to the crime-fighter's arsenal.

Not surprisingly the possibility of designing an 'electronic nose' has already been under investigation for some years, notably by the Olfaction Research Group at the University of Warwick. The first requirement is to understand exactly what it is that an animal's nose does.

The nose reacts to volatile chemicals in the atmosphere which are then analysed by the brain which identifies molecules of different shapes and dimensions which relate to individual smells. An experimental instrument is already being tested consisting of twelve tin oxide sensors each of which responds in a slightly different way. The electrical outputs construct between them a pattern which can be expressed graphically on a VDU screen. The 'artificial nose' has already proved capable not only of distinguishing between wine and coffee, but between different wines and different coffees. To add a slightly Sherlockian air, it can also distinguish between the smells of different cigarettes and cigars.

The problem is that human body odour is infinitely more complex, and subject not only to the many pollutants in the atmosphere and applied cosmetics, deodorants, etc., but is modified by what the body eats and drinks. It has been discovered, however, that behind all this confusion there is a unique identifiable 'smell'.

At the University of Leeds Department of Forensic Medicine, Dr Barbara Somerville is seeking that 'constant component' which is unaltered by other overlying odours and which is unique to the individual. Her work to date has concentrated on the analysis of sweat, and by comparing individuals in sets of twins. Dr Somerville had started from the basis that twins have a shared genetic code and the presumption that some of the several hundred components of sweat are genetic; it is this component that is the 'fingerprint'. Sweat concentrated in an odour-trapping resin is placed in a gas Chromatograph (see **Chromatography**) in order to separate the sample out into its constituent chemical parts. The resulting chromatogram trace represents these constituents in graphic form. Ironically, Dr Somerville has at times reverted to the use of a trusty canine tracker in order to isolate the genetic odour component from the other constituent parts making up the sample.

So we can see that if an odour sample can be retrieved from the scene of a crime – from an article touched or handled by the criminal (even if he is wearing gloves) – its chromatogram can be compared electronically with a sample from a suspect. Although this information is, in theory at least, 'scientific', it has yet to be tested in a British court of law.

In the Netherlands the Dutch 'politie' have enjoyed many successful convictions based on odour identification given not by sophisticated laboratory equipment but by – police dogs! Odour is 'lifted' from the scene of a crime, absorbed in a special soft sterile cloth (say, by wiping a weapon held by the criminal) and stored against such time as a suspect is taken into custody and exposed in an 'odour line-up'. This involves the suspect plus five volunteers showering to remove extraneous body odours and being dressed in sterile clothing. All six are then lined up in separate cubicles. The sniffer dog is exposed to the 'control' cloth and then released along the line of cubicles. Rarely does the dog fail to identify a guilty suspect, and so proud is he of his force's record that Brigadier Jan de Bruin of the Rotterdam police has founded the world's first 'bank' of odour samples taken from convicted criminals and stored for future comparison; the storage system will apparently keep the odour reliably 'fresh' for at least three years.

By way of a postscript, a woman whose handbag had been stolen in an English nightclub, in 1991 was able to identify the two thieves later when she caught a whiff of her own expensive perfume as they brushed by her!

OPIUM

Opium is rather better known as a nineteenth-century soporific introduced by Chinese sailors and smoked by the shady denizens of opium houses that sprang up in the Chinatown districts of seaports around the world. It was the main constituent of the one-time universal panacea, Laudanum (opium dissolved in alcohol). The following description of its harvesting dates from this same 'golden age' of opium:

Opium is the juice of the *Papaver somniferum,* the opium poppy. No more beautiful sight can be imagined than to see the whole countryside ablaze with purple and white poppies from which the valuable extract is obtained. The native cultivators guard their fields very carefully when they see that the flowers are about to fall. Then, as soon as the petals have been shed, leaving the familiar capsule containing the seeds, the time for reaping the harvest has come. Armed with a slender knife, wrapped round with cotton or string to within a quarter of an inch of the point, the ryot passes rapidly from plant to plant, making two little slits, one on each side of each capsule. The thick white juice of the poppy oozes out of the slits, and soon dries to a brownish, gummy matter on the side of the capsule. That evening the cultivator goes round again and scrapes the gum off the plants, making more slits for a fresh supply of juice to be ready the following morning. About six incisions in each capsule is as much as the plant can stand, and then it commences to die.

The sticky juice is collected and warmed, and then rolled up into balls which are covered with leaves; this product is crude opium. The refining is effected by means of mixing carefully with water and filtering, then drying the product and treating it with other solvents. It is then ready for conversion into the various forms under which we know it.

Despite its comparatively ready availability, raw opium was never popular with poisoners, possibly because of its slow action and distinctive smell, and outside the case of Eugene Chantrelle, no classic cases of opium poisoning can be found in the records.

Because opium's most active constituent is morphine, the symptoms of opium poisoning are the same as those described for morphine below.

Case Study

EUGENE MARIE CHANTRELLE

Chantrelle was born in Nantes, France, in the year 1824, son of a wealthy ship-owner who ensured that young Eugene enjoyed the most favourable education, completed by a course of study at the Nantes Medical School. That Chantrelle was forced to postpone his medical instruction can be blamed on nothing but his own improvident nature.

A shiftless boy, at the age of seventeen he espoused the Communistic ideals fostered by the French Revolution, and fought actively behind the barricades. The ultimate success of the Napoleonic party making France an insecure homeland for his like, Chantrelle decamped for the United States. In 1862 he came to England, and with some distinction devoted himself to teaching the French language. In 1866 he transferred his activities to Edinburgh, Scotland, where he enjoyed considerable popularity as a private tutor, not only in his native French, but also in German, Greek and Latin.

It was during Chantrelle's period of service at the exclusive Newington Academy that he became involved with a fifteen-year-old pupil named Elizabeth Cullen Dyer, and as a direct consequence of the intimacy, the unlikely couple were married on 11 August 1868.

The first of their four children was born just two months after the wedding, though already in so short a time Chantrelle had begun the resentful ill-treatment of his wife that would characterize the next ten miserable years of her life. Time after time she would be driven by his brutality to seek refuge in the comfort of her mother. Twice the police were summoned to protect her from her husband's threatening behaviour – threats that prophetically embraced the declaration that he had the knowledge to poison her by means defying all detection.

Very soon his drinking and womanizing began to erode the financial stability of an already diseased marriage, and Chantrelle was rapidly becoming unemployable, shunned by those who once saw his services as a gracious favour. In October 1877, with the spectre of ruin shadowing him, Eugene Chantrelle insured his young wife's life for the sum of £1,000, being at pains to ascertain that the policy was valid in the case of 'accidental death'.

On New Year's Day 1878, Elizabeth Chantrelle became ill and took to her bed. When the servant returned from her day off she was asked by Madame for a glass of lemonade and a piece of orange. On the following morning, the servant-girl rose at 6.30 to find her mistress unconscious in bed and moaning most desperately. In a state of alarm she summoned the master, and Chantrelle entering the room asked the girl whether she did not smell gas. She replied that she did not, but shortly afterwards was aware of so strong a smell that she turned the gas supply off at the meter.

Meanwhile, Chantrelle had summoned Dr Carmichael, who in turn sent for Dr Littlejohn, the Edinburgh medical officer, to whom the apparently distraught husband once again suggested a gas leak. Littlejohn had Elizabeth Chantrelle confined to the Royal Infirmary where her case was taken over by Dr Maclaglan, but she died shortly. Maclaglan decided that it was narcotic poisoning, not coal-gas, that had laid Madame so low, though whilst proving the latter true, the post-mortem failed to reveal any traces of drugs. Nevertheless, the samples of vomit brought up by Elizabeth Chantrelle on the previous night had been scraped from her nightdress and bed linen and subjected to analysis; unmistakable evidence of the presence of opium was found. On the afternoon of 5 January 1878, Eugene Chantrelle was arrested immediately after his wife's funeral, and conveyed to Calton Gaol.

On Tuesday 7 May, Chantrelle was put on trial, indicted that on 1st and 2nd January of that year he murdered his wife by administering opium in her lemonade; and further that by his maltreatment and threats he had frequently put her in fear of losing her life.

During the four days of the trial, the Crown sought to prove that, though the post-mortem failed to support a conclusion that Madame Chantrelle had been poisoned by opium, the deposits found in her vomit indicated that her death was a direct consequence of the unlawful administration of that drug. It was emphasized that the prisoner, as a result of his medical studies, was well aware of the uses and effects of poisons, and that he was at the time of his wife's death in possession of opium. Furthermore, his suggestion that a gas leak had been the cause of Elizabeth's death was entirely spurious. Though it was not incumbent on the prosecution to prove motive, the jury was, nevertheless, reminded of the impoverished state of Chantrelle's finances, and of the convenient insurance policy that he had taken out in case of his wife's 'accidental death'.

The defence presented on behalf of the prisoner was, by comparison, lacklustre, relying as it did upon a simple refutation of the charge. Indeed, at the end of his counsel's brief plea, even Chantrelle was forced to demand: 'Is that *all* the evidence for the defence?'

On the afternoon of Friday 10 May, the jury delivered their verdict: 'The jury unanimously find the panel guilty of murder as libelled'; he became the first prisoner to be hanged in Edinburgh after the passing of the Capital Punishment Amendment Act of 1868, making execution within the walls of the prison mandatory.

Morphine

The fine white crystalline alkaloid was first extracted from opium in 1805 by the German chemist Friedrich Serturner (which, incidentally, first proved the existence of organic bases containing nitrogen). Its invaluable properties as a powerful analgesic meant that morphine's availability was widespread, particularly among the medical fraternity. Quite how many homicidal deaths might be attributed to morphine poisoning in the early days of its discovery will never be known, for even in 1823, when the Frenchman Dr Edme Castaing was accused of poisoning two of his patients with the drug, there was no scientific means of proving its presence in the victims' bodies; Castaing was convicted on evidence of financial advantage from the deaths.

A fatal dose of the drug varies from one person to another, but about 5 grams (325 milligrams) normally causes respiratory failure within a few hours. The symptoms of morphine (and opium) poisoning onset within ten to thirty minutes of an orally ingested overdose, and more rapidly if the drug has been injected. Death has resulted from anal administration, and where morphine has been mixed with a poultice applied over broken skin. The characteristics are that the victim becomes drowsy (though at first sometimes mildly euphoric) and is afflicted with nausea and occasional vomiting; the face may be swollen and highly coloured. Gradually the victim slips into unconsciousness, and the skin may be cool and clammy, although the patient complains of feeling cold; the face exhibits cyanosis (blueness) and the extremities are livid. As the victim goes into coma, the muscles become increasingly relaxed and flabby. Breathing is slow and noisy, the pulse slow and weak until finally respiration ceases.

One of the best-known symptoms of morphine poisoning is the pin-point contraction of the pupils of the eyes, until conjunctival reaction degenerates and the pupils will no longer respond to light or dark.

Case Study

THE EYES HAVE IT

It was the invariable characteristic of the pupils pin-pointing that almost allowed another murderous medic, this time in the United States, to avoid discovery. Dr Robert Buchanan was a Scottish-American who had studied at Edinburgh and in 1886 returned to practise in New York. His fondness for the city's low life led two years later to Buchanan divorcing his wife in favour of Miss Anna Sutherland, the wealthy proprietress of a successful brothel. In the spring of 1892 the new Mrs Buchanan fell seriously ill, and when she died a short time afterwards it was certified as a brain haemorrhage; and Buchanan became richer by $50,000. One person who was less than happy with the result of the autopsy was Anna Sutherland's former amour (and one of her pimps), whose suspicions were championed by the *New York World*. Despite some very active harassment, the medical examiner flatly refused to reconsider his opinion, stating that morphine poisoning could not have been the cause of death as no tell-tale pin-pointing had been observed. It required even more active harassment of the New York coroner through the columns of the *World* to persuade that gentleman to order an exhumation and second post-mortem. This time the examination was undertaken by the foremost of America's toxicologists, Professor Rudolf Witthaus. Witthaus declared that the remains contained one-tenth of a grain of morphine, which by extrapolation could be estimated as a fatal dose of between two and three grains. In March 1893 Robert Buchanan was put on trial.

Witnesses were summoned who recalled for the benefit of the court conversations with Buchanan during which the doctor referred to the convicted morphine poisoner Carlyle Harris as a 'bungling amateur'. Harris (himself a medical student) had been tried the previous year for the disposal of an inconveniently pregnant girl-friend by means of an overdose of morphine. The prosecution medical expert testified to the pin-pointing of the victim's pupils being a universally accepted characteristic of morphine poisoning; that medical expert was the same Professor Rudolf Witthaus. Buchanan's disparaging remarks about his fellow-poisoner were for his not thinking to put a few drops of belladonna in his victim's eyes which would effectively have arrested the contraction of the pupils. Other witnesses at Buchanan's trial remembered that *he* had – for no apparent reason at the time – put drops in *his* wife's eyes shortly before she died.

To settle the matter a cat was brought in to court, administered a lethal dose of morphine, and while its life ebbed away drops of belladonna were applied to prove its effectiveness in halting the pin-pointing process.

On 8 May 1893, Carlyle Harris was executed in the electric chair at Sing Sing prison. On 2 July 1895, Dr Robert Buchanan met the same fate in the same chair.

The other well-known by-product of opium is heroin (diamorphine), and although it may be responsible for misery and even death on an alarming scale, it is rarely encountered in cases of murder; see entry under **Drugs**.

P

PAINT ANALYSIS

The suitability of paint to highly specific identification techniques makes it one of the most useful contact traces, particularly in vehicular cases such as hit-and-run accidents. Traces of paint from window and door surrounds which have been damaged during forced entry and fragments of which have become attached to the suspect's clothing are also frequently encountered in the chemistry laboratory.

There are two ways in which paint fragments can be matched to their source, the most obvious being a physical fit. This may only be practical with comparatively large chips, and the more reliable method of comparison is the matching of paint layers. The longer a building has been standing the more layers of paint there are likely to be, reflecting the varying tastes of the people who have lived or worked in it. Although the range of colours and shades make duplication unlikely, a convincing match can only be made when there are sufficient layers to eliminate chance.

The layers of paint on motor vehicles, because they are so strictly controlled and monitored, provide excellent material for comparison, the layer pattern of paint often being confined to very few models produced between verifiable dates. Most motor mannfacturers keep extensive records and sample lists of all paints used in production, which are available to police laboratories, most of which hold reference collections.

Comparison of samples can normally be carried out under a microscope, but if identification is difficult or inconclusive, paint is suitable for analysis by **Chromatography** and **Spectrometry** (in particular, emission spectrometry).

In one British serial rape case, the suspect had driven his victim off the motorway into a wooded area during the course of which the rear of the car struck a tree branch and chipped off a small flake of paint which lodged in the bark. By simple visual comparison a colour match was made and cross-checked against the motor manufacturers' samples. It turned out that only one maker used the colour Harvest Gold with any regularity, and other information at the scene of the crime indicated that the car was a hatchback. By a process of elimination the field was narrowed down to one model – an Austin Allegro manufactured between May 1973 and August 1975; and of course the suspect car would also be missing a small fragment of paint from the rear, forty-five inches from the ground (the height of its collision with the branch).

Successive victims had already identified the rapist by his accent as coming from north-east England, and while checking a computer list of known crinunals from the area working in the Home Counties a man was questioned. Outside the London flat an Austin Allegro was parked; it was Harvest Gold with a chip of paint missing from the rear pillar at a height of exactly forty-five inches. Along with other forensic evidence found in the vehicle, the paint ensured the conviction of one of the country's most notorious rapists.

A postscript to the subject of paint appeared with the announcement by a Swedish company that it had developed a paint which is capable of *absorbing* between forty-nine and ninety-five per cent of noxious fumes. As well as its application to rid public areas of the smell of tobacco smoke, and to freshen lavatories, it is suggested that the paint could find a welcome use in mortuaries and post-mortem rooms.

PALMARS

In principle, prints from the ridge patterns of the palms of the hands and the soles of the feet are as reliably identifiable with their source of origin as fingerprints. In practice, they are less easily classified and no extensive reference collection is kept in any police bureau.

That said, palmprints left at the scene of a crime – perhaps by pushing open a door or window to gain access, or by moving furniture – will be developed and preserved against matching with a future suspect. This procedure will also be followed in the less likely event of **Barefoot Prints**.

Palmprints have been acceptable as evidence in courts of law throughout the world for many years (though the first time that such evidence was produced in a murder case in Britain was in 1942). It was, however, in the United States as early as 1918, that the first major legal debate over the admissibility of palmprint evidence took place. A man named Kuhl had been convicted of the murder of a stage-coach driver named Fred Searcey. The conclusive evidence had been a bloody handprint on an envelope stolen from the mail-bag cargo. Kuhl's defence attorney appealed the validity of the evidence before the Nevada Appeal Court, and the judicial decision created a landmark in palmar print evidence.

Having confirmed that fingerprint evidence was now generally accepted as irrefutable in cases of identity, the court went on to state:

The lines of the palms of the human hand and the soles of the feet, which form the basis of individual identification, are the papillary ridges [which] form figures, patterns or designs which research, study and science have divided into classes . . . These patterns, while they have been discussed principally in connection with finger impressions . . . are found with equal importance and equal persistency in the human palm and the sole of the human foot . . . We have gone at length into the subject of palmprint and fingerprint identification, largely for the purpose of evolving the indisputable conclusion that there is but one physiological basis underlying this method of identification; that the phenomenon by which identity is thus established exists, not only on the bulbs of the finger tips but is continuous and co-existing on all the parts and in all sections and sub-division of the palmar surface of the human hand.

Case Studies

BRITAIN'S FIRST PALMPRINT CONVICTION
SAM DASHWOOD and GEORGE SILVEROSA

The date is Thursday 30 April 1942; the place, a small shop in east London's Hackney Road; the victim, a septuagenarian pawnbroker named Leonard Moules. The crime is murder, a sordid, pointless exercise in greed and incompetence, but one that will add another landmark to the history of fingerprinting.

Moules had been found by a beat policeman, lying unconscious in his shop from a series of savage blows to the head and face, probably from the butt end of a pistol. Despite emergency treatment at the nearby Bethnal Green Hospital, the 71-year-old pawnbroker died without regaining consciousness.

One of Scotland Yard's most experienced detectives, Detective Chief Inspector Ted Greeno, wasted no time in combing the scene of the crime for clues; also attached to the team was Detective Superintendent Frederick Cherrill, head of the Fingerprint Bureau. Among the countless prints found around the shop only one did not match those of Moules or his assistant. On the inside surface of the plundered safe Cherrill found a palmprint. The problem was that the Yard maintained only a small collection of palmprints – about 4,000 – and none of them matched.

It was not until a witness recalled seeing two men near the scene of the murder that the case picked up momentum. The witness vaguely knew the men as 'George' and 'Sam', and he had seen them handling a gun. It is true that the eyes and ears of the law are everywhere, and it was only a matter of time before 'George' became George Silverosa, a twenty-three-year-old machinist with a palmprint identical to that left on Leonard Moules' safe. No hero, Silverosa was quick to admit the robbery, even quicker to point the finger of guilt for murder in the direction of his accomplice 'Sam' – Sam Dashwood. Dashwood, of course, blamed Silverosa, and the ungracious couple were still squabbling among themselves when they faced judge and jury.

Both men refused to give evidence; both refused the services of a counsel; and quite deservedly both men were found guilty of murder. Dashwood and Silverosa were hanged at Pentonville on 10 September 1942 – the first British victory for palmprints.

MASS PALMPRINTING AT POTTER'S BAR
MICHAEL QUERIPEL

On the evening of 29 April 1955, forty-six-year-old Mrs Elizabeth Currell made her daily pilgrimage to the Potter's Bar golf course with her pet corgi. It was almost a ritual – the path along the railway embankment, past the wartime pillbox and on to the links. But tonight it would be different; lurking in the dark of the pillbox was the last person who would see Mrs Currell alive. As she reached the seventeenth tee, the man pounced, trying ineffectually to strangle her, then punching, struggling, till his hand reached out and grabbed the heavy iron tee-marker.

At dawn the next day a police constable found Elizabeth Currell's body. Pathologist Dr Francis Camps confirmed that she had been battered to death; rape had clearly been considered, but abandoned. The killer had left one clue – a fragmentary palmprint on his weapon, a mark that, but for his youth, would have hanged him.

It is often rightly assumed that a rapist, thought to be on foot, lurking in a particular dark and isolated place, will be a local. It was based on this assumption that a decision was made to carry out a mass palmprinting in the Potter's Bar area, including the male occupants of close to 7,000 homes, plus the employees who travelled into the area to work. A team of fifty-seven detectives was mobilized to take the prints, while twelve experienced officers from the fingerprint branch were responsible for the work of comparison.

By the middle of August – four months after the murder – 9,000 palmars had been taken and the experts were half-way through comparing them. On the 19th of the month, print 4,605, taken from seventeen-year-old Michael Queripel, matched.

As profiled earlier, Queripel was a local youth, living with his parents and brother in a house close to the golf course. In fact, he had already been questioned by the police five days after the murder. On 3 July he had refused to have his palmprint taken claiming that it was 'against his principles'; only the intervention of his brother persuaded Queripel to comply.

After insisting that Mrs Currell was already dead when he found her on the golf course, Michael Queripel confessed to her murder. His trial lasted a bare five minutes and he was ordered to be 'detained during Her Majesty's pleasure

PATHOLOGISTS
England and Wales

The chief responsibility of the forensic pathologist is to undertake the **Post-Mortem** examination of bodies discovered in what are termed 'suspicious circumstances', that is to say where there is a suspicion of murder, manslaughter or infanticide. The object of the primary examination is to determine, as far as possible, the cause of death.

The next stage of the investigative procedure then frequently rests on the pathologist's professional judgement – whether the case is dealt with by a coroner at inquest, as in the finding of suicide, accident or natural causes; or by the police as a criminal investigation (though in this latter eventuality also, a coroner's preliminary, or 'opening', hearing is required).

In the usual course of events, the forensic pathologist summoned by the police will first examine the body of the victim at the scene of the crime, often in far from agreeable conditions and surroundings, before attending the body in the mortuary to conduct a detailed post-mortem and prepare a report on his findings. Once he is 'on the case', the pathologist will be an occasional, though key member of the investigation team, working in collaboration with the police and the local forensic science laboratory. Finally, he may be required to prepare expert testimony for the Crown Prosecution Service and to act as an expert witness for the prosecution in any subsequent criminal proceedings.

Forensic pathologists and murder investigations are always connected in the popular imagination, though to see this in perspective it is necessary first to look at statistics. The figures for one recent year, 1987, were as follows: 175,769 deaths were reported to coroners in England and Wales, of which seventy-seven per cent (135,961) were the subject of post-mortem examinations. Less than one per cent of these cases, about 1,500, were in the nature of 'suspicious' deaths where the pathologist was summoned by the police, and in only 630 cases was a homicide recorded. Anecdotally, one report states that July, August and Christmas are the 'busiest' times.

So much for the man in the white coat. His specialism, forensic pathology, has emerged from the wider discipline of forensic medicine. Whereas previously the subject would have incorporated toxicology, biochemistry, materials analysis, ballistics, etc., each of these now forms its own specialized department, and the pathologist, while having a broad grasp of many related disciplines, now relies on experts in the other, increasingly complex technical fields, such as odontology, microbiology, serology, chemistry and clinical pathology.

In 1990 there were about four dozen recognized forensic pathologists on call to the police forces of England and Wales, partly comprising the so-called 'Home Office list' of practitioners generally associated with the provincial universities or regional Home Office forensic science laboratories. Historically, the 'list' does not include the many eminent pathologists based in the capital's medical colleges, who serve the Metropolitan and City of London police forces.

United States

In the United States, the investigation of deaths in 'suspicious circumstances' is undertaken either by a **Coroner** or the department of the Medical Examiner, depending on the system adopted by a particular state. Because the coroner system is based on politics and so liable to corruption, the medical examiner option is gradually replacing the coroner. Here a fully qualified and experienced forensic pathologist is employed full-time by the state and is in charge of a custom-equipped building and a team of qualified scientific staff.

The Continent

Unlike the haphazard (and rapidly declining) availability of forensic medicine facilities in England, the rest of Europe (East and West) and Scandinavia have a healthy, efficient and well-financed network of forensic science institutes, usually attached to the universities, and in the charge of a professor (there are fewer than half a dozen forensic pathologists with the status of professor in the whole of England and Wales). These operate in many ways similarly to the American medical examiner's department, though the high level of research and refinement that they undertake puts countries like Denmark ahead of the rest of the world.

PHOTO-FIT

It was in 1971 that Britain saw the introduction of what became the successor to the Identikit system – the Penry Facial Identification Technique, called 'Photo-FIT'. Superficially, the system closely resembled Identikit with its images photographic rather than hand-drawn. However, in an article published simultaneously in *The Criminologist* and *Forensic Photography* in 1974, Jacques Penry opens: 'I should like to make it clear that Photo-FIT is a completely original conception, and not a development of any other facial identification system. It was in 1938, while selecting faces to be photographed to illustrate my first book *Character From the Face* that the idea of face building came to me by accident.' In 1968 Penry, a specialist in physique/personality links, approached the Home Office Police Research and Development Branch and was put under contract to produce a 'kit'. By 1969 Penry had completed the prototype 'Front-view Basic Caucasian Kit' which was capable of composing five billion faces. 1970 saw the production of the Afro-

Asian Supplement (500 million possibilities of 'Coloured' faces). Supplement followed supplement (including a North American Indian supplement produced in collaboration with the Royal Canadian Mounted Police). However, it was not until 1974 that a Female Supplement was introduced.

The scope of the full kit can be judged from the current Caucasian Basic Kit, which alone contains:

> 204 Foreheads/Hairstyles
> 96 Pairs of Eyes
> 89 Noses
> 101 Mouths
> 74 Chin/Cheek sections
> Plus various 'accessories' – headwear, moustaches/beards, spectacles, age lines, ears.

It is possible to compose about 15 billion faces with this kit.

Nevertheless, as Penry so perceptively warned – the effective use of Photo-FIT depends upon a combination of three important factors:

1. The efficiency of the system itself – its range and flexibility.
2. The ability of the witness to recollect, describe and compare facial characteristics.
3. The operator's skill in interpreting the witness's description without prompting him, and skill in the use of the system.

Penry's Photo-FIT found, and in many cases is still finding, favour with police and security forces throughout the world. However, the rapid advances made in computer-generated graphics technology have had their beneficial effect on facial recognition techniques. One of the recent improvements over Identikit and Photo-FIT is that an image can be created 'in the round', adding depth, colour and texture.

PHRENOLOGY

> 'A very fantastical, and, in our humble judgement, most absurd hypothesis.'
>
> Francis Jeffrey in *Edinburgh Review,* 1826

In 1796, a Viennese physician, Dr Franz Joseph Gall, announced to the world the revolutionary theory of *Phrenology*. At the basis of his system was the presumption that as we think we actively affect the shape of the brain, and this in its turn affects the shape of the bony cranium – resulting in the irregularity of surface which laymen called 'bumps' and phrenologists called 'faculties'.

Each of these 'faculties' (according to the system adopted, as many as forty-two) corresponds to a facet of a person's overall personality. Consequently an assessment could be made of character by reading the state of development of the faculty, or bump.

One of the problems, even during its Victorian heyday, was that there was no strict agreement on where the appropriate bumps should be. The sample given below has been compiled from several sources.

The Seven Sentiments, or Propensities	*Faculties*
1. Domestic Propensities	1–6
2. Selfish Propensities	7–12
3. Self-regarding Sentiments	13–16
4. Moral Sentiments	17–21
5. Self-perfecting Faculties	22–26
6. Intellectual Faculties	27–28
7. Reflective, Reasoning and Intuitive Faculties	29–42

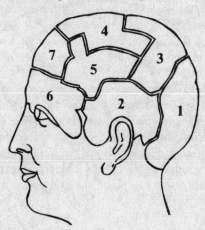

The Forty-two Faculties
1. *Amativeness:* Love and Sexuality
2. *Philoprogenitiveness:* Parental and Filial Love

3. *Conjugality:* Marriage; Fidelity
4. *Adhesiveness:* Friendship
5. *Inhabitiveness:* Love of Home; Patriotism
6. *Continuity:* Concentration and Perserverance

7. *Combativeness:* Courage and Determination; Pugnacity
8. *Destructiveness:* Self-protection; Aggressiveness
9. *Alimentiveness:* Love of Food
10. *Aquativeness:* Love of Drink
11. *Acquisitiveness:* Love of Possessions; Thrift
12. *Secretiveness:* Discretion; Diplomacy

13. *Cautiousness:* Self-preservation
14. *Approbativeness:* Need for Attention and Popularity
15. *Self-esteem:* Self-confidence
16. *Firmness:* Determination

17. *Conscientiousness:* Moral Conviction; Integrity
18. *Hopefulness:* Optimism
19. *Spirituality:* Belief in Spiritual Existence; Psychic Powers

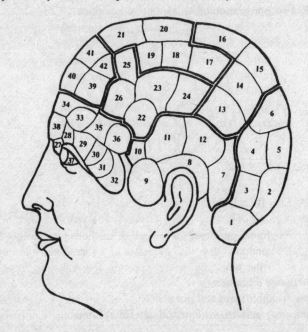

20. *Veneration:* Respect for Social Conventions
21. *Benevolence:* Kindliness and Generosity

22. *Constructiveness:* Mechanical Ability; Mental Development
23. *Ideality:* Desire for, and Love of, Perfection and Purity
24. *Sublimity:* Desire for the Magnificent; Ambitious Conceptions
25. *Imitativeness:* Need for Conventionality; Ability to Mimic
26. *Mirthfulness:* Sense of Humour; Joviality

27. *Form:* Visual Memory
28. *Size:* Ability to Assess Proportions

29. *Weight:* Perception of Gravity; Precision of Movement
30. *Colour:* Appreciation of Deeper Significance of Colour
31. *Order:* Organization; Control
32. *Calculation:* Comprehension of Mathematical Principles; Analytical Tendencies
33. *Locality:* Relationship to Environment; Sense of Direction
34. *Eventuality:* Memory; Knowledge; Experience
35. *Time:* Punctuality; Regulation of Life and Society
36. *Tune:* Appreciation of Music
37. *Language:* Facility in all Forms of Communication; Foreign Tongues
38. *Individuality:* Awareness of Identity; Discrimination
39. *Causality:* Facility for Reasoning, Planning and Deduction
40. *Comparison:* Analytical Judgement
41. *Human Nature:* Character Assessment; Intuition
42. *Agreeableness:* Ability to Communicate Socially

Case Study

FRANÇOIS BENJAMIN COURVOISIER

On the morning of 6 May 1840, seventy-three-year-old Lord William Russell was found murdered in his bed in his house in Norfolk Street, Park Lane, London. There was evidence of a forced entry through the back door to the house but there were too few valuables missing to make robbery a likely motive for the attack.

The household below stairs consisted of two maids, a manservant, a coachman, and a groom. And Françis Benjamin Courvoisier, a young Swiss, who for the past five weeks had occupied the position as Lord Russell's valet. It transpired that his Lordship was in the habit of trusting the valet to act as the head of this small ménage and had the previous morning given Courvoisier a number of instructions to transmit to the rest of the staff. One of these messages was that the coachman should be ready to collect Lord Russell from his club at five in the evening. As the valet omitted to pass that order on, it is understandable that when the master arrived home at last in a hired cab he should express some dissatisfaction with his valet's competence. It transpired that Courvoisier greatly resented this slight.

All this was noted by the investigating officers (Inspector Nicholas Pearce and Sergeant Frederick Shaw). They felt that this misunderstanding, in combination with clues like a small amount of missing jewellery being found in the valet's pantry, and bloodstained clothes in his room – not to forget his depositing some choice pieces of the Russell silver with Madame Piolaine, a Leicester Square hotelier – indicated a large measure of guilt on the part of Monsieur Courvoisier. And after sentence of death had been passed on him Courvoisier obligingly confessed his crime:

> His lordship was very cross with me and told me I must quit his service. As I was coming upstairs from the kitchen I thought it was all up with me; my character was gone, and I thought the only way I could cover my faults was by murdering him. This was the first moment that any idea of the sort entered my head. I went into the dining room and took a knife from the sideboard. I do not remember whether it was a carving knife or not. I then went upstairs. I opened his bedroom door and heard him snoring in his sleep; there was a rushlight in his room burning at the time. I went near the bed by the side of the window, and then I murdered him. He just moved his arm a little; he never spoke a word.

The execution was carried out at Newgate on 6 July 1840, and shortly afterwards George R. Lewis published *Illustrations of Phrenology*, the first and only issue of which was devoted to the late François Courvoisier. As was the custom, a cast had been taken of Courvoisier's head after death, and this was used as a basis for phrenological study by a Dr Elliotson, who was also a pioneer of hypnosis as an anaesthetic.

No one acquainted with Gall's discoveries who has seen the cast of Courvoisier's head will wonder at the following details. It presents one of the worst cerebral developments.

The cast is that of a large powerful head, being 23A inches in circumference. But its magnitude arises from the great size of the sides and back, and of the posterior central part of the summit, and from the length of the lowest central part of the forehead. The forehead is very narrow and its upper portion retreating, while the lateral portions of the crown slope down gently, rendering it keel-shaped.

In the sides and back and in the posterior portions of the crown reside the dispositions which are as powerful in brutes as in man – love, sexual, parental and friendly; the disposition to resist, to do violence, to act with cunning, to possess, to construct; self-estimation; love of notice; cautiousness; and firmness.

The organs of the whole of these are *very large,* with the exception of those of Parental and Friendly Love, which are but *mean* or ordinary, and of Constructiveness, which is only *large*. The part now considered by Dr Hoppe as the seat of the Disposition to Feed, and situated just before the organ of the Disposition to do Violence, is also *very large* . . .

Benevolence is actually *small* . . . In regard to the intellect, there is but one organ very large, and this is the organ of General Observation – the Sense of Things, in the language of Gall – and which is frequently large in brutes . . .

The history of a being so unhappily organized as Courvoisier must suggest the most serious reflections to every thinking and humane person upon the improvements necessary in education, in the views and arrangements of society, and in punishments and prison discipline.

PHYSIOGNOMY

We all intuitively read other people's character from their faces a dozen times a day; it is often our only way of measuring our reaction to them. So it is no surprise that the formulation of a system of 'divination' by physiognomy should have been with us for millennia, becoming increasingly sophisticated and enjoying periodic favour among those criminologists tirelessly seeking a formula by which to anticipate a criminal mentality.

This illustration is from a seventeenth-century treatise by Porta, and attempts to interpret the faces of men through animals and their brute characteristics.

Case Study

REPORT ON MISS LIZZIE BORDEN

The murder of Mr and Mrs Borden in Fall River, Mass.,* at midday some months since, and the mystery which hung over the case for days and weeks and filled the land with wonder and terror, and finally the suspicion that settled upon Lizzie, the daughter, and her commitment to prison for trial for the murder, has been the melancholy marvel of the season.

Lawyers and others who have an interest in criminal jurisprudence, as well as writers historical or sensational, bring to our office [the *Phrenological Journal*] photos, or send us woodcuts, smooth or rough, from every part of the country for our opinions of the character. Anxious mothers come with or send a photograph of a young man who is a candidate for the honour or emoluments of the position of son-in-law, to get our opinion of his talents, worth character, social qualities or capacity for making a living, and especially if he is adapted to be the husband of a daughter who is present in person or by picture. It is therefore no surprise when a person says: 'Please give me your opinion verbally or in writing of the original of that picture.'

On the 27th of October last, a photo was sent to our office with a request for a brief estimate of the character, which was given as printed below. It was published in the Chicago *Evening News* of 4 November, a copy of which was sent to us.

The photograph of Lizzie Borden, from which the accompanying illustration was made, was given to Mr Sizer without a possible clue by which he could discover its identity. At the end of fifteen minutes'

*The controversial axe-murders of Fall River are probably America's best-known 'classic' crime. In August 1892 Andrew Borden and his second wife were found dead in their home, their heads brutally smashed with an axe. Daughter Lizzie was accused of the killings, though by the time her trial opened in 1893, popular opinion seemed to favour her innocence. Lizzie Borden was acquitted of the murders and returned to a comparatively quiet life in Fall River, where she died in 1927. As befits a case of this celebrity, its story has been turned into films, musicals, plays, and a library of books and magazine features; nor is there any shortage of passionately held theories about the outcome of the trial and Lizzie's guilt or innocence.

examination he gave me this 'analysis and criticism', to use the technical phrase of Phrenology:

We see in this portrait latent talent. The fullness across the lower part of the forehead evinces large perceptive faculties as a group, making her bright, quick to see, to know and to remember, giving the talents necessary for practical education, for art, mechanism and for business. The head seems to be broad in the sides above and about the ears, showing bravery, energy, severity and a strong desire for ownership, and laying the foundation for good business talent and the tendency to push the cause which has business involved in it to a successful termination. The face indicates power. The broad cheekbones and the prominence of them, the massiveness of the lower jaw, as it makes an angle to get up towards the ear, show vital power and the tendency to be thorough and severe. The mouth indicates determination and resolution. The breadth of the head above and about the ears shows courage, selfishness and executive ability. She appears to have large firmness, that is shown by the height of the head, on a line from the opening of one ear to that of the other over the top. We think she has a pretty good share of self-esteem. She is self-willed, courageous, high tempered, secretive, fond of property. She is not a thinker and reasoner; she is a critic, but she is rather light in the reasoning power, though amply developed in the abilities which relate to practical knowledge and the ability to be ingenious and artistic. If the back and top of the head were available it would be an aid to the full estimate of her character. She appears to have more courage than prudence, more determination than pliability, more force than restraint of mind.

Phrenological Journal, No. XCIV, December 1892

POISONS

Toxicology is one of the busiest departments of the forensic chemistry laboratory, and the toxicologist's work is divided between the twin menaces – **Drugs** and poisons. By 'drugs' here is meant 'illicit' drugs, those that have been used for pleasure or through addiction.

Poison is generally defined as 'a substance that when introduced into or absorbed by a living organism may destroy life or injure health'. In the forensic laboratory the 'living organism' is always human, and the effect has usually been to 'destroy life'. In all other respects the range of poisons dealt with is as broad as the definition. As Goethe observed: 'There is no such thing as poison; it all depends on the dose.'

Nevertheless, there are traditionally those substances which are toxic enough to cause death with very small doses which have, sometimes over millennia, become associated with the craft of the poisoner – arsenic, cyanide, strychnine . . . It is this list of poisons most commonly encountered in homicide that will be dealt with here.

Accident? Suicide? Homicide?

Before embarking on a more detailed study of the effects of the main poisons, one subject must be addressed that is of vital importance to the investigation of death by poisoning – was it accident, suicide or homicide?

Although homicidal poisoning are still committed, by far the greater number of fatalities are due to accident or suicide.

Accident

Accidental poisoning most frequently occurs in young children. The sources are infinite, but poison berries, medicines that look like sweets, and substances, such as turpentine and petrol, in soft drinks bottles are among the biggest culprits.

Many Acts of Parliament have been passed over the years that have restricted the general availability of poisons, and from times not so long ago when just about everything from cosmetics to sheep-dip seemed to contain **Arsenic**, it is now comparatively difficult to purchase the toxins historically so beloved of the poisoner. It is for this reason that a high proportion of poisoning cases has involved members of the medical profession, among whom the means to kill is never far from hand.

Accidental poisoning can still arise from industrial causes, where toxic substances are essential to the working process; and natural gases, such as methane and **Carbon Monoxide**, are hazards in the mining industry. Just as the various Poisons Acts have restricted the availability of poisons, so statutory regulations controlling working conditions and safety in industry have reduced the number of accidental deaths by poisoning in the workplace. However, it is a fact that one cannot legislate against carelessness and stupidity.

Suicide

Suicidal poisoning accounts for as many as 25,000 admissions to hospital in Great Britain every year. Most are half-hearted gestures, cries for help of one kind or another, and of the total only between one and two per cent are fatal. However, there are further thousands who perish from the effects of self-administered toxins before they can be treated; these are the serious suicides.

Although there tend to be 'fashions' in the suicidal poisons, the top four substances tend to be barbiturates, salicylates, carbon monoxide and tranquillizers – between them responsible for around ninety per cent of suicides. Additionally, many suicides are accompanied by a greater or lesser ingestion of alcohol.

Homicide

For reasons partly connected with availability and partly with highly developed laboratory detection techniques, poisons account for a very small proportion (about six per cent) of all homicidal deaths. The latest available figures at the time of writing show that in 1989 there were seven* confirmed cases in England and Wales and twenty-eight cases in the United States, out of a total of 576 and 18,954 respectively.

Statistics include only *confirmed* cases of homicidal poisoning, making no allowance for suspicious deaths that *may* have been homicidal poisoning, or deaths which at the time were certified as due to 'natural causes' and could have included some undetected poisoning cases.

Police officers investigating sudden or rapid death among people vulnerable to *natural* death – the chronically ill, the elderly, alcoholics, the mentally disturbed, young children – should be particularly aware

*Both sets of figures combine homicides by poison *and* narcotics.

that these categories are also naturally vulnerable to homicide, as they could be seen by some to represent a 'domestic nuisance'.

The Main Poisons

There is no truly satisfactory system for classifying poisons, particularly the many recent chemical formulations, and so the system followed here is broadly derived from the classifications given by Dr Gerald Roche Lynch in his important treatise, *Toxicology: Homicidal, Suicidal and Accidental Poisoning*. Some of the major 'homicide' poisons have been referred to in separate entries throughout this book (indicated in the following list by bold type), but brief notes are given here on the other significant substances that are or have been encountered by the forensic toxicologist.

1. GASES
   Carbon Monoxide (see page 99)

2. CORROSIVES
   Acids (see page 15)
      Hydrochloric
      Nitric
      Sulphuric

Alkalis

   Potassium hydroxide (Caustic potash): A highly corrosive poison which, when taken orally in concentration, will cause burning from the mouth to the stomach, and cause lips and tongue to become swollen. Retching and vomiting follow, first of food and mucus, then a brownish liquid containing alkaline haematin and necrotic shreds of mucous membrane. The skin feels cold and clammy to the touch and the pulse feeble and rapid. Death may occur rapidly through shock or asphyxia from corrosion of the larynx, or more slowly by a combination of symptoms – breathing dead material into the lungs causing broncho-pneumonia, damage to the stomach retarding gastric functions, even, rarely, perforation of the stomach.

   The highly corrosive nature of caustic potash, and its facility for dissolving human tissue, has not gone entirely unnoticed by a handful of killers anxious to dispose of the remains of their handiwork.

Case Study

ADOLPH LOUIS LUETGERT

Luetgert arrived with the great German migration to America of the 1870s, and once there settled in Chicago to establish a sausage-making business, a business that was to prove most expedient when, in 1897, he finally bade farewell to his wife.

The master sausage-maker was a large man with a large sexual appetite, and he must, despite his hulking seventeen stone weight, have been attractive to women. Certainly the flow of mistresses through his factory necessitated a bed being installed in the office.

It was on 1 May 1897 that Louisa Luetgert disappeared from her home. There had been frequent quarrels, and it was clear that Mrs Luetgert was getting more than a little agitated over her husband's amours – he in his turn saw no reason to persevere in a relationship with a woman he no longer even liked and who was an increasing impediment to his future happiness with Miss Harriet Becker, whom he had promised to marry.

It was some days before Louisa's disappearance was reported to the police – and then not by Luetgert himself, although he had been provident enough to pay a visit to the local police station *in advance* of his wife's 'elopement' to confide his fear that she *planned* to run away with an amorous New Yorker. To her family, Adolph had broken the tragic news that Louisa had left him, and that he had hired a private detective to try to track her down.

When police searched the sausage factory and drained down the three giant steam-vats, they found that the greasy sediment in one contained pieces of human bone, some teeth and two gold rings. Mrs Luetgert had not *completely* disappeared.

At Adolph Luetgert's trial for the murder of his wife, the prosecution case drew from police evidence the unavoidable conclusion that Louisa Luetgert had been killed – probably with one of the many sharp butchering knives used in the factory – cut into manageable pieces . . . and turned into sausages.

It would have transformed a sensation into a *cause célèbre* if Adolph Luetgert had really made human sausages; as it was, he most likely first coated the dismembered pieces of Mrs Luetgert with caustic potash, then tossed them into one of the steam-vats where a combination of the action of the potash, heat from the furnace, and boiling water, dissolved the bone and tissue sufficiently to flush away – or very nearly.

There was not really much evidence the prisoner could bring to indicate otherwise. He was emphatic that he had not killed his wife, and equally emphatic that the rings found in the steamer had not belonged to her, despite their identification by relatives and despite the initials 'L.L.' engraved on one of them. As to the evidence of human remains, Luetgert maintained that they were porcine in origin and not human. But he would, wouldn't he?

It didn't help his case that, in one sensational appearance after another, several of Luertgert's mistresses took the stand to testify against him. One told the court that the prisoner had said of poor Louisa: 'I could take her and crush her', another said that Luetgert had asked her to look after a bloodstained knife for him.

In an unsurprising verdict, Adolph Louis Luetgert was found guilty of first-degree murder, and sentenced to life imprisonment. He served his time in Joliet State Penitentiary where, protesting innocence with his last breath, he died from a heart attack in 1911.

Sodium hydroxide (Caustic soda): Like potassium hydroxide, this is a highly corrosive poison which, owing to its common use in clearing sinks and drains, is often found in domestic kitchens. Considerable quantities are also employed industrially. Same effects as potassium hydroxide.

Ammonia: A colourless, pungent-smelling gas and liquid (so named because ammonium chloride used in soldering was formerly made from camel dung in the neighbourhood of the Libyan temple of the god Ammon). Rarely encountered in homicide, though occasional accidents and suicides are still recorded.

If ammonia is ingested in concentrated liquid form, death can be very rapid, with corrosion of the larynx and obstruction of the glottis. Post-mortem examination will reveal congested lungs containing much frothy fluid which is also apparent in the upper air passages. The blood appears dark and is resistant to clotting.

The effect of exposure to ammonia gas is an immediate sensation of suffocation followed by severe burning pains from the mouth to the stomach, retching and vomiting. The vomit smells of ammonia and may contain altered blood.

3. SYNTHETIC ORGANIC SUBSTANCES
Acetylsalicylic Acid (Aspirin)

Probably the commonest medicinal drug used by humankind – and one of the commonest agents of suicide. In the stomach acetylsalicylic acid decomposes into aspirin, salicylic acid and acetic acid. Symptoms are nausea, though not necessarily attended by vomiting, and tinnitus. This is followed by mental confusion and hearing difficulty; sleepiness is succeeded by coma. Breathing is deep and slow, pulse rate high.

Post-mortem appearances: Dehydration and, due to the large doses taken in fatal cases, some undissolved traces should be found in the stomach. There is general congestion of the viscera, and the lungs particularly are oedematous. Marked degeneration of the liver and kidneys. Urine will be very acid, contain albumin and show granular casts.

Barbituric Acid

Synthesized in 1863 by the German chemist Adolf von Bayer and called, rather romantically, after a lady friend named Barbara. At the turn of the century Fischer and von Mering isolated two of the derivatives of barbituric acid – barbital and phenobarbital – as effective sedatives. The former was called Veronal (after the city of Verona), the latter Luminal. If they had known the unending misery that their discoveries would cause by the end of the twentieth century all three eminent men might have thought twice.

As early as 1913 the leading English toxicologist William Willcox was warning of the dangers of Veronal, but it was not until the 1950s that the true menace of barbiturates as drugs of addiction was fully appreciated. More information on this aspect will be found in the entry on **Drugs.**

The average sedative dose is between 10 and 70mg taken orally in tablet form, the drug entering the blood through the walls of the small intestine. In themselves the doses are relatively safe, but prolonged use leads not only to physical dependence but also to body tolerance – in other words, larger doses will be required to have the same sedative effect. Accidental overdosing is not uncommon, and death has resulted from as little as twice the prescribed dose; barbiturates are particularly dangerous in combination with alcohol. The ubiquity of barbiturates and their effectiveness as an agent of suicide puts them far and away above any other means of self-destruction.

A fatal dose will first induce headache, vertigo, and an inability to control the bodily functions. The subject falls asleep and after a short period during which he can be roused with difficulty, slips into coma. There may be a brief onset of hallucinations, but then coma becomes profound and the body exhibits no reflex actions. Pupils of the eyes are small, but not pin-point, and will not react to light; in terminal stages the pupils may begin to dilate. Surface of the body will be cold and clammy to the touch, the pulse quick but feeble. Breathing is loud and heavy, and towards the end may stop periodically and then start again. Death results from respiratory paralysis.

Post-mortem appearances: The lungs are oedematous and heavy, preventing aeration. The air passages contain a frothy fluid, and the bronchi may contain pus and show areas of broncho-pneumonia; there is little or no fluid in the pleural sacs. The brain is congested and softened by oedema. The liver shows some fatty change, and the bladder is usually found full. Urine should always be collected, carefully protecting against contamination with blood or other matter, as cases of barbiturate poisoning can be confirmed by the characteristic red colour when urine is in an acid solution, changing to purple on the addition of ammoma.

Case Study

AN UNNATURAL FATHER

Five-month-old Terence Armstrong died at his home in Gosport, Hampshire, 22 July 1955. At first it was thought that he had been the victim of infant curiosity in eating poisonous red berries – not an unreasonable assumption in view of the red skins found in the child's throat and stomach during post-mortem examination. However, subsequent laboratory analysis of the contents of the stomach showed that the 'skins' were none other than the soggy gelatine capsules that had once held the barbiturate drug Seconal. By this time the parents, neither of whom seemed particularly distressed, had been given permission to bury their son, and it was necessary to apply for an **Exhumation** order that a second autopsy could be performed – this time confirming the presence of traces of Seconal.

John Armstrong, the father, was known to have access to the drug in the course of his duties as a naval sick-bay attendant, but as he denied ever having had Seconal in the house, and as there was no proof to the contrary, the inquest on Terence Armstrong's death returned an open verdict.

It remained open for a year, during which marital strife between Armstrong and his wife Janet became so intolerable that in July 1956 she applied for, and was granted, a legal separation on grounds of cruelty. Then Mrs Armstrong had quite a lot to tell the police about the tragic death of her son. Her husband *had,* according to her written statement, brought Seconal capsules home from the hospital where he worked, and after little Terence's death one afternoon when John Armstrong was alone in the house with him, she was made responsible for disposing of the remainder of the drug.

Facing charges of murder at Winchester Assize Court, John Armstrong continued to plead his innocence in the face of his wife's claim that he had killed their son. From the evidence it transpired that Terence Armstrong was the innocent victim of his parent's inability to cope with the responsibilities of family life. John and Janet Armstrong, twenty-five and nineteen years old respectively at the time of their son's death, already had one three-year-old daughter, Pamela, who had been stricken with a mysterious illness two months earlier, but had recovered in hospital. Mrs Armstrong had also given birth to a second child who died in 1954 at the age of three months, of the same strange symptoms that had brought Pamela so close to death. When his wife became pregnant with Terence, John Armstrong made it clear that he could not afford any more children, and when the child arrived it became, quite simply, an expensive nuisance. At the end of the Armstrongs' trial John was found guilty of murder and sentenced to death (though he was later reprieved). Janet Armstrong was acquitted, but in a sensational revelation one month later, admitted that she had given a Seconal capsule to Terence to help him sleep.

Chloroform *and Chloral Hydrate*
Chloral hydrate is a sedative chemically related to chloroform (see page 107); a crystalline solid which is soluble in water. An average fatal dose for an adult is about 120 grains, taken orally. Although the toxic effects are similar to those of chloroform it does not depend on the formation of chloroform in the bloodstream. Death occurs in coma between six and ten hours later from cardiac and respiratory collapse.

Post-mortem appearances: The organs will be found congested and slightly cyanosed; the brain is swollen and engorged, lungs congested, with considerable oedema, and the bronchi filled with fluid.

Chloral hydrate was once notorious as the 'knock-out drops' used by press gangs in seedy dockside bars around the world. John Thompson, the English forensic scientist who spent his life working in Africa recalled that: 'In tough bars in seaports, and elsewhere, the proprietor keeps a bottle of chloral hydrate behind the bar, and if one of his well-oiled customers becomes aggressive and looks likely to start a fight that will wreck the premises, the bartender slips a spoonful of chloral hydrate into his next drink. A few minutes later the would-be trouble-maker passes out . . . and the bar proprietor has saved himself a great deal of trouble and expense.'

Case Study

CHARLIE PARTON

The mystery began on a cold Manchester afternoon in February 1889. Close to where the grey cathedral was trying to lose itself in a drifting fog, two men stood braced against the icy wind. To their ears came the rattle of a horse carriage making its way across the damp granite streets; when it closed on them the two men saw that it was a hackney, and hailed the driver to stop. As they stepped into the cab the driver noticed that one of his passengers was quite elderly, the other young; it was the young man who shouted instructions to drive to a public house in Deansgate, and as the door of the cab slammed the driver urged his horse on.

When the carriage was reined-in outside the tavern his two passengers left the driver with instructions to wait, and they disappeared into the Lounge, letting out as they did a blast of warm air and tobacco smoke.

Huddled into the comfort of his greatcoat, head down in his collar, the cabbie must have dozed, because he was startled to find his two passengers below him on the street, the younger ordering the cab to Stretford Road.

Dusk had caught up with Manchester by now, and it was only by his shouting that the hansom driver was aware of the man on the pavement just ahead of him: 'Stop! Look!' – waving his arms now – 'Stop!'

By the time the driver had reined his horse to a stop the man needed to run to catch him up: 'The door's open, your cab door's open. I just saw somebody jump out and run off down there.'

The cabbie climbed down and looked to where the man was pointing. What was the use? Manchester seemed to have become full of people who wanted a cab but didn't want to pay. He gave a sigh and shrugged inwardly. He thanked the good citizen and turned to close his carriage door. 'Wait a minute! There were two of them, we've still got one!' He reached across the seat to where the older of his two passengers seemed to snooze in the corner.

'Sir! Better wake up, sir!'

'Go away'

'Sir, the other gentleman . . . Wake up, sir.'

'Leave me alone.' The old man still did not stir, did not even open his eyes: 'Go away and leave me alone.'

The cabbie faced his dilemma stoically, drove his carriage back to the city centre, and called a policeman. 'Better come along with me to the station, and bring him with you,' said the constable, who had in his turn been rebuffed irritably by the cab's occupant. The policeman wearily hauled himself into the cab, thankful to be out of the damp and cold. The horse had barely got into its stride when the window of the cab flew open and the agitated face of the constable shouted up: 'Better go to the hospital first, I don't like the look of this one.'

At the infirmary a doctor took charge of the situation and needed little time to pronounce the old man dead. No evidence of violence; could be heart; smells of drink.

'But he was alive a minute ago,' moaned the constable. 'I'll have to make a report out now.'

'And what about my fare?'

We don't know, but the policeman probably replied that life wasn't getting any easier for working men like them, and together they set about writing down a description of the dead man's young companion – not very tall, about five-three; brown suit, felt hat, clean-shaven. The cabbie mentioned taking the men to a public house, and this seemed to suit the constable's superior. The whole tragic episode was set down to old age, cold weather and too much to drink. The young man, they supposed, had panicked at his companion's illness and taken the easy way out – saving himself the cab fare at the same time.

But there is a legal obligation that goes back a very long time in Great Britain's legal history; when a person dies in mysterious circumstances a **Coroner** must convene an inquest, and a qualified physician must perform a post-mortem examination in order to report to that inquest. In most cases the autopsy reveals that the deceased became that way due to natural causes, misadventure or suicide. Occasionally the coroner's jury is obliged to return a verdict of murder.

In the case of the Hackney Carriage Mystery, it was likely that just such a verdict would be reached; the victim had died as a result of being poisoned with chloral hydrate. Nevertheless, before this information could be discussed by a coroner's court the inquest was deferred subject to police inquiries. The inquiries of one policeman in particular – Jerome Caminada, a plain-clothes detective with the Manchester force, a native Mancunian who knew the streets and the inhabitants of his city like the back of his own hand.

It took Caminada no time at all to deduce the reason why on arrival at the infirmary the dead man's pockets were empty; it took no longer to deduce why the address in Stretford Road given by the young man was a red herring to get the cab moving somewhere, anywhere. And the motive explained why the young man should have made a hasty departure after poisoning his companion in the back of the hackney carriage.

What puzzled Jerome Caminada was why the wealthy senior partner of a long-established Lancashire paper manufacturer, county councillor and Justice of the Peace should be sharing a cab with a man likely to kill him for the contents of his wallet and a gold watch. It was no less mysterious when Caminada discovered that the victim had left his home outside Manchester on the morning of his death with the intention of travelling to Knutsford, where he was to spend the following few days. He took a business lunch in town, and arranged to meet a long-standing friend for an early supper at 7.00 p.m. So why was he sharing a cab . . .

Perhaps it was characteristic of the guilelessness of the times, perhaps of the ingenuity of the early detective forces, but disguises were as essential to the Victorian policeman as computers are to his modern counterpart. So, beneath a stubble of beard and in a suit of soiled 'civvies', Caminada set off on a round of cheap drinking dives, gambling dens and back-street brothels; he kept the company of drunkards, thugs and whores – putting a nose in here, pulling a scrap of information out there. Information about a young man with too much money and a thick gold watch chain with seals; a flash young man who liked to ride in cabs. Then Jerome Caminada struck lucky; he found a cab-driver who remembered the showy youth, remembered taking him to a pub known to be the haunt of the seedy denizens of the fight game – pugilists, managers, touts and gamblers, the kinds of underworld hangers-on that dogged every sport where a dishonest penny could be turned. Things were beginning to fit into place; chloral hydrate – it was used by doctors as an anaesthetic, but to the criminal world it was known as 'knock-out drops', and was especially valued by the promoters of crooked fights.

In one of those flashes of inspiration that make good detectives great, a name ran through Caminada's head – Pig Jack. That was it – Pig Jack Parton. He had his publican's licence taken away after drugging customers' drinks so that his cronies could rob them when they left for home. Jack had gone into boxing – promotions; crooked promotions; and when Jack's boy looked like losing there was always a drop of something to add to his opponent's mouthwash water.

There was something else – Pig Jack Parton had a son. But when the detective went to have a word with young Charlie Parton he had the sense to take a couple of companions as tough as himself – the Partons were not celebrated for their cooperation with the forces of law and order, least of all when one of the clan was under threat of arrest. As it turned out, Pig Jack, Charlie, and the rest of the Partons had already departed their run-down back-to-back in flight from the bailiffs – to the undisguised joy of their neighbours. These neighbours, with the immediate threat of intimidation removed, had quite a lot to say to the police about the affairs of the Parton family, and especially of the family business of drugging customers; the business in which young Charlie had received his apprenticeship.

When Charlie Parton was arrested – as he had clearly anticipated he would be – there was a ready alibi on his lips – Liverpool; a coursing meeting, he could even remember the name of the street he was in. Which was silly of Charlie, because it was the street that he had been in a few days before the murder, and the chemist from whom he had stolen a jar of chloral nitrate had a good memory for faces!

The magistrate agreed with the police – Charlie Parton had a capital charge to answer. Jerome Caminada had already outlined his reconstruction of the afternoon, with Charlie smoothly talking to a rich-looking gent while pouring a few 'knock-out drops' into his glass; 'helping' the now groggy man into a cab and taking him on to a low pub where he plied the confused man with yet another loaded drink. Then back into the cab for the fatal ride, give the driver an address, anywhere far enough away to give him time to rifle the old swell's pockets. It is unlikely that Charlie Parton meant to kill, he could have just misjudged the dose; but it was more probable that the old man's bodily resistance was just too weak to withstand the drug. Intentionally or not, Charlie Parton had killed, and a determined detective was going to make sure he paid the price.

The trial was held in Liverpool's St George's Hall where extra police were needed to control the disorderly crowd. Try as he would, Charlie Parton could not get even close to a defence of mistaken identity. There were too many people who knew him; there were too many people to testify to having been mysteriously drugged while in Charlie's company and waking up a lot later and a lot poorer in some back alley.

Charlie was condemned to death, but his youth – and perhaps the frank confession that he eventually made – saved him from the ultimate retribution and he spent much of the rest of his life in Walton Gaol. Jerome Caminada retired in 1899 with a special commendation from the Manchester Watch Committee, after thirty years' successful fight against crime. Charlie Parton was one who could vouch for that.

Sulphonal Group
  Sulphonal
  Methylsulphonal
  Tetronal

Hydrocyanic Acid (Prussic acid)
  See **Cyanide** (page 129)

Metacetaldehyde (Meta, or metaldehyde)
Still readily available in two forms – one as solid blocks, or sticks, which are used as solid fuel for camping and sinular stoves; and in proprietory brands of slug killer for use in the garden. Fatal doses vary between 360 and 600 grains.

Vomiting is the first symptom (the meta itself, although not particularly enjoyable to eat, is not unpleasant), followed by restlessness, tremors of the arms and mild delirium. Tremors are succeeded by cramps and convulsions and the subject slowly becomes unconscious, slipping into coma. Death from respiratory failure is expected within three or four days.

Nitrobenzene (Oil of Mirbane)
A poisonous yellow oil favoured in the perfume trade as an inexpensive substitute for oil of bitter almond, and also used in the aniline dye industry.

Fifteen to twenty drops have occasionally proved fatal, though recovery has followed much larger doses. Nitrobenzene is a blood poison: the red cells become haemolyzed and the circulating haemo-globin is converted into methaemoglobin. The poison also paralyzes the central nervous system.

Depending on the size of dose taken, the symptoms begin with a burning sensation in the mouth and throat followed by tingling and numbness. Pallor is followed by lividity, then unconsciousness, and death from respiratory failure occurs inside two hours. With smaller doses the symptoms onset only after the passage of an hour or more; there is ataxy, vomiting, and eventual coma. The subject appears cyanozed and there are muscular twitchings and involuntary vacuation of the bladder and bowels. Death occurs in coma in up to twenty-four hours.

Post-mortem appearances: Pronounced cyanosis. The organs will smell of bitter almonds and the analyst must guard against confusing this with a symptom of poisoning by hydrocyanic acid. The blood is dark and viscous and may show the spectrum of methaemoglobin. The stomach presents a bright reddish congestion with submucous haemorrhages. The urine may contain amino-bodies derived from the nitrobenzene.

Oxalic Acid (Salts of lemon, salts of sorrel)
Widely distributed in the vegetable kingdom as a solid white powder. At one time in general use in the home as a cleaning and bleaching agent, where it had contributed to the roll of accidental poisonings by its resemblance to Epsom salts. Oxalic acid is also present in the leaves of rhubarb (though not its stems) and fatalities have resulted from people boiling and eating the leaves as a vegetable. The poison has the effect of removing calcium from the blood, and ingestion of the powder is followed by stomach pains, muscle tremors, rapid respiration, convulsions, coma and death. About fifteen grains have proved a fatal dose.

Post-mortem appearances: One of the most striking post-mortem effects is the precipitation of solid calcium oxalate in the tubules of the kidneys.

Paraldehyde
Colourless liquid with a burning taste and unpleasant smell; similar in effect to chloral hydrate (see above). It is possible, despite its odour and taste, to become addicted to paraldehyde as it induces feelings of euphoria. It also damages the digestive system resulting in emaciation.

Continued use will cause mental degeneration, memory loss, hallucination and delusion. Although toxicity is low, and several fluid ounces are needed to cause death, this is by no means an unknown quantity for addicts to take over the course of a day.

Lysol and Phenol

Lysol, widely used as a disinfectant, contains about fifty per cent cresol, a violently corrosive substance which if swallowed – even in dilution – can cause extensive damage from the mouth to the stomach, depression of the central nervous system, damage to the liver and kidneys and death from respiratory failure or cardiac paralysis. In the case of pure cresol as little as 14 grams can prove fatal.

Roche Lynch records an extraordinary case of accidental poisoning in which a man carrying a bottle of Lysol in his hip pocket fell asleep and the bottle broke. The skin of one leg was soaked from hip to heel with Lysol, from which he died forty-five minutes later.

Phenol (carbolic acid) is a colourless crystalline deliquescent solid which in corrosive effect resembles cresol, and like it is used as a disinfectant when in dilution with water.

4. ALKALOIDS

Aconitine (see page 17)

Belladonna (extracts)

Atropine: An odourless powder, sharp to the taste, atropine is present in all the nightshades, and in its pure form is a poison capable of causing death with as little as one and a half grains (though still not as deadly as aconitine). Symptoms begin with a dryness of the mouth and tongue and difficulty in swallowing. The skin is flushed, developing into a rash on the upper body; headache and giddiness give way to hallucination and then to maniacal delirium. Respiration is speedy and the pulse rapid. Later, signs of paralysis appear, passing into sleep, then coma during which death occurs due to respiratory failure or collapse of the heart.

One of the most distinctive appearances of poisoning with this group of drugs is the dilation of the pupils, to such an extent that the eyes appear completely black; this led to the controlled use of atropine in ophthalmic practice. It was also fashionable at one time for ladies to use drops of atropine in order to make their eyes 'larger' and more alluring, leading to the drug's popular name, 'eye-bright'.

Atropine can be absorbed through the skin, particularly where it is thin, and through the mucous membranes, causing it to be the stock in trade (or stock in cauldron) of witches, whose hallucinatory flights were the result of using atropine ointments massaged into their vaginas.

Hyoscyamine: A drug similar in effect to atropine and hyoscine, derived from the plants henbane and thorn-apple.

Hyoscine (see page 295)

Cocaine

A powerful stimulant to the nervous system, much favoured by drug addicts. An overdose, which could be about one gram, will overstimulate the heart to the extent that the subject dies. Cocaine is not a substance that occurs with any frequency in homicidal poisoning cases, and a fuller discussion will be found in the entry on **Drugs**.

Colchicine

Pale yellow crystals extracted from the meadow saffron (*Colchicum autumnale*) and bitter to the taste. About one-third of a grain is lethal, though deaths have occurred from as little as one-tenth of a grain. Symptoms do not onset for several hours, and then a burning sensation in the throat is accompanied by vomiting, stomach pains, diarrhoea and bladder spasms. Death results from paralysis of the respiratory system in between seven and thirty-six hours.

Coniine

An oily liquid similar to nicotine extracted from the poison hemlock *Conium maculatum*, which is best known as the means of judicial execution of the Greek philosopher Socrates. The effects of the drug, so eloquently described by Plato, are not painful; the body becomes increasingly numb until the lungs fail or the heart is paralysed. There are no post-mortem signs save those found in cases of **Asphyxia**.

Gelsemium

An alkaloid rarely encountered in homicide (or indeed suicide). The symptoms are muscular weakness accompanied by slow pulse, and dilated pupils, and death occurs from respiratory failure.

Opium *and Morphine* (see page 350)

Nicotine

Occurs in tobacco in a liquid state and is the only alkaloid apart from coniine (whose effects it shares) which is not solid at normal temperatures.

Pure nicotine is a pale yellowish oil, but it discolours dark brown in light. Although it is present in minute quantities in cigarettes, it is from the horticultural preparations in which nicotine acts as an insecticide that most poisoning results. Accidental poisoning can take place when insecticides are used as a spray, or suicide when drunk. Less than one grain can induce a fatal paralysis of the respiratory system, and in addition nicotine can be absorbed through the skin.

Large doses produce a burning sensation in the mouth, down through the oesophagus and in the stomach. Vomiting and diarrhoea follow, then mental confusion and giddiness. If the subject is not yet dead, muscular twitching becomes spasmic, and convulsions will be succeeded by unconsciousness and death. According to Roche Lynch death can occur within a few minutes, and only hydrocyanic acid (see above) acts more rapidly.

Case Study

HIPPOLYTE DE BOCARMÉ

An early, and rare, case of murder by nicotine poisoning took place in France in the middle of the nineteenth century.

As a child Hippolyte de Bocarmé was troublesome and undisciplined, and as an adult developed into a crook and a womanizer. In 1843 he succeeded to his father's title and took possession of the family château at Tournai – his behaviour was about to get a lot worse.

As like tends to attract like, the Comte de Bocarmé made a self-seeking marriage to Lydie Fougnies in the belief that her father, a grocer of Mons, was wealthy. She had no less fond hopes of a substantial inheritance, and it came as a bitter disappointment to the greedy couple to discover that at the time he died the old man was rather poorly off; to add to their grief, the little that remained had been left to Lydie's brother Gustave.

Acting on the principle that anything is better than nothing, the Count and Countess invited Gustave to the château, where he was later found sprawled dead upon the floor by a servant. Despite de Bocarmé's insistence that his brother-in-law had died of apoplexy the police suspected poisoning, and acting on information given by the servant (who had obviously been taking lessons in treachery from his master) they found the Count's laboratory where he was accustomed to experiment with perfumes and grow exotic plants; it was also where he kept a bottle of pure nicotine, and the apparatus with which it had been distilled. An internal examination of Gustave Fougnies' body revealed a lethal quantity of nicotine.

The Count and Countess de Bocarmé stood trial at the Palace of Justice at Mons in May 1851 – each indignantly blaming the other for poisoning poor Gustave. In the end it was the Count who lost his head to the guillotine – grumbling the while that he hoped the blade was sharp enough – and Countess Lydie was acquitted.

Physostigmine (Ersine)

Extracted by some tribes from the calabar bean and used in ceremonies as an 'ordeal' poison. The effects of ingestion are mental excitement and hallucination; an overdose of the drug causes vomiting, epigastric pains, and in severe cases interferes with the function of the heart causing death.

Strychnine *and Brucine* (see page 477)

5. CANTHARIDIN

The so-called Spanish fly *(Cantharis vesicatoria)* which from time immemorial has enjoyed a completely undeserved reputation as an aphrodisiac. The poison is a powerful irritant derived from the crushed bodies of the insects which, when applied to the skin, sets up local inflammation accompanied by small blisters which later spread into one large blister.

Taken orally as little as one-third of a grain will result in serious kidney damage. Greater amounts will cause pain in the mouth and leave a trail of inflammation down through the oesophagus to the stomach. Vomit, faeces and urine will all contain blood, and headache, delirium, convulsions and finally coma lead to death.

Case Study

ARTHUR FORD'S FANTASY

As befits cantharidin's rather exotic nature, homicides featuring it are few and far between. One of the most sensational took place in England in 1954, and involved a forty-four-year-old wholesale chemist's manager named Arthur Kendrick Ford.

Arthur Ford, a married man, had conceived a romantic desire for two of the young women who worked for him – twenty-seven-year-old Betty Grant and seventeen-year-old June Malins. While serving in the army Ford had heard of the legendary aphrodisiac properties of Spanish fly; his downfall was learning that its proper name was cantharidin and that stocks of it were kept at the very place where he worked.

Not that it was as easy as that. Cantharidin is a scheduled poison, and Ford was obliged to apply to the firm's senior chemist, Richard Lushington, if he hoped to get hold of any. His reason, preposterous as it might sound, was that his neighbour was hoping to breed rabbits and thought that a little Spanish fly might jolly along the mating process. Whatever Mr Lushington thought of Ford's contribution to his neighbour's enterprise, he did not hand over the drug; Arthur Ford had to return later to steal it.

On 26 April 1954, Ford purchased a bag of coconut ice, a sugary pink and white confection into which he pressed a tiny amount of cantharidin; he then gave a piece each to the Misses Grant and Malis, and popped a morsel into his own mouth. Within hours all three were being rushed to nearby University College Hospital. It was the last place Betty Grant and June Malis ever saw – the drug had literally burned their insides out. Arthur Ford just survived. When post-mortems on the two women revealed cantharidin, there was nothing else for Ford to do but confess and make his not very adequate apologies: 'I have been an awful fool,' he is reported as saying. A lethal fool, Arthur Ford went on trial at the Old Bailey later that year, where he was convicted of manslaughter and sentenced to five years' imprisonment.

6. INORGANIC AND METALLIC POISONS

Antimony (see page 35)

Arsenic (see page 40)

Barium

One of the heavy metal poisons which can be lethal in all its soluble compounds. The salts are classed as:

1. Those soluble in water, for example barium chloride, all of which are acute irritant poisons.
2. Those soluble in body fluids, such as barium carbonate, which is also an irritant poison and used in rat bait.
3. Those that are insoluble, for example barium sulphate, which is harmless and used in the 'barium meal' given before X-ray of the digestive system.

Of the other barium salts, the sulphide is used externally as a depilatory, the nitrate produces the green flames in fireworks, the carbonate is used in dyeing, and the chromate as a pigment. A fatal dose can be regarded as between 70–100 grains, but as with all the irritant poisons the early symptom of vomiting is responsible for getting rid of some of the dose. Vomiting is accompanied by severe stomach pain and vacuation of the bowel – faeces will contain blood. Barium particularly affects the muscle tissue causing contractions. Heart-beat is increased and the blood-pressure rises, resulting in severe cases in the organ stopping. The poison also attacks the central nervous system and death might result from coma and paralysis.

Post-mortem appearances: Characteristic of the irritant poisons there is heavy inflammation of the pharynx, oesophagus, stomach and rectum. The viscera are congested and exhibit parenchymatous degeneration.

Lead

Extremely dangerous metallic poison usually encountered in the form of one of its salts – notably lead acetate (sugar of lead). Fatal doses can vary between ten grains and half an ounce, and the symptoms are stomach pains with vomiting and diarrhoea, followed by coma and death.

Recent research has shown that very small amounts of lead taken into the body can cause mental deterioration, and considerable concern has been expressed over the mental health of young children exposed to the high levels of lead released into the atmosphere from petrol fumes. One former hazard – lead water pipes – has been all but eradicated through the widespread use of alternative materials.

Mercury

A liquid metal whose soluble compounds are extremely dangerous. The numerous salts of mercury find wide application in medicine, horticulture, paint manufacture, and wood preservatives, and the metal is used in a variety of scientific instruments, most commonly thermometers. The clinical symptoms, fatal periods and post-mortem appearances differ so greatly according to individual salts and size of dose that space restricts any lengthy discussion here; one example is mercuric chloride, a corrosive sublimate, of which about 15 grains will cause severe burning and swelling of the mouth, damage to the stomach and heart failure. It should be noted that the vapour of metallic mercury is also highly toxic.

Phosphorus (Yellow)

Rarely encountered these days outside the chemistry laboratory, since the use of yellow phosphorus in the manufacture of matches and in rat poison has been prohibited. Acute poisoning has been caused by as little as one grain, resulting in damage to the liver, convulsions, delirium and coma. One of the characteristics of chronic cases – common among industrial workers with phosphorus – was 'phossy jaw', a condition of necrosis of the upper and lower jaw causing the teeth to fall out.

In July 1991 the Perth, Australia, newspapers carried the story that two hospitals and a number of streets were evacuated when lethal fumes leaked from a body being carried between the buildings. The corpse was that of a man who had committed suicide by ingesting phosphorus insecticide which had reacted with his body fluids to create a poisonous gas. Fire officials in protective clothing and masks neutralized the gas, while the ambulancemen transporting the body were given emergency oxygen treatment.

Case Study

LOUISA MAY MERRIFIELD

The end came on 14 April 1953; Sarah Ricketts died at 3.15 a.m. in her home at Devonshire Road, Blackpool. Her sole companion in her last hours was Mrs Louisa Merrifield, housekeeper.

It had begun with a knock on the front door just a few weeks earlier, on 12 March. When seventy-nine-year-old Mrs Ricketts, a widow for many years, opened the door, she was confronted by a stoutish, bespectacled woman of forty-six; matronly was probably the word one would have used – at least until getting to know her.

She announced that she was Mrs Merrifield and had come in answer to an advertisement in the local newspaper for a housekeeper. What Mrs Ricketts did not know when she engaged Louisa Merrifield was that she had been similarly employed no fewer than twenty times in the previous three years, had collected an impressive criminal record and served a term of imprisonment for various dishonesties connected with ration-books. Nor did Mrs Ricketts know of the existence of Louisa's elderly and somewhat senile husband; it was only after the arrangements had been made that Mrs Merrifield mentioned seventy-one-year-old Alfred as an obligatory extra. Still they must have given some satisfaction, for despite a modicum of grumbling that she was not given enough to eat, Mrs Ricketts was pleased enough with the service to make the Merrifields sole beneficiaries of her will. And then she died.

The police were soon swarming all over the bungalow looking for clues to support their suspicion that the old lady had been murdered. For her part, Mrs Merrifield engaged the local Salvation Army band to stand outside the house and play *Abide With Me* while they were searching. It may have been this eccentricity that prompted officers to take a peek into Louisa Merrifield's handbag; it was here they found a teaspoon bearing traces of the unlikely combination of rum and phosphorus. Which by coincidence was what Mrs Ricketts had died from. Before long a chemist in town recalled selling old Alfred Merrifield a tin of phosporus-based rat poison.

Things looked black indeed for the Merrifields as they stood in the dock at Manchester jointly charged with the murder of Mrs Sarah Ricketts. Evidence proved that although the victim had collapsed in the early hours of the morning, it was not until eleven hours later that a doctor was called. 'It was not such a nice time in the morning to go out on the streets and call a doctor,' Mrs Merrifield explained. She was guilty, of course; guilty of inflicting an excruciating death on an elderly woman whose last act had been to bequeath her a bungalow worth £3,000. Mrs Merrifield had already admitted as much. She had told friends: 'We went living with an old lady and she died and left me a bungalow.' Who was the old lady, they asked, and when did she die? 'Oh she's not dead yet,' Louisa replied, 'but she soon will be.'

Louisa Merrifield was hanged on 18 September 1953, at Strangeways jail. Her husband, who throughout the trial had seemed to be in a world of his own, was an enigma. The first jury were undecided on a verdict, and before a retrial could be arranged everybody had lost interest and the case against Alfred was dropped. He lived out the rest of his life supported jointly by his share of Mrs Ricketts' will and occasional appearances as a side-show attraction on Blackpool sea-front.

Thallium (see page 491)

7. **FUNGI** (POISONOUS) (see page 263)

8. POWDERED GLASS

It was something of an eccentricity for Roche Lynch to include powdered glass on his list of poisons, and he admits as much: 'It is not a poison. Its action is purely mechanical, and therefore it might properly be described as wounding. Occasionally cases are recorded in England in which an attempt, generally unsuccessful, to cause grievous bodily harm or to kill is made by the incorporation of fragments of glass in food.'

In fact, it would be fair to say that this myth, apparently created by historical fiction, is an impossibility; indeed one toxicologist suggests that finely powdered glass *can* be eaten 'by the spoonful' without ill effect, and a doctor named Johns, writing in the *Lancet* in 1825, recommended that two spoonfuls *should* be given to children as a cure for worms.

To be of any use as a tool of murder, glass must retain its integrity of *sharp edges,* like a thousand small blades to cut the lining of the stomach and intestines. But it is next to impossible to disguise fragments of such a size as to be effective.

In a letter to her lover and co-conspirator Frederick Bywaters, Edith Thompson wrote of an attempt on her husband's life: 'I'm going to try the glass again occasionally – when it is safe. I've got an electric light globe this time.' Three weeks later, in another letter, Edith was obliged to report: 'I used the light bulb three times but the third time he found a piece – so I've given up . . .'

In fact, the present author has also given up – given up trying to find a single authenticated case of powdered glass being fatal.

POLICE ARTISTS

There is a long tradition of using the talents of artists within the police force, and it should be remembered that until the introduction of **Identikit** in the 1960s, followed by its more sophisticated descendants **Photo-FIT** and Video-Fit, the skill of the artist was relied on to piece together the portrait of a suspect from witness descriptions. Even today there is a place for police artists in the same role, because no mechanical kit system can ever recapture a witness's *feeling* about a suspect – they can get the right shape of eyes, of noses, of mouths, but they can never show *expression,* never give any indication of the way the suspect *used* his features. An outstanding example of the way in which a victim and a police artist can work together was the remarkably animated portrait of the man described by Stephanie Slater as having kidnapped her in February 1992.

Police artists are also accustomed to alter and embellish photo-fit likeness to add small personal details such as moles and scars, or to give extra refinement to features. In the case of unidentified victims, an artist may be asked to produce a composite picture based on mortuary photographs and the clothing found on the body, a technique particularly favoured when the victim's face has become disfigured and it is important for likenesses to be shown to members of the public during police inquiries.

More mundane tasks entrusted to the police artist are recording the scene of crime and preparing the subsequent annotated scale plans of the scene for possible use by counsel during a trial. There have even been cases in the recent past of policemen with a talent for carpentry being commandeered to construct three-dimensional models of crime scenes for court use.

Larger than Life

Some police artists become celebrities in their own right, such as the American Ector Garcia working with the Los Angeles Police

Department. Garcia graduated from Woodbury College with a degree in commercial art and an ambition to become a cartoonist with a film animation studio; he eventually settled for the marginally more attractive salary as editorial cartoonist on the Seattle *Post-Intelligencer*. Later, Ector Garcia took himself to southern California where, in 1951, he applied to join the police force. Soon Garcia was happily combining the duties of street patrol with occasional help of a more artistic kind drawing stolen cars and criminal suspects for circulation to other patrolmen. It was while they were on assignment with the homicide division in 1959 that Ector Garcia and his partner Detective Jose Costellanos were ambushed in an attack that left Garcia blind in one eye. Disabled from street duties he put down the gun and took up the pencil against crime as a full-time police artist; he became, in the words of his biographer, 'the Michelangelo of Murder, the Dali of Death'.

Among the major crimes in which Ector Garcia exercised his special talents were the Tate-LaBianca multiple murders committed by Charles Manson and his followers. Garcia was called to the Polanski residence at Cielo Drive where the film director's actress wife Sharon Tate and four friends had been savagely killed on 9 August 1969; it was Garcia's grisly task to record the **Scene of Crime**. Later the artist was assigned to speak with members of one of the victims' family to try to get enough information on which to compile composite drawings of some mysterious unidentified acquaintances of Voytek Frykowski who may have been implicated in the murders.

Ector Garcia had always entertained a low opinion of the Identikit system, once boasting to a colleague: 'Who needs some fancy kit? I bet I can call the victim [on the telephone] and draw a better composite than you can piece together with your kit.' It is recorded that when both the Identikit and Garcia's portrait were placed next to the suspect the artist was indeed closer to the original.

POLICE COMPUTERS
H.O.L.M.E.S.

The frightening picture that the word 'computer' once projected has long since been demystified, and since the 1980s microcomputers have become familiar features of home, school and office. The computers' powers may seem limitless, but they still cannot achieve anything which a human brain cannot (at least, not yet); what they can do is work at astronomical speeds, manipulating information at previously undreamed-of rates.

Despite their long-time commitment to the use of new technology, it comes as some surprise to learn that it was not until comparatively recently that the British Home Office provided regional police forces with a computer system to carry out the vital police task of storing and cross-referencing the tens of thousands of pieces of information accumulated during a major investigation, and transferring it to the Police National Computer for access by other regional forces.

A case that dramatically illustrated the need for a computer facility was the five-year hunt for the Yorkshire Ripper. There were, throughout the inquiry, the links in a chain of evidence that should have identified Peter Sutcliffe as the main suspect – one officer who interviewed him said as much – but they were all overlooked in the increasing morass of paperwork. In fact, Sutcliffe was interviewed on nine separate occasions, and was only taken into custody by chance when two officers on patrol saw him acting suspiciously. Had all the information gathered during the investigation into the Ripper been accumulated on a computer it would at the very least have highlighted the numerous points at which Sutcliffe's name appeared in relation to the inquiry.

In 1987 the Home Office responded to the demand by announcing what it chose to call, despite the tautology, H.O.L.M.E.S. (Home Office Large Major Enquiry System); the 'twenty-first century detective' was designed to make use of the existing Police National Computer. By 1988 considerable progress had been made, and the facilities of H.O.L.M.E.S. were available to regional forces throughout the country. Its basic function is to allow an investigating team to enter information such as statements and interviews, building up a huge index which can be instantly cross-referenced and relevant material retrieved. If, say, the computer were to be asked to locate all witness mentions of a suspect who walked with a limp and drove a blue delivery van, up on the screen would come the information. The computer has a capacity of one gigabyte (about 100 million words). In one inquiry alone (by the West Yorkshire police into the murders of three children between 1982 and 1986) it was anticipated that H.O.L.M.E.S. would be fed 42,656 statements, a nominal index of 105,000 names, almost as many addresses, 15,000 telephone numbers and a range of specialized information categories and description indexes.

In the United States the Federal Bureau of Investigation had already been using a similar system – it too had a silly name, it was called Big Floyd. The programming of the American machine began by conducting lengthy interviews with experienced investigators in both the police and

Justice Department in order to assemble a sequence of questions which would normally be asked in a major inquiry. This information was then translated into computer language – in other words, the machine would be asked to draw conclusions from the information available; it can, for example, highlight the most likely from among a list of suspects. Of course, a team of police officers could also do this by sifting through the same huge amount of data – the difference is that Big Floyd can do it in seconds. One senior FBI agent was reported as claiming: 'If you saw it operate you would think it was a human being doing it . . . Before, it was a time consuming job to make inquiries before putting a case together, now Big Floyd checks all the basic data for the agent and analyses the results immediately.'

PNC2

The second generation Home Office Police National Computer (called sensibly PNC2) was installed at Hendon in north-west London in December 1991. It will give police forces nationally twenty-four-hour access to information such as fingerprint records, stolen vehicles, vehicle registrations and disqualified drivers. It will also, it is claimed, bleep a warning signal when some important piece of information attaches to a name – for example, that the person is known to be HIV positive. PNC2 has double the processing capacity and nearly five times the memory of its predecessor, and is capable of responding to each of its anticipated 125,000 queries a day in about three seconds. There is spare capacity for a computer base for the planned NCIS (National Criminal Intelligence Service) – a British equivalent of the FBI, and a project to computerize all criminal records and make them instantly available to courts of law.

However, the debate continues apace between the civil liberties group Liberty who, understandably, are concerned about the degree of accuracy of information stored on such a wide-ranging system and the uses to which it will be put, and the police who, though they seem to appreciate some of the public's misgivings, are equally understandably reluctant to compromise a system which offers the potential of huge advances in rates of detection in the face of huge rises in national crime figures.

The burgeoning of the Internet over the 1990's brought advances and setbacks to the field of forensic computing. More efficient police computers can now share detailed information worldwide, greatly enhancing multinational police operations – for example, in cracking down on paedophiles that travel abroad to find victims.

On the other hand, the crime of hacking (that is electronically breaking into private computers to steal information or alter official records) is becoming ever more advanced. At the same time, computer viruses (covert autonomous programs designed to invade computers via the internet and damage their software) have ceased to be a minor annoyance created by a few cyber-vandals, and now do billions of dollars worth of damage worldwide every year – indeed, many now count virus-creation as a form of international terrorism.

As of this writing (September 2003) there has been no reported incident of serious damage being done to a police national computer either by hackers or a virus, but it seems increasingly likely that this might happen sometime in the future.

NOTE: Although in Britain H.O.L.M.E.S. was not operational until the late 1980s, the lessons of the Yorkshire Ripper case were well learned much earlier. In 1985, the police of four forces collaborated successfully on compiling a computer-based information bank during the hunt for the rapist and serial killer John Duffy. (See **Psychological Profiling** Case Study.)

POLICE SURGEONS

Of the two medico-legal professionals who are likely to be called upon to assist in police work the first on the scene of any major incident is usually the police surgeon; the forensic **Pathologist** is called out only when it is apparent that murder has been committed, and from that point he is in sole medical charge, through post-mortem to a possible appearance in court to present the medical evidence. However, in cases of sexual assault it is customarily the police surgeon who persists with the case.

The job of police surgeon is almost as old as the force itself, and at one time it was his sole responsibility to cater for the medical needs of the policeman and his family. This aspect of the work has now been largely absorbed by the local general practitioner. At the same time police surgeons themselves are nearly always GPs with a local practice who have received supplementary training in order to assist the police with a number of important medical functions.

Alcohol Abuse

The police surgeon will always be called to a police station in cases where alcohol abuse is thought to have resulted in a crime. Most frequently it will be a matter of drink/driving, and it is the police surgeon's responsibility to attend to the taking of blood or urine samples after the patrolman has confirmed excessive blood/alcohol by giving a breathalyser test at the roadside. The police surgeon will also make observations when persons thought to be inebriated are taken into custody on other charges. This is important, for what may look like drunkenness to the untrained beat officer may in reality be the symptoms of some illness or disease. (For fuller explanations of these duties see entry on **Alcohol**.)

Sexual Assault

In cases where women (or more rarely men) complain of having been raped or sexually assaulted the first important step is to ascertain whether an offence has actually been committed (there is a surprisingly high number of fraudulent accusations dealt with by police, usually from younger girls acting out of spite or fantasy). The police surgeon, preferably a woman if the victim is female, has received special training in dealing with sensitive cases of sexual assault, and there is a strict procedure for the examination of the victim – indeed the process has been formalized to the extent that specially prepared 'rape kits' are available containing the sterilized swabs, etc. that will be required by the laboratory for subsequent analysis.

Death and Injury

The police surgeon will be routinely summoned to the scene of an apparently suspicious or violent death. His main function will be to ascertain that the victim *is* dead, and if he is not then his priority becomes the administration of medical help until an ambulance arrives. It is always impressed upon the police surgeon that he must not disturb the body more than is absolutely necessary before the scene-of-crime photographs have been taken and the pathologist has seen the body; in effect, the police surgeon's duty ends with the pronouncement of death. Other occasions on which the skills of the police surgeon may be needed are the now frequent brawls and violent incidents that arise in places of public entertainment, and it must sometimes seem a thankless task examining and patching up a cell-full of drunks with assorted cuts and abrasions, bumps and bruises.

Training

The following programme shows how much additional training a qualified doctor is required to undertake before he or she is appointed as a police surgeon.

Stage 1

Six weeks attachment to a Senior Police Surgeon; attendance in doctor's own time.

Stage 2

Completion of basic training requirement within twelve months of appointment; attendance in doctor's own time:

Basic Training Requirement

a. Visit to Force Headquarters to meet principal officers; explanation of administration and tour of departments and Control Room.
b. Visit to Forensice Science Laboratory.
c. Visit to Scenes-of-Crime Department for demonstration of technique and discussion.
d. Visit to Crown Court, Magistrates Court and discussion with Crown Prosecution Service regarding legal matters and evidence.
e. Attachment to Coroner's Department for attendance at inquest and discussion with coroner. Attendance at Post-Mortem.
f. Based on experience:
   i. Attendance at Area Review Committee (re Child Abuse); and
   ii. Attendance at Case Conference held in respect of Child Abuse; and
   iii. Meeting with NSPCC Child Protection Scheme.
g. Visit to Drug Squad.
h. Attendance on police courses to receive the following presentations:

CID Junior Initial Course:

   i. The work of the Police Surgeon (Injuries or Death);
   ii. Pathology;
   iii. Forensic Odontology;
   iv. Forensic Science;
   v. Child Physical Abuse;
   vi. Murder Exercise.

Sexual Offences Course:
   i.   The work of the Police Surgeon (Sexual offences);
   ii. Interviewing Child Victims;
   iii. Rape Trauma/Rape Crisis.

Stage 3
Attendance on training courses held by the Association of Police Surgeons of Great Britain. Held on six weekends over an eighteen-month period. Attendance in doctor's own time.

Stage 4
Completion of the 'Diploma in Medical Jurisprudence' within five years of appointment.

Refresher Training for Police Surgeons
Police Surgeons to undertake two days training per annum; one day in-house and one day external. Attendance in doctor's own time.
In-house Training: Contents of the seminar will be decided on by the police surgeons themselves, based on current priorities and perceived needs.
External Training: Each year police surgeons will be expected to attend a course held by the medico-legal profession. There are a number of alternatives available and doctors will choose one that is appropriate to their circumstances.

POLYGRAPH

The *polygraph* or 'lie detector' enjoys a controversial history, and seems to have found lasting favour only in the world of detective fiction. As an instrument of scientific accuracy the polygraph is flawed on almost every count – not least in that it *cannot* determine whether a person is telling lies or not – only whether there has been a change in their metabolism.

Basically the instrument is a device for measuring autonomic nervous system responses in terms of blood pressure, pulse rate, respiration rate, and galvanic skin response. In theory, when a person tells a lie, fear of detection causes uncontrollable reactions in these physiological areas which the polygraph indicates with inked lines on a moving paper scroll.

As people's responses differ one from another, it is first necessary to calibrate an individual's response to 'normal' questions and to deliberate lies; this is followed by a series of 'filler' questions interspersed with 'key' questions. The responses to key questions are compared with responses to deliberate lies.

The polygraph is a cumbersome process which even its champions rate only between 73–90 per cent accurate – and only in the hands of an expert. The problem is that there are few 'experts' with sufficient training in anything but the mechanics of the polygraph, lacking the psychological and physiological knowledge essential to eliminate natural error. For example, it is impossible to secure any useful reading for a subject who is mentally disturbed – the problem is identifying the disturbance.

There is no quick, reliable method for judging the psychological origin of a positive reaction to, say, a question about a death by shooting. It is just possible that the subject himself *has* just shot somebody. He may, however, have once had a member of family or circle of friends who was shot dead, or he may have witnessed a fatal shooting – the polygraph needle does not distinguish.

This quest for the 'perfect' subject has resulted in the United States (one of the few consistent users of the polygraph) issuing the following list of individuals entirely unsuited to polygraph testing:

1. Psychopathic liars
2. Demented or abnormal persons
3. A person who is emotionally upset
4. One with a heart condition (stress could provoke a heart attack)
5. A person who has been imprisoned for a long time (they tend to be 'hardened and unresponsive')
6. Somebody who is hungry or thirsty
7. Drunks
8. Children under the 'age of reason'
9. Persons under medication or narcotics
10. Those overtired
11. People with colds, sneezing, or coughing
12. People suffering from emphysema (irregular respiration)

The Volumetric Glove

An ancestor of the polygraph which operated on not dissimilar principles was the 'volumetric glove', invented by Patrizi, a contemporary of **Lombroso** and described by him:

It consists of a large gutta percha glove, which is put on the hand and hermetically sealed at the wrist by mastic. The glove is filled with air, and the greater or smaller pressure exercised on the air by the pulsation of the blood in the veins of the hand reacts on the aerial column of an india-rubber tube, and this in its turn on Marey's tympanum (a small chamber half metal and half gutta percha). This chamber supports a lever carrying an indicator which rises and falls with the greater or slighter flow of blood in the hand. This lever registers the oscillations on a moving cylinder covered with smoked paper. If, after talking to the patient on different subjects, the examiner suddenly mentions persons, friends or relatives who interest him and cause him an amount of emotion, the curve registered on the revolving cylinder suddenly drops and rises rapidly, thus proving that he possesses natural affections. If on the other hand, when alluding to relatives and their illnesses, no corresponding movement is registered on the cylinder it may be assumed that the patient does not possess much affection.

L'Uomo Delinquente, 1876

POROSCOPY

Although this system had some early success in the hands of the celebrated Dr Emond **Locard**, the practical uses of Poroscopy are severely limited. Locard observed that along the papillary ridges there are microscopic pits – called 'pores'. Under a glass, between eight and sixteen of these pores can be counted per mm; the arrangements of pores do not change with age and are as individual as fingerprints.

The discovery was first put to practical use during the investigation of a burglary in Lyon in 1912. Fingerprints left on a jewellery box matched those of a crook named Boudet, whose prints were on record at the Laboratory of Police Techniques at Lyon. Boudet and his accomplice were arrested, though there was no shred of evidence to support the then new and mistrusted 'dactylography'. By means of photographic enlargements of a section of Boudet's fingerprint and that taken from the jewellery box, Locard demonstrated that each contained exactly 955 pores.

However, due to the microscopic nature of the pores, variable factors like quantity and consistency of ink in taken prints and inconsistencies in pressure, could clog and obliterate the true pattern, rendering any comparison unreliable. Poroscopy was awarded a single, dismissive paragraph in Frederick Cherrill's official manual of the *Finger Print System* and relegated to being an historical curiosity.

PORTRAIT PARLÉ

One of the most important and far-reaching developments of Alphonse **Bertillon**'s experiments with **Anthropometry** was the *portrait parlé,* or 'word portrait'.

With several major successes to his credit, Bertillon had turned his attention to the possibilities of the new science of photography; it was he who first improved the Sûreté's 'rogues' gallery' by recording both full-face and profile, a practice which was adopted, and remains standard, in police forces throughout the world. Using this by now vast store of facial types, Bertillon observed common characteristics of features which, used selectively, could be combined to produce a descriptive facial picture.

Lecture courses on *portrait parlé* were given to detectives at the Paris police headquarters (and subsequently at the Detective Training School in London), as described by Dr Hans **Gross** in his *System der Kriminalistik* (1893):

The theoretical course consists of lectures or classes in which the professor describes in exact and scientific terms the various characteristics of the forehead, the nose, the ear, the lips, the mouth, the chin, etc. The walls of the lecture-room are covered with numbered life-size photographs of heads, so that when the description is finished the pupils can look around and point out heads containing the characteristics described. Here, for instance, is the description of the *nose,* quoted from the 'Table of descriptive marks, as entered in the model descriptive card', which is a summary of the lectures on the *portrait parlé.*

The Nose: Depth of the root: small, medium, large.
Profile: concave, rectilinear, convex, arched, irregular, sinuous.
Base: raised, horizontal, depressed.
Height: ⎫
Projection: ⎬   small, medium, large.
Size: ⎭

Particularities: The root of the nose may be very narrow; or very large; high or low; the root may be broken. *The profile* may be in the shape of an S; it may be flat, fine or broad; or the nose may be broken; it may be curved to right or left. *The tip* may be tapering, or thick, or bi-lobar, or flat; twisted to right or left; blotched and pimpled. *The partition (septum)* may be disclosed or hidden. *The nostrils* may be stiff or mobile, recurved, dilated, pinched up.

All the features and the general contour of the head are thus examined and described in succession with perfect precision. The next lesson is on colours: the colour of the iris, the hair, beard, complexion; then morphological characteristics, first in profile, then full-face. As the professor describes a trait he draws it upon the board, and asks the students to search for it among the photographs on the walls. The eye is quickly trained, and after a course the student is able to construct a speaking likeness, or to search for a person by the aid of a speaking likeness, which he has either written on the card or fixed in his head.

Practical work also helps him. From the second month of the course a descriptive card serially numbered and drawn up in conformity with the principles of the *portrait parlé,* is prepared for every person arrested and brought daily to the office for anthropometric measurement. These cards are given to the students, and when all the criminals are assembled in the great hall, the students are ordered to go amongst them, and pick out and bring up the person or persons whose card or cards they possess. In a very few days the students can pick out their men in two or three minutes. At the end of the second month, on leaving the school, they are provided with a formidable and accurate instrument for the recognition of malefactors.

From the days of Vidocq and Bertillon police officers were trained in the construction of *portraits parlé* in France and at the Detective Training School in London. It is a tradition that was still going strong in the 1950s with the publication of a manual by Superintendent A.L. Allen of the Metropolitan Police Training School at Hendon entitled *Personal Identification*. In it Mr Allen covers all aspects of identification, placing appropriately strong emphasis on facial features and the problems of accurate recall.

POST-MORTEM PROCEDURES
Introduction

Throughout this book the terms *post-mortem examination* ('examination after death') and *autopsy* ('self-examination') have been interchanged as there is no difference in definition save that the latter was at one time more commonly associated with practice in the United States. The more accurate description *necropsy* ('examination of the dead') has been avoided simply because of its archaic associations.

The practice of examining the bodies of those who have suffered violent or inexplicable deaths is ancient. The first post-mortem examinations are said to have been conducted in the third century BC by two Alexandrian physicians named Erasistratus and Herophilus. The pair regularly dissected corpses in the course of their study of the cause of disease – though not, as far as we know, in the pursuit of murder. The analysis of murder was to come hundreds of years later; one of the most frequently quoted early examples is the Roman physician who examined the bloody corpse of Julius Caesar and declared that of his twenty-three stab wounds, only one was fatal – it had pierced the emperor's heart.

Towards the end of the first century AD the Greco-Roman physician Galen, who began his study of medicine at the age of sixteen and gained his first-hand experience of treating wounds while serving as surgeon to the gladiators at Pergamum, made great contributions to the understanding of human anatomy through dissection. Galen's influence was far reaching, and many of his treatises on anatomy and surgery remained standard works until the Middle Ages.

The *Hsi Yuan Lu* was published in China in 1248 and dealt with, among other medical subjects, the examination of murder victims in the context of pursuing and prosecuting their killers. It covered the post-mortem appearances of **Drowning**, **Strangulation**, and other untimely deaths, as well as the identification of instruments used in stabbing cases.

The remarkable illustrated book of dissections made by the Flemish anatomist Andreas Vesalius appeared in 1545 under the title *De Humani Corporis Fabrica;* shortly afterwards it is recorded that Pope Clement VI ordered autopsies on the victims of the Black Death in order to discover its cause.

There followed the work of the French surgeon Ambroise Paré, surgeon to Henry II and a specialist in the study of vital organs, the Roman Paolo Zacchia, and Fortunato Fidelis of Palermo; all three of whom wrote extensively on the effects of homicidal wounds and other matters of medico-legal significance such as criminal culpability.

The seventeenth and early eighteen century saw a new 'father of modern pathology' in the person of Padua-born Giovanni Battista Morgagni, professor of anatomy and founder of the discipline of pathological anatomy. A scrupulous recorder of post-mortems on both the diseased and the murdered, Morgagni made many notable discoveries as to the origins of disease, and was the first to describe cirrhosis of the liver.

In 1642 the first rudimentary teaching of forensic medicine began at the University of Leipzig, followed by similar courses at Prague and Vienna. The French physician Fodere published his *Traité de médecine légale* in 1796, and at about the same time in Vienna Johann Franck published a work entreating his fellow physicians to treat legal medicine as seriously as their clinical practice.

A tradition was begun in Scotland in the year 1801, when surgeon Andrew Duncan began to lecture in legal medicine at Edinburgh University, for not only was Scotland to become one of the world's great seats of medical learning, but one of the great seats of forensic medicine, with the universities of Edinburgh and Glasgow producing many of the most eminent forensic pathologists in British medical history. In 1807, Duncan's son (also Andrew) was appointed the first Professor of Forensic Medicine.

In 1813 the United States appointed as their first Professor of Medical Jurisprudence the New York surgeon/lecturer James S. Stringham. With his example, and that of his disciple T.R. Beck, forensic medicine as a subject spread to all the major American schools of medicine.

The middle of the nineteenth century witnessed the publication of two seminal books on forensic medicine compiled by Johann Ludwig Casper of Berlin. In 1850 his work on Forensic Dissection (*Gerichtliche Leichenöffnung*), and in 1856 *Praktisches Handbuch der Gerichtliche Medezin* (Practical Manual of Forensic Medicine), both of which became international standard textbooks.

There followed a worthy stream of successors to the memory of Erasistratus and Herophilus. Some of them have their separate entries in this book – Professor **Lacassagne** at Lyons, and his pupil **Locard**; in Britain, William Wallace and Bernard **Spilsbury**; Sydney **Smith**, John **Glaister**, and later the 'Three Musketeers' – Keith **Simpson**, Francis **Camps** and Donald **Teare**. The United States produced such giants of forensic medicine as Milton Helpern, Alan Moritz and Michael Baden.

Procedure for Post-Mortem

Preliminary

The body, which should still be wrapped in a plastic sheet after removal from the **Scene of Crime**, is weighed and measured. When the covering is removed attention will be paid to collecting any debris that may have become detached from the clothing – hairs, fibres, particles, etc. The plastic bags that had been put over the head and hands at the crime scene to prevent loss of any contact traces are now removed and scrutinized. Any debris will be carefully sealed in clean specimen jars or plastic bags for examination in the forensic laboratory.

Examination of the Clothed Body

This operation must be carried out systematically from the head to the feet, making certain that all 'foreign bodies' and stains are recorded, collected and stored in separate containers. Dried blood can be either lifted with a moist swab or scraped into a jar. Care must be taken to collect scrapings from beneath the victim's fingernails as they may contain clothing fibres, blood, body tissue, etc. from an attacker. Each fingernail is scraped and the debris stored separately.

A photographic record will be made throughout the post-mortem procedure – colour photographs and, in many present-day investigations, videotape. During this stage of the examination note must be made of any damage to the clothing associated with injuries bullet-holes, stab cuts, etc. These may later provide vital information on angle of wounds and relative positions of attacker and victim.

Removal of Clothing

Clothing must be removed carefully from the body and stored separately in plastic bags. Damp articles should be air dried before packing lest shrinkage alter the relationship between holes and wounds. In cases of **Strangulation** with a ligature, the position of the knot should be noted before the ligature is cut off some inches from the knot, preserving it for further investigation.

External Examination of the Body

First the presence of any matter exuded from the body during or after death should be looked for – sometimes bloodstained froth will appear around the nostrils and mouth in some cases of **Asphyxia**, particularly **Drowning**. Samples of the froth should be taken for later tests which may also reveal traces of poison.

Whether or not sexual interference is immediately apparent, vaginal and rectal swabs will be required to check for the possible presence of **Semen**. In female victims injury to the perineum may be consistent with rape, and in either sex damage to the anus will suggest anal penetration. Swabs are also needed from the mouth.

Close examination of the conjunctivae (the membranes connecting the inner eyelids to the eyeballs) is often rewarding; in cases of asphyxia they will reveal bloodspots caused by haemorrhaging, and when **Carbon Monoxide** has contributed to death colour changes will occur.

The whole surface of the body must be meticulously searched for injuries and external signs of disease. The sites of wounds and injuries are usually plotted on to a pre-printed diagram of the human body along with details and measurements. Needle marks may be found consistent with homicidal injection of poison or self-administration of drugs.

Finally, it is surprising how easy it is to forget to inspect the back of the body. Here the most obvious post-mortem sign is likely to be **Hypostasis**, though the same check for wounds and injuries must be made as for the front of the body.

Dissection of the Body
Before internal examination commences the body is washed clean of any blood and dirt, and samples taken of scalp, eyebrow, facial and pubic hairs, both plucked and cut, which are then labelled and stored separately. X-ray examination is also conveniently carried out at this stage, a procedure that has proved particularly useful when investigating suspected cases of baby battering, where evidence of healing fractures will contribute proof of repeated injury.

As each pathologist will have his own systematic procedure for postmortem dissection so he will have a favoured method of opening the body. In most cases, a simple incision is made down the middle of the body from the neck to the pubis making a detour around the navel (which consists of tough tissue, difficult to cut and even more difficult to sew up afterwards). Where strangulation is suspected it is common to make a V-shaped incision so that the front of the neck can be taken out for separate examination and the larynx removed.

Collecting Body Fluids
The collection of specimens for subsequent laboratory examination is one of the main requirements of autopsy, and although not all of the following samples may be required, it is usual to take them anyway as

part of the procedure. Care must always be taken not to contaminate samples with blood or other extraneous fluids; needless to say all equipment should be kept scrupulously clean.

Blood
Blood is the most frequently required body fluid and may be wanted for one or more tests including:

1. Detection of **Alcohol** content
2. Blood grouping
3. Detection of **Carbon Monoxide**
4. Detection of carbon dioxide
5. Detection of poisons (e.g. barbiturates)
6. Detection of glucose

At least 20ml of *clean* blood, preferably more, should be taken and stored in a sterile container; blood for alcohol determination is often kept in bottles containing sodium fluoride, which inhibits further production of alcohol as the result of breakdown of sugar and bacterial action.

Blood samples are usually taken at the start of the autopsy when the neck has been opened allowing access to the jugular veins; otherwise, any of the main veins will do. Only as a final resort should heart blood be used as a laboratory sample as it is often clotted or contaminated with blood from the liver.

Urine
Easily obtained with a ladle or pipette through an incision in the dome of the bladder and stored in a labelled sterile container. The most frequent tests on urine are:

1. Detection of alcohol
2. Detection of metallic poisons, barbiturates, opiates, amphetamines, etc.

Cerebro-Spinal Fluid
Collected by lumbar puncture before post-mortem begins. Most easily obtained with the needle of the syringe between two spines of the vertebral column with the body in a sitting-up, head-between-the-knees position. Alternatively, CSF can be taken straight from the brain with a syringe and long needle.

Stomach Contents
The exposed stomach must be slid away from the other abominal organs
and maneouvred over a large container. The wall of the stomach is
opened with scissors and the contents collected. In cases such as
suspected poisoning it is customary to detach the whole stomach and
include it in the container. Great care must be taken to avoid contamination with blood.

Intestinal Contents
It is usually the small intestine that is preserved for laboratory analysis,
tied and cut at the end of the jejunum and the ileo-caecal junction and
stored whole. In the event that the large intestine is also required (as in
some cases of suspected metallic poisoning) it too is preserved separately.

Liver
Vital organ in the determination of poisoning as it naturally stores and
concentrates the toxin. Once the pathologist has made any incision
necessary to his visual examination, the whole liver, or the greater part
of it, is put into a container for analysis. In any event the total weight of
the liver must be recorded on the label to enable a calculation of the total
amount of poison.

Vitreous Humour
The jelly-like fluid behind the lens of the eye which is particularly
resistant to post-mortem change. The sample is extracted by means of a
fine-needled syringe. For purely cosmetic purposes, an equal amount of
water is injected back behind the eye to prevent collapse. The vitreous
humour has recently come to favour as a more accurate indicator of
Time of Death than the traditional rigor mortis.

After Post-Mortem
When the autopsy has been completed, all the organs weighed and the
cadaver sewn up, the pathologist should finalize his report as soon as
possible. It is the current practice for a pathologist to make use of a
microphone suspended over the post-mortem table to record a running
commentary as he proceeds. Any necessary additions and corrections
will be made to a typed transcript and then the report, along with photographs and other documentary material relating to the autopsy, will be
forwarded to the coroner and the findings made known to the police
investigation team.

In cases of homicide, where it is possible that a year or more may elapse between post-mortem and examination and trial, the body may have to be preserved for some time intact and as fresh as possible under refrigeration.

For one thing, it may be that a defence counsel will want to commission an independent post-mortem examination with the purpose of finding conflicting evidence in favour of his client. Some of the important body parts (such as the larynx in a suspected strangulation) will be preserved in formalin for subsequent examination and possibly even used as tangible evidence in court. Specimens taken for tissue analysis will be sent to the laboratory, but returned to the pathologist who may require to demonstrate them during the course of presenting expert testimony in court.

All samples taken at the post-mortem – including microbiological specimens such as swabs – will pass into the hands of an experienced scenes-of-crime officer who will label all material and have specimens countersigned by the pathologist before ensuring that they are transported safely to the laboratory.

Post-Mortem Instruments

Although individual pathologists will have their personal preferences, there are basic requirements for the carrying out of a post-mortem examination. The following brief notes are derived from the work of Professor Bernard Knight, one of Britain's foremost forensic pathologists:

Dissecting Knife: In constant use throughout the autopsy both for incisions and the removal of organs. Modern instruments consist of a metal handle in two parts which open to receive four-inch long disposable blades.

Brain Knife: In order to make long, clean cuts through the brain a knife with a straight twelve-inch blade is used. Also employed in sectioning large organs such as the liver.

Scissors: About eight inches in length with both ends rounded, having long handles and short blades. Some pathologists like also to have a smaller pair of sharp-pointed scissors about five inches in length.

Saws: For cutting through bone; the saw must be very sharp and its teeth finely set. Although some pathologists use the hand saw for removing the skull cap, it is now common for a special electric saw with oscillating safety blades to be available.

Skull Key: Purpose-designed chisel in the shape of a 'T' allowing firm leverage when removing the skull cap.

Scalpels: Not entirely necessary for post-mortem work, except in the case of examinations of infants. Instruments with small disposable blades are currently favoured.

Forceps: A strong pair about five inches long with a serrated tip is most useful, though 'for most post-mortem operations, the fingers are better tools than forceps'.

Chisels: Used in conjunction with a metal mallet, these instruments (usually one-inch and half-an-inch wide) are used in bone work.

A Question of Identity

The post-mortem examination of human remains in the event of suspicious death follows a strict sequence developed to reveal as much information as possible as quickly as possible. The evidence of the pathologist and his staff will be vital to the investigation of the case.

Basic information such as probable cause of death and time of death will already have been estimated by the **Pathologist** or **Police Surgeon** at the scene of the crime, though speculation of this kind can only ever be provisional on post-mortem results.

Where a body has suffered extensive mutilation following death, or where putrefaction is so advanced as to render visual identification impossible, it is essential for the forensic scientists to make a positive identification of the victim, often before the investigation can properly proceed. In cases such as the murder and dismemberment by Dr Buck Ruxton of his wife and maid (see page 149), identification becomes a remarkable feat of detective work in itself.

The notes which follow on the post-mortem identification of human remains derive from the procedure developed by Professor Francis Camps, which has become, with minor regional variations, an international standard.

The Identification of Dead Bodies and Skeletal Remains

A. BASIC FACTS

a. *Sex:* Clearly the genitalia are the most reliable guide to the sex of the victim, though in cases of post-mortem decomposition, it is useful to know that the uterus is the last organ to putrefy.

If only skeletal material remains, the skull and pelvis are the most certainly indicators of sex.

More recently, a method of determining female body cells by **Serology** (nuclear chromatin) has been developed. Tests require the skill of an expert technician.

b. *Age:* A criterion fraught with problems once maturity has been reached, but below the age of about twenty-five years the development of the teeth follows a remarkably consistent pattern.

Pathological changes, such as arthritis and arterial degeneration, together with other anatomical indicators are customarily the province of the specialist.

Skulls can be useful for broadly determining age in that around the age of forty, the sutures of the skull vault begin to close at a fairly standard rate.

c. *Height:* When a corpse is intact, measurement presents little difficulty; but in cases of dismemberment, where a body or skeleton is incomplete, measurement can be calculated because of the relationship between the limbs and the total height of the body. Accurate measurement of one of the 'long bones' will give total body length with an accuracy of plus/minus one inch (25mm).

The table derives from the work of Dupertius and Hadden:

Male

Length of femur	× 2.238 + 27.200 inches (69.089cm)
Length of tibia	× 2.392 + 32.161 inches (81.688cm)

Female

Length of femur	× 2.317 + 24.178 inches (61.412cm)
Length of tibia	× 2.533 + 28.572 inches (72.572cm)

The figures are correct for dry bones (without cartilage) but measurements must be made using a special osteometric board, not a tape measure.

d. *Race:* While there is no problem identifying general racial groups in a fresh, intact body, recourse must be made to the anatomical structure of the head and face, teeth and long bones in the case of skeletal remains.

e. *Fingerprints:* (including foot and palm prints) Even where putrefaction is extensive, it has been possible to obtain a print (see **Fingerprints** – Fingerprinting the Dead).

f. *Blood Group:* Apart from the possibility of helping to identify a victim through their blood-group – or at least to eliminate those who do not share it – blood from the remains will be compared with staining on possible murder weapons and on the clothing of a suspect. (See also **Serology**.)

In November 1987 rapist Robert Mellas became the first person to be convicted as a result of so-called 'genetic finger-printing' evidence. The technique of **DNA Profiling** was discovered by Dr Alec Jeffries of Leicester University in 1984 and compares the pattern of DNA molecules found in every cell of the human body – a pattern which is different for every person.

B. TOPOGRAPHICAL FEATURES

In general, note should be taken of such topographical details as facial features – colour of eyes, shape of ears, etc.; hair and general shape of head; build of body and any deformities of limbs, etc. As identification is commonly the purpose of this minute examination, advantage must be taken of all the clues that a corpse might silently offer – such as **Tattoos** and scars.

1. *Head and Face*
   i   Eyes (shape, colour, etc.)
   ii Nose (shape – broken, etc.)
   iii Mouth and Teeth
   iv Ears
   v   Hair (colour, texture, etc.)
   vi Shape of Head
   vii Scars and other special peculiarities
2. *Trunk*
   i   General Shape
   ii Clothing (name tags, laundry marks, etc.)
   iii Tattoos, scars, other special peculiarities
   iv Circumcision
3. *Limbs*
   i   Size
   ii Occupational marks and deformities (callouses, staining, etc.)

    iii Tattoos, scars, amputations, other special peculiarities
    iv Social status based on observation of care of hands, feet, etc.

C. PATHOLOGICAL INFORMATION

This information will be revealed during post-mortem opening of the body, which may show evidence of previous surgical treatment, or current medical conditions – gall stones, cardiac disease, ulcers, etc., for which records of treatment may be matched.

1. Specific already known conditions – gall stones, ulcers, fibroids, skin disease
2. Prior surgical treatment – scars, absence of organs, etc.
3. Evidence of previous accidents – scars, mended fractures, etc.
4. Changes that may help establish age – arthritic condition, cardio-vascular disease, etc.
5. Specific pathological changes – malaria, sickle cell anaemia, etc.

D. SPECIAL PROCEDURES

1. X-ray studies of bones.
2. Special studies of tissues.
3. **Odontology**: One of the most vital aspects of forensic identification. In cases of severe mutilation, the teeth are often the *only* clue remaining to a victim's identity.
4. Photography: Special photographic techniques have been developed to aid identification of badly mutilated or decomposed bodies; notable is the process of overlaying a transparency of a known portrait of the supposed victim on a photograph of the skull that has been found. First developed in the Ruxton case, the technique was subsequently used successfully in the Dobkin case (see page 114).
5. Other procedures.

PSYCHIATRY

Forensic psychiatry is the youngest of the medico-legal disciplines, having developed over the past thirty years or so from the wider field of general clinical psychiatry. Broadly, the forensic psychiatrist deals with the several aspects of work related to the mentally abnormal offender – advising courts, lawyers, the probation and prison services, and, where appropriate, advising on treatment. One foremost consultant has described his work as 'at the interface between psychiatry (and health service facilities) and the legal (criminal and civil) system'.

In Britain, although several senior psychiatric consultants had acquired reputations for their work in criminology, this was in the main confined to Broadmoor and other special hospitals and prisons. However, by 1966 the pioneering efforts of these few specialists were rewarded by the first official appointments of Consultants in Forensic Psychiatry to coordinate efforts throughout the health regions and begin to assemble a rudimentary forensic psychiatry 'service'.

In 1971 the notorious poisoner Graham Young was released from Broadmoor, where he had been confined for nine years for poisoning his family. Within months, he had killed two of his work colleagues and made a half-dozen others severely sick with thallium poisoning. The alarm felt at the premature release of so dangerous a man who had gone on to offend again, led directly to the appointment in 1972 of the Butler Committee on Mentally Abnormal Offenders. The Committee had made wide-ranging proposals for changes in the prevailing system, including the procedures for defence pleas based on claims of insanity, diminished responsibility and competence to stand trial (less optimistic is the fact that few of these recommendations have been acted upon). However, the Butler Committee did see success in the growing support for the new discipline of forensic psychiatry, and the establishment of a Regional Secure Unit programme for the treatment of mentally abnormal offenders. There are currently around fifty fully qualified full-time forensic psychiatrists providing a service mainly to the Regional Forensic Psychiatry Service, and each of the fourteen health regions operates at least one Regional Secure Unit, which runs a graduated system of parole to reintegrate patients into the community in a safe and controlled way.

Duties of the Forensic Psychiatrist

That life is far from dull for the practising forensic psychiatrist was admirably expressed by Dr Jeremy Coid, a Consultant and Senior Lecturer in Forensic Psychiatry at St Bartholomew's Hospital Medical School:

> I would like to describe a regular daily routine, but in fact I have to remain flexible. Two ward rounds and an out-patient clinic are the only two regular weekly fixtures. One week I can be visiting a

man remanded to Brixton Prison for armed robbery to prepare a report for his solicitor, the next I might travel to Broadmoor to assess a chronic schizophrenic who killed his mother ten years ago. The following week I make a trip to Parkhurst Prison where a drug-dealer is serving a seven-year sentence and has now developed a psychotic illness, is refusing food, and needs transfer for psychiatric treatment. In between, the letters and phone calls come in for advice, and a large patient is smashing up the ward in a local mental hospital and would I take him away please? Being called to the Old Bailey at short notice to give evidence in a contested case of diminished responsibility will disrupt any vestige of routine.

Criminal Justice Matters, No. 4, Summer 1990, London

Defences to Murder

Because of the seriousness of the crime, murder has always been of special concern to psychiatrists, and in coping with the wide range of motivations to kill, a number of possible medical defences are available to the offender, each of which will need to be assessed by the forensic psychiatrists whose reports will be presented as expert evidence in court:

Diminished Responsibility (see page 145)

Insanity (see page 314)

Automatism (see page 57)

Infanticide: A special plea where a mother may claim that at the time of her child's death (the infant must be under one year old) the balance of her mind was disturbed because she had not recovered fully from the effects of giving birth or the effects of lactation. A successful plea will result in a conviction for manslaughter.

Unfit to Plead (see Competence to Stand Trial, page 111)

The assessment is usually made at the request of the court or the prosecutor and carried out at the prison hospital in which the accused is held awaiting trial. The assessment is carried out by staff of the prison medical service, though if a psychiatric disorder is suspected they may choose to summon a psychiatrist from outside the service. The defendant himself, through his solicitor, may also request a psychiatric report from an independent psychiatrist of their choice. Although they may attach different weight to the answers, psychiatrists for both the Crown and the defence will seek to answer one of a number of fundamental questions in their report to the court:

1. Is the defendant fit to plead?
2. Was the defendant mentally disordered at the time the offence was committed, to the degree that he was without responsibility within the meaning of the McNaghten Rules?
3. Was the defendant suffering from a mental abnormality at the time of the offence which would have substantially diminished his responsibility?
4. Was the defendant so disordered at the time of the offence as to be able to plead the defence of automatism?
5. Was the woman charged with the murder of her child sufficiently disturbed to be brought within the Infanticide Act?

Psychological Profiling

In addition to the forensic psychiatrist's duties in connection with offenders, his skills and insights have become increasingly valued by police officers investigating crimes and attempting to compile a 'profile' of the as-yet undetected offender. This work was pioneered in the United States by the leading American psychiatrist James Brussel, and his legacy has passed to the specialized Behavioral Science Unit of the FBI, where officers using advance **Psychological Profiling** actively collaborate with convicted killers, families, victims, and forensic psychiatrists in an attempt to combat the growing menace of serial murder.

Understanding Violence

At the basis of any criminological work – of an investigative, preventive or curative nature – is the need to understand the rudimentary motivations to violence, and it is in this field increasingly that the forensic psychiatrist is making use of his acquired knowledge and experience for the study and treatment of delinquency.

PSYCHOLOGICAL PROFILING

Although in response to the growing menace of serial murder the psychological profiling of killers has seen a recent upsurge of awareness not only among the general public, but also within the law enforcement agencies, the technique is by no means new. Indeed, it is tempting to suggest that Cesare Lombroso's concept of '**Criminal Man**' encompassed a rudimentary form of profiling. For example in his *L'Uomo Delinquente* (1876), Lombroso matches crimes with occupational temptations:

Many persons, cooks, tavern-keepers, confectioners, etc. exercise callings that have a deleterious effect on the central nervous centres and encourage an abuse of alcohol; others, like bakers, have night work, which is equally harmful. Professions which bring poor men, servants, secretaries, cashiers, etc. into close contact with wealth, are sometimes the cause of dishonesty in those who, in the absence of special temptations, would have remained upright. Others provide criminaloids with opportunities or instruments for accomplishing some crimes, as in the case of locksmiths, blacksmiths, soldiers, doctors, lawyers, etc.

But it is the American psychiatrist James A. Brussel who can truly be called the father of psychological detection, the 'Sherlock Holmes of the couch' as one reporter described him, the 'Psychiatric Seer', according to another. Brussel's simple standpoint was that any psychiatrist can study a man and make some intelligent predictions about what he may do in the future, how he would respond to certain situations. What Dr Brussel did was to reverse that process – by studying a man's responses and actions to deduce what sort of person he may be.

James Brussel has a long list of achievements resulting from this disarmingly modest technique – in 1957 he identified New York's 'Mad Bomber', George Metsky, who used **Explosives** in his one-man crusade against his former employer, the Consolidated Edison Company. Although there were no fatalities during Metsky's sixteen-year campaign of terror, the bomb placed in the Pennsylvania railroad station during rush-hour in January 1953 injured several people. Metsky was finally trapped by Brussel's brilliant profile which in part read: 'Single man between forty and fifty years old, introvert. Unsocial but not anti-social. Skilled mechanic. Cunning. Neat with tools. Egotistical of mechanical skill. Contemptuous of other people. Resentful of criticism of his work but probably conceals resentment. Moral. Honest. Not interested in women. High school graduate. Expert in civil or military ordnance. Religious. Might flare up violently at work when criticized. Possible motive: discharge or reprimand. Feels superior to critics. Resentment keeps growing. Present or former Consolidated Edison worker. Probably case of progressive paranoia.

In 1964 Dr Brussel was equally precise in his description of Albert de Salvo, 'The Boston Strangler', who sexually assaulted and killed eleven women during 1962–3. Among his predictions were that the murders were all the work of the same man (contrary to the official view that there were two stranglers), and that he was around thirty years of age, average height but strongly built, with a head of thick dark hair but clean shaven, unmarried, and of Spanish or Italian origin. He was also, Brussel warned, a paranoid schizophrenic.

It was in the early 1970s that psychological profiling was given structure and status. Mainly as a result of the pressure imposed by a concern over the escalation of serial killings, and the virtual impossibility of applying the time-honoured techniques of traditional homicide investigation in these cases, senior instructors at the FBI's National Academy at Quantico established the Behavioral Science Unit. FBI agents began working on a system of 'psychological profiling' which would use the disciplines of the behavioural scientist, the psychologist and the psychiatrist, to help analyse evidence, both tangible and intuitive, collected by officers at the scene of the crime.

A profile is built by the careful analysis of elements such as victim traits, witness reports, method of killing, and eventually comprises a physical and psychological 'portrait' of the wanted killer and his behavioural patterns. A useful list of elements might be: age group, gender, marital status, race, occupation, criminal record, sexual preferences, etc. Clearly a considerable amount of intuitive guesswork is involved, and no law enforcement agent would dismiss suspects from his investigation simply because they did not fit the profile. However, profiling has proved increasingly accurate in narrowing the field of inquiry.

Following his work on the case of John Duffy (see Case Study below), the British professor of behavioural science and applied psychology David Canter explained: 'A criminal leaves evidence of his personality through his actions in relation to a crime. Any person's behaviour exhibits characteristics unique to that person, as well as patterns and consistencies which are typical of the sub-group to which he or she belongs.'

In 1985, the enterprising FBI Academy introduced an additional investigative tool under the name Violent Criminal Apprehension Programme (VI-CAP). The programme is a central information system which collects and analyses reports from all over the United States with the primary objective of revealing early serial killing patterns. One of the most constructive projects to emerge from the FBI Behavioral Science Unit has been the personality profiles compiled during 1979–83 from information contained in extensive interviews with some two dozen convicted serial killers, with contributions from their families, from doctors, psychiatrists, neurologists and social workers. The results are profiles of serial killers which may ultimately help in the apparently impossible task of identifying individuals who may be predisposed to this kind of deviant behaviour.

Although the problems of coordination and analysis of information are on a much smaller scale in Britain, the massive and frustrating investigation into the murders of 'Yorkshire Ripper' Peter Sutcliffe exposed the vulnerability of a regional police force without access to a central body of information compiled from around the country, and some means of processing it quickly and efficiently. In the wake of the Ripper inquiry, regional police forces have been offered the use of the Home Office computer system called **H.O.L.M.E.S.** (see page 396).

Although psychological profiling has clearly had its successes, and appears to be riding on the crest of a wave in the wake of such popular cinema entertainments as *The Silence of the Lambs*, it still has many detractors. Although it may save considerable manpower and resources by screening a list of suspects, it is no *substitute* for vigilant 'scientific' policing. After all, serial killer Ted Bundy was on a short-list of five suspects on two separate occasions, but despite his reasonable match with the profile, he was never contacted by the police.

Over the 1990's, psychological profiling became so highly refined and diversified that big businesses now sometimes employ profilers to help when hiring key employees – aiming to find ideal personalities rather than habitual criminals, of course. There is even a new forensic technique, *geographical profiling*, that allows an expert to map the likely home area of a serial criminal.

Taken at its most simple level, geographical profiling is based on the idea that criminals have set 'prowling areas' – rather like hunting tigers. This area will not be too close to the criminal's home district, for fear that they might be recognized by an acquaintance. On the other hand, the prowling area will only stretch as far as the criminal has easy access – indicating further clues as to his method of transport and financial situation.

By running many varying factors thrown up by a case through a computer, a geographical profiler can offer the police a reasonably precise area from which to interview suspects. The technique is still in its infancy, but initial results have been positive.

For example, police in Lafayette, Louisiana, called in geographical profiler Kim Rossmo when they failed to catch a serial rapist who had attacked at least fifteen women over eleven years. Public response had been rather too helpful and the investigators had over 2,000 tip-offs and over a thousand suspects to interview. Rossmo ran the profile program and highlighted a particular area in which the rapist was likely to live. Investigators targeted suspects in this area and soon, using traditional methods as well as DNA matching, caught the rapist: a sheriff's deputy called Randy Comeaux, who confessed and was sentenced to three life sentences.

Case Study*

JOHN FRANCIS DUFFY

Known throughout the long investigation into his three murders as 'The Railway Killer', Duffy was the first criminal in English legal history to be identified by the procedure known as psychological offender profiling (POP).

A petty criminal described variously as 'weak', 'immature', 'lazy', 'lying', 'insignificant', and 'almost invisible', John Duffy nevertheless compensated for his inadequacies by throwing a blanket of fear over the activities of young women around north London and parts of the Home Counties. And far from describing him as 'insignificant', Duffy's wife told an Old Bailey jury how he had become 'a raving madman with scary, scary eyes' (he was also nicknamed by the press 'The Man with the Laser Eyes'), who used to tie her up before sex and frequently bragged: 'Rape is a natural thing for a man to do.'

The first attack that has been linked to Duffy was a rape in 1982, during which two men attacked a twenty-three-year-old woman in Hampstead, close to the North London Link railway line. It was the first of a four-year series of rapes, in eighteen of which Duffy worked with an accomplice. In July 1985 there were three violent attacks in a single night and the police, frustrated by lack of progress, launched 'Operation Hart', which was to develop into the most comprehensive manhunt in Britain since the search for the Yorkshire Ripper, and involved officers from four forces – Scotland Yard, Surrey, Hertfordshire, and the British Transport Police.

In the following month, August, John Duffy was arrested and charged with offences involving violence, but quite unconnected with the

*Text adapted from an entry in *The Encyclopaedia of Serial Killers,* by Brian Lane and Wilfred Gregg, Headline, 1992.

'railway rapes'. Against police recommendations, Duffy was released on bail. Nevertheless due to the nature of the crimes he was routinely entered on the suspect file of Operation Hart. Shortly after his release, Duffy attacked another young woman in north London, though in her confused 'rape trauma' condition she was unable to bring herself to identify her attacker until December of the following year. By that time he had killed three times.

On 29 December 1985, John Duffy dragged nineteen-year-old secretary Alison Day off an east London train and took her to a squalid block of garages in Hackney where he garrotted her with what is known as a 'Spanish Windlass', a kind of tourniquet favoured by carpenters (the trade Duffy once followed). Seventeen days later Miss Day's body was recovered from the river Lea.

The connection was not finally made with the 'Railway Rapist' until three months later, when a fifteen-year-old schoolgirl, Maartje Tamboezer, was killed on her way to the shops in West Horsley, Surrey. Duffy had tried to remove clues by burning his victim's body, but left semen traces and a set of uncommonly small footprints (it later transpired that Duffy had always been sensitive about his diminutive five feet four inches). At this point information on the two murders was included in the computer-based files of Operation Hart, and the hunt was accelerated.

On 18 May 1986, Mrs Anne Lock, who worked for London Weekend Television, disappeared on her way home from the studios; her body was not found until July.

In the meantime, forensic scientists had been working on eliminating suspects from the Operation Hart file by matching semen samples from Maartje Tamboezer's body with blood from those on the suspect list. The register of more than 5,000 was thus reduced to 1,999 men, of whom John Dnffy was No. 1,505. Duffy was interviewed in July but refused (as was his right) to provide a blood sample, and after bribing a friend to 'mug' him, put himself voluntarily into a psychiatric hospital to recover from the trauma.

Psychological profiling was a relatively unknown factor, in Britain at least, in the arsenal of weapons being made available by the rapidly emerging science of forensic psychiatry. Increasingly concerned by their own lack of progress, the police enlisted the professional help of Professor David Canter, an expert in behavioural science and professor of applied psychology at Surrey University. Canter carefully built up a projectural profile of the 'Railway Killer' based on statistical analysis of police witness statements. From these reports, Professor Canter was able to make deductions such as that the killer lived in the Kilburn-Cricklewood area of north-west London, was married, childless (this turned out to be a particular source of anguish to Duffy), and surrounded by domestic disharmony. In all, Professor Canter's profile was to prove accurate in thirteen out of its seventeen points; he explained: 'A criminal leaves evidence of his personality through his actions in relation to a crime. Any person's behaviour exhibits characteristics unique to that person, as well as patterns and consistencies which are typical of the sub-group to which he or she belongs.'

While the police were awaiting David Canter's report, Duffy struck again. This time the victim was a fourteen-year-old girl who was blindfolded before her ordeal. During the struggle this mask slipped and she caught a glimpse of her attacker; why Duffy did not kill the girl is inexplicable on the basis of his former *modus operandi*. When the psychological profile was run alongside the computer file of Operation Hart it came up with the name that officers had been waiting years for: John Francis Duffy. After a short period of intensive surveillance, Duffy was arrested at his mother's home where scenes-of-crime officers recovered sufficient forensic clues to build a watertight case against him.

John Duffy's trial took place during the first two months of 1988. He offered a weak and unsuccessful defence of amnesia, and on 26 February Mr Justice Farquarson, who described him as 'little more than a predatory animal who behaved in a beastly, degrading and disgusting way' sentenced Duffy to seven life sentences adding the recommendation that he serve at least thirty years. His Lordship added: 'You should not depend on that being the total amount of time you will serve.'

In the case of Anne Lock, Mr Justice Farquarson had directed the jury to return a verdict of not guilty on account of insufficient evidence.

In January 2001 Duffy gave evidence against his former school friend, David Mulcahy, alleging that he had been his partner in many of the rapes and murders. Duffy's detailed evidence, together with conclusive DNA fingerprint evidence, convinced the jury and Mulcahy was found guilty of ten counts of rape and three of murder. The judge sentenced the forty-one-year-old father of four to life imprisonment.

Cynics who suggested at the time that Duffy was giving evidence against Mulcahy in order to improve his own chances of early parole got a surprise two months later. Duffy voluntarily admitted to a further seventeen rapes and was sentenced to a further twelve years in prison.

Duffy himself admits he is unsure how many women he raped, on his own and with Mulcahy, and the police investigation into the Railway Rapists remains open-ended.

PUTREFACTION (POST MORTEM)

When a human body dies, when its functions cease, the process of decomposition begins. Some cells remain chemically active and live longer than others (which makes transplants possible) but by the time *rigor mortis* departs the body (see **Time of Death**) putrefaction has begun, and its progress can be seen on the following table:

Period	Change to body	Change if immersed in water
Hours		
	Cooling of body	
0–12	1½–2°F (approx.) per hour	3°F (average) per hour
12–24	¾°F (approx.) per hour	1½–1°F (average) per hour [5–6 Hrs – body *feels* cold 8–10 Hrs – body *is* cold]
10–12	Body *feels* cold to touch	
20–24	Body *is* cold (internal and surface)	
	Lividity	
3–5	Begins to develop	Cutis anserina ('goose *flesh*') *and whitening of the skin*
	Rigor Mortis	
5–7	Begins in face, jaw and neck muscles	Variable development
7–9	Arms and trunk, then legs	
12–18	Full rigor mortis	
24–36	Rigor mortis leaves body in the same order	Rigor mortis often still present [2–4 days] Rigor disappears
Days		
	Putrefaction	
2	Green staining on flanks of abdomen	
2–3	Green and purple staining of abdomen, body begins to distend	
3–4	'Marbling' of veins; staining spreads to neck and limbs	Root of neck discolours
	Abdomen swells with gases. Skin blisters	Face and neck swollen and discoloured

Period	Change to body	Change if immersed in water
6–10		Body floats. Decomposition of trunk

Weeks		
2	Abdomen tightly distended. Organs disrupted by gases	Skin beginning to peel and hair easily pulled out
3	Vesicles burst; tissue softens; organs and cavities bursting	Face further bloated and discoloured
4	Disruption and liquefaction of soft tissues	Body greatly bloated with gases; organs crepitant; hair so loose as to be wiped from scalp; finger and toe nails easily removed

Months		
	Formation of **Adipocere** (if conditions are damp)	
4–5	Established on face and head	Develops less quickly as temperature is lower
5–6	Established on trunk	

These are the chronological processes in detail:

1. Greenish discoloration on right flank of abdomen. (Colour changes result from changes in the blood due to the action of bacteria.)
2. Staining spreads over the whole of the abdomen, and begins to appear on other parts of the body.
3. Face begins to swell and discolour.
4. Swelling and discoloration of the scrotum (in a male) or vulva (female).
5. Abdomen distended with gases. (Generally the gases arising from putrefaction are sulphuretted hydrogen, phosphoretted hydrogen, and ammonia.)
7 Skin develops blisters of various sizes which subsequently burst accompanied by the shedding of large areas of the epidermis.
8. Fluids escapes from nostrils and mouth; eyeballs liquefy.
9. Whole body discoloured; abdomen greatly distended.
10. **Insect Infestation** of body.
11. Finger and toe nails loosen and shed; hair loosens and falls away.

12. Tissue begins to soften and liquefy; face becomes unrecognizable.
13. Abdominal and thoracic cavities burst.
14. Tissues progressively dissolve.

The speed with which putrefaction is achieved will depend upon several factors.

External Factors

Presence or not of micro-organisms: If there is a free circulation of moist air around the body and a degree of warmth, bacteria will begin to develop and more rapidly decompose the surface.

Presence or not of air: As a general rule air will encourage decomposition and lack of it will retard decomposition. Thus a clothed body will decay less quickly than a naked one, and a body buried in light porous soil will decay faster than one buried in dense, heavy soil.

Temperature: Putrefaction onsets at around 50°F (10°C) and favours temperatures in the range 700 to 100°F (21°–38°C). Greater temperatures, between 100° and 212°F (38°–100°C) will retard the process due to the drying out of body fluids (which in turn may result in *preservation* by **Mummification**).

Moisture: The presence of moisture is vital to the process of putrefaction and normally the body's own fluids are sufficient. However, additional moisture, particularly in a warm atmosphere, will greatly accelerate decomposition.

Type of medium (air, earth, water): The general principle established by John Glaister (in *Medical Jurisprudence*) is that a body decomposes in air twice as quickly as it does in water, and eight times as quickly as in earth. (Some observations on body changes in water are noted in the table above.)

Internal Factors

Age: Young people decay more rapidly than old because of the relative absence of fat in the latter.

Sex: No influence unless a woman has died of childbirth (particularly from septicaemia) when putrefaction will be accelerated.

Size of body: Or more correctly, bodily condition – the relatively greater fluid and fat content hastening decomposition in overweight people.

Nature of death: People who die suddenly while in good health putrefy less rapidly than people suffering from a disease, particularly an infective disease. Where large areas of flesh have been exposed by trauma bacterial action will hasten decay. However, certain poisons such as **Arsenic**, **Antimony** and Zinc Chloride tend to preserve the body tissues and attack the organisms of putrefaction.

Q

QUICKLIME

The legendary properties of quicklime as an agent for disposing of unwanted human remains (whether the debris of assassin or hangman) owe more to popular fiction than to biological reality. Who has not felt the shudder provoked by Oscar Wilde's chilling description of the fate of the recently executed corpse of Trooper Charles Wooldrige as it lies in its coffin packed with quicklime:

> And all the while the burning lime
>   Eats flesh and bone away,
> It eats the brittle bone by night,
>   And the soft flesh by day,
> It eats the flesh and bones by turns
>   But it eats the heart alway.*

In the majority of cases, quite the contrary effect is achieved.

For all practical purposes, there are three states in which lime (CaO) is commonly encountered:

1. *Quicklime:* Produced by strongly heating limestone to form calcium oxide; it has the appearance of irregular white lumps.
2. *Slaked lime:* Calcium hydroxide, a dry white powder produced by adding water to quicklime.
3. *Chlorinated lime:* Product of the action of chlorine gas on slaked lime; at one time widely used as a disinfectant.

*The Ballad of Reading Gaol, Oscar Wilde, 1898.

Contrary to the legend that used to recur with pathetic regularity in tales of murder, the truth is that when a body is buried in quicklime which is then slaked with water, only a small degree of superficial 'burning' will result, and the intense heat generated by the chemical reaction will simply dry out, or 'mummify', a certain amount of the body tissue. When slaking occurs gradually by absorbing the body's own water or water from the soil in which it is buried, there will again be partial desiccation of the tissues. In both these instances the effect will be to retard putrefaction and *preserve* the body against external decomposing agents. In the case of chlorinated lime, the effect is much the same, though it has been used more often for its disinfectant properties, serving to mask effectively the stench of decomposing flesh. When Henry Wainright shot an 'inconvenient' mistress in London in 1874, he interred her remains packed in a half-hundredweight of chlorinated lime in his Whitechapel workshop. So well did the lime preserve poor Harriet Lane's corpse that one year later the physicians were able to prove her identity by a triumphant twelve points of similarity; twelve points that sent Wainwright to the gallows.

The first forensic scientist to investigate systematically the effects of different forms of lime on dead flesh was Alfred Lucas. Lucas obtained the results shown in the table (see page 433) using young pigeons as subjects; the birds were plucked but otherwise left intact and buried in boxes on the roof of his Cairo laboratory in the month of July.

The results, according to Lucas's report were that: 'First, the lime is a preservative; and second, that the act of slaking lime in contact with a dead body, whether this is brought about gradually or done suddenly, does not destroy the body.'

Case Study

'THE BERMONDSEY HORROR'

Maria de Roux was born in Switzerland in 1819. Her early means of livelihood was as a lady's maid, and in 1846, while travelling from England to join her mistress, Lady Blantyre, on the Continent, she first met Patrick O'Connor. O'Connor was a forty-nine-year-old Irishman, a Customs Officer in the London docks, but earning a considerable second income from money-lending. Shortly afterwards, Maria met Frederick George Manning, a railway guard on the Great Western Railway and a man of somewhat dubious reputation.

Pigeon	24 Hours	3 Days	5 Days	15 Days	6 Months
A Buried in dry earth			Disagreeable smell; maggots and beetles observed in box	Active decompositon; disagreeable smell	Considerable smell of decay; areas of flesh disappeared
B Buried in freshly slaked and sifted lime				No apparent decomposition; little smell; flesh soft	Slight smell; flesh soft but shrunken, skin pliable/unbroken
C Buried in fresh chlorinated lime		Pigeon partially uncovered due to swelling from putrefaction; objectionable smell. Lime wet and pasty.		Decomposition in progress; very objectionable smell	Considerable smell of putrefaction; still decomposing; swollen.
D Buried in quicklime (small lumps)				Lime slaked. Flesh dry and intact. No burning or rupture of skin.	Flesh in good condition; dry, hard and shrunken. Skin unbroken.
E Buried in small lumps of quicklime which was immediately slaked with water.	Lime turned to a fine white powder. Pigeon discoloured and drier and firmer; otherwise undamaged by chemical heat.			Flesh dry and firm; faint discoloration but no rupture of skin.	In good condition; flesh dry, hard, brittle and shrunken; skin unbroken.

In the following year, 1847, Maria married Manning and the couple moved to Taunton, in Somerset, to run the White Hart Inn; Maria, though, persisted in her previous close friendship with O'Connor. Manning himself was still working on the railway, but after being implicated in a £4,000 bullion theft, and arrested and then released following a mail robbery, the Mannings decided that a move to London might be advisable. They opened a beer shop in Hackney Road. Shortly afterwards Maria took it into her head to abscond with O'Connor. Manning went in hot pursuit, and he was able to effect an uneasy reconciliation.

The Mannings' next address was in Minver Place, Bermondsey, where to make ends meet, it was necessary to take in a lodger, in the person of a medical student called Massey. Manning suddenly developed a previously undeclared interest in medicine, and seemed anxious to question Massey about various matters related to that youth's intended profession. The effects of chloroform, for example, and whether a person could sign cheques under the influence of narcotics; the effects of shooting somebody with an airgun, and where the weakest point of the skull is. These were prominent among the queries which began to arouse Massey's suspicion; Massey's suspicion in its turn resulted in the unfortunate man being put out of the house. It was about this time that Manning took delivery of a crowbar and a quantity of quicklime.

O'Connor had throughout continued to be on terms of some intimacy with Mrs Manning, and on 8 August 1849, he was invited to tea; it was on the same day that Manning bought a shovel.

O'Connor was never seen alive again.

Mrs Manning had shot him through the head, and according to Manning's final confession, 'I found O'Connor moaning in the kitchen. I never liked him very much, and battered in his head with a ripping chisel.' He was then buried under the flagstones in the kitchen, well covered with the quicklime.

On the following day Maria Manning visited O'Connor's lodgings and removed a quantity of money and shares, and two gold watches. William was sent out to sell the shares, on which he raised £110. At this point Mrs Manning decided to ditch her husband and, after putting her belongings in the left-luggage at London Bridge Station, she fled to Edinburgh. Manning sat it out at Minver Place a couple more days and then he also fled; to the Channel Islands.

O'Connor's acquaintances were quick to notice his disappearance and contacted the police. An official search of the house at Minver Place revealed two newly cemented slabs in the kitchen floor; Patrick O'Connor's remains beneath them. Mrs Manning was speedily arrested in Edinburgh, but Manning was able to lay low until 21 August, when he was recognized and taken near St Helier, in Jersey.

The trial of Frederick and Maria Manning opened on 25 October 1849, before Mr Justice Cresswell, with the Attorney General prosecuting. The case aroused huge public interest, with Frederick and Maria each trying to put the blame on the other for the murder. It was all to no avail, and both were duly sentenced to death. At the end, just before the day of execution, Manning confessed; but Maria still maintained her innocence, claiming 'There is no justice and no right for a foreign subject in this country.'

Maria and Frederick Manning were executed on 13 November 1849 in front of Horsemonger Lane Gaol. A crowd of fifty thousand spectators witnessed the hanging, including Charles Dickens, who complained to *The Times* about the levity of the crowd and the barbarity of the scene.

Maria wore a black satin dress on the scaffold and it is said that this put the material out of fashion for ladies' dresses for a period of at least twenty years.

R

RADIOCARBON DATING

The non-metallic element carbon (C), together with hydrogen, occurs as a component of all organic compounds and is one of the basic requirements for life itself. For example, carbon compounds are found extensively in the earth in the form of carbonates (limestone, chalk, etc.), in the air as carbon dioxide, as cellulose in plants, and as starch and sugar in animals. Consequendy, it is the *organic* matter left by past civilizations which is suitable for dating by the radiocarbon method.

The existence of radiocarbon in living matter was first proposed by Willard Libby, Professor of Chemistry at the University of Chicago, in 1946. The following year he published a paper detailing experiments to detect radiocarbon in biological material, and by 1950 had achieved results on samples of known age and shortly afterwards measurements of specimens of unknown age. In recognition of this vital work, Libby was awarded the 1960 Nobel prize for chemistry.

Principles of Radiocarbon Dating

Carbon has three naturally occurring isotopes (that is, having the same atomic number but different atomic weights) with the atomic weights 12, 13, 14. Carbon consists of 99 per cent ^{12}C, 1 per cent ^{13}C, and only about one-million-millionth part of ^{14}C (or 'carbon fourteen') – which unlike the other two is radioactive (hence *radio*carbon). Carbon fourteen is also formed in the upper atmosphere where it combines with oxygen to form carbon dioxide. This carbon dioxide dissolves into the oceans, and is absorbed by plants as part of the process of photosynthesis which converts the carbon dioxide into carbohydrates such as glucose; in turn this then enters animal life forms via the food chain.

This carbon exchange occurs at a constant rate and so, in principle at least, all living organisms contain a constant level of carbon fourteen.

When a living organism dies it ceases to absorb carbon fourteen, the concentration of which decays at a constant rate (the law of radioactive decay). Put at its simplest, the number of atoms left in the sample after a period of time indicates its age. It has been established that with each period of 5,730 years the number of remaining atoms is halved, so if the number of radiocarbon atoms remaining and the initial number can be evaluated, then the time that has passed since the sample's 'death' can be determined.

Methods of Measurement

Until recently, the methods of measuring radiocarbon in a sample were to wait until it decayed and then count the beta particles in a gas proportional counter or a liquid scintillation counter. Both these variants have the disadvantage of requiring large samples of material. However, with the advent of the accelerator mass spectrometer (AMS), the radio-carbon atoms can be separated and counted, and the method requires minute samples (as small as a few tens of milligrams). It was this development that finally persuaded its conservators to allow a tiny fragment (about 50 milligrams) of the controversial Turin Shroud to be removed for radiocarbon dating of the fabric, which proved it to be a medieval fake.

Suitable Subjects

As we have seen, all organic materials are in theory capable of radio-carbon dating, though due to the allowance necessary for margin of error, dating is only of significance in samples of some age – making the process ideal for archaeological purposes. Consequently, the range of materials that survive over long periods of time is more limited. In the context of forensic science the most commonly tested material is probably bone, where the date of death of a subject is important. Otherwise, radiocarbon dating is mostly used in the testing of antiquities and works of art, when forgery is suspected.

RADIO TRANSMISSION OF FINGERPINTS

The first successful experiments in telegraphing fingerprints took place during 1945–6. The method was never much used, coinciding as it did with improved air-mail services, the speed of which was usually adequate for the purpose. Exceptions were when fingerprint evidence needed to be communicated quickly over very long distances, such as to the Antipodes and Far East.

On 5 January 1946, information was prepared at Scotland Yard on an Australian man due to be charged with a crime in London. It took just seven minutes to transmit an image of his fingerprint the 10,750 miles to Melbourne, Australia, and by the following morning his criminal record had been received in London via the same wireless telegraph.

The standard form on which information is collected and sent measures approximately 7½ × 6½ inches. It allows space for a profile and full-face portrait of the subject and a brief physical description. At the top left is a panel for one distinguishing fingerprint (tests had proved that an impression of the same size as the original did not transmit well and enlargements were henceforth used). Ten boxes gave information on the ridge patterns of all ten fingers using a letter code; this code, say E for a Radial Loop, is followed by the ridge-count – E6. The box relating to the sample print sent was usually blocked in.

The numbered boxes represent:

1. Right Thumb
2. Right Forefinger
3. Right Middle Finger
4. Right Ring Finger
5. Right Little Finger

6. Left Thumb
7. Left Forefinger
8. Left Middle Finger
9. Left Ring Finger
10. Left Little Finger

The pattern cipher:

A   Plain Arch
B   Arch with ridges showing Radial slope
C   Arch with ridges showing Ulnar slope
D   Tented Arch
E   Radial Loop
F   Ulnar Loop
G   Central Pocket (Inner ridge tracing)
H   Central Pocket (Outer ridge tracing)
I   Whorl (Inner ridge tracing)
J   Whorl (Meeting ridge tracing)
K   Whorl (Outer ridge tracing)
L   Lateral Pocket (Inner ridge tracing)

M   Lateral Pocket (Meeting ridge tracing)
N   Lateral Pocket (Outer ridge tracing)
0   Twinned Loop (Inner ridge tracing)
P   Twinned Loop (Meeting ridge tracing)
Q   Twinned Loop (Outer ridge tracing)
R   Composite (Inner ridge tracing)
S   Composite (Meeting ridge tracing)
T   Composite (Outer ridge tracing)
U   Accidental
V   Finger amputated
W   Finger injured or scarred beyond classification

REFRACTIVE INDEX
(see Glass)

RICIN POISONING
Ricin is a protein derived from the castor oil seed, though the oil is uncontaminated when extracted. The toxin ranks alongside botulinus as one of the deadliest known to mankind; just one gram of the substance is sufficient to kill around 36,000 people. Indeed, so powerful are its possible effects that during the Second World War it was under serious consideration for use as an agent in chemical warfare; its present status as a potential weapon remains shrouded by military secrecy. The symptoms of ricin poisoning are a high temperature, vomiting and diarrhoea, and giddiness; its effect is to agglutinate the red blood cells before proceeding to attack the other body cells.

Although ricin has been known for some time, it was not until the late summer of 1978 that it made headlines, in the Case of the Umbrella Murder. On 7 September Georgi Markov, a Bulgarian writer who had defected to Britain, was returning home from a day working with the BBC's World Service where he made occasional broadcasts to his native country. As he stood at Waterloo Bridge waiting for a bus, Markov felt in his thigh a sharp jab that seemed to come from behind; when he turned, Markov saw a man stooping to pick up an umbrella. The man muttered an apology and immediately hailed a cab; it was thought he was a foreigner by the difficulty the cabbie had understanding his destination. That night Georgi Markov was running a temperature of 104, and vomiting; the following morning he was admitted to hospital. During a routine exalnination of his body, the doctor noted a small area of hardening around what appeared to be a tiny puncture wound on Markov's thigh. X-rays, however, revealed nothing. Markov's symptoms continued to give great cause for alarm during the following days, and at 9.45 on the morning of 11 September his heart stopped. Subsequent testing of the Bulgarian's blood showed an unbelievable white blood cell count of 33,000 per cubic millimetre; the normal count is 5–10,000. Death was attributed to blood poisoning.

Since he had felt the jab in his thigh, Georgi Markov had been muttering darkly about political assassination, and although nobody but his wife took it seriously at the time, the dramatic manner of his death caused Scotland Yard to have the area of flesh around the deceased man's thigh wound removed and sent for analysis to the sinister Porton Down government microbiological research establishment – at that time Britain's laboratory for research into biological and chemical warfare. The result of pathological investigation was the find of the now-famous microscopic pellet, 1.77mm in diameter bored with two minute holes and clearly intended to contain some deadly poison. As the pellet had most likely been forced into Markov's leg by the foreigner's umbrella tip, the defector's suspicions began to be taken a lot more seriously. The pellet would contain less than half a milligram (500 micrograms) of a substance, which greatly reduced the available poisons. When the remaining possible toxins were eliminated because they did not match the dead man's symptoms, the Porton Down pathologists were left with ricin. The appropriate amount was injected into a pig, and when the unlucky animal died twenty-four hours later its post-mortem appearances were identical to those of the equally unlucky Georgi Markov. Furthermore, reports were now circulating about an earlier victim, another Bulgarian exile, who had lived in Paris; he had died mysteriously after feeling a stinging pain in his back while travelling on the Metro.

The case has never really been put to rest. Markov's widow, Annabel, and her family and friends have maintained a constant pressure on the Bulgarian government to make a statement about its implication in her husband's death. In June 1991, Bulgaria's interior minister Khristo Danov was reported to have stated officially: 'No one can convince me that the writer Georgi Markov was not assassinated by the Bulgarian secret services.' Later, senior officials laid the blame for ordering Markov's assassination on the country's former communist leader Todor Zhivkov, and intimated that he and others may be charged with conspiracy to murder. Needless to add, Mrs Markov was delighted: 'If the assassin is not found, but Zhivkov and the other organizers stand trial, the whole family will be satisfied . . . It will be the trial of the regime – a symbolic trial for crimes carried out against the Bulgarian people during the years of totalitarianism.' In February 1992 a former Bulgarian intelligence chief, Stoyan Savov, committed suicide while awaiting trial on charges of destroying official papers relating to the Markov incident.

As it turned out, Savov may have killed himself unnecessarily. A few months after his death, Bulgarian prosecutors announced that their investigation had proved too inconclusive to allow them to press charges against anyone suspected of involvement in the Markov murder. The case remains open, but has shown no developments in over ten years.

At the time of writing (September 2003) ricin is again in the news. In January of this year, police, acting on a tip-off, raided a flat in Wood Green, North London. There, it is alleged, they found evidence of ricin production and arrested four men of North African origin. The case has yet to come to court, but it is claimed the accused planned to use the ricin in an act of mass terrorism.

RIGOR MORTIS
(see Time of Death)

RUGOSCOPY
By no means as reliable as other means of dental identification, the morphology of palatal rugae (the 'ripple' marks and bumps on the roof of the mouth) may be used as supporting proof if there is some record of its ante-mortem state. This is most frequently achieved when matching upper dentures (or fragments of dentures) which will have picked up a mould of the wearer's rugae.

S

SALIVA
(see Scene-of-Crime Procedures, Serology)

SCANNING ELECTRON MICROSCOPY

While a simple reflected light **Microscope** can enlarge samples by a factor of about 1000×, the scanning electron microscope, by focusing a beam of electrons across a specimen instead of light, can produce three-dimensional enlargements of up to 150,000×. Day-to-day forensic work rarely requires magnification of more than about 10,000×.

The scanning electron microscope scans a sample with an extremely fine electron beam or microprobe, which generates electron emissions – rather like television – feeding back information depending on the contours of the sample. The messages are amplified by a photo-multiplier as they pass into a display cathode ray tube where they modulate the brightness (again similar to television) and form a micro-graphic image on the screen of a television-type monitor; a 'zoom' facility gives control of the enlargement factor. The apparatus also allows high quality photomicrographs to be taken as a record and for possible use as court evidence.

The technique is particularly useful in comparing evidence like paint fragments, fibres, paper and wood, and is capable of working with samples in the order of one-hundred-thousandths of an inch.

This facility to enlarge minute samples has made scanning electron microscopy invaluable in the examination of potentially very valuable articles, for instance in the scientific study of the Vinland Map. The map purported to date back to the fifteenth century, and depicted the coastlines of Greenland and North America; if it was genuine it would prove that the Vikings discovered America. Scientists examining the document were at first inclined to believe it authentic because the paper on which it was drawn and the watermark seemed genuinely from 1450 – decades before Columbus's well-documented voyage of 1492. Then the ink was tested. About fifty samples were taken across the map, each weighing approximately one-billionth of a gram, and subjected to a range of tests including examination by scanning electron microscopy, which identified titanium dioxide in the pigment in a form known as anatase; it was not commercially available until the early 1920s!

SCENE-OF-CRIME PROCEDURES

It is no exaggeration to say that the observation of proper procedures during the primary investigation of the scene of a crime can make the difference between a solved and an unsolved crime, a proved and an unproved case; or at the very least hasten or delay a solution.

Securing the Scene of Crime

In most instances, irrespective of the gravity of the crime, the first police representative on the scene will be a beat constable or a mobile uniformed officer alerted by radio. These officers are not trained as investigative detectives and are expected to confine themselves to as little activity as necessary in the immediate vicinity of the crime; this will insure against inadvertently destroying or contaminating potential evidence.

The primary duty of the first officer at the scene is to 'secure' the site by setting a boundary (if necessary with a physical barrier) within which no unauthorized person may pass. Crime scenes can be literally anywhere, and for convenience and recording are categorized as:

1. Indoors, residential
2. Indoors, place of entertainment
3. Indoors, other
4. Outdoors, street/public place
5. Outdoors, private place
6. Other, e.g. vehicle

It will depend upon the accessibility of the crime scene as to how easy it will be to secure – a private dwelling is obviously easier to secure than a public park, where an officer may be obliged initially to control the knots of morbid sightseers who are inexplicably drawn to scenes of tragedy. However, as most police officers are now able to be in immediate radio contact with their local station, the first on the scene will rapidly assess the situation and call in for any necessary assistance as soon as possible.

For example, if he comes upon a scene where a person is badly injured, his first duty is to give what assistance he can and call for medical aid to remove the victim to hospital (in this case the officer will note the position from which the injured party was removed, so that it can be marked on the scene-of-crime chart). If a person is found hanging, they must be taken down in case it is possible to administer artificial respiration successfully. However, where it is obvious that a person is dead, then the body must not be touched or moved in any way until it has been examined by a police surgeon or pathologist and photographed.

Police academies are at pains to instruct young police officers that they have the potential to be the investigation team's own worst enemy. One senior officer tells the story of a case of death by shooting in which everything pointed to suicide; except that the gun was inexplicably found on a mantelshelf on the other side of the room. It was obvious from the severity of the wound that death had been instantaneous – so perhaps it had been murder. Fortunately, the 'murder' investigation had not proceeded far before one of the constables early on the scene admitted obligingly moving the gun from where it lay next to the body – in case it got in anyone's way!

Recording the Scene of Crime
By this time the senior detectives who will lead the investigation (in the case of a serious crime such as homicide or sexual assault) will have arrived along with the **Police Surgeon** or **Pathologist**, and specially trained scenes-of-crime officers – some of whom will be experts at recording crime scenes in detail.

Photography
The photographer, using a combination of single-shot and videotape cameras, will, in the event of a homicide, first take record pictures of the body and its position in relation to the location, as soon as the medical officer has confirmed death. He is then at the disposal of the pathologist to make such records of wounds and other medical features as will help the future investigation.

When the body has been removed the photographer works alongside the exhibits officer, recording clues *in situ* before they are collected, bagged and labelled for the laboratory.

Once he has finished at the scene of the crime, the photographer may be required to follow the corpse to the mortuary where he will record details of the **Post-Mortem** examination.

Sketching

In addition to photographs, detailed sketch plans are drawn of the site on which is entered vital information, such as the position of furniture, doors and windows open or closed, exact measurements of distances and heights, angles and position of bloodstains, position of weapons and other clues.

Evidence Before the Court

On 24 October 1983, Arthur Hutchinson, already on the run after escaping from custody on a charge of violent rape, broke into the home of Sheffield solicitor Basil Laitner and his family. The Laitners had just been celebrating the wedding of their eldest daughter and had seen off the last of the guests. Hutchinson, in an orgy of mindless destruction, knifed to death Mr Laitner, his wife and his son before subjecting the younger daughter to rape at knifepoint. Although at his subsequent trial at Durham Hutchinson denied ever being at the house, he was faced with overwhelming forensic evidence consisting of palm-prints, a match of his rare blood-group, and bite-mark evidence left in a piece of cheese. On 7 September 1984, two colour television sets were installed in the well of Durham Crown Court and a two-minute extract from a police scene-of-crime video was shown to the court and jury. The film opened with an outdoor shot of the victims' house, followed by a brief view of a wooden staircase on which the body of Mr Laitner lay face down in his bloody pyjamas; detail was shown of bloodstaining on the stair carpet which was believed to be footprints. Four days later – after rejecting the prosecution counsel's wish to protect them from 'some of the nastier shots' – the jury asked to be shown the police video in its seven-minute entirety, with details of the victims' injuries being explained by a Home Office pathologist. This was the first time that a scene-of-crime video had been shown to a jury in a British murder trial, and despite the judge's caution that they should not be influenced by 'horror and revulsion' at the film, it is unlikely to have been far from the jury's mind when they returned verdicts of guilty against Arthur Hutchinson.

Medical Evidence

It is vital that the scenes-of-crime officers and the medical officer work as a team, each understanding and respecting their clearly defined roles in the investigation; above all, this ensures that no part of the examination is overlooked. The tasks undertaken by the investigating officers and by the police surgeon/pathologist complement each other, and they will exchange information – a matter of particular importance at the scene of the crime.

Murder

In the same way that the first officer on the scene is entrusted with preventing deliberate or accidental interference with the surrounding area, it is also vital that he ensures the body itself is not touched or moved before the pathologist arrives to make his preliminary examination.

When death has, for all practical purposes, been established (usually earlier by a police surgeon), it is the first job of the pathologist to determine the three key factors involved:

Cause of death: The pathological condition that produced death.

Manner of death: The instrument or physical agent employed.

Mode of death: The motivation or intent, viz:

1. Accident
2. Suicide
3. Homicide
4. Natural causes

Much of this information may only be available after post-mortem examination, but the pathologist will pass on such enlightened opinions as he may form at the crime scene to the senior investigating officer.

For example, before the body is removed to the mortuary for autopsy, he may hazard a preliminary estimate of the **Time of Death** as indicated by body cooling, *rigor mortis*, etc.

The medical officer will then attend to the following:

1. Placing plastic bags over the head, hands and feet of the deceased to ensure that any trace evidence that may be adhering to those parts of the body is not lost.
2. Overseeing the laying of the whole body on a clean sheet for the same reason.

The body may now be removed (preferably in the position in which it was found) for post-mortem. Only now will the pathologist signal scenes-of-crime officers to examine the floor or ground beneath the body.

The pathologist may remain briefly at the scene of the crime to assist in the search for medical clues, and to record such impressions of the scene as may be useful to his assessment of the events surrounding the crime. For example, his experience of interpreting the vital clues offered by the shapes and configurations of **Bloodstains** may provide detectives with information on the logistics of the act of killing.

It is customary to complete the post-mortem as soon as possible after removal from the crime scene as not infrequently pathological clues fade or change if the corpse is kept in mortuary storage.

Case Study

PATRICK DAVID MACKAY

Mackay's father, a violent alcoholic who regularly assaulted his wife and children when drunk, died in 1962, when Patrick was ten years old. From this point the boy seems almost to have taken over his father's role as the local bully. He was always in trouble at school, mostly for beating children younger and weaker than himself, and he became fond of torturing small animals. This behaviour inevitably resulted in frequent visits both to mental institutions and to approved schools. Twice Mackay was released from Moss Side Hospital – 'Liverpool's Broadmoor' – against the strong advice of his doctors.

The young Patrick Mackay enthusiastically embraced the theories of the German Nazis, styling himself 'Franklin Bollvolt the First' and fashioning crude uniforms by sewing and sticking various Nazi emblems on to his everyday clothes. Like his father, Patrick also became dependent upon drink, and reacted violently under its stimulus. He was also now a more-or-less fully employed crook, specializing in theft, street robbery, and aggravated burglary – all his victims were elderly women. On 14 February 1974, Mackay broke into the London home of Isabella Griffiths, and in the course of robbing her, stabbed the eighty-four-year-old woman to death. Just over a year later, Mackay knocked at the door of Mrs Adele Price to ask for a drink of water; when invited in, he strangled her.

Father Anthony Crean, a benevolent sixty-four-year-old Roman Catholic priest, had helped Mackay two years previously when he was having problems at home, and by way of thanks Patrick robbed him.

Then on 21 March 1975, Mackay returned and attacked Father Anthony at his home in Shorne, Kent. He stabbed his former benefactor several times and then split his head open with an axe before putting him, still alive, in a bath of water and sat on the edge for an hour watching as his victim floundered and groaned, and then died.

Given the nature of the previous relationship between the priest and the unworthy recipient of his generosity, local police had Patrick Mackay under arrest within forty-eight hours. In the meantime, pathologist Professor James Cameron had made his model report of the medical aspects of the scene of crime:

The small window in the bathroom was open and a traycloth was over the wash-hand basin. The pipe from the shower attachment appeared to have been torn off. The blood-stained water was up to the level of the overflow. There was much blood-staining of the top of the bath and all over the wall at the back of the bath and over the wall over the top of the bath with slight blood-staining over the edge of the front of the bath, but there was no evidence of water or dampness on the floor of the bathroom. No naked eye evidence of blood-stained marks on the taps of the wash-hand basin. The top of the head appeared to have a towel wrapped over it. A sample was taken of the bath water and the level of the blood-stained water was marked before the plug, which did not have any attached chain, was removed to release the water. The body was removed from the bath and placed on a plastic body sheet. I remained at the scene whilst this was being carried out and whilst the body was totally wrapped within the body sheet and removed from the bathroom by police officers into the hallway from which it was moved, in my presence, by the undertakers. In conjunction with Detective Superintendent Irvine, I visited the other rooms in the house and was present when Superintendent Irvine found a box underneath the stairs in which there was a blood-stained axe. During this preliminary view of the scene I saw no evidence of a blood-stained cutting weapon. I remained at the scene until the body was removed to the mortuary. Later the same day, at 6.00 a.m., within the mortuary of Gravesend and North Kent Hospital, Bathstreet, Gravesend, I carried out a post-mortem examination on the body of the man previously identified to me by Detective Chief Inspector Hart as being Anthony Joseph Crean.

As for Patrick Mackay, he was charged with a total of five murders and questioned about a further six. He was judged to be sane and fit to plead at his trial, and subsequently found guilty of murder and sentenced to life imprisonment.

Sex Crimes

Photography

Any injuries that the victim may have sustained as a result of the attack must be carefully photographed in colour with a ruler alongside to indicate scale and perspective. In the United States there is a curious exception to this common-sense rule: a court may deem photographs 'inflammatory', and therefore not admissible as evidence, if they show a woman's nipples or genital area. Injuries to the breast must therefore be shot in close-up, and the genital area only when injuries are considered to be 'remarkable'.

Evidence from a Victim

The doctor or **Police Surgeon** summoned to a case of sexual assault will have had special training in the collection and handling of relevant evidence:

1. *Swabs:* Vaginal swabs (plus anal swabs and oral swabs if relevant) are taken to determine the presence of seminal deposits.
2. *Hairs:*   a) Hair *combed* from the victim's pubic region which may, by transfer, also contain hairs from the attacker.
   b) Hair *plucked* from the pubic region to be used as a control (some may have been transferred to the attacker).
   c) Hair *plucked* from the head, to be used as a control (some may have been transferred to the crime scene and to the attacker).
3. *Blood:* Sample taken from victim's vein to provide information on blood type.
4. *Saliva:* Sample taken to determine whether victim is a secretor (see **Serology**).

Seminal stains: In sex crimes seminal fluids are the fundamental evidence proving the fact, and stains may be found on the victim's clothing, bed linen, paper tissues, floor coverings and used towels. The area of staining, if still wet, should be allowed to dry in the air before being circled with a special marker pen and packaged for examination in the laboratory (plastic bags should not be used).

Victim's clothing: Clothing not covered by the previous paragraph should also be carefully collected and packaged for subsequent examination for **Trace Evidence**, such as hair and fibres.

Evidence from a Suspect

At such time as investigating officers take a suspect into custody, the police surgeon will be called on to collect physical evidence for the purpose of comparison.

1. *Clothing:* Should be taken for laboratory examination for blood and semen traces and contact trace evidence, such as hairs and fibres from the victim or from the scene of the offence.
2. *Hairs:*
   a) Hair *combed* from the suspect's pubic region which may, by transfer, also contain hairs of the victim.
   b) Hair *plucked* from the pubic region to be used as a control.
   c) Hair *plucked* from the head to be used as a control (some may have been transferred to the crime scene and to the victim).
3. *Blood:* Sample taken from suspect's vein to provide information on blood type.
4. *Saliva:* Sample taken to determine whether suspect is a secretor (see **Serology**).

Collecting Evidence

Evidence collected at the scene of the crime will be of two kinds:

1. *Verbal evidence:* From witnesses, victims, suspects.
2. *Physical evidence:* Tangible clues which will later assist in supporting a case arising from the crime.

For the purpose of this book, only Physical Evidence is discussed.

Although there are minor differences in personnel and procedure, most of the world's police forces have separately designated *Scenes-of-Crime Officers* (in the United States called Crime Scene Officers and in Canada, rather confusingly, Identification Officers). It is the specialized task of these officers to observe, record and collect potentially valuable clues from an often bewildering muddle of traces at the crime scene. Specimens are carefully stored in individual labelled bags or containers for transport to the forensic science laboratory. Occasionally during their search of the site, scenes-of-crime officers will encounter evidence the interpretation of which will require a visit by a forensic specialist to the scene.

Scene-of-crime operations are arguably the most important stage in any criminal investigation, and errors and omissions now can cause irreparable damage to the future of an inquiry. Here, more than anywhere, the meticulous, painstaking attention to detail and strict adherence to system that characterizes good police work is needed. Of course, there will be a time and place for imaginative deduction, but the 'Sherlock Holmes' element is of little use in a court of law without tangible evidence to support it – and no amount of scientific wizardry in the laboratory can ever bring back the overlooked clue, the carelessly erased fingerprint, the lost hair . . .

List of most commonly found types of Physical Evidence

Arson traces
Biological (Sexual – semen, etc.)
Biological (Other – saliva, faeces, etc.)
Blood
Clothing
Documents
Drugs/drug paraphernalia
Dust/powders
Explosives/residues
Fibres
Fingerprints
Firearms; other weapons
Footwear
Glass
Glove(s)
Hair
Impressions (footprints, tyreprints, etc.)
Paint
Poison
Soil and Minerals

Tools/tool marks
Wood; other vegetable matter

It is also important that officers on the scene of a crime do not 'import' any confusing debris, and it is customary for a small area away from the main scene to be designated for jobs like changing photographic films where packaging can be deposited, and for fingerprinting small objects so that the scene does not become contaminated with powders.

Case Study

MURDER AT THE FARM

On the vast majority of occasions the work of the police scenes-of-crime team is impeccably carried out and provides the inquiry with the support it needs to bring a case to a successful conclusion. However, nothing can be perfect as long as it contains the possibility of human error – and this includes police work; indeed, we can learn a great deal from those few cases where errors have been made.

In the early hours of an August morning in 1985, the station officer received an agitated telephone call from a young man giving his name as Jeremy Bamber and claiming to be anxious about the safety of his parents. He told the policeman that a few minutes earlier his father had telephoned to say that his daughter Sheila – Jeremy's sister – was at their Essex farmhouse home going berserk with a semi-automatic rifle. Then there had been the sound of a shot and the line had gone dead.

When an investigating team arrived at White House Farm, they found the battered and shot bodies of Nevill and June Bamber, the 'insane' daughter Sheila Caffell, and her own twin children Daniel and Nicholas. From the state of the bodies and the story of his sister's mental instability enthusiastically related by Jeremy, it looked like a clear case of murder followed by suicide – the young woman, a bullet through her brain, was still holding the .22 Anschutz.

This was the one insurmountable psychological disadvantage to the police inquiry – the 'killer' had already been named; and it was with this misinformation at the forefront of their minds that investigating officers found themselves, in effect, looking for clues to fit the story of the young woman's mad rampage, in the process misinterpreting what did not fit the murder/suicide theory.

Information was there for the looking, and even if no other suspect came immediately to mind, then at least all the evidence indicated that Sheila Caffell *could not* have committed the murders. It was later learned that she suffered impaired hand-eye coordination anyway, and had no experience whatever of handling firearms. Nevertheless, she is supposed to have fired twenty-five accurate shots into her family, stopping twice to reload the gun. It might have seemed inconsistent, even to the untrained eye, that such extensive ballistic activity could have been carried out without the slightest damage to the 'killer's' perfectly manicured fingernails, and leaving her hands free of oil and powder deposits. What was more, the soles of her feet were found to be as clean 'as though she had just stepped out of a bath' – despite having run around the house on a bloody massacre.

Nobody thought to ponder how this slim, 5ft 7in woman had bludgeoned her healthy, sturdily built, 6ft 4in father with the rifle butt, which broke under the impact, without suffering injury herself. Incidentally, because of their assumption of her guilt, the real killer, Jeremy Bamber, who probably *was* bruised and marked in the struggle, was not examined by the police for four weeks.

The pathologist's report revealed that Sheila Caffell could not possibly have killed herself; either one of her wounds would have been instantly fatal, and besides, detailed examination had shown that while one of those wounds had been inflicted with a gun in its normal state, a silencer had been used during the other shot – even the most inexperienced officer might have felt that this represented an unusual extravagance for a suicide. Besides, she would have needed much longer arms to have shot herself in the head with a gun lengthened by a silencer.

Ignoring the clues offered by this victim's body was not the only area of the investigation that proved wanting. Fingerprinting procedure was, by all reports, rather lackadaisical, and many were surprised when experienced scenes-of-crime officers moved the murder weapon with bare hands. Not all of the bodies were fingerprinted at the time, and the cremation of the victims so soon after the crime rendered the situation unsalvageable. Ironically, the police took the real killer's prints six *weeks* after the shooting. By now Jeremy had developed an almost theatrical display of filial grief. Blood was obligingly washed off the farmhouse walls, and bloodstained bedding and carpets removed and burned.

One week later the inquest on the victims opened before the deputy coroner, and in evidence, a detective inspector outlined the scenario as seen by the police, and emphasized once again that the official view was to regard the young woman as guilty of the murders.

Rather less happy with the outcome were the surviving members of the Bamber family, in particular two of Sheila's cousins. David Boutflour and Christine Eaton were convinced that she was incapable of killing anybody, least of all the twins she adored. In more practical terms, they knew that Sheila's bad coordination made pouring a cup of tea without spilling it difficult enough – so how could she manage to shoot her whole family? Adding a certain 'Miss Marple factor' to this already bizarre scenario, the amateur detectives visited the farmhouse and retraced the steps of the police search. They entered the study where, as the police had done before them, they found the gun cabinet. To the police it had contained nothing significant; to David Boutflour and Christine Eaton it contained a bloodstained gun silencer of a type that fitted the murder weapon. They lost no time in alerting the police to this vital piece of evidence that they had already missed the first time round. And vital it most certainly was, for the silencer provided indisputable evidence that their suspect could not have shot herself; the blood that had seeped into the silencer's baffles was her own – which made it rather difficult to explain how it got into the gun cupboard if she, the last to die, had killed herself.

Although the information was not revealed until the trial, the silencer, when it came into police possession, had a single grey hair adhering to it. This hair – presumably from the head of either of the elder victims – was lost by police while in transit to the forensic laboratory for testing.

The true perpetrator of this brutal and cynical act of familicide turned out to be none other than the young man who had so unashamedly pointed the accusing finger at his own sister. But when Jeremy Bamber stood in the dock he was not the only person to find himself on trial. For fairly or not, the whole of the initial police inquiry came under scrutiny in court. The judge himself remarked that the examination by officers at the scene of the crime 'left a lot to be desired'; and the Deputy Chief Constable of the force concerned added that 'with the benefit of that perfect science, hindsight, the judgement made at the scene of the crime . . . was misdirected'. Finally, the then Home Secretary called for an urgent report on police handling of the murder inquiry.

It is not the purpose in selecting this case study further to malign experienced police officers of otherwise excellent professional records; however, it does demonstrate most graphically the vital part played by the scenes-of-crime officers in determining the future success or failure of a serious crime inquiry.

SCOPOLAMINE
(see Hyoscine)

SECRETORS
(see Semen, Serology)

SEMEN

This reproductive fluid ejaculated by the male of the species is of vital forensic importance in cases of rape and sexual abuse. Human semen is composed of upwards of one hundred million sperm cells (spermatocytes) suspended in a high-protein serum.

When seminal stains are found at the scene of a crime it is usually on bed linen or furniture coverings, carpets or the victim's clothing. The material must be dried naturally in the air (in the same way as blood traces) and then covered with a clean sheet of paper before being bagged; note should be made that it was found wet, and if there is sufficient quantity a liquid sample must be taken before drying. Clothing is never folded across the stain, but so that the stained area remains flat.

Laboratory Testing

It is normally easy to identify the starchy-looking semen stain on garments, but if the sample is not obvious to the naked eye, examination under ultraviolet light will reveal the stain as a white or blue-white fluorescence (though it must be remembered that other substances produce the same effect – for example urine – so the test may be invalid on undergarments).

Identifying the stain as semen is done initially by means of a microscope which will show the spermatocytes. However, in certain conditions, such as where a suspected attacker had undergone a vasectomy, or in the case of those suffering from low sperm count (oligospermia) or no sperm (aspermia) it is necessary to resort to chemical tests.

Acid Phosphatase Colour Test: Detects the presence of the acid phosphatase enzyme in semen, and although the enzyme is present in other body fluids it is not in such great concentration. [The presence of semen is indicated by a purple-blue coloration when the stain is treated with a mixture of calcium alpha-naphthyl phosphate and II-naphthalin diazo blue-B.]

Grouping from Semen

It was discovered in 1925 that some eighty per cent of individuals are what is called 'secretors'; that is, they secrete their specific blood group information in other body fluids. This makes it possible to subject semen to tests to reveal that blood group. The limitation is that semen is capable of division into only three systems – secretor/non-secretor, ABO, and one enzyme sub-group, PGM. This is a very low specificity compared with the possibilities of blood grouping (see **Serology**).

More important, semen is ideal material for **DNA Profiling**, and since the discovery of the process by Dr Alec Jeffreys in 1984, many rapists have been convicted on the convincing evidence of their genetic 'fingerprint' left at the scene of the crime in the form of semen.

SEROLOGY

In most cases of traumatic death blood will be one of the most important traces found and sent to the forensic laboratory for examination. It may have been found on a weapon, or on a suspect's clothing; stains may have been left at the scene of the crime, in a vehicle, and so on. It is virtually impossible to remove all traces of blood, and analysis can now deal reliably with microscopically small particles. However, it is vital that suspected traces are first tested to see that they *are* blood, to prevent elaborate experiments being set up to determine the blood group of a banana stain!

Kastle-Meyer Test

The so-called 'Peroxidase' test is a simple experiment capable of being carried out in the most modest laboratory or at the scene of crime. It is based on the fact that peroxidase, a constituent enzyme of blood, will release the oxygen from hydrogen peroxide. There are several variations on the test, though the most commonly used is the Kastle-Meyer. A small portion of the suspect stain is placed on a dry filter paper. A drop each of the reagents phenolphthalein, alcohol and hydrogen peroxide is used to activate the sample, which will produce a pink coloration in the presence of blood.

Having established that the sample *is* blood, the next stage is to determine the source – whether it is human or animal (indeed, if necessary, which animal).

The Preciptin Test

In 1901 Paul Uhlenhuth was an assistant professor in the University at Greifswald, Germany; he had been developing the earlier researches of a Belgian named Jules Bordet, arguably the true father of the science of serology. Bordet had been working on the inoculation of animals against diphtheria by injecting them with diphtheria toxins which produced protective antibodies in their blood serum. Uhlenhuth found that if he injected protein from a chicken's egg into rabbits, then mixed the rabbit serum with egg white, it caused the egg proteins to separate from the clear liquid and form a cloudy precipitate (preciptin). It was a short step to being able to produce rabbit-based serums that would, by the same process, precipitate and therefore identify the proteins of the blood of any animal, including humans.

In modern practice a liquid sample containing the suspected human blood is deposited in a depression on a gelatine-coated glass slide next to a similar sample of the biological reagent (the anti-serum). When an electric current is passed through the glass by means of electrodes, the protein molecules in the two samples filter outwards through the gelatine towards each other and if a preciptin line forms where the antigens and the antibodies meet the sample is human blood.

Anti-serums are available for testing most animals' blood, though laboratory stocks are rarely kept for those other than domestic pets and farmyard beasts.

The preciptin test is extremely sensitive, requiring minute samples. Positive results have been obtained on human blood that has been dried for as long as fifteen years, and experiments on tissue samples of mummies several millennia old have proved successful.

Case Study

LUDWIG TESSNOW

A very early triumph for the infant science of serology cut short the gruesome career of the man known either as 'The Monster of Rugen' or 'The Mad Carpenter of Rugen'. It was on the first day of July in the first year of the twentieth century that two young brothers, eight-year-old Hermann and six-year-old Peter Stubbe, failed to return to their home at Gohren on the island of Rugen in north Germany, after being out at play. It was not until the following morning that horrified villagers searching for the boys began to find the dismembered and disembowelled fragments of the Stubbe brothers, scattered over a wide area of local woodland. Ludwig Tessnow, a journeyman carpenter from the neighbouring village of Baabe, who had been working at Rugen and was seen talking to the children on the day they disappeared, was detained for questioning. During a routine search of his home, boots and clothes were found that bore dark stains, and others had obviously been recently washed. Tessnow's explanation was that the stains were wood dye – a common enough material, after all, to craftsmen in his way of business.

Unfortunately for Ludwig Tessnow, the examining magistrate at Greifswald before whom he appeared, had a long memory. Three years earlier, Johann Schmidt recalled, there was a similar case in the village of Lechtingen, near Osnabruck, where seven-year-old Hannelore Heidemann and her friend Else Langemeier were found mutilated and dismembered in a wood near their home. A man seen hanging around the woods on the day of the murder had been picked up and his clothing was found to be stained. The man's name was Ludwig Tessnow, and when he told the police that the stains were simply wood dye from the job which they had just interrupted, he was absolved of any further suspicion. What if . . . thought Herr Schmidt. Then he remembered the sheep. Three weeks before the savage murder of the Stubbe brothers, on 11 June, a farmer had seen a man running away from one of his fields, and when he went to investigate he found seven of his sheep eviscerated, hacked to pieces and strewn around the field. At an identity parade, the farmer picked out Tessnow as the man he had seen.

However, Tessnow was denying everything – and apart from the undefinable stains on his clothing (remember, this is 1901) there was no direct evidence on which to base a case against him. But that was to reckon without the persistence of magistrate Schmidt and his prosecutor, Ernst Hubschmann. Hubschmann had just heard of the entirely new and remarkable tests developed by a young German biologist, Professor Paul Uhlenhuth, which was able to determine not only the existence of bloodstains, but tell human blood from animal blood.

On 8 August 1901, Uhlenhuth submitted his report: of the stains on Ludwig Tessnow's clothing the large number on the suit and shirt were human, others on the jacket were sheep's blood. Tessnow was executed at Greifswald Prison in 1904.

Blood Group Analysis

Detailed characterisation of blood requires the more specialist skills of the serologist, and its classification into group systems has become very complex. The simplest system, and the one with which the lay person is most familiar, is the ABO system.

That blood could be categorized into several different 'types' was first discovered by the Viennese-born biologist Karl Landsteiner in 1901. Knowing that red blood cells contain a number of antigens – substances responsible for the production of antibodies to combat infection and disease in the body – Landsteiner found that the presence or absence of two of these antigens (which he called A and B) in human blood formed four distinct groups:

A – antigen A and antibody B present
antigen B and antibody A absent

B – antigen B and antibody A present
antigen A and antibody B absent

O – antigens A and B absent
antibodies A and B present

AB – antigens A and B present
antibodies A and B absent

Each human being belongs to one of the broad groups A, B, O, or AB. In Great Britain and the United States, for example, the percentages are approximately: A = 42 per cent, B = 9 per cent, O = 46 per cent, AB = 3 per cent.

So it can be seen that if traces of blood belonging to group O are found on a murder suspect's clothing, and he belongs to group A, then the blood is not his own. Further, if the victim's group was O then it could – but only *could* – have come from him.

In 1927, Landsteiner and his co-workers discovered further grouping factors M and N. Landsteiner and Weiner then began to experiment with other primates by injecting the blood of an Indian Rhesus monkey into guinea pigs, and found hitherto undiscovered antigens which they named Rhesus (Rh). The injected animals were observed to produce an anti-Rhesus antibody which also agglutinated human cells. Resulting tests proved that human beings could be divided into the two phenotypes *Rh positive* and *Rh negative*.

Subsequently, other important typing systems emerged including divisions based on components of the red blood cells – haemoglobin and haptoglobin, and a variety of enzymes contained in the serum:

ENZYMES AND PROTEINS USED TO CLASSIFY BLOOD

Blood Factor	Abbreviation
Adensosine deaminase	ADA
Adenylate kinase	AK
Carbonic anhydrase II	CA II
Erythrocyte acid phosphatase	EAP
Esterase D	EsD
Glucose-6-Phosphate dehydrogenase	G6PD
Glyoxase I	GLO I
Group-specific component	Gc
Haptoglobin	Hp
Peptidase A	Pep A
Phosphoglucomutase	PGM
6-Phosphogluconate dehydrogenase	6PGD
Transferrin	Tf

Returning to our murder suspect's sample of group O blood, we can subject it to a further *hypothetical* system to try to reduce the odds of 46 per cent of the population. Call this hypothetical system BPL, and let it contain four groups i, ii, iii, iv. We know also that the population is divided i = 50 per cent, = 30 per cent, iii = 15 per cent, iv = 5 per cent. Tests reveal that our bloodstain group O is also group iii in the BPL system. Thus it may be deduced that of the 46 per cent of the population who belong to group O (in the ABO system) only 15 per cent will belong to group iii (in the BPL system). Then only 6.9 per cent (15 per cent of 46 per cent) belong to both groups – a significant reduction in the odds.

There are now some 300 group systems, and there is optimism that a key will eventually be found to identify positively individual bloodstains. However, the current preoccupation with DNA 'fingerprinting' may eventually render this objective obsolete.

Secretors
Serologists were presented with a bonus when, in 1925, it was discovered that some 80 per cent of the population belong to a group called 'secretors'. This means that their other body secretions, saliva, semen, urine, perspiration, etc. carry the same substances as their blood, and so can be used to determine blood groupings.

Example
The following example demonstrates the way in which the 'secretor' factor can materially influence the strength of a case against, say, a rape suspect:

Tests made after the incident showed that both the victim and the suspect shared blood group A; material tested from the vaginal swab also indicated group A. On the face of it the evidence was all but useless. However, a mouth swab taken from the victim revealed that the saliva was free from blood grouping antigen factors – in other words, she was not a secretor. Thus the A traces in the vagina could have originated from the suspect. Additional elecrophoresis tests were made – which separated charged protein molecules by means of an electrical field – for the presence of PGM (phosphoglucomutase) groups. The suspect proved to be PGM type 2, the victim PGM 1. The vaginal traces were PGM 1–2, showing the presence of both types. The presence of type 2 enzyme (which could not have come from the victim's own metabolic system but *could* be from the suspect's) provided further evidence.

From this information it was possible mathematically to shorten the odds in favour of the suspect having committed the crime:

Blood of type A occurs in about 40 per cent of the population.

PMG type 2 occurs in about 6 per cent of the population.

Approximately 80 per cent of the population are 'secretors'.
Therefore:

$$0.40 \times 0.06 \times 0.80 = 0.019 = 2 \text{ per cent}$$

The suspect is a member of that 2 per cent, a fact which, with other corroborating evidence, should be sufficient to secure a conviction.

Barr Bodies
In 1949, two British scientists, Barr and Bertram, discovered that it was possible to distinguish between the nuclei of male and female body cells. This effect was most noticeable in the white blood cells and the mucosa of the lining of the mouth. In a large percentage of female cells they found a small darkly staining chromatin body in the rough shape of a drumstick; it does not occur in male cells. The body was subsequently named after Barr in recognition of his discovery, though it is now usually called the sex chromatin body.

A Question of Heredity
It has for some time been possible to *exclude* putative fathers in paternity disputes by means of a simple ABO blood test. However, it cannot state with certainty that a child comes from specific parents (only that it

does not). The determination of parentage is now routinely carried out by **DNA Profiling**, which gives *specific* results. The table below shows the heredity factors in blood-grouping:

Parent 1	Parent 2	Children's Groups Possible	Children's Groups Impossible
O	O	O	A,B,AB
O	A	O,A	B,AB
O	B	O,B	A,AB
A	A	O,A	B,AB
A	B	AB,B,O,A	Al possible
B	B	O,B	A,AB
O	AB	A,B	O,AB
A	AB	AB,A,B	O
B	AB	AB,A,B	O
AB	AB	AB,A,B	O

Research into hereditaty factors in blood-grouping (mainly for the purpose of establishing paternity) cannot state with certainty that a child comes from spectfic parents; it can, however, ascertain whether a child is not the offspring of a given couple.

SEXUAL ASPHYXIA
(see Hanging)

SEXUAL OFFENCES
(see Police Surgeon, Post-Mortem Procedures, Scene-of-Crime Procedures)

SHOE-PRINTS
Many shoe-prints fall into the category of **Impressions**. However, the skilled analysis that can now be applied to the matching of glove prints may be applied to those of shoes. Convincing 'points of correspondence' will include the overall design, shape, size and dimensions, characteristic worn areas, manufacturer's marks, stitching patterns, etc.

Making It Easy

In the ever-escalating race to sell more and more of the same commodity, the main manufacturers of designer 'training shoes' (Reebok and Adidas to name but two) have put on the market a bewildering array of variations and styles of the basic trainer – each with its own distinctive and very often complex pattern of moulded sole. While not as individual as a fingerprint, there are enough of these designs to make the *elimination* of suspect footwear considerably easier, and contribute to reducing the odds when it comes to individual characteristics such as wear marks.

Case Study

FOOTPRINTS IN BLOOD

Ironically it was only a week before St Valentine's Day 1984 that teenage sweethearts Robert Vaughan and Michelle Sadler were murdered on the premises of the firm where Robert worked in south London. Michelle Sadler had been sexually assaulted and strangled, Vaughan had died from a cut throat. Early the following day their killer, also an employee at Courier Display Systems, returned to the scene of his crime and loaded the bodies of his victims, now in makeshift shrouds of plastic sheeting, into a trolley and wheeled them to a nearby park and left them in a builder's dumper truck.

At his Old Bailey trial the following December, David Carty, who had been working overtime with Robert Vaughan on the evening of the murder, claimed that he had left Robert and Michelle, who had come along to help out, and gone off to do some shopping. When he returned, he said, he found the couple dead, and in a panic disposed of the bodies. Not an entirely impossible defence, but it was badly damaged by police evidence that a trail of bloody footprints led along the basement corridors of the scene of crime. The prints were later matched by the forensic team to the very characteristic pattern on the soles of Carty's trainers; in combination with other material evidence, it helped seal the prosecution case. Still protesting 'I had nothing to do with it', David Carty was convicted and sentenced to life imprisonment.

Electrostatic Mat

In cases where traces can just be seen, or it is believed that a faint shoe-print may have been deposited on such surfaces as linoleum, wooden and concrete floors, tightly woven carpet, etc., an Electrostatic Mat may be used to raise the image. A weak current of electricity is passed through a sheet of foil sandwiched between two sheets of black acetate; the static charge which is created attracts the evidence to the surface of the mat. Viewed and photographed at an oblique angle to light the black surface may reveal an incriminating print which in its previous state would have been too weak to be useful.

SIMPSON, CEDRIC KEITH (1907–85)

One of the foremost medico-legal pathologists of the twentieth century, Keith Simpson entered the field at a time when it was completely dominated by the personality of Bernard Spilsbury, and within a short time had established himself at the head of his profession and, more rarely, as a brilliant teacher. Simpson was the pioneer of forensic dentistry (or Odontology), writing in the *Medico-Legal Review* in 1951: 'Dental data, it is now realized, has come to provide detail of a kind comparable with the infinitesimal detail that was previously thought likely to be provided only by fingerprints.' A prolific lecturer and writer, Simpson adopted the pen name Guy Bailey for his more popular published offerings.

Cedric Keith Simpson was born on 20 July 1907, the son of a doctor, at Brighton, Sussex. After an education at Brighton and Hove Grammar School he entered Guy's Hospital Medical School in 1924, the institution with which he was to be associated in a variety of roles throughout his professional life. In 1930 Simpson graduated after an outstanding studentship during which he won five major prizes including two gold medals; he was immediately appointed to a teaching post.

In the following half century Keith Simpson's career embraced one triumph after another – 1932–7, Senior Demonstrator in Pathology at Guy's; 1937–46, appointed Lecturer in Forensic Medicine at London University; 1946–62, Reader in Forensic Medicine; 1947, first edition of *Forensic Medicine*, which in 1958 won the Royal Society of Arts Swiney Prize for the best work on medical jurisprudence to be published during the preceding ten years; 1961, appointed lecturer in Forensic Medicine to Oxford University; 1961–3, elected President of the Medico-Legal Society; 1962, first edition of *A Doctor's Guide to*

Court; 1962–72, appointed the first Professor of Forensic Medicine at London University; 1965, first successful prosecution of a baby batterer for murder – Simpson had been the first to identify what became known as Battered Baby Syndrome; 1966–7, elected President of the British Association in Forensic Medicine; 1975, created CBE; 1978, Simpson's autobiography, *Forty Years of Murder,* published by Harrap; 1983, caused a controversy by refusing to carry out a post-mortem examination on a suspected Aids sufferer – a decision endorsed by the Department of Health.

A great internationalist, Simpson lectured around the world spreading the excellence of British forensic medicine. He was a member of the Société de Médecine Légale, and of the American Academy of Forensic Sciences, a co-editor of the *Zeitschrift für Rechtsmedizin* and holder of an honorary doctorate from the University of Ghent.

According to himself, Simpson entered the outwardly grim world of forensic pathology out of *squeamishness* – he could not bear to see sick and dying people, people in great pain and distress. Of his own discipline he wrote: 'Forensic, or legal, medicine provides one of the most fascinating of all chapters in the practice of medicine. The study of the body, usually dead, the quiet scientific evaluation of the evidence it bears, and the construction of reasonable inferences based on these observations cannot fail to give interest and satisfaction.'

A man happy with his lot in life, Simpson would say: 'I enjoy life; I'm only sorry it is so short.' On 21 July 1985, he died from a brain tumour at the age of seventy-eight.

Celebrated Cases

1942. *Harry Dobkin* Pioneering work by Simpson in forensic odontology (see page 140).

August Sangret 'The Wigwam Murder'.

1946. *Harold Hagger*
Neville George Clevely Heath

1948. *Goringe Case* Killer identified by the teeth marks left on his victim's breast (see page 83).

1949. *John George Haigh* 'The Acid Bath Killer'. One of the most celebrated crimes of the century, in which Simpson was responsible for the remarkable identification of Haigh's victim (see page 118).

Frederick Radford Murdered his wife with arsenic-laced fruit pie.

1964. *William Brittle* Accused of the murder of Peter Thomas, whose decaying body was found in a wood near Bracknell, Berkshire. Brittle's alibi was destroyed when Simpson testified that maggots of the common blue-bottle found on the remains had not pupated which, given the life cycle of the insect, established time of death (see page 319).

1967. *Stephen Truscott* Tried and convicted in Canada of the murder of twelve-year-old Lynne Harper in 1959, fourteen-year-old Truscott was sentenced to life imprisonment. In 1967, the controversy raised by a re-examination of the evidence resulted in a retrial at the Ottawa Supreme Court. The array of internationally famous forensic experts was unprecedented; Francis **Camps**, Keith Simpson, and Milton Helpern of New York among them. The testimony centred around the rate of digestion and stomach emptying in the human body, and whether or not it could be reliably used to estimate time of death. Although doubt continues to hover over the outcome, the evidence of Simpson and Helpern was preferred to that of Camps and Dr Charles Petty for the defence, and Truscott was returned to prison.

SKELETON
(see Anthropology, Post-Mortem Procedures)

SMITH, SYDNEY ALFRED (1883–1969)

One of the celebrated products of the Edinburgh University Medical College, Smith was the equal, though in a more self-effacing manner, of his contemporary, Bernard **Spilsbury**. An all-rounder in the field of forensic science, Smith contributed a great deal to toxicology, microscopy and ballistics, as well as casting his brilhance on to pathology. A great champion of the comparison microscope, which he had used to such startling effect in Cairo in the case of Sir Lee Stack, it was largely through Smith's influence that the instrument achieved recognition in Britain. Arguably, Sydney Smith's greatest contributions were in the fields of **Firearms** and **Gunshot Wounds**, on which his textbooks became standard references.

Sydney Smith was born on 4 August 1883, in the small New Zealand village of Roxburgh. After leaving school he served an apprenticeship with a local apothecary and then spent the two years between 1906 and

1908 as a part-time student at the Faculty of Science, Victoria College, Wellington. During the rest of his waking time, the young Sydney Smith worked as a chemist's assistant. He invested his wages in a steamship ticket to Britain where he enrolled at Edinburgh University. In 1912 he graduated – M.B., Ch.B. with first class honours and the offer of a research scholarship. At first Smith had decided on opthalmology, but as a position arose as assistant to the celebrated Professor Harvey Littlejohn at the department of forensic medicine, and as the post also carried an annual salary of £50 Smith came, almost by chance, to the discipline of which he was to become an acknowledged master.

The first major murder in which Sydney Smith became involved was of the Higgins children at Hopetoun, and he was personally selected by Littlejohn for the job (see page 22). The following year, 1914, Smith received his master degree with honours, at the same time picking up the Diploma in Public Health. The Great War was about to shatter the peace of the world, and Sydney Smith returned to New Zealand to serve with the Army Corps and also perform the role of civilian Medical Officer of Health.

In many respects the life-work of Sydney Smith began in 1917 with his appointment as Principal Medico-Legal Expert to the Egyptian Ministry of Justice; he later founded the chair in forensic medicine at the University of Cairo and became its first Professor. There followed eleven of the most productive and rewarding years of Smith's life, which came to an end only with the death of his old friend and mentor, Professor Harvey Littlejohn in Edinburgh. With the first edition of his *Textbook of Forensic Medicine* just two years behind him, Sydney Smith returned to his old university as Regius Professor to take up the vacant chair in 1927. He occupied the position for the next twenty-five years, being appointed Dean of Faculty in 1931, and knighted in 1949. Sir Sydney retired from Edinburgh in 1953 with the honours of Professor Emeritus, Rector and, two years later, Honorary Doctor of Law. His autobiography, *Mostly Murder,* was published by Harrap in 1959 – and is still in print more than thirty years later. Professor Sir Sydney Smith died on 8 May 1969.

Celebrated Cases

1913.   *Patrick Higgins* Despite their almost complete transformation to **Adipocere**, Smith managed to identify as Higgins's sons the two small corpses taken from the Hopetoun Quarry, near Winchburgh, Scotland.

1930. *Sidney Harry Fox* Retained by the defence to oppose **Spilsbury** in this celebrated case of matricide.

1931. *Sarah Ann Hearn Case* Smith was retained by the defence to oppose the evidence of Dr Roche Lynch for the Crown that Mrs Hearn had poisoned her friend and neighbour, Alice Thomas, with sandwiches laced with **Arsenic**. Mrs Hearn was acquitted (see page 83).

1934. *Jeannie Donald* Accused of murdering eight-year-old Helen Priestley in Aberdeen. Smith and fellow Scot John **Glaister** matched **Hairs** and **Fibres** found in the sack in which the victim was discovered with Mrs Donald's by use of Smith's comparison microscope (see page 284).

1935. *The Shark-Arm Case* An Australian classic in which Smith proved the shark 'innocent' (see page 486).

   Dr Buck Ruxton Notorious dismemberment case which established the reputation not only of Smith, but of his two Scottish contemporaries, John Glaister and James Brash (see page 149).

1952. *Regina v. Sathasivam* Smith was invited to Ceylon to present expert testimony in the case of Sathasivam, who stood accused of murdering his wife.

SMOTHERING
(see Suffocation)

SPECTROMETRY

The principle of the spectrometer and spectrograph is that they analyse *light* when it passes through a solid, liquid or gaseous sample, or is emitted from a material that has been subjected to a high temperature which has raised it to a high energy.

First it is necessary to understand that light – visible, or white, light – is composed of all the colours of the rainbow (red, orange, yellow, green, blue, indigo, violet); and a glass prism is able to separate a beam of white light back into these component colours. Each colour has a different wavelength, and some colours, because they are invisible to the eye, can only be determined by measuring their wavelengths (the best-known are infra-red and ultra-violet, which are out of the visible range at each end of our spectrum).

Spectrophotometer

When infra-red light, a radiation source, is directed at a sample it will pass through slightly 'diluted' where the sample has absorbed some of the wavelengths of the light. Which wavelengths have been absorbed, and to what degree they have been absorbed, depends upon the chemical structure of the sample. The spectrophotometer measures and records the intensity of the light transmitted at each wavelength as it has passed through the sample; these measurements are recorded on a graph, or absorption spectrum.

Large reference collections of sample spectrographs of known substances have been catalogued and indexed for easy comparison with the spectrographs of unknown substances.

The preparation of samples will vary according to the type of radiation source being used; for example, ultraviolet absorption spectra are normally obtained from samples dissolved in a suitable liquid held in a glass cell. The ultraviolet spectrum is far simpler than the infra-red, and is by no means as specific in its results.

Emission Spectrograph

One of the oldest spectrometric techniques, the emission spectrograph is commonly used in the qualitative and quantitative identification of metals, glass, paint, and elements such as iron, gold, silver, lead, etc. It is a destructive technique, though it can work with relatively small samples (10mg).

The method is to burn the sample between two carbon electrodes which will give a brilliant multicoloured flame. Sometimes the energy is generated by heating to high temperatures, and more recently with a laser beam or electron beam. The resulting wavelengths of light are passed through lenses and a prism which breaks the light up into its special colours which are recorded on a photographic plate. When the plate is processed a series of lines appears depicting the component frequencies of the sample.

Atomic Absorption Spectrophotometry

Based on the principle that an atom when vapourized will selectively absorb light, and in this respect it is not unlike ultraviolet spectrometry. Although the technique has been in use since around 1955, atomic absorption spectrophotometry is a cumbersome process which has not found wide application in the forensic laboratory.

The specimen is presented as a liquid which is heated to the degree where its atoms are vapourized (usually achieved with an air-acetylene flame); the atoms are exposed to radiation from a light source. The result is only specific if this source is a discharge tube made of the same element that is being analysed in the sample. For instance, if one wished to test a sample for the presence of mercury, the instrument would be fitted with a mercury lamp so that the specimen would absorb light only when it contained mercury. When the radiation has passed through the sample and a diffraction grating which isolates the required radiation frequency, it is converted into an electrical signal which in its turn is recorded on a chart.

Although a high degree of accuracy can be achieved with the apparatus, it can only test for one element at a time, and it requires the lamp to be changed for each different element.

SPILSBURY, BERNARD HENRY (1877–1947)

The man who would be described as 'the greatest medical detective of the century' was born in January 1877 at Leamington Spa, Warwickshire. In 1896 he was admitted to Magdalen College, Oxford, and when he came down three years later he had decided to enter the medical profession. It was later, under the inspired influence of his tutors at St Mary's Hospital Medical School, that he took a specialized interest in 'the beastly science' as pathology was then called. He entered St Mary's, Paddington, in 1899 as an exhibition student, and with a voracious appetite for learning immersed himself in the study of psychology, chemistry, histology, anatomy, biology, pharmacology, microscopy, and the emerging science of pathology. In this he was encouraged by the brilliant trio of Drs A.P. Luff, William Willcox, and A.J. Pepper, under whom he was appointed Resident Assistant Pathologist upon his graduation in 1905. In 1908 Spilsbury was elected to the Medico-Legal Society.

The turning point in Dr Spilsbury's career came in 1910 when he was called in to examine the mutilated remains of Mrs Cora Crippen; it was his first murder case, and a landmark in the development of medico-legal evidence. In order to satisfy the legal requirement to identify the victim positively, the existence of an abdominal scar had to be proved. The defence contended that the so-called 'scar' was simply a fold in the skin. Spilsbury, in presenting his counter-evidence, brought a microscope into court and encouraged the jurors to examine for themselves the slides of tissue samples that he had prepared. It was this ability – and willingness – to explain clearly and patiently the most complex scientific problems to a lay jury that ensured his formidable reputation as an expert witness; indeed, the accusation has often been levelled against him that the respect, almost reverence, for his every utterance blinded everybody to even the *possibiliiy* that he might be wrong. Typical of the adulation of his contemporaries is this extract from the summing-up of Mr Justice Darling in the case of Major Herbert Rowse Armstrong, accused of poisoning his wife:

> Do you remember Dr Spilsbury? Do you remember how he stood and the way he gave his evidence? Do you remember how if there were any qualifications to be made in favour of the defence he always gave it without being asked for it? Did you ever see a witness who more thoroughly satisfied you that he was absolutely impartial, absolutely fair, absolutely indifferent as to whether his evidence told for one side or the other, when he was giving evidence-in-chief, or when he was being cross-examined?

Between the Crippen case and his death in 1947 Spilsbury performed around 25,000 post-mortems, and although only one per cent of these were homicidal deaths it was the one per cent that made his name a legend. In 1920, after twenty years at St Mary's, Bernard Spilsbury moved to the Lectureship in Morbid Anatomy and Histology at St Bartholomew's Hospital, and three years later was knighted and made a Freeman of the City of London. Following the tragic deaths of his two sons, from which he never recovered, and long periods of overwork resulting in ill-health and a decline in his mental alertness, Sir Bernard took his own life by coal-gas poisoning on 17 December 1947, in his laboratory at University College, London; it was an irony that so much of his life's work had been concerned with suicides. The man who carried out the post-mortem on 'the post-mortem man' was Dr R.H.D. Short.

Celebrated Cases

1910.   *Hawley Harvey Crippen*

1911.   *Frederick and Margaret Seddon* Spilsbury and Dr William Willcox examined the exhumed body of Eliza Barrow and were able to confirm cause of death as acute arsenical poisoning (see page 46).

1915.   *George Joseph Smith* The 'Brides in the Bath Case'. With Willcox, Spilsbury worked out the method used by Smith to drown his 'wives' – putting his left arm under their knees and pushing the head downwards and under the water with the right hand. While attempting to demonstrate his technique in court, Spilsbury nearly drowned the nurse on loan from St Mary's for the occasion.

1917.   *Lonis Voisin*

1918.   *David Greenwood* 'The Button and Badge Murder'.

1922.   *Frederick Bywaters and Edith Thompson*
Herbert Rowse Armstrong Spilsbury examined the exhumed body of Armstrong's wife to prove incontrovertible evidence of arsenic poisoning.

1924.   *Patrick Mahon* Spilsbury responsible for piecing together what was left after the butchering and burning of Miss Emily Kaye's body, at Eastbourne, Sussex. Horrified to see detectives touching with their bare hands the victim's putrid remains Spilsbury collaborated with Dr Scott-Gillett in evolving the now famous 'Murder Bag' (see page 120).
Norman Thorne Tried for the murder of his fiancée, Thorne maintained that she had hanged herself. In court, Spilsbury's evidence was seriously challenged (effectively for the first time) by Dr Robert Bronte giving evidence for the defence. The judge, however, considered Spilsbury's opinion 'undoubtedly the very best that can be obtained'. Thorne was hanged.
Jean-Pierre Vaquier Poisoned his lover's husband with a strychnine hangover cure.

1926.   *John Donald Merrett* Greatly swayed by what turned out to be misleading evidence by Spilsbury and ballistics expert Robert Churchill, a jury acquitted Merrett of murdering his mother. In 1954, now using the name Chesney, Merrett killed twice more before committing suicide.

1927.   *John Robinson* 'The Charing X Trunk Murder'.

1929.   *William Henry Podmore* Bludgeoned to death Vivian Messiter in a garage in Southampton (see page 168).
Sidney Harry Fox Tried in 1930 for the murder of his mother in a Margate hotel room. Spilsbury conducted the post-mortem during the course of which he found a bruise on the larynx consistent with strangulation. The subsequent natural disappearance of the bruise led to the pathologist's evidence being seriously disputed by Professor Sydney **Smith** who had been retained by the defence (see page 302).

1930.   *Alfred Arthur Rouse* 'The Blazing Car Murder'.

1931.   *Oliver Newman and William Shelley* Two itinerant labourers
        who murdered a fellow vagrant, Herbert Ayres.

1934.   *The Brighton Trunk Murders*

1937.   *Leslie Stone* Remarkable forensic detective work leading to
        the identification of Stone as Ruby Keen's murderer, by
        matching soil and fibre particles from the scene of the crime
        with those embedded in Stone's trousers (see page 192).

1938.   *William Butler*

1942.   *Gordon Cummins* 'The Wartime Jack the Ripper'.

1943.   *Harold Loughans* In a rare appearance on behalf of the
        defence, Spilsbury's evidence was instrumental in Loughans'
        acquittal of the murder of Portsmouth publican Rose
        Robinson. Twenty years later, when Loughans emerged from
        a term of imprisonment on a quite separate charge, he
        confessed to the Portsmouth murder (see p. 475).

1947.   *Jenkins, Geraghty and Rolt* The last appearance in court for
        Spilsbury (and, coincidentally, for firearms expert Robert
        Churchill). Two months after Geraghty and Jenkins were
        hanged Spilsbury himself died.

STABBING
(see **Knife Wounds**)

STRANGULATION
Strangulation with a Ligature

Death is caused by a constricting force around the neck exerted by
means of some pliable strip, such as a rope, necktie, etc., but unlike
Hanging is not dependent on the suspended weight of the victim's
body. The ligature may have been knotted, tied into a running noose, or
simply had the ends crossed over; in any event, in cases of homicide
some agent other than the victim will need to have pulled the ligature
tight in order for strangulation to occur. Death is by **Asphyxia**, and can
result from accident, suicide or homicide.

Ligature marks usually consist of a furrow (or furrows) impressed
horizontally around the neck; because the weight of the body has not
been pulling against the noose, the mark will be lower than that charac-
terizing hanging, and less well defined. The nature of the ligature and
the degree of pressure exerted will dictate the physical appearance of

the marks – a wire noose will produce a thin deep mark, while the mark made by a soft scarf may hardly be noticeable.

Suicidal strangulation is effected by the victim himself tying and tightening the ligature, and it is common to find a double knot used, or the ligature wound round the neck more than once – this ensures that pressure is maintained even when the victim has passed into unconsciousness.

It is vitally important that any ligature is photographed *in situ* around the victim's neck at the scene of the 'crime'; it is equally important that in removing the ligature it is *cut* in such a way that the knot is preserved intact to give what clues it might – for example, in the notorious case of the 'Boston Strangler' thirteen-times killer Albert de Salvo tied knots in such a characteristic way that it was immediately obvious when a murder was the Strangler's handiwork.

Manual Strangulation

Sometimes described as 'throttling', manual strangulation is caused by compression of the throat by the hands and fingers of an assailant. There are three ways in which the natural functions of the body are impeded by strangulation – the obstruction of respiration, obstruction of the blood supply to the brain, and pressure on the carotid nerve plexuses. Although they may put up a struggle – and the physical signs of that struggle may be observed on the body – throttling renders victims helpless very quickly as they fall into unconsciousness.

Post-Mortem Appearances
Ligature Strangulation

The nature and extent of injury will depend on the degree of force exerted, and little damage may be caused to the underlying muscles, except that they may show blood due to ruptured vessels. The cartilages of the trachea and larynx are generally intact, except in cases of homicide where it is frequently the case that an assailant will exert far more pressure than is required and fractures in the cartilages result. Homicidal strangulation will almost always cause fracture of the hyoid, suicide and accident almost never.

Other post-mortem appearances, both external and internal, will be consistent with forms of death by asphyxia.

Manual Strangulation

Bruising to the victim's neck will depend upon the way in which the attack was made and the relative positions of the victim and assailant. Marks are produced by the fingers and thumbs at the points where pressure is exerted and appear as roundish bruises about half an inch in diameter. If the attacker has long fingernails, these may inflict crescent-shaped indentation marks. There may be damage to the tongue through pressure on, or being trapped between, the teeth. A victim's face may exhibit other signs of bruising and abrasion received during a struggle.

Internal appearances will be a greater or lesser degree of muscle bruising depending on the severity of the attack and the amount of violence used, likely damage to the thyroid and crocoid cartilages, and almost certainly fracture of the hyoid bone. In addition, there may be bruising to the tongue, the floor of the mouth, epiglottis, and lining of the larynx. The usual signs consistent with asphyxial death will be found.

Case Study

HAROLD LOUGHANS

The killing of pub landlady Mrs Rose Robinson in 1943 was by no means a 'classic' murder in the true sense of that term – it was the squalid, not particularly remunerative result of a burglary. However, it was the one occasion on which an unscrupulous killer was acquitted on the expert testimony of Sir Bernard **Spilsbury**.

On the night of Sunday 28 November 1943, Mrs Robinson's cellarman at the *John Barleycorn* public house in Portsmouth closed up for the night and left at about half-past ten. Rose Robinson transferred the evening's takings from the till to her handbag and went upstairs. On the following morning she was found strangled in her ransacked bedroom; her handbag was empty. The killer had entered through a rear window beneath which police officers found a small black button with a broken thread.

The pathologist was Dr Keith **Simpson**, who concluded that Mrs Robinson had been strangled as the killer sat astride her: 'The finger-marks told a clear story – a deep bruise on the right side of the voice-box, presumably made by a thumb, and three lighter bruises in a line on the other side. Right-handed, four inches across. There were no curved fingernail impressions immediately related to these marks, but there were several scratches on the neck that could have been made by Mrs Robinson as she struggled to prise away her attacker's hands.'

It was in London a month later that a shabby, suspicious-looking man attracted the attention of a couple of policemen who followed him into a café, where the man tried to sell a pair of new shoes. Taken into custody for questioning Harold Loughans told his captors: 'I'm wanted for things more serious than this; the Yard wants me. It's the trap-door for me now.' He went on to confess to a string of burglaries, concluding: 'I want to say I done a murder job.' It was the still-unsolved *John Barleycorn* killing.

There was no shortage of forensic evidence to back up the confession **Fibres** linked Loughans to the murder of Rose Robinson, and his coat was missing all its buttons – pulled off when he discovered he had left one behind at the scene of his crime.

The one problem as far as the police were concerned was that Harold Loughans had no fingers on his right hand; a fact which they relayed to Dr Simpson with some anxiety. Simpson was unperturbed, Loughans still had a thumb and four half fingers, and if he was sitting astride his victim just the weight of his body pressing down on the hand could have proved fatal. Loughans' condition also explained why there were no fingernail impressions.

By the time Harold Loughans stood trial at Winchester Assizes in March 1944, he had had the opportunity to ponder his future; the trap-door. He had decided to plead not guilty to murder and swore the police had coerced him into making a confession. His defence attorney paraded three witnesses before the court who testified they had seen Loughans in an air-raid shelter in London on the night of the crime (remember we are in the middle of the Second World War). The jury failed to reach agreement, and a retrial was held two weeks later, this time against the backdrop of the world's most famous criminal court, the Old Bailey. Loughans again pleaded alibi, but by now the defence had a new weapon. They had retained the services of Sir Bernard Spilsbury. Simpson for one was dumbfounded. His colleague had not had a chance to see the victim's body, had made no independent post-mortem examination, had not even inspected the medical evidence assembled by Simpson for his own testimony. Apparently Sir Bernard had visited Loughans in Brixton Prison, had been impressed by his flabby handshake, and told the court: 'I do not believe he could strangle anyone with that hand.' Nor would he budge; and it is a tribute to the awe in which his expert testimony was held that Spilsbury's bald statement was accepted as the undeniable truth and Harold Loughans was acquitted.

In time the case was forgotten, which is the way of things, and besides Loughans was swiftly rearrested and put in jail convicted on a charge of aggravated burglary. Then in December 1960 the *People* newspaper serialized the memoirs of Mr J.D. Caswell, the Crown prosecutor in the Loughans case. Caswell intimated that Loughans was very lucky to have been acquitted, and Loughans responded by taking out libel proceedings against the paper. The suit failed, and in doing so presented the uniquely bizarre situation of a jury going against a high court judgement and, in effect, finding Harold Loughans guilty of the *John Barleycorn* murder. Whatever happened he could not be tried twice for the same crime, so three months after his libel action failed, Loughans wrote his confession – with the 'bad' hand – for the *People:* 'I want to say I done that job. I did kill the woman in the public house in Portsmouth.'

STRYCHNINE

Nux vomica, or poison berry, is said to have been known to the Arabians as far back as the fifth century. The first really reliable record of the existence of the berries *Strychnos nux vomica* in the pharmacy is met with in the textbooks of medicine in the seventeenth century, where the powdered berries are recommended for poisoning vermin and birds. But though *nux vomica* was not used as a medicine till the end of the seventeenth century, its active principle, strychnine, produced its medicinal effect, being administered in the form of 'St Ignatius's Bean', a berry brought back from India by the Jesuit missionaries. This bean, which was administered for fever and as a tonic, contains about 1 per cent of strychnine, and was a very safe method of administration.

In 1818 the celebrated chemists, Pelletier and Carenton, investigated the properties of several of the medicinal herbs and berries which were brought from the East, and among them the two berries *Strychnos nux vomica* and St Ignatius's Bean *(Strychnos ignatii).* Exhaustive experiments showed them that the active principle of both these drugs was a white crystalline substance which they named 'strychnine', and since *nux vomica* is far more plentiful than the Jesuits' famous berries, it became the principal source of the alkaloid.

The *Strychnos nux vomica* shrub from which the valuable seeds are obtained, is a member of the botanical family *Loganiaceae,* and has the dark shiny leaves so typical of that family. When in seed, it produces long, cylindrical beans, or pods, from which a number of disc-shaped seeds about the size of a 5p piece are extracted. The seeds are slightly hollow on one side, and the centre of the opposite side is raised correspondingly. They are covered with fine silky hairs, which radiate from the centre to the edge, and give the seed a very striking appearance owing to the reflection of the light falling on it. In colour *nux vomica* seeds are light brown, greenish-grey, or silver grey, according to the state of maturity at which they were gathered. They are very tough, and difficult to powder in a mortar.

The principal source of supply is the Malabar coast of India, where the inhabitants are said to eat the seeds as a prophylactic for snake-bites; some authors claim that the strychnine eaters enjoy immunity even from the venom of the cobra.

Strychnine produces a colourless solution with an intensely bitter taste, which can be distinctly detected even in dilutions as weak as one part in 600,000 of water. It is a very powerful poison, and it must be considered that a dose of one-third of a grain administered by mouth, or one-twentieth of a grain injected, constitutes a dangerous dose. One and a half grains (100 milligrams) is generally set as the fatal dose, though one-third of a grain is known to have been fatal within twenty minutes.

The symptoms of strychnine poisoning are very marked. Some time after the administration of the drug, the victim experiences a sense of restlessness, accompanied by a feeling of impending suffocation. Then the face is drawn into a characteristic grin, due to the contraction of the facial muscles. This grin is known as the *risus sardonicus*. Following this the muscles are violently and spasmodically contracted, the patient being bent and doubled up into all sorts of shapes. At one moment he may be bent double like a bow, resting on his heels and head – a phenomenon known as opisthotonos; at the next he may be jerked off the bed through violent contractions of other muscles. The paroxysms last for several minutes, and are succeeded by a period of rest, during which the sufferer complains of great exhaustion, and of intense thirst. Then another longer and more violent attack comes on, and the patient suffers further agony. The muscles of the stomach become hard and tense, the face livid, the eyeballs staring and prominent. Still the patient is fully conscious, though often unable to speak owing to the fixture of the jaw by a variety of lockjaw. The slightest touch will often throw the sufferer into violent convulsions. The pulse becomes so rapid during the spasmodic attacks as to be uncountable. As the effect progresses, the attacks follow one another with increasing rapidity, and in one of them the victim dies from suffocation, due to the paralyzing of the respiratory muscles. There may be an interval between the administration of the drug and the commencement of the symptoms of two or even three hours, but once the symptoms are developed it is a question of speedy death or equally speedy recovery. Strychnine poisoning has been mistaken for tetanus and also epilepsy – though the consciousness of the victim throughout the ordeal should rule out epilepsy.

Until the turn of the century there was no way of accurately detecting strychnine in the body after death, and it was on this that Dr Palmer, the Rugeley murderer, relied for safety when he poisoned his wife, brother and friend with strychnine. However, shortly before Palmer started on his poisoning career an absolutely accurate test for the poison had been discovered, and had the country doctor kept up his medical knowledge instead of neglecting his profession for the turf, he would never have selected strychnine as his weapon. There is no doubt that with the knowledge of the effects of strychnine and the accurate methods of analysis which have now been perfected, no person can administer a fatal dose of the alkaloid to another without detection. A minuscule trace can be separated out of the body, and to this absolutely distinctive tests can be applied.

Brucine

Although the active principle of *nux vomica* is strychnine, the seeds also contain another alkaloid called brucine, which resembles strychnine in all its characteristics, but is only one-sixth of its strength. It was with this drug, Dumas tells us (in his novel *The Count of Monte Cristo*), that Madame de Villefort attempted to poison half a household. It is worth recording that in the nineteenth century a number of brewers were heavily fined for putting brucine into their beer to enhance its bitterness.

Case Study

THE DOG IT WAS THAT DIED

In the case of the death of Arthur Major the police would have been unaware that there had even been a crime to solve had it not been for an anonymous letter – the writer of which remains unknown to this day.

On 26 May 1934, Inspector Dodson of the Horncastle force received the following:

Sir, Have you ever heard of a wife poisoning her husband? Look further into the death (by heart failure) of Mr Major, of Kirkby-on-

Bain [Lincolnshire]. Why did he complain of his food tasting nasty and throw it to a neighbour's dog, which has since died? Ask the undertaker if he looked natural after death? Why did he stiffen so quickly? Why was he so jerky when dying? I myself have heard her threaten to poison him years ago. In the name of the law, I beg you to analyse the contents of his stomach.

'Fairplay'

A quick check revealed that forty-four-year-old lorry driver Arthur Major had indeed died – on 24 May. The symptoms – violent spasms and painful muscular contortions – had begun two days before, shortly after Mr Major had eaten his supper of corned beef. The doctor had been summoned and found the patient in great discomfort, foaming at the mouth, unable to speak and sweating profusely. On examination, the surface of Major's body was blue, and the physical contact set off another spasm. During the following thirty-six hours it seemed that almost anything would throw the unfortunate Arthur Major into convulsions – voices, movements in the room, the touch of the bedclothes against him. Then at 10.40 on the night of the 24th he died in extreme agony; certificated cause of death *Status epilepticus* – epilepsy.

Dodson acted swiftly in getting a coroner's order to prevent the funeral taking place at its appointed time on 27 May and it must have been a uniquely disturbing experience for the mourners assembled at the Majors' house ready to follow the coffin to see the police remove it in front of their very eyes.

Meanwhile, Dodson's officers had confirmed that a wire-haired terrier belonging to the Majors' next-door neighbour had died during the night of 23 May after suffering muscular spasms. The direct cause of the unfortunate beast's untimely death could not elude the redoubtable Dr Roche Lynch, distinguished analyst to the Home Office. Nor could the reason for Arthur Major's recent demise – both had succumbed to a fatal dose of strychnine – in Major's case, probably two doses.

An account of his first meeting with Ethel Major is conveniently supplied by the Scotland Yard officer who was placed in overall charge of the case, Chief-Inspector (later Commander) Hugh Young:

She impressed me as a cool and resourceful woman suffering no pangs of sorrow at the loss of her husband. In fact, she seemed quite callous about the whole affair, and even informed me that she felt 'much better in health since he was gone'. She began, however, by telling me that she was sure her husband had died through eating corned beef. She appeared over-eager to impress me with the fact that she had nothing to do with providing his meals, explaining that for a fortnight before her husband's death she and her young son had not slept at home, but had stayed with her father . . . 'My husband bought his tinned beef himself,' she went on, adding with great insistence: 'I know that I never bought any. I hate corned beef and think it is a waste of money to buy such rubbish.' This obvious desire to dissociate herself from any provision or purchase of corned beef seemed to me rather important, because corned beef was the last meal eaten by Arthur Major before he was seized with his fatal illness on the night of 22 May.

Commander Hugh Young, *My Forty Years at the Yard*

Further investigation began to colour in many of the details of the Majors' unsettled married life; for a start, they couldn't stand the sight of each other – in fact Ethel, a cantankerous, arrogant woman, was pretty much disliked throughout the neighbourhood. Arthur was also sinking financially as a result of what he saw as his wife's extravagance. A development worthy of note, in the circumstances, is that in the week he died Major had arranged to have a notice published in the *Horncastle News* dissociating himself from all the debts accumulated by his wife – an arrangement countermanded by Mrs Major immediately her husband died. Jealousy also emerged as a potential motive. Ethel claimed to have found two letters written by Mrs Rose Kettleborough (a neighbour) to Arthur; to her detriment Ethel showed these letters to her doctor with the accompanying comment: 'A man like him is not fit to live, and I will do him in.'

When Chief-Inspector Young next interviewed Mrs Major she claimed: 'I've never had any strychnine poison.' 'I never mentioned strychnine,' the detective replied, 'how did you know about that?' 'Oh, I'm sorry. I must have made a mistake.'

When she came up for trial at Lincoln Assizes, Ethel Lillie Major was defended by Mr Norman (later Lord) Birkett. He could not have faced a more daunting task in the whole of his long career. The evidence against his client was overwhelming.

The police had proved access to the poison when they found a key in Ethel Major's purse that opened a box containing a bottle of strychnine belonging to her ex-gamekeeper father. He had used the poison to exterminate vermin, and vaguely remembered having mislaid his spare key some years before. The corned beef from which Mrs Major had been at such pains to distance herself was proved to have been bought by the couple's fifteen-year-old son – on his mother's instruction.

Norman Birkett would surely have been one of the first to concur with the claim made by his learned colleague for the Crown, Mr Edward O'Sullivan KC: 'The case is really on the evidence unanswerable.' The defence called no witnesses, and Ethel Major did not take the witness stand. When the jury filed back into court with their verdict after one hour, Birkett already knew that he had lost.

Mr Justice Charles passed sentence of death on the prisoner, and relayed the jury's inexplicable recommendation to mercy. This latter was not acted upon by the Home Secretary and Ethel Lillie Major was executed at Hull Prison on 19 December 1934.

SUFFOCATION

One of several causes of death by asphyxia, with which it is convenient to include Smothering, Choking and Crush (or Traumatic) Asphyxia. Post-mortem appearances will be those of anoxia (see **Asphyxia**).

Suffocation

Death will occur if the oxygen in the atmosphere drops below a certain level and is replaced by carbon dioxide. Death is then attributable to a combination of anoxia and carbon dioxide poisoning. Suffocation is usually associated with a person's entrapment in a confined, airtight space, and the length of time it takes to die will depend upon the size of the space and the metabolism of the victim. Suffocation is usually accidental (mine and lift accidents, becoming trapped in a cupboard or packing case, etc.), and children are often the victims. Death can also result from poisonous gas being produced in an unventilated space (see **Carbon Monoxide Poisoning**).

Homicidal suffocation could result from deliberately locking a victim in an airless atmosphere.

Smothering

Death is caused by the accidental (or homicidal) obstruction of the mouth and nose preventing respiration. This can occur accidentally if a very old, very young or very intoxicated person becomes entangled in heavy bedding or if their head becomes 'buried' in a soft pillow or cushion. The same effect, of course, results from deliberately holding a pillow or cushion over a victim's face cutting off the air supply. Putting the head in a plastic bag – either accidentally or suicidally – will cause smothering, which is a particular hazard to young children.

Homicidal smothering can result if pressure, say from an attacker's hand, is applied over the nostrils and mouth, and at the same time the weight of the assailant's body applied over the victim's chest preventing movement of the diaphragm. This was the murder method favoured by William Burke and William Hare, the notorious Edinburgh body snatchers; the method became called 'Burking' in recognition of their enterprise. As the bodies were required for anatomical demonstration, smothering ensured that the subjects were free from unsightly injury.

Choking

Caused by blockage of the air passage by foreign bodies. These can originate from inside the body – such as inhaled vomit, or blood from a mouth or throat injury; or from outside the body – partly masticated food, or granular material, such as sand and coal dust in construction and mining accidents. Accidental choking on food so resembles a heart attack that the French call these incidents 'café coronaries' (and the prudent physician will bear this in mind when making his examination).

Choking is rarely encountered as a method of homicide, except in some cases of infanticide where it is easy to interrupt the baby's breathing by forcing foreign bodies into its mouth (a death which may subsequently be claimed to have been accidental). Cases have also been recorded of victims choking on material used to gag their mouths during the course of some other crime such as burglary.

Suicidal deaths have occurred of subjects deliberately forcing objects down their own throat with the intention of inducing choking. John Glaister cited one case of a man suffering from mental instability being placed in a padded cell and shortly afterwards being found dead. Inside the patient's mouth was a piece of flannel about twelve inches long and one inch wide, and behind it were two more strips of similar length. The last of these was so firmly packed over the epiglottis that it was withdrawn only with difficulty. He had obtained the cloth by tearing his blanket.

Crush (or Traumatic) Asphyxia

Almost always the result of an accidental fall of a heavy substance – earth from the sides of a trench, bales from a stack, a piece of machinery – which compresses the chest and prevents movement of the diaphragm, making respiration impossible. Due to the nature of the death, post-mortem appearances are severe, with deep engorgement and cyanosis accompanied by large haemorrhages beneath the skin from mid-chest to head. There is additional haemorrhaging of the conjunctivae and oedema of the eyeballs. A further common cause of traumatic asphyxia is being crushed in a crowd.

SUICIDE
(see Carbon Monoxide Poisoning, Gunshot Wounds, Hanging, Poisons, Strangulation)

T

TATTOOS

The omnipotent presence of Professor Alexandre **Lacassagne** of Lyons was felt in many aspects of the emerging science of Medical Jurisprudence and it was he who recognized the potential of tattooing as a contribution to a system of visual **Identification**. Lacassagne had been commissioned as an Army surgeon and served in North Africa with as rough a collection of reprobate soldiers as France could muster – all of whom sported these often unique and virtually ineradicable pictorial 'identity cards'.

In fact, the marking of slaves was practised as far back as Roman times, and there are reports that in the coarser days of the Senior Service some ships' captains recorded details of their crew members' tattoos in the log, the easier to identify deserters. Quite how this helped in the face of perennially favoured designs is uncertain – especially as the criminally inclined tar would be sure to have a crucifix etched into his back in the belief that the cat o' nine tails would shrink from the sacrilege of striking the sacred relic. More recently it was the custom among sailors of the American merchant marine to have a pig tattooed on the sole of their foot as a sure protection against drowning.

Although sophistication of the technique and visual artistry has made tattooing a body ornament now finding favour across the social classes, it is their traditionally favoured place among the 'criminal class' that render tattoos of such 'enduring' value to the forces of law and order. Nor is identification confined to criminals on the run – a photographic record of skin decorations on bodies discovered in suspicious circumstances is made in the event that the tattoos might be a vital source of identification. Even when putrefaction has rendered a tattoo indistinct it is possible, by careful removal of the loose epidermis, to photograph a clearer image on the underlying dermis. This technique is particularly useful in relation to bodies recovered from long periods in water.

Tattoos as a sign of membership have always been favoured by the Chinese secret societies, and their use as a means of identification is certain to increase, in the fight against alarming escalations in Triad activity among the residents of the world's Chinatown districts.

In present-day America, tattoos of a 'home-made' variety are common among drug addicts and other criminal and antisocial elements, and the messages themselves are appropriately antisocial – 'Born to Lose', and 'I Don't Believe in Friends' being popular. In December 1991 the burned and battered body of a man was discovered in Essex, England; among other tattoos were the words 'Eat Your Heart Out'. Chief US Medical Examiner Michael Baden says resignedly of tattoos: 'An amazing number of people who are murdered are adorned with them.'

Case Study

THE SHARK-ARM CASE

April 25th, 1935; it was Australia's annual Anzac Day celebration, and despite the country being caught in the slough of an economic depression, a day off work – if you were lucky enough to be working – was cause enough for seeking any cheap entertainment that was on offer. The attraction at Coogee certainly pulled the crowds – for a few bob they could lap up the spectacle of a fourteen-foot-long tiger shark, recently caught by local fishermen. And if, on that sultry afternoon, they had known of the dramatic finale that was to be played at Coogee, every sensation-seeker in Sydney would have turned out.

Until then the shark had been something of a disappointment. In a state of deep shock and resentment at its capture, the creature had refused to eat, bare its teeth, or even move about very much; in fact, the spectators were moving on from boredom more than horror. Then, at precisely five o'clock, in front of the sleepy Anzac crowd, the shark suddenly went berserk, thrashing wildly with its tail, snapping its huge jaws, torpedoing in circles around its tank; *now* the audience gasped in horror, as a dark mass was emitted from the foaming jaws. As the disgusting mess dissipated in the tank the crowd caught its breath again, unable to believe its eyes. Surfacing from the slime spewed from the shark's belly were the outstretched fingers of a human hand attached to a burly, tattooed human arm, a length of rope floating out from the wrist. Anzac Day 1935 was something none of them would forget in a hurry.

For the authorities there were other considerations; such as how a shark captured eight days earlier could have stomached a perfectly preserved human relic for this length of time?

There was, and is, no shortage of experts on 'sharkology' in Sydney. Local expert Dr Coppleson suggested the arm had been preserved because the shark had been in a state of shock since its capture and had eaten nothing. He added that, from his many years' experience seeing victims of sharks, the creature need not be guilty of amputating the man's arm – it was not consistent with the work of a shark's teeth – the limb had more likely been hacked off with a sharp knife, and the shark had merely taken advantage of a floating snack.

Clearly, a single arm begged the question, what happened to the rest of the body? In an attempt to find the corpse, searches were made by beach patrols, divers, and by air force aerial units; all without success. In an operation taking several weeks, the fragile flakes of skin from the tips of the fingers were removed and stabilized sufficiently to allow fingerprints to be taken from them – a process that has subsequently been widely used in identifying corpses suffering extensive putrefaction. A search of criminal records proved the prints to belong to James Smith, described as 'construction worker, billiard-marker, engineer, road labourer, and boxer; age 40'; known to the police as a forger and petty thief. Furthermore, Smith's wife had reported him missing on 8 April; she later made a positive identification of Smith's arm from the tattoo depicting two sparring boxers. The question now was not *who* had died, but how and where.

Mrs Smith could provide no clue to the identity of her husband's companion on the fishing trip from which he failed to return, but police did eventually locate the cottage in which the anglers had stayed. Subsequent questioning of the owner revealed that a mattress and a tin trunk were missing. If Smith had been killed at the cottage, a tin trunk might be a handy receptacle. A boat belonging to the cottage had also been plundered of three mats and a coil of rope matching the description of that tied to the wrist of the severed arm. One reconstruction was that the killer had tried to cram the body into the tin trunk, and finding it an impossible fit lopped off one of the arms and lashed it to the outside of the trunk with rope from the boat; the trunk was then dumped offshore, the arm providing a shark's breakfast.

It was a theory that had the support of the celebrated English forensic pathologist Sir Sydney **Smith**, who was in Sydney on his way to a meeting of the British Medical Association in Melbourne. It became Smith's task to determine whether, as police now suspected, James Smith's arm had been severed after he had been killed, or, as others suggested, the limb had been chewed off by the shark while the man was still alive, which would have favoured either accident or suicide.

Sir Sydney recalled: 'I found that the limb had been severed at the shoulder joint by a clean-cut incision, and that after the head of the bone had been got out of its socket the rest of the tissues had been hacked away. In my opinion it was certain that it had been cut, and not bitten off by a shark. The condition of the blood and tissues further suggested that the amputation had taken place some hours after death.'

Then inquiries into James Smith's recent activities left little doubt that he had been caught up in the evil machinations of a thriving underground drugs trade. At the time of the 'murder' Sydney was virtually the world centre of heroin and opium smuggling; the business was getting uncomfortably overcrowded, and the result was an ugly dog-eat-dog war of hijackings, sinkings, torture and murder. Intelligence sources identified Smith as recently occupied as 'minder' of the smuggling boat *Pathfinder*. What the police needed now was to trace the owner of the craft – Reginald Holmes.

Holmes was unexpectedly cooperative; yes, he had employed James Smith to look after *Pathfinder*, and had been sorry to let him go when the boat was 'mysteriously' sunk. Naturally he knew nothing about smuggling, but he did think that Smith was being blackmailed – by a man named Patrick Brady, owner of a cottage to which Smith had recently gone for a holiday!

In no time, Brady was in custody, and police began to feel that at least they were in the lead; but that optimism reckoned without interference from the twilight world of Australia's drug-runners.

It was a couple of days after the arrest of Patrick Brady that somebody tried to shoot Reg Holmes dead as he was out in his boat; he finally managed to lose the assassin after suffering a superficial head wound; clearly somebody was determined that Holmes would be out of circulation by the time of the inquest. In a gesture of almost unbelievable stupidity, the police rejected the common-sense expedient of placing Reg Holmes in protective custody and Sydney's star witness was turned loose on the streets again.

The hit-man must have thought he was dreaming; surely, he could never have expected a second chance at Holmes, and in the small hours of 13 June – the day set for the inquest on James Smith's arm – Holmes was put beyond the call of all but the celestial coroner. The police had lost their witness, and with him, any chance of a case against Brady.

On its twelfth day, the inquest on Smith was halted by order of Mr Justice Hulse Rogers of the Australian Supreme Court, who ruled that: 'A limb does not constitute a body', and a body had 'always been essential for the holding of an inquest'. This was based on an English statute enacted in 1276, subsequently ignored in all modern legal decisions, and ultimately forgotten – except by Mr Justice Hulse Rogers.

Three months later, Patrick Brady was brought to trial before Justice Sir Frederick R. Jordan. Hardly surprisingly, the case fell flat on its face without Holmes on the witness stand, and Brady was acquitted.

In their desperation to salvage some dignity, the police authorized a £1,000 reward for information linking the murders of Holmes and Smith. But it was too late; the blanket of silence had fallen over the Sydney underworld once again.

On 12 December 1935, less than nine months after it had been opened, the file on the Shark-Arm Case was closed. In the murky drama of gangland intrigue, all the players are potential victims, many are potential murderers; the only innocent party in the whole grisly scenario was the shark!

TEARE, ROBERT DONALD (1911–79)

A third member, along with Francis **Camps** and Keith **Simpson**, of what became known as 'The Three Musketeers'. A less flamboyant character than his two colleagues, though it has been suggested by at least one observer that he might have been the best pathologist.

Donald Teare was born on 1 July 1911, and was educated at King William's College on the Isle of Man before transferring to the mainland to study medicine at Gonville and Caius College, Cambridge, and St George's Hospital, London; from which he graduated and where he stayed on to become a consultant pathologist.

The Three Musketeers shared the workload of London's wartime murders – Teare notably being associated with the killing by Hulten and Jones of a London taxi driver in what became popularly known as 'The Cleft-Chin Murder'. During that time he also regularly shared the supper table with his two illustrious colleagues at Soho's French restaurant *L'Etoile*. At one meeting their mentor Sir Sydney **Smith** was invited, and the four pathologists founded the Association in Forensic Medicine. Although the Three Musketeers eventually went their own ways, all enjoyed a brilliant future, the only slightly sour note being when Francis Camps, after some disagreement, went off to form his own Academy of Forensic Sciences in 1960.

Donald Teare continued to enjoy the favour of London's Metropolitan Police, and he was involved in many of the capital's most notorious murder cases – Daniel Raven, Timothy Evans and John Christie, Hume, Straffen and Podola. By this time Teare had been appointed Lecturer in Forensic Medicine at St Bartholomew's Hospital Medical College, and in 1963 he became Reader in Forensic Medicine at Charing Cross Hospital Medical School, where he was appointed Professor in 1967. In 1975 Donald Teare retired with the position of Professor Emeritus and four years later, on 17 January he died.

Celebrated Cases

1944. Karl Hulten and Elizabeth Jones The American GI in London – and his girl-friend who formed a wartime Bonnie and Clyde relationship ending in murder. Hulten claimed he killed taxi driver George Heath when the gun went off accidentally, but with the aid of a skeleton propped up in the cab's driving seat, Teare proved that the trajectory of the bullet could be consistent only with intentional murder.

1948. *James Camb* One of the few examples of a trial without a body (see **Corpus Delicti**). Camb appeared at Winchester Assizes charged with the murder of showgirl Gay Gibson aboard an ocean liner out of Durban, and of disposing of her body through the cabin's porthole. For the Crown, Donald Teare gave evidence that the blood-flecked saliva on the victim's bed-linen and the fact that her bladder had opened just before death and stained the bed with urine were indications of manual **Strangulation**.

1949. *Daniel Raven* Hanged for the murder of his mother- and father-in-law.

Timothy Evans and John Christie In the tragic case of the murder of Evans' wife Beryl in 1949 it was Donald Teare who carried out the post-mortem on the victim after Tim Evans had confessed to her murder. In 1953 Beryl Evans was exhumed and subjected to a second autopsy. Evans had already been executed but now Christie, the Evans family's neighbour at the notorious address 10 Rillington Place, was in custody charged with murdering his wife, and admitted responsibility for the deaths of five other women, including Beryl Evans. The second medical examination was undertaken by all three of the Musketeers – Camps had been nominated by the Attorney General, Simpson represented the interests of Christie's defence, and Teare was in attendance having undertaken the first post-mortem. In the end, the new autopsy did not add significantly to Christie's confession and he was tried and executed for the murder of his wife. Considerable doubts were raised over the safety of the Evans conviction, and after years of strenuous campaigning on his behalf Evans was granted a posthumous pardon in 1966.

THALLIUM

Thallium, a heavy metal closely related to mercury and lead, but more toxic than both, was discovered by Sir William Crookes in 1861. Its usefulness to industry has been mainly limited to incorporation into pesticides, although as in the case of arsenic before it, the sale of thallium-based products is no longer permitted in many countries.

As an instrument of murder, thallium occurs rarely in homicide records (England's Graham Young being the most celebrated, if not the first, to use it – see page 418). Nevertheless, its properties suit it ideally to the purposes of the poisoner; its salts are colourless, almost tasteless, and can be easily dissolved in water-based liquids; furthermore, the symptoms of thallium poisoning can be confused with those of a number of common virus diseases, such as influenza.

Biologically, the human body seems to confuse thallium with potassium – which is essential for the sustenance of cells and nerves – and so interferes with several different systems at the same time. It upsets the metabolism of the B vitamins, inhibits the absorption of iron and calcium, and disturbs the nerve cells. Uniquely, thallium causes the hair to fall out, and until the recognition of its dangers, thallium acetate was used by dermatologists to remove body hair in the treatment of fungus diseases such as ringworm.

Case Study

'AUNT THALLY'

She had frequently been described as 'a kindly old lady', one to whom 'people looked in time of trouble', so it took her neighbours aback when sixty-three-year-old Mrs Caroline Grills was put on trial in Sydney, Australia, charged with four counts of murder and two of attempted murder by the administration of the metallic poison thallium.

The first to suffer was Mrs Grills' stepmother, Christina Mickelson, who died suddenly in 1947 at the advanced age of eighty-seven; it was probably a relief to Caroline Grills because she had never really seen eye to eye with Mrs Mickelson since she married her son in 1908.

Shortly afterwards a family friend died, Mrs Angeline Thomas – also a venerable octogenarian. Sixty-year-old John Lundberg, another relative, was the next in Mrs Grills' circle of family and friends who fell ill; first his hair fell out, and in October 1948 he died. Mary Ann Mickelson, taken ill with similar symptoms, was the next to die, then the late John Lundberg's widow and daughter began to lose their hair and feel a heavy deadness in their limbs.

None other than Caroline Grills took it upon herself to nurse them in their sickness and she never seemed happier than when soothing her patients with cups of tea. As the two women slowly weakened, a relative began to put two and two together and arrived at the answer, 'poison'. When one of the cups of tea was analysed by the police chemist it was found to contain thallium – just in time to save the Lundbergs' lives.

Following a short investigation, Mrs Grills was arrested and charged with murder, though in advance of her trial, the prosecutor elected to proceed only on the charge of the *attempted* murder of Mrs Eveline Lundberg – who had now gone blind as the result of her experience with thallium. The prosecution contended that the pivotal motive for murder had been gain, but that there had been a secondary interest in Caroline Grills' clear desire to exercise the power of life and death over her victims. She was found guilty of the charge against her and sentenced to life imprisonment.

In jail, Mrs Grills became affectionately known as 'Aunt Thally' by her fellow inmates.

THROAT-CUTTING
(see Knife Wounds)

TIME OF DEATH

The problem with scientific methods of determining how long a body has been dead is that until very recently they have all been notoriously unreliable; in fact, they can often only be treated as rough indicators of time of death.

The three standard measurements have been Body Temperature, **Hypostasis**, and Rigor Mortis (frequently called in America *algor mortis, livor mortis* and *rigor mortis* respectively). All are subject to variation due to ambient (atmospheric) temperature, location, physique and condition of health of the subject, alcohol or drug ingestion, etc.

Body Temperature

After death the body stops generating heat, and such temperature as it has is gradually lost. At first cooling is relatively rapid (in the region of 1.5°F per hour), but after a few hours the rate slows until the temperature is the same as that of the surrounding atmosphere. Allowing for many variables, the heat-loss process for the body's surface generally takes from eight to twelve hours. Even so the body does not cool evenly, the extremities losing heat more rapidly than, say, the trunk. Furthermore, the interior of the body requires additional time to reach ambient temperature – about twenty to thirty hours in all.

At the scene of a homicide as soon as the fact of death has been established, the attendant police surgeon or pathologist must take the rectal temperature of the victim's body. A low-reading chemical thermometer is used rather than the customary clinical one, and at the same time a note is taken of the atmospheric temperature. It is advised that both temperatures are taken again before the body is removed to the mortuary so that an estimate can be got of the rate of cooling.

The following formula is widely used for estimating time since death:

$$\frac{\text{Normal Temperature (98.4°F)} - \text{Rectal Temperature}}{1.5} = \text{Approximate hours since death}$$

The following graph shows the variation in the cooling curves of a naked adult in a room temperature of 60°F (15.5°C) depending upon his build (data from *Gradwohl's Legal Medicine*, 1968):

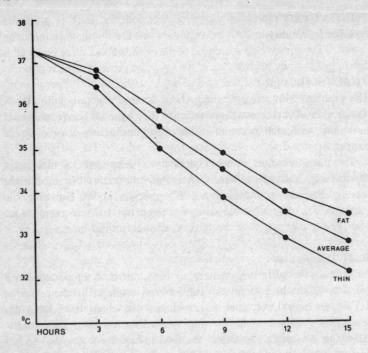

Hypostasis

Hypostasis, or post-mortem lividity, commences shortly after death and is visible thirty to sixty minutes later. The condition reaches its maximum in between six and ten hours and is fixed at about twenty-four hours (thus rendering the time-bands of this phenomenon even less useful than body temperature and rigor mortis as a means of ascertaining time of death).

Rather dramatic manifestations of hypostasis occur when the cause of death was **Carbon Monoxide Poisoning** and the lividity is bright cherry red, with **Cyanide** poisoning and the lividity is pink, and the deep bronze of sodium chlorate poisoning.

Rigor Mortis

A term to which much mystical significance has been attached by some crime fiction writers which, despite their firmest beliefs, is a singularly unreliable method of assessing accurately time of death, and one which, like body temperature, is subject to fluctuation depending on local conditions.

The complete muscular relaxation that follows death is gradually replaced by rigidity in both the voluntary and the involuntary muscular systems. It begins with a stiffening of the eyelids about three hours after death, followed by the muscles of the jaw. The process spreads progressively down through the face and neck to the thorax, the upper extremities, trunk and lower extremities. The process is generally complete in about twelve hours, though many factors affect the rate of development – weather, muscular condition of the subject during life, cause of death, temperature, and so on. In the majority of subjects the stiffening will have begun to wear off within about thirty-six hours, and the muscles in which rigor first appeared are those which are released first, until the body is once again supple in about forty-eight hours. However, the impossibility of 'calibrating' the time span has led one experienced forensic pathologist, Professor Bernard Knight, to observe: 'If a body does not have any perceptible rigor it has either been dead less than six hours or more than forty-eight hours.'

A further complication for the medical examiner are those conditions which simulate the stiffening of rigor mortis but have different origins.

Bodies exposed to intense heat, such as those which die of **Burning**, frequently stiffen into a 'sparring' pose like a boxer – called the 'pugilistic attitude'. This effect is also induced by immersion in hot liquids and is caused by the coagulation of albuminates in the muscles. The condition *replaces* rigor mortis and the stiffness persists until **Putrefaction**.

Another false rigor is 'cadaveric spasm', a phenomenon that can occur at the instant of death, most commonly causing the muscles of the hand to tighten in a vice-like grip, holding fast anything that it may be clutching – such as a weapon of self-destruction or tools held at the time of accidental electrocution. More rarely the condition will affect the whole body like true rigor. To date there is no reliable explanation of this mechanism.

Recent Developments

Clearly such an important consideration as the time that a victim died could not be left forever to inspired guesswork, and biologists have been industriously searching for a more accurate method of determining the 'hours since death'.

One current practice promising a greater degree of precision is an analysis of the amount of potassium contained in the fluid of the eye. The test was developed by John Coe, Chief Medical Examiner of

Hennepin County, United States, who observed that as red blood cells break down following death the potassium in them enters the vitreous fluid at a slow but predictable rate. This reaction is unaffected by temperature and its reliability is proving a useful guideline on both sides of the Atlantic.

TOOL MARKS

Almost any implement fashioned by man to do his work can be called a 'tool', and almost any tool will leave behind some mark of its use. There are three categories of tool marks – *Impressions* such as might be made by a hammer or a jemmy; *Cut Marks* made by wire cutters, saws, etc.; and *Scratch Marks* perhaps made by the scraping of a knife blade over a surface. Like other forms of contact trace evidence, tool marks can provide a lot of information for eyes trained to see them, and lead to the identification of the implement which made them, and so placing the tool's owner suspiciously near to the scene of the crime.

One of the most frequently found examples of tool impressions is the 'jemmy' mark at the site of a forced entry where the implement – a tyre lever, perhaps, or a chisel or screwdriver – is wedged between a door and its jamb or a window and its frame and pressure exerted. The much harder metal will compress the wood into an impression of its contour.

A significant category of tool marks are those found impressed and carved on bullets and cartridge cases by the parts of the guns which fire them; this subject is discussed in the entry on **Ballistics**.

One of the more macabre incidents in which tool marks proved vital to the solution of a brutal double murder was in the case of Danny Rosenthal. Both Rosenthal's mother, visiting London from her home in Israel, and his father, who lived in Paris, disappeared in the early autumn of 1981. Leah Rosenthal had last been seen at the home of her twenty-seven-year-old schizophrenic son Danny.

Danny Rosenthal was a virtual recluse, and had turned over the greater part of the bungalow in which he lived to a 'laboratory' in which he experimented with live chickens. Acting on the suspicions of Mrs Rosenthal's friends, police searched the squalid building and a forensic team found human bloodstains on the floors and around the skirting board. In one of the workshop rooms Dr Mike Sayce of the Aldermaston Central Forensic Research Establishment found a hacksaw which, despite cleaning, had retained traces of human bone and tissue around the blade-locking nut. Meanwhile, it had been discovered that Milton

Rosenthal had disappeared from his apartment in the suburbs of Paris – at about the same time that his son had paid a visit. The apartment bore traces of blood and tiny fragments of bone, and again a contaminated hacksaw blade was found.

Back in England Danny was saying nothing; and there was little enough evidence on which to bring a charge of murder. Then the French police unearthed the dismembered remains of a man whose physical characteristics matched those of Milton Rosenthal, though the corpse lacked the head and hands which might have provided positive identification. Nevertheless, with the ingenuity which has earned him a reputation as one of the country's leading forensic scientists Dr Sayce, in collaboration with the French pathologist Professor Michel Durignon, compared the saw-marks on the bones of the dismembered limbs with the hacksaw blades now proved to have been bought by Danny Rosenthal. Sayce used the saw blade to cut through a block of wax and, by brushing carbon powder across the resulting 'tool marks' to make them more visible, was able to make a convincing match with the saw-marks on the bones. This evidence greatly contributed to Danny Rosenthal's subsequent conviction for murder.

TOXICOLOGY
(see Drugs, Poisons)

TRACE EVIDENCE AND THE EXCHANGE THEORY
At the very foundation of forensic science is a principle first recognized as early as 1910 by Edmond **Locard** at the University of Lyon. The theory states simply that a crimmal will always take something away from the scene of his crime and leave something behind.

A simple illustration is the drunk driver who crashes his car into a lamp-post before speeding off. The impact will have transferred flakes of paint from the car to the lamp-post and vice-versa. More subtle contact traces such as hairs and minute fabric fibres, blood and other body fluids might be exchanged between a killer or rapist and his victim; or fingerprints may be deposited at the crime scene. As cases of murder in which there is an eye-witness are understandably rare, such 'circumstantial' evidence is vitally important in placing a suspect at the scene of a crime.

The following example shows how evidence of this type might be built up piece by piece into a watertight case. There has been a homicide and scenes-of-crime officers have identified a cloth cap as 'foreign' to the scene – that is, nobody who knew her could remember the elderly female victim or any of her few visitors having such a hat. However, a suspect *is* known to have possessed an identical piece of headwear; so have thousands of other people he points out. But the laboratory has turned up three human head hairs from the crown of the cap – and they match the suspect's hair! Now the suspect remembers – he did have such a hat; he left it behind in a diner months ago, hasn't seen it since, and he certainly wasn't in Brooklyn at the time of the murder. In the meantime, the forensic team have been examining the clothing worn by the suspect when he was picked up, and which he claims he was wearing on the day the crime was committed. From one of the large topcoat pockets scientists recovered some small splinters of **Glass** which are proved to have the same refractive index as the broken window pane through which the killer had gained entry to his victim's home. Furthermore, a chip of paint in the pocket gave a perfect match when compared with the coloured layers of paint on the window frame. So by the mutual exchange of 'dust, dirt and debris' it would be fair for a jury to conclude that the suspect, no matter how emphatically he may deny it, is inseparably linked to the scene of the crime.

TRUTH SERUMS

So-called 'truth-drugs' (commonly sodium amytal or sodium brevital) were a by-product of interrogation techniques developed during the Second World War. The effect is, quite simply, to inhibit that part of the brain which acts as a 'censor', rendering the subject incapable of anything but a spontaneous response to questions. Unfortunately there is a chasm of difference between a flow of uninhibited speech produced by a lowering of the defences (equally easily facilitated with alcohol) and what would, in legal terms, be considered incontestable 'truth'.

In cases such as this and, indeed, such as polygraph reports, results should not be considered of any value outside 'lead-generating', that is, opening additional avenues of research for an investigator. Results should never be used as 'evidence' in a court of law.

TYPEWRITER IDENTIFICATION
(see Disputed Documents)

TYRE MARKS
(see Impressions)

U

'UNIVERSAL' REGISTERS

Ever since the discovery of the unique characteristics of fingerprints, there have been calls for a 'Universal', or at least national, register containing the prints of every citizen. The logistics need pose no problem since one of the fundamental properties of fingerprints is that they do not alter with age, and such a scheme could be incorporated into one of the many 'medical' procedures undergone by children while at school – screenings, X-rays, moculations, etc. Opponents reason that any collection of data on a population constitutes *per se* an infringement of civil liberty – regardless that it may assist the apprehension of criminals, help identify victims of mass disasters unrecognizable by visual means, or put a name to the scores of unidentified corpses that pass out of mortuaries every year into unmarked graves.

The 'father' of fingerprinting, Juan Vucetich, was among the first to advocate a national record. On 18 July 1916, a bill was passed by the Argentine Parliament making the fingerprinting of all citizens and foreign residents compulsory. Immediately a large section of the community refused to cooperate (for what reason we can only conjecture), and the General Register building was attacked and severely damaged. In less than a year the scheme was abandoned, and in an attempt to appease the protestors many records were publicly destroyed.

In the United States efforts to assemble a Universal Fingerprint File have been 'voluntary' – mainly because compulsory registration would contravene existing law. However, some interesting results emerged from the limited exercise undertaken by the US Civil Service who required all job applicants to submit to fingerprinting; it was discovered that among 300 candidates for the police force, seven had served prison sentences.

On 17 November 1937, Britain got its chance to institute a national register. Mr Rupert de la Bere MP tabled a question in Parliament as to whether the Home Secretary would consider a scheme for nationwide fingerprinting to make easier the identification of people suffering from amnesia. Such a scheme was apparently contrary to the 'British spirit', and it was ignored. Undeterred, Mr de la Bere reworded his question for the benefit of the then Foreign Secretary, suggesting that the right thumb print of the bearer should be impressed on passports alongside the signature – a similar procedure to that already discussed at the 1937 International Police Convention with a view to preventing passport forgery. Again the honourable Member was fobbed off with excuses, and there the matter rested.

To many honest, thoughtful citizens a central fingerprint registry makes a lot of sense. Indeed, it seems to have disadvantages *only* for those whose criminous activities might suffer. If proof is needed, take just two of the cases highlighted in this book.

The body of Caroline Manton (see Case Study below), stripped of physical identification and so badly bludgeoned as to render the face unrecognizable, lay in a mortuary for months awaiting the spark of genius offered by Fred Cherrill – identifying a fingerpint on a pickle jar that could have been on a record card. And Peter Griffiths (see page 248) almost slipped through the net of mass-fingerprinting that could have left him at large long enough to kill again. His careless print could have been identified within hours from a national record.

So there they all are, awaiting identity – the unknown dead, the vagrants, runaways, suicides; the accident victims and victims of murder; the crooks and killers; even Mr de la Bere's amnesiacs. Crime increases, the physical resources of the police decrease; we may soon have no choice.

Case Study

THE LUTON SACK MURDER

A heavy fog had settled over London and the Home Counties. On this gloomy afternoon of 19 November 1943, two sewer-men were measuring the water level of the river Lea where it flows through Luton. Lying in six inches of water they found a bundle; it contained a naked female corpse.

In any homicide investigation the vital first clue is the identity of the victim; in the case of the Luton sack victim police were faced with a double problem: not only had every identifiable accessory been removed, but her injuries had rendered the woman's face unrecognizable.

Then, on 21 February, from amongst a heap of old rags retrieved from a rubbish dump, a fragment of dirty black cloth yielded the clue that not only identified the victim, but led to her killer. Attached to the cloth was a dyer's tag bearing the number 'V 2247' – the number allocated to a coat deposited by Mrs Caroline Manton of 14 Regent Street, Luton.

Chief Inspector William Chapman called at the address in person, and interviewed 'Bertie' Manton, a former boxer. Manton's story seemed plausible enough: after a violent quarrel Mrs Manton had packed her bags and left. Bertie produced a letter from her – addressed from 'Hamstead'.

Unhappy with Manton's story, Chapman called in Scotland Yard's leading fingerprint expert, Frederick Cherrill. In his own account, Cherrill describes his search:

Opening the door of a cellar-like place under the stairs, I found its walls grimed with dust. In the gloom I could make out a shelf on which were stacked quite a number of bottles of all shapes and sizes, from medicine-phials to beer-bottles.

I started to examine them. The walls of the cellar *may* have been grimed with dust, but there was no dust on these bottles. They had obviously been as scrupulously cleaned as had the crockery in the kitchen. It struck me that somebody had been reading detective stories, and that somebody had gone to great pains to remove any trace of finger-marks. Why?

One by one the bottles were tested, without result. It looked as though my search was to be fruitless. The examination was nearing its end when, lurking in the shadows of the remotest corner of that shelf, I came across the last bottle of all.

It was a pickle-bottle! I handed it carefully – almost lovingly, for it was my last hope. It was the one remaining article in the whole of that house which had not been tested . . . This bottle had not been cleaned like the others [and] I found a thumb-mark which corresponded with the left thumb impression of the dead woman, whose fingerprints had been sent for comparison weeks before.

Chapman now looked afresh at the letters supposed to have come from Manton's 'estranged' wife; and noticed the spelling of 'Hamstead'. He asked Manton to write out the text of the letters, and true to expectation Manton left out the 'p' in Hampstead.

Bertie Manton was found guilty of murder and died three years later in Parkhurst prison.

DNA Register

As the threat of the 'serial' killer and the 'serial' rapist grows, particularly in the United States, demands are being made for an even more sophisticated form of 'Universal Register' – of DNA samples. It is suggested that as, like fingerprints, the genetic composition does not change, samples could be routinely taken as part of a national programme during infancy or childhood. This unique genetic information would then be classified and stored against the need to test against samples of blood, semen, even a single hair, deposited on a victim or at the scene of a crime.

Mass 'blooding' was undertaken in Britain as early as January 1987 in the case of two fifteen-year-old girls in Leicestershire who had been sexually assaulted and killed. Working on the assumption that their murderer was a local man, around 2,000 blood samples were taken from males aged between sixteen and thirty-four living in the villages of Enderby, Narborough and Littlethorpe. The exercise led, albeit indirectly, to the arrest and conviction of Colin Pitchfork for the double murder.

In the summer of 1991 the British Home Office outlined its plans to set up a national DNA database founded on blood samples, and it was alleged that at least one police authority was already keeping on file DNA records of people even though they had been eliminated as suspects; this is in direct contravention of the Data Protection Act which states that information collected for one purpose should not be used for another.

Such extensive record-keeping exercises as a DNA national register clearly pose problems for individual freedom that require reassurance from the Home Office. Already the National Council for Civil Liberties, which has studied the question of DNA tests, has called for the drawing up of guidelines before they become more widely used.

The NCCL has three main concerns:

1. That Home Office plans for the DNA index were being made without provision for public or parliamentary debate.
2. That data was already being assembled by police without the subjects' knowledge or consent.
3. That there is a lack of adequate safeguards to control the ways in which information contained in DNA profiles would be used.

V

VOICE ANALYSERS

Two recent devices have emerged on the US market, variations of the voice analyser. The advantage of these machines over the **Polygraph** lies in their not requiring to be physically attached to the subject under investigation. The analyser picks up sub-audible tremors in speech claimed to be characteristic of those telling untruths, and transfers them on to digital tape.

For the 'Mark II Voice Analyzer' it is claimed that accurate results can be obtained from a recorded voice, live speech, or over a telephone; furthermore, only three questions are required which take less than ten seconds to ask, process and evaluate.

A second instrument, the 'Psychological Stress-Evaluator' also functions on the principle of analysing stress-related components of the human voice. The hard print-out using a heated, inkless stylus on thermographic paper resembles the results that appear on polygraph rolls.

VOICEPRINTS

Although its champions claim it to be as unique to an individual as a fingerprint, the human voice is still working towards recognition as a forensic means of identification. One problem has been developing a system that will reliably transcribe sound into a graphic image that can be analysed and demonstrated as evidence in a court of law. There has always been a small place for such subjective witness descriptions as 'a gruff voice', but it was of limited value as proof of identity.

The early groundwork was carried out during the Second World War when it was useful to be able to identify the voices of field radio operators. The task was carried on by a group of scientists and engineers at the Bell Telephone Laboratories in New Jersey; among them was Lawrence G. Kersta. It was Kersta who made the breakthrough in 1963 when he developed a technique of electronically measuring the pitch, volume and resonance of the human voice and transcribing it graphically on to a spectrogram.

Kersta wrote in an introduction to his system:

> The chance that two individuals would have the same dynamic use of patterns for their articulators [the lips, teeth, tongue, etc. which modify sound] would be remote. The claim for voice pattern uniqueness, then, rests on the improbability that two speakers would have the same vocal cavity dimension and articulator use patterns nearly identical enough to confound voiceprint identification methods.

The Voice Spectrograph

The spectrograph records a 2.5 second band of speech (the ten most common words used are: a, and, I, is, it, on, the, to, we, you) on high-quality magnetic tape and then scans it electronically. It takes eighty seconds to scan the 2.5 seconds of tape, and the output is recorded on a rotating drum by an electric stylus. There are two types of voiceprint output:

Bar Voiceprint

The most common type to be encountered in a courtroom. The horizontal axis records the length of time (2.5 seconds, say), the vertical axis records the frequency, or intensity, of sound – the denser the print-out the louder the sound.

Contour Voiceprint

Again the horizontal axis represents time, and the vertical records frequency, but in this case points of equal density are connected by contour lines – in much the same way that gradient contours are marked on a map. In the illustration below the same word has been spoken by two people but with very different print-out results:

Contour prints of three separate individuals speaking the same word

Lawrence Kersta described the first official application of voiceprints by police in Connecticut, which actually proved the *innocence* of the suspect:

A man is free today because his voiceprints showed that he was not the depraved caller who made violent death threats to a family. During an emotional scene at police headquarters the principal victim proclaimed insistently that it was the suspect who made threatening telephone calls. He, just as vigorously, protested it was not him. As the debut of voiceprints in a police case, tape recordings were made of the death threat calls and the suspect's voice. The proof of his assertions by using voiceprint identification gave him his freedom and subsequently established the guilt of two suspects picked up later who eventually pleaded guilty. The nature of the disguises these men used during the frenzied telephone calls tricked the ears of the victim, who was not even aware that two men were involved.

The Future

Although voiceprinting is spreading slowly in the United States, it has yet to make any impact on British law enforcement. It is clear that there are areas of investigation in which the voiceprint has a serious potential in confirming identity. The telephone is now in such common use that it has become an everyday tool of the criminal just as it has of his more honest compatriots – ransoms are demanded by telephone, bomb threats are made, as are obscene calls, messages are phoned in to police and newspaper offices – often by the culprit himself – giving information on crimes . . . When a suspect is taken into custody and asked to repeat selected phrases or words the resulting voiceprints can be compared with the telephone recordings in much the same way as **Fingerprints**, making note of points of similarity.

Another area in which the individual quality of the human voice is being exploited is security. Engineers at the United States Air Force Systems Command are developing a voiceprint system to give clearance to personnel in restricted areas. The authorized person records a sequence of short phrases on to a computer memory and in use the computer will ask the person to repeat one of the phrases. If there is a match the doors open, if not the computer selects another phrase and the process is repeated. Tests have proved ninety-nine per cent reliability, and it was found that the system was even proof against professional impersonators who enjoyed less than one per cent success.

It is reported that one New York county police department is looking the practicalities of what it calls a 'Talking Rogues' Gallery', where voice samples are routinely taken, along with fingerprints and other personal details, of felons convicted of crimes which are 'appropriate' to voiceprinting – viz. telephone frauds, obscene calls, etc. The voice recordings would be used like mug-shots and played for witness identification.

Index